J. VANSINA

ART HISTORY IN AFRICA

AN INTRODUCTION TO METHOD

Drawings by C. Vansina

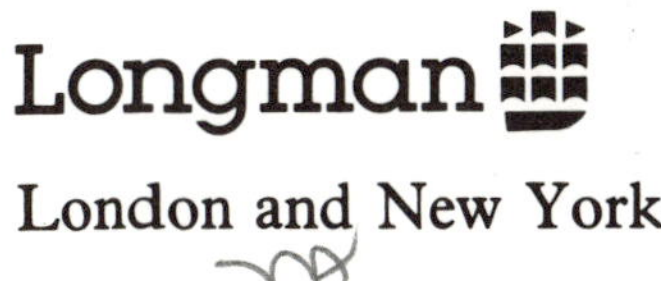

London and New York

Longman Group Limited
Longman House, Burnt Mill, Harlow, Essex CM20 2JE, England
and Associated Companies throughout the World.

Published in the United States of America
by Longman Inc., New York

First published 1984

British Library Cataloguing in Publication Data

Vansina, Jan
Art history in Africa.
I. Arts, African
I. Title
709′.6 N7380

ISBN 0-582-64367-8
ISBN 0-582-64368-6 Pbk

Library of Congress Cataloging in Publication Data

Vansina, Jan.
Art history in Africa.

(Longman studies in African history)
Bibliography: p.
Includes index.
I. Art, African. I. Title. II. Series.
N7300.V36 1983 709′.6 82-21644
ISBN 0-582-64367-8
ISBN 0-582-64368-6 (pbk.)

Printed in Hong Kong by
Sheck Wah Tong Printing Press Ltd.

Dirk Vansina

Ter Nagedachtenis

CONTENTS

PREFACE

As a child artworks enthralled me. They seemed to struggle to speak, to whisper about their times, their landscapes, the people that roamed the roads in those days when everything was as different as the characters in a fairy tale are from real people. But the eye could never understand all by just gazing at this window into a world as far away as the mirror image at the bottom of a deep well. This feeling never left me completely, but I came to understand that works of art must be helped, not by the imagination, but by the retrieval of as full an historical setting as research can uncover.

This is as true for Africa as for any other continent. And yet how often are works of African art viewed as if they came from nowhere, as if they did not raise questions about where and when they were created? Even today most commentaries deal only with ethnographic context or parallel, and with form. How often they therefore remain flawed and shallow! Still, on the whole the concerns, goals and tools of art history are beginning to appear in the study of art in Africa, albeit as timidly as the first crocuses appear after the tide of winter. And yet an awareness of the historical setting needs to permeate all research about art, if art is to make sense at all. The greatest masterpiece is timeless only because it captures the evanescent spirit of its own time. Art cannot properly be understood at all without history. This book has grown out of that conviction.

Several scholars have read and generously commented on this manuscript in earlier forms. It is a pleasure to thank Professors J. Watrous and F. Neyt, Dr D. Henige who read and commented on the whole manuscript as well as Professor S. Feierman who shared his thoughts about the chapters dealing with society and culture. I also owe a debt of gratitude towards the sometimes intemperate reviewer for Longman whose frankness was enhanced by his anonymity. The book, I hope, is better because of his comments. So thanks to J.P. also. I have been greatly assisted in the background work for this book by the assistants, especially Dr B. Fulks, who helped me with the teaching of a course on art history in Africa. The manuscript became clear thanks to the superior skills of Mrs Rosso who typed it. But the text is only part of such a book. The individuals and the institutions who graciously allowed me to reproduce their photographs in this book should not be forgotten in any acknowledgements. The list of illustrations records their names. The Vilas Research Fund of Madison (Wisconsin) is also gratefully remembered. Its support gave me time to think and write while providing some of the necessary travel funds as well.

And then I come to the collaborators. First Claudine, whose talents produced all the drawings, diagrams and maps. She has been the most persistent commentator and one endowed with the gift of seeing. Then there are my parents, both painters, who taught me art history. My father was also an art historian whose formidable knowledge was matched only by his genius for interpretation. This book is dedicated to his memory.

J. Vansina

LIST OF PLATES*

* *Acknowledgements:* the first mention refers to the photographer, the second to the owner if different from the photographer or if not a public building.

LIST OF FIGURES

ACKNOWLEDGEMENTS

The publishers are grateful to the following for permission to reproduce photographs in the text: J. de V. Allen for pl. 11.1; Erwin Böhm for pl. 8.6; Collection Troppenmuseum, Amsterdam for pl. 2.6; Comte B. de Grunne for pl. 10.3; Courtesy of the Trustees of the British Museum for pls 3.2 (Museum of Mankind), 5.7 (Museum of Mankind), 6.2 (Museum of Mankind), 8.4 (Museum of Mankind), 10.1 and 10.2 (Museum of Mankind); Marie-Claude Dupré, Centre National de la Recherche Scientifique, Ouagadougou for pl. 7.2; Etnografisch Museum, Antwerp for pls 2.2 and 5.6; Werner Forman Archive for pls 4.2 and 4.4; Frobenius Institute for pl. 10.4; Peter Garlake for pl. 7.4; T. Garrard for pl. 11.2; The Johns Hopkins University for pls 4.8, 7.1 and 8.8; Koninklijk Museum voor midden Africa, Tervuren, Belgium for pls 3.3, 3.4, 4.6, 5.5, 6.3, 8.2 and 11.3; M. Jean-Dominique Lajoux for pl. 6.4; Musée de l'homme for pl. 3.1; Musée de Louvres for pl. 6.8; Museo Nationale Preistorico ed Etnografico for pls 2.1, 2.4 and 5.2; Museum für Volkerkunde W. Berlin for pls 2.3, 3.5, 5.3, 6.1, 8.3 and 11.6; Natal Museum for pl. 10.5 (Tim Maggs); F. Neyt for pl. 5.4; Société d'Arts Primitifs for pl. 11.5; Staatliches Museum für Völkerkunde, München for pls 4.3 and 6.7; Ulmer Museum, Ulm, W. Germany for pls 1.1 and 9.1 (Collection Weickmann); University Museum, Philadelphia for pls 5.1 and 11.4; University of Wisconsin Press/Dr. Thompson Webb for pl. 4.7; J. Vansina for pls 4.5, 6.6; Walters Art Gallery for pl. 7.3; L. Wunderman for pl. 2.5; Yale University Art Gallery for 8.5; pl. 4.1 was taken from the publication 'The Heart of Africa' by G. Schweinfurth published by Sampson Low, 1878; pl. 6.5 appeared in Wreszinski, 'Atlas Zur' published by J. Hinrichsen Leipzig, 1923 Atlag licher Kulturgeschichte.

The cover photograph was kindly supplied courtesy of the Trustees of the British Museum (The Museum of Mankind).

CHAPTER ONE

INTRODUCTION

AFRICAN ART, ARTS OF AFRICA

'African art' is the label usually given to the visual and plastic arts of the peoples south of the Sahara, especially those of western and central Africa. Not only have students of African art limited themselves to a portion of the continent but they have been primarily concerned with the aesthetic appeal of sculpture and a description of the uses and functions of the objects in an ethnographic context. Thus the historical evolvement of the art forms, even the sculptural forms, has not been a subject of sustained research and, furthermore, other kinds of art have received scant attention. Thus defined, 'African art' is not the Art of Africa. Northern Africa, almost half of the continent in size, has been excluded from those studies because its arts clearly belong to widely flung traditions centered on the Mediterranean and the worlds of Christianity and Islam. These traditions can be called *oikoumenical*, from a Greek expression (oikoumenikos) meaning 'the whole world'. They transcend local and regional cultures over many lands. The contrast with the regional traditions of art elsewhere is great. We cannot amputate half of Africa and then call a portion of what remains 'African art'. Moreover, by its emphasis on sculpture even among regional traditions, the artistic expressions of eastern and southern Africa where sculpture is not the major form of artistic expression in recent times are also slighted.

Because of this, the present book deals with art in Africa and its history. It is not an art history of Africa. There are as yet not enough monographs to write such an art history, as too many scholars in the field of 'African art' have been allergic to historical pursuits. But we deal here with historical problems of the art of Africa before A.D. 1900. This book is an exposé of the approach to art history in general as it relates to Africa. It is an introduction to the questions art historians should ask about the objects of study and to the ways they should follow when seeking answers to such questions. It applies the general epistemology and methods used in the discipline to the specific situation of art in Africa. It should also be of help in evaluating historical hypotheses made about art in Africa. If this book becomes a stimulus to historical study, its purpose will be fulfilled along with the hope that one day it will indeed be possible to write an art history of Africa.

ART AND ITS HISTORY

Art is a term of western culture but a very inexact one. The threshold between what may be judged a work of visual art and another kind of man-made object is often a matter of dispute. For example, in our time, the distinction between what was once considered to be music and what noise has become frayed. A lapidary definition of art is therefore meaningless. All we can say is that art deals with form and expresses images or metaphors (Layton, 1981:4–15).

Yet an 'aesthetic' drive is universal. Everywhere and at all times people have made objects or manufactured decorative patterns that are unnecessary from the point of view of use. Even cooking pots are not entirely determined by use. Their shapes vary from place to place over time and archaeologists use them as prime determinators of 'culture'. There exists everywhere a need for the formal expression of values by metaphorical means, an appeal to the senses of sight and touch. The visual and plastic arts are means through which this need can be satisfied. Any made-made object studied from the point of view of form may be an art object, and form is a major concern of any study of the arts, whether or not the objects will be lasting, whether or not the object was made just to express form, whether or not the object is a man-made thing or merely an embellishment of some other object, such as painting on the human skin. Art historians also investigate iconography, the characteristics and meanings of pictorial renderings or of symbols whose arrangements, and even specific location in compositions, affect the form of the art or, conversely, the form affects the iconography. They further study media and technologies as methods and materials that allow a concordance between the artistic conception and the aesthetic form of the work of art.

In practice our illustrations are mostly taken from architecture, especially public architecture, sculpture and ɔainting or drawing, whether figurative, stylized or decorative only. The illustrations like the text are but an introduction to the field. Hence they represent such works of art as can be most easily linked to historical concerns, leaving such art historical problems as

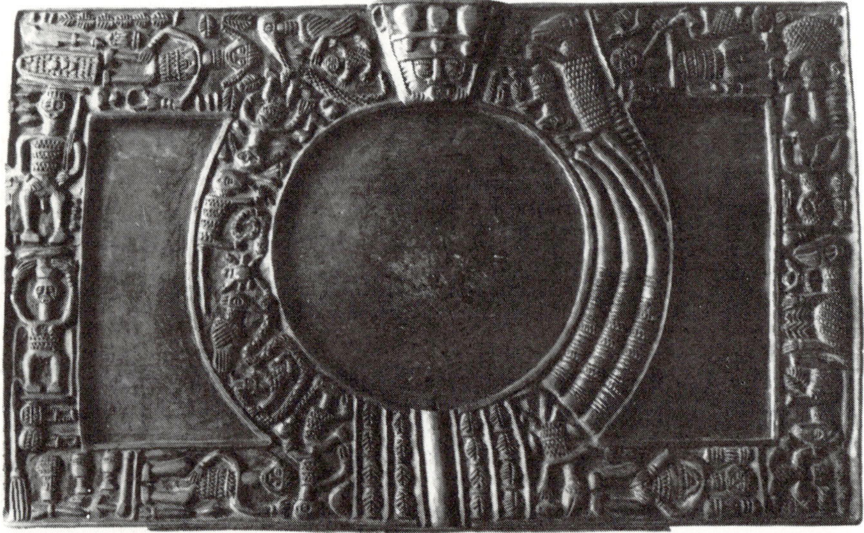

Plate 1.1 *Divination board. Wood. Used in* ifa *divination. Ardra, Republic of Benin. Ulmer Museum. Height 55cm, Width 34cm. Before 1659*

body painting in East Africa or sculptured hairstyles in southern Angola aside altogether, because those manifestations of art are ephemeral, and thus very difficult to document in the past. If we consider a work of art as in Plate 1.1, we can illustrate the types of questions it raises. Is this a tray? Where does it come from? When was it made? How was it made? Is it what it pretends to be? Is it unique in its general form or one of several or only a copy of something else? What was it used for? What did it mean? How does it fit in the whole of artistic production in Africa and elsewhere? Who made it? For whom? A jumble of questions pours out. The job of art history is to answer these and to do so in an orderly manner, first identifying the object as to authenticity, place and time of production, the artist, the manner of fabrication, the style, the meaning and the socio-cultural context relating this to the whole culture. Then it examines the idiosyncrasy of the object in comparison to others, that is, the conditions, circumstances and quality of its creation both internal and external. Finally it places the object in a general framework of the evolution of similar and related art forms in Africa, and by inference, in the world. This book follows this order of asking questions throughout.

As to the art object cited, it is authentic. It came in the seventeenth century (before 1656) to Europe from Ardra, a town on the coast of the present Republic of Benin (Dahomey). Its maker, the exact location of the workshop in which it was made, and the date of manufacture are unknown. Our information about it stems from a catalogue in 1659:

> A sacrificial board carved with strange, marvelously rare and horribly devilish images, which the King in Ardra, who is a vassal of the great king of Benin, and his most important officers and people of the same province, use to employ for the sacrifices to their gods or fetishes and on which they are wont to sacrifice to them. And this sacrificial board has been desecrated* by the ruling king of Ardra himself and has been used by him (*Exoticophylacium*: 52).

It was a board used for divination. *Ifa* is the name for a god linked to it, for the system of divination of which it was a tool, and for a cult whose priests are the diviners. The face on the board may be Ifa's or Legba's, another god who tricks people into offending the gods. Many details of its iconography are still not understood. Most occur on other objects from the seventeenth to the nineteenth and twentieth centuries. *Ifa* boards are still made in the general area. It was probably not the first *ifa* board of its type to be made, although it is the oldest of those recovered. 'Foreign' influence has not been detected in it. In general it belongs to a great tradition of sculpture in western Nigeria labelled 'Yoruba art' of which it is the earliest dated specimen. Note that the object was not found in a town inhabited by Yoruba speakers (Willett 1971).

Why should there be an art historical study of Africa for until recently there have been doubts that it was possible or even desirable (Volavka 1979)? First, perhaps, because art from remote times exists there. Some graphic works survived from dates as remote as 25 000 B.C. in Namibia and 6000 B.C.

* 'Infestiert' not in dictionaries (Grimm, Duden). Presumably: 'desacralized'. Amended to 'Investiert' it would mean 'commissioned' which would make more apparent sense in the context.

in the Sahara. African visual and plastic arts have a long and complex past. Secondly, works of art are always transformations of whatever kinds of realities people experience. And, in a given time, the nature of the art of a culture evolves as a response to realities – seen, felt or taught – which artists then record, with as much perfection of form as their talents can summon, in objects that may be descriptive or expressive, symbolic or decorative. As social and cultural values of a people change with time, so do the substances, statements and aesthetics of their art. This is history, and the more we can know about the art of successive times and places, the better we are able to understand the perceived realities of a people as expressed in their art.

The art history of African regional traditions, however, is still in its infancy. There are various reasons, of which the one of most concern is that only the merest fraction of art has survived, compared to the mass that was once in existence. As this book will argue, however, we can still recover much of the history of these traditions. The main reason for a lack of interest in the history of these arts was simply the haphazard development of the field of 'African art' and the circumstances surrounding the 'discovery' in Europe that Africa had an art.

For a long period the study of regional arts in Africa were contained in the expressions of a Western aesthetic response, as if it were a wonder of nature or of outer space, an exotic specimen in the gallery of visual images in Europe. Later, more serious students turned to the determination of style and the position of the work of art in its social and cultural milieu, but – barring a few exceptions – without considering any time scale, instead they used an immobile 'ethnographic present' tense to describe the object in its context. It was as if creativity in Africa had been frozen after some genesis when the known types of icons were crafted by the hands of some hero of a founding myth. Clearly this approach will not do. It still deprives works of African art of the full measure of attention and study they deserve if they are to be properly understood. It is faulty because even the contexts described for some objects may not apply to older works of art, created in circumstances very different from the ones observed by anthropologists. An historical analysis is absolutely necessary before a study of art in Africa, initiated by descriptions of style and context, can be completed.

If history and a methodical approach to history are essential to the study of art, art history is also relevant to any general history. It is essential because any history cannot be called general if it does not include art, and because art is a contemporary and authentic expression of the concerns of an age and a community, while changes in art reflect changes in such concerns. Because historians of Africa have also neglected the history of its art, the last chapter in this book briefly discusses how art can contribute to the general enterprise of historians. For art objects are often primary evidence of times long past.

AFRICAN GEOGRAPHY

Africa, the second largest continent and the most massive in outline, forms with nearby Asia and Europe the Old World. And an old world it is, as mankind itself evolved in Africa and spread from it to the rest of the world. The continent is deeply marked by its vegetation belts and its orography. From north to south a belt of mediterranean vegetation fades into the largest desert of the world, the Sahara, crossed only by the oasis ribbon of the Nile. Further south grasslands, called the Sahel in West Africa, gradually covered with dry

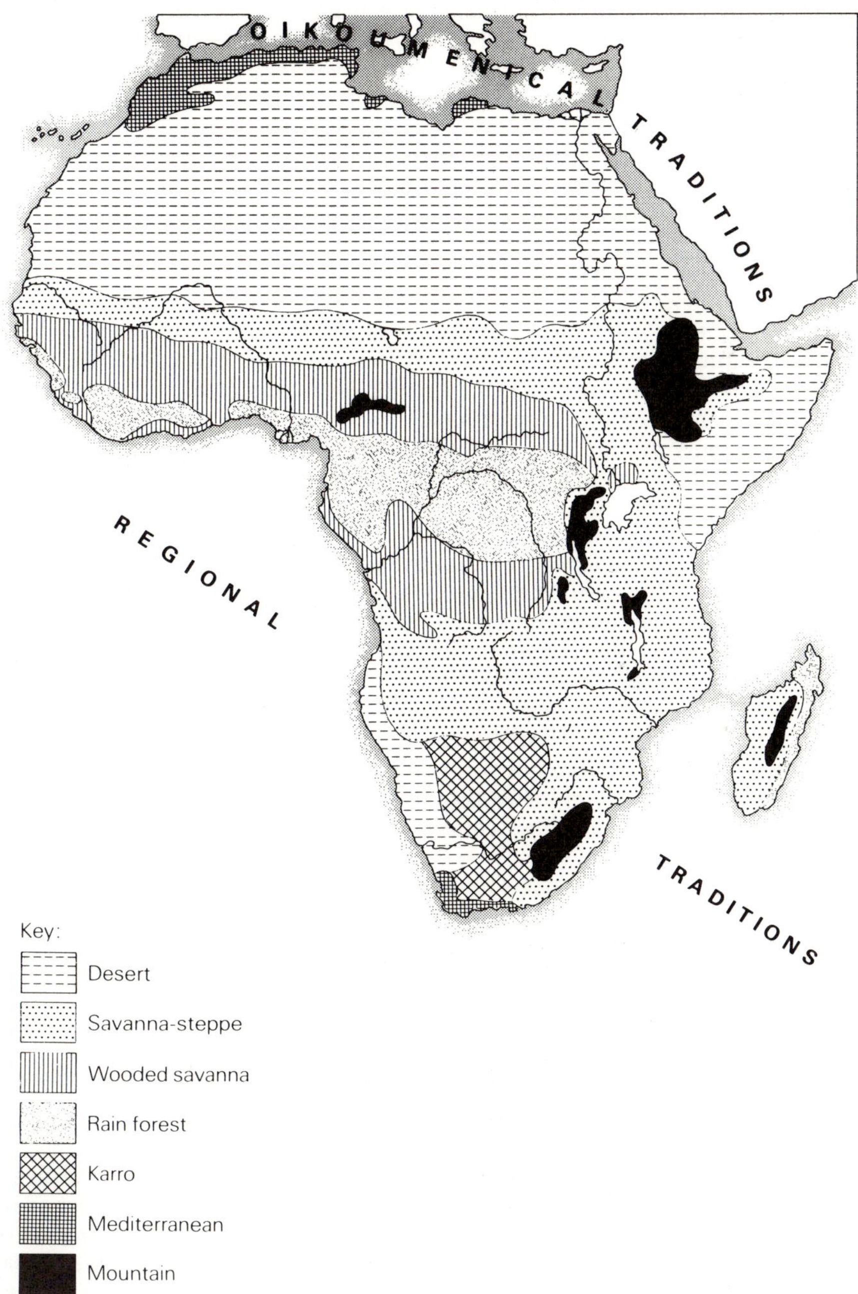

Fig. 1.1 *Vegetation zones and art traditions of Africa*

forest as one moves south, give way to rain forest near the coast of West Africa and all across central Africa. East Africa's elevations keep a wide corridor of grassland of various sorts open to the south. At about lat. 4° south of the Equator grasslands and dry forest appear again only to fade in more open country further south and finally run into the deserts and extremely dry lands of Namibia and the interior of Cape province. There, a mediterranean type of vegetation suddenly appears again in a tiny portion of the continent around the Cape proper.

Gradually the vegetation belts have shifted and the Sahara has not always been a desert, but the rain forest has always been there. These facts are important because the desert and the forest have acted not as absolute, but as partial barriers to communication. Thus the shape of the continent and the vegetation belts show that southern Africa was the most isolated from the rest of the world, central Africa was cut off from the lands north by the forest and the desert (after *c.* 2000 B.C.) separated West Africa from North Africa. East Africa communicated with southern Africa, but the existence of a great geological rift containing a string of major lakes separated it from Central Africa and hampered communications.

The oceans around the continent provided their own highways and barriers. East Africa was part of an Indian Ocean world in which the monsoons regulated the seasons for trading. The currents and winds of the Atlantic Ocean prevented any passage west of the Sahara until the caravel, that space-shuttle of the Renaissance, was developed. When the door opened from *c.* 1450 onwards European ships could reach all of Africa's coasts, but not its interior defended by deltas, waterfalls and lethal tropical diseases unknown to Europeans. The Mediterranean in the north has served at all times as a link, more than as a barrier. It was the heart of what was to become the *oikoumene* around it. That the *oikoumene* encompassed all northern Africa and all northeastern Africa as well as its eastern seaboard to Mozambique – the limit of the monsoons – is therefore not surprising. Because the Sahara dried up only gradually and last of all on its western flank, and because of its gold deposits, West Africa never totally lost contact with the *oikoumene,* but still never became a part of it.

One effect of the geography of the continent has been that in certain areas droughts were numerous and populations had to be nomadic or migrate often, preventing the creation of bulky works of art. Thus sculpture and a complex architecture were precluded in large portions of the interior of eastern Africa, and in southwestern Africa.

THE DAWN OF ART IN AFRICA

Some two thousand years and more before the first Pharaoh was enthroned, hunters and pastoralists in the Sahara were both engraving and painting on rock. Indeed, ancient Egyptian graphic art owes something to the great Saharan tradition that both preceded it and ran parallel to it for most of its history. Painting and engraving are typical for nomadic people, and were probably practised all over the continent before the spread of settled life. Although rock art dated to very early times has only been found in southern Africa and the Sahara, later rock art is known from almost anywhere where rocks were available. Apart from tiny sculptures in the Sahara and in southern Africa, architecture and sculpture truly developed only with more sedentary ways of life. Fishing, agriculture and some forms of husbandry allowed such developments in places from about 7000 B.C., and then increased with the spread of cereal agriculture and the domestication of animals a thousand years later.

Metallurgy, first developed for copper, bronze, gold and silver, existed by the dawn of the Pharaonic Age, *c*. 3000 B.C., and then spread from northern Africa to Mauritania where Akjoujt's mines were exploited between the ninth and the fifth century B.C. By that date iron technology had become well established. The smelting of iron may have first reached Africa with the Phoenician colonies from *c*. 1000 B.C. onwards. By 700 B.C. at the latest their technology had crossed the Sahara and had been refined at such foundries as Taruga in Nigeria. By 500 B.C. iron was worked in Ethiopia and by the same date people in the Great Lakes area of East Africa were melting iron at high temperatures, perhaps developing a process first elaborated in India. Be that as it may, from the last centuries B.C. onwards, both West and East Africans were producing high carbon steel directly from the furnace. Not long after the turn of the era, iron metallurgy had reached Natal (Van der Merwe 1980; Schmidt 1981). The sophistication and the independent innovations in African metal technologies at such early dates should place historians of art on the alert. Even if we have no works of art in metal dating directly from such remote times, there remains the probability that they were made. We do have evidence for complex ceramic sculpture called *Nok* in Nigeria from 700–500 B.C. onwards. It was a mature art and one may think that sculpture was also practised in other more perishable media as well.

By that time the separation between the *oikoumene* and the regional arts of Africa began to appear. *Nok* flourished at the time of Herodotus (485–425 B.C.), whose reports show that the Sahara was then almost as dry as it is now, although it still could be, and was, crossed by horse-drawn chariots. Most of the Saharan populations had moved southwards before the onslaught of drought, including perhaps some forebears of those who crafted the works of the *Nok* tradition. The gulf between the Mediterranean and the continent beyond had opened.

THE *OIKOUMENE*

At first the dominant arts of the *oikoumene* were tied to political developments, and their associated religions. The Pharaonic achievements first, then Carthaginian and Greek colonies, later still the expansion of the Roman Empire, all affected the spread and growth of the arts and provided subject matters, uses and functions. Then from the first century A.D. onwards, religion – less and less tied to empire – became the driving force.

Christianity reached African shores from its first generation of believers onwards. After long struggles it was recognized by the edict of Milan in A.D. 313, the date conventionally assigned to the onset of Coptic art in Egypt. Eastern Christian art spread to both Nubia and Ethiopia in the next centuries, in both areas succeeding arts already influenced by the *oikoumene* for more than half a millennium at least. The flight of the prophet Muhammad from Mecca in

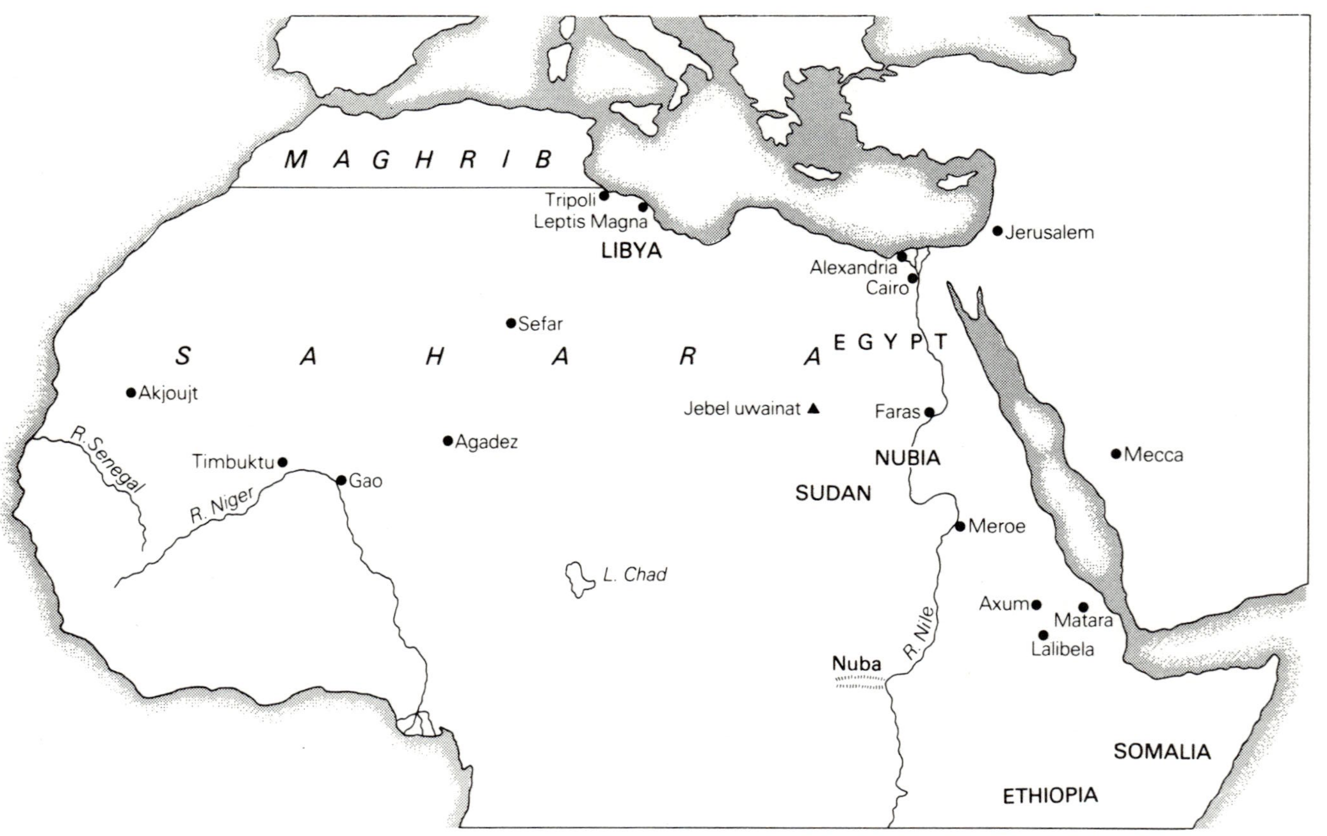

Fig. 1.2 *Northern Africa*

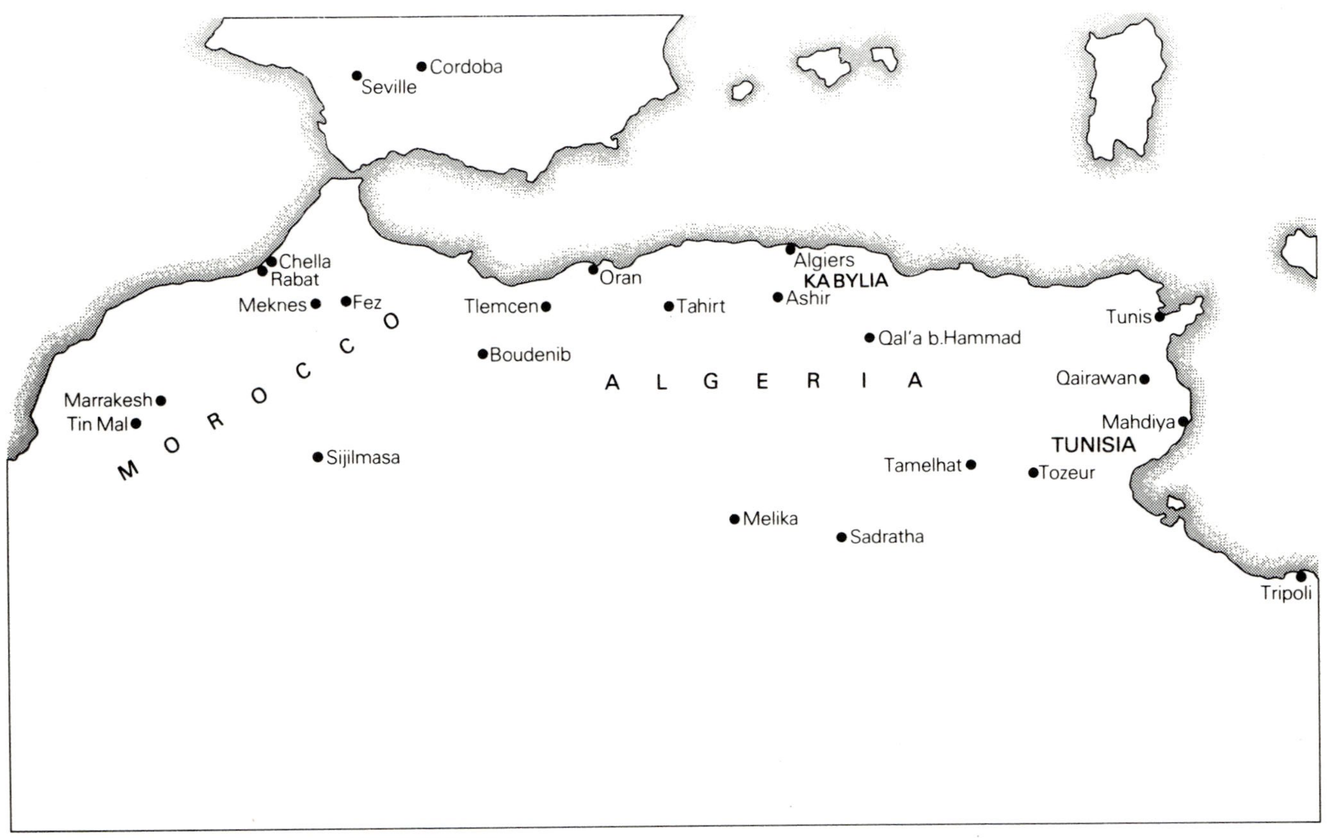

Fig. 1.3 *The Maghrib*

622 signalled the birth of Islam. The new religion and the new Empire, still developing its own artistic expression, entered Egypt in 639. The first conqueror of the Maghrib, 'Uqba ibn Nafi', founded the first mosque at Qairawan in 670. But Muslim forces were not well entrenched in the Maghrib before A.D. 710. From then on, however, Muslim art began to develop and displayed major local expressions a century later. In Egypt, meanwhile, masterworks of Islamic art had appeared even earlier. Islamic art spread with the later expansion of religion and of Arabs over northern Africa, already reaching the East African coast as well as portions of Madagascar from the ninth century onwards, and West Africa in the eleventh century A.D. But Christianity and its art did not fade overnight. Even in Egypt, Coptic art continued to *c.* A.D. 1200, when Christian Nubia was overrun, although Christian backwaters survived in Nubia until A.D. 1500 and perhaps later. And Islam never overwhelmed the Ethiopian highlands. There Christian arts survive to our own day.

Although Islamic art in northern Africa is divided into periods and given dynastic labels, the changes in dynasties do not always correspond to changes in style. Dynasties by themselves do not shape the arts, but the variations in the extent of the territories ruled led to variation in artistic influences. Also, particular religious motivations were often adduced as legitimation for new dynasties, and exerted some influence on the arts.

Architecture was dominant in the arts of Islam. The congregational mosque found an early 'classical' expression in Tunisia during the ninth century. This type of building also led to a distinct Hispano-Maghrebi tradition that was to last until the twentieth century. From 1169 onwards with the conquest of Egypt by Salah al-Din (Saladin), Egypt developed characteristics, often labelled Mamluk art, which survived until about 1800. Meanwhile, in Libya and in the Sahara, a distinct tradition developed from the 'classical' congregational mosque. Finally, from the sixteenth century onwards, Ottoman traditions, creating new local styles, took root in Algeria, Tunisia and Libya. Egypt, dominated by Istanbul since 1517, resisted Ottoman influences. When Egypt adopted them wholeheartedly, they were already competing with European influences (Marçais 1954; Creswell 1952–9).

THE REGIONAL TRADITIONS

Only three major upheavals affected almost all of Africa south of the Sahara and that to different degrees. The first was the huge expansion of Bantu languages throughout the southern third of the continent from the Cross River basin on the border between today's Nigeria and Cameroon to southern Africa. The expansion began some time before 500 B.C. and probably reached the eastern Cape area in the first centuries A.D. This was *not* a single migration of a culturally superior people, implanting a Bantu culture everywhere. There is no Bantu culture and there are no Bantu arts (Vansina 1979/1980)! It was a diffusion of languages only. At best one can recognize a substantial common heritage among Bantu speakers of southeastern Africa and portions of East Africa, where Bantu speakers seem to have carried the practices of agriculture, husbandry, metallurgy and settled life. But even that is not established beyond doubt.

The second and third upheavals were the work of Europeans. They had rounded the coasts of Africa and began trading between *c.* 1440 and 1500. In the seventeenth century, the slave trade became dominant over all other commerce, and from the 1650s to *c.* 1850 a massive transplantation of Africans to the New World ensued. Various Afro-American arts evolved out of this great migration. But this European impact did not directly affect the arts in most of Africa to any great degree. The third upheaval was caused by the industrial revolution and the cheap products that flooded into the continent from 1800 onwards. The increased European presence culminated in the colonial partition of the 1880s which led to the demise of the classical regional arts in most parts of the continent. But even before formal partition, increased and varied trade had affected the arts in many parts of the continent.

WEST AFRICA

By A.D. 750 at the latest, West Africa's past was dominated by the gold trade across the Sahara, and by the development of kingdoms and cities. The earliest state of the Sahel may date from the first centuries A.D. The largest and best known empires were Ghana, from perhaps A.D. 500 onwards, and then Mali and Songhay, which collapsed in 1591 (Levtzion 1973). Further east, cities arose in northern Nigeria from perhaps A.D. 1000, while cities, royal residences and states are attested in southern Nigeria from A.D. 800 and later. Around Lake Chad, the state of Kanem was flourishing from the same date or earlier. But apart from southern Nigeria, sculpture, a well-known art of West Africa, does not seem to have been focused around royal courts. Very little evidence of the northern imperial arts has survived; rather, more remains of the ceramics of the upper Middle Niger, probably focused around the city of Jenne (1100–1600).

With the arrival of the Europeans, the lands on the seaboard came into the forefront of West African trade, rather than being the last trading nations on the road to North Africa. The gradual settlement of the forest was finished by 1450 at the latest, and various forms of societies based on associations (e.g. in Liberia) or chiefdoms were flourishing. Gradually some evolved into larger kingdoms such as Asante and Dahomey in the eighteenth century. Meanwhile in the Sahel smaller successor states had replaced the empires over a large portion of their territory, and in Upper Volta new state forms had arisen. Early on, the cities, the courts, the trading settlements, the association lodges, all became centres of artistic production, since masterpieces from the fifteenth century onwards have survived. The earliest known ceramic sculpture in the east of the area, in the delta, dates from the onset of our millennium (Ke) and from the Cross River since the sixteenth century.

The evolution of the arts in West Africa never led to a massive tradition emerging and covering most of the area, mainly because the institutions they were associated with had no universal aspirations. Islam abhorred representational sculpture, while trading institutions, though contributing to some spread, were not inherently tied up with an art of their own. West Africa was strongly influenced by northern Africa, especially in metal technologies of casting, in textiles and for some decorative designs. West African arts also exercised, we believe, some influence on North Africa, but again, all proof is lacking so far.

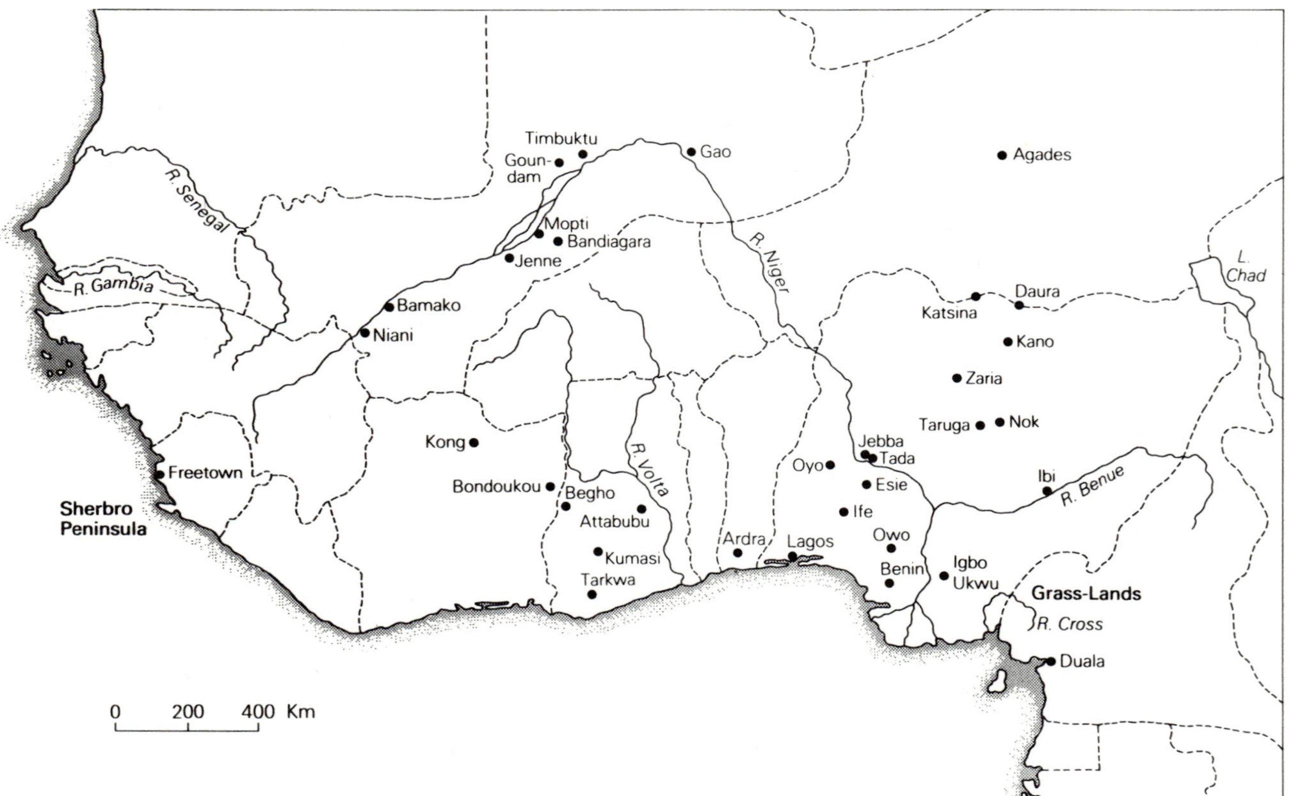

Fig. 1.4 *West Africa*

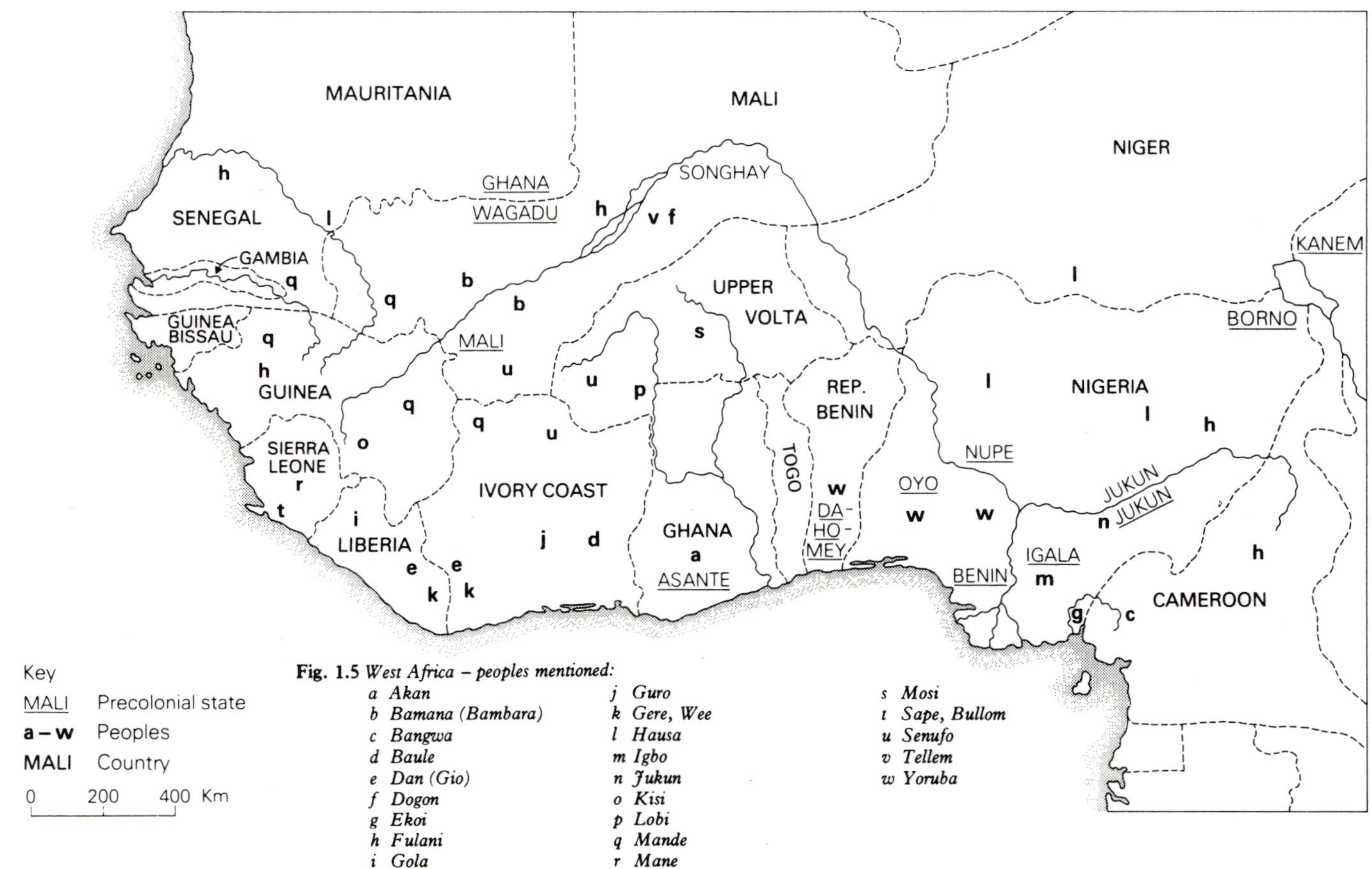

Fig. 1.5 *West Africa – peoples mentioned:*

a Akan
b Bamana (Bambara)
c Bangwa
d Baule
e Dan (Gio)
f Dogon
g Ekoi
h Fulani
i Gola
j Guro
k Gere, Wee
l Hausa
m Igbo
n Jukun
o Kisi
p Lobi
q Mande
r Mane
s Mosi
t Sape, Bullom
u Senufo
v Tellem
w Yoruba

CENTRAL AFRICA

Central African history falls into several sharply divided segments according to environments. The northern savanna saw the rise of states near its Saharan fringe and the development of architecture as a dominant art certainly after 1500 and perhaps earlier. Islamic influences were, by then, already strong in the states. Further south, people lived scattered over the land and, except for portions in what is now Cameroon, no larger political units arose. With the exception of the lower Shari region, no known early works of art have survived, barring a few pieces of sculpture from the nineteenth century.

In the Central African forest, sculpture was practised in small communities where the foci of art were the public men's houses, centres of government, the village temples in Gabon that fulfilled the same role, the paraphernalia of associations and in parts the shelters where memorials for the ancestry of local leadership were built. In almost the whole area, such sculpture exhibits common traits, such as the economy of means to render expression. Here, too, no works of art older than the nineteenth century have survived, although some known works (e.g. in ivory) may be much older and the traditions certainly were at least a few centuries old. On the southern margins of the forest grew a major kingdom labelled the Kuba kingdom. Distinctive and rich traditions in architecture, sculpture, textiles and decoration developed there from the seventeenth century onwards (Cornet 1972, 1975, 1978; Neyt 1981; Perrois 1979).

South of the forest, eastern Central Africa has left us a few traces of wood sculpture (Van Noten 1972, D. Clark personal communication) and also ceramics from the last centuries of the first millennium. From A.D. 900 onwards, trade in copper products became important and indirect connections with Indian Ocean trade existed. In Shaba (Zaïre) chiefdoms, then larger states, gradually grew. They flourished in the eighteenth century; some, such as the Lunda empire, grew in direct relation to the slave trade. The Lunda empire and the main Luba state deeply influenced all local cultures around them from 1700 onwards at the latest. They also exercised mutual influences on one another. This is clearly shown by the positions of central Angolan and northern Shaban foci of sculpture. Nevertheless, some local traditions remained unaffected, especially in the area between the Kasai and Kwango rivers, and in the Kasai and Maniema (Zaïre) areas north of the Luba empire. The earliest sculptures in wood from Angola date from the second half of the first millennium. Near the coast, sculpture, decorative design and textiles were flourishing before 1500 in the kingdom of Kongo and adjoining regions. With the arrival of Europeans, especially missionaries, Christian European art forms dominated among the elite of that state until *c.* 1700 when local traditions assimilated them. Further south, central Angolan art assimilated many borrowings from Portuguese art.

Even in the southern savanna one cannot speak of a massive art tradition for much the same reasons as in West Africa. Nevertheless, three traditions of art only, coastal Zaïre and Angola, central Angola, and northern Shaba, clearly dominated the southern savanna.

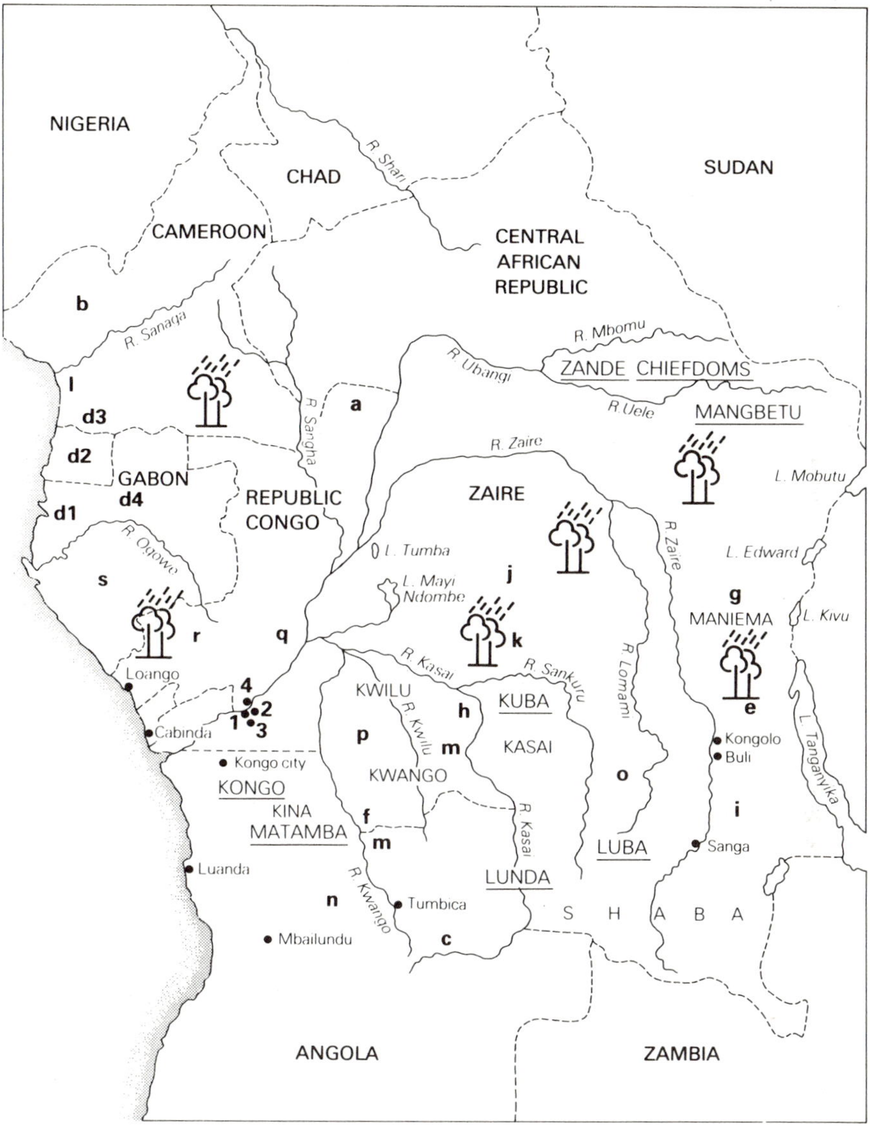

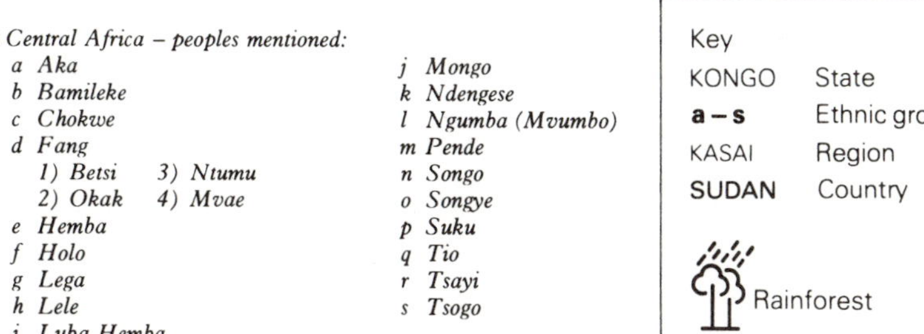

Fig. 1.6 *Central Africa – peoples mentioned:*

a Aka
b Bamileke
c Chokwe
d Fang
1) Betsi 3) Ntumu
2) Okak 4) Mvae
e Hemba
f Holo
g Lega
h Lele
i Luba Hemba
j Mongo
k Ndengese
l Ngumba (Mvumbo)
m Pende
n Songo
o Songye
p Suku
q Tio
r Tsayi
s Tsogo

Others known by the name of a state: e.g. Kuba, Kongo, Luba

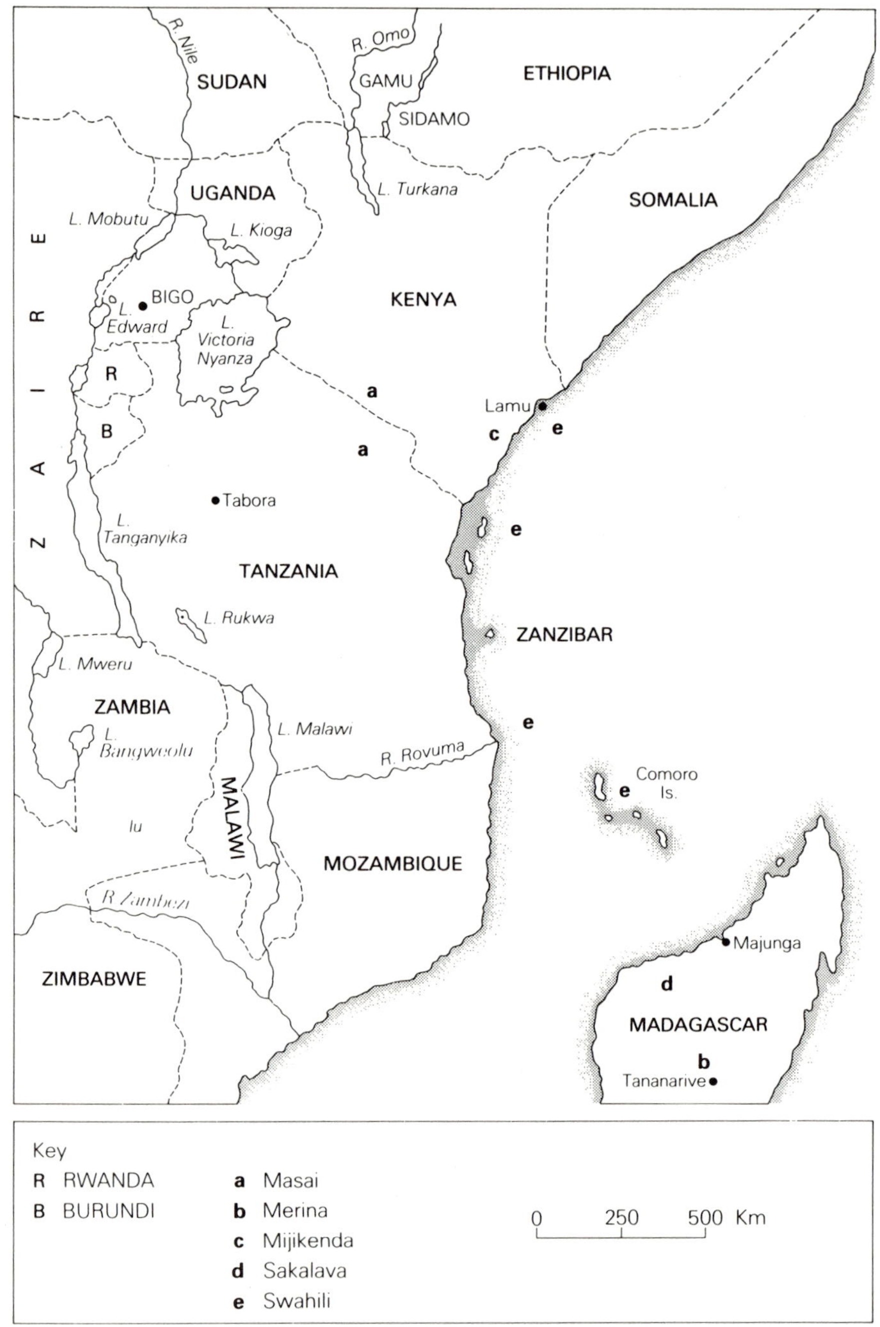

Fig. 1.7 *East Africa*

EAST AFRICA AND SOUTHERN AFRICA

East Africa is the geographic area of the continent where art traditions have been the least studied and were the most varied (Hartwig 1978; Holy 1967). Apart from the coastal architecture influenced by Islam, architecture was a major art in a set of kingdoms in the Great Lakes area that had developed by the sixteenth century, although earlier architectural traces have been found at Bigo. In the truly drought-prone lands of southern Sudan, northern Uganda, portions of Kenya and Tanzania, the main expression of visual art was painting on rocks, on portable objects such as shields, and on human bodies. Funerary pole sculpture occurred in southern Ethiopia, nearby portions of Sudan, near the Kenyan coast and in parts of Madagascar. In much of Tanzania the situation is less clear. Some sculpture in clay and on wood was centred near the Rovuma River extending from northern Mozambique as far as Malawi. None of the arts of inland East Africa is dated and most remains are probably of recent origin, with the exception only of rock paintings and a few ceramics from Uganda and Bigo. But we do not even know when hunters, herders or farmers stopped painting on rocks.

East Africa's history has been one of coastal trading settlements since A.D. 700 and even earlier, of sizeable migrations by herders, herder/farmers, or farmers in much of the drought-prone area, of the rise of higher densities of population and states only in the interlacustrine area and of trade routes at first only from Malawi through southern Tanzania to the coast and then, in the late eighteenth but especially in the nineteenth century, from the coast to beyond Lake Tanganyika, the Great Lakes and northern Kenya, led by Muslim Swahili speakers from the coast. This corresponds well with what we know about the practice of the arts, which is clearly far too little.

History south of the Zambezi shows a development of agriculture and later specialized herding as well as the opening up of gold mines and the export of gold to the Indian Ocean by A.D. 1000. Thereafter, centres characterized by both architecture and sculpture arose first at Mapungubwe in the Limpopo valley, then in Zimbabwe, where centralized regimes dominated the area until well after Portuguese settlement on the coast.

From Zambia to Transvaal, small-sized ceramic sculptures are found from *c.* 1000 onwards. Earlier still, ceramic sculpture had flourished in Natal and southern Transvaal between *c.* A.D. 500 and 800 (Maggs and Davison 1981). In later times, well-watered southeastern Africa developed a mixed economy of herding and farming. Groups there began to form various chiefdoms, until the nineteenth century when a Zulu leader, Shaka, built a large army and a large state and plunged the whole region into turmoil. New political formations of large size appeared as far north as western Zambia. This upheaval ended a long sequence of artistic evolutions in Zimbabwe, Transvaal, and portions of the Orange Free State that had been characterized for many centuries by architecture in stone. The great miseries in the area from the 1830s onwards resulting from the Zulu upheaval and from the Boer migration into Transvaal, probably brought most artistic traditions to an end.

The western half of southern Africa is desert or at least very drought prone. Since the end of the first millennium, only pastoral nomads shared these lands with hunters. The rock art of South Africa and Namibia from

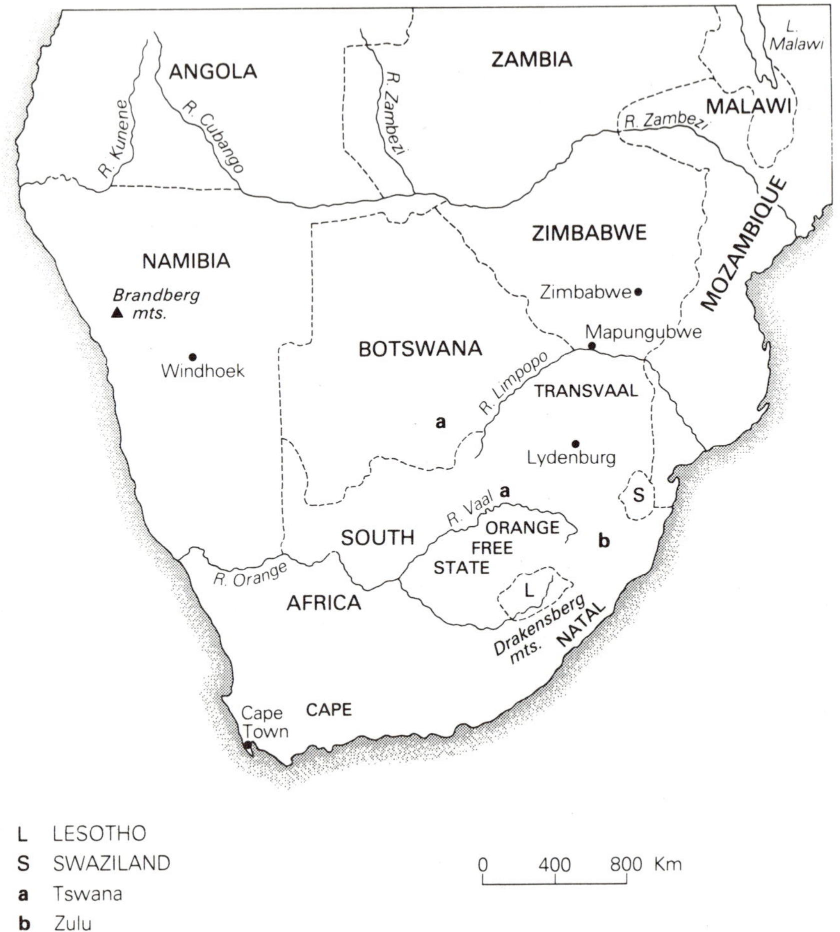

Fig. 1.8 *Southern Africa*

earlier than 27 000 years ago is the work of these hunters (Inskeep). The tradition died out in the late nineteenth century as they were decimated by Bantu speakers and Europeans alike. The arrival of the Europeans on the Cape and the Dutch settlement there from 1652 onwards brought European styles into the area. But they had little effect on the arts beyond the areas of their settlements. In fact, European art influenced the African arts less here than on the West African coast. Although there was some expansion from the Cape settlers before the 1830s, an emigration of Dutch speakers, the Boers, dissatisfied with British rule, occurred in that and the succeeding decades. This led to the expansion of European settlement ultimately all over southern Africa. Wherever they settled, African classical art died out.

Madagascar was settled by immigrants from southeast Asia and from the nearby African shores before A.D. 1000. As nodes of population slowly grew on the island, larger political units gradually arose. A kingdom of the Sakalava dominated in the seventeenth and eighteenth centuries, while a state of the Merina overtook it from the late eighteenth century onwards. By the 1890s the Merina had control of more than two thirds of the whole island. The arts of the island have always centred around tombs. Some Islamic tombs of East African parentage are found in the northwest and may be older than 1500. Elsewhere the architecture of tombs, their sculpture and their decoration is wholly original, but the age of this tradition is not well known. As towns developed – first Majunga on the West Coast, later Tananarive in the centre – architecture became more important. In the nineteenth century a Malagasy architectural style became prominent. It was heavily influenced by European models as well as by older methods of construction in planks. The affiliations of Malagasy art and architecture are not at all clear. Indian, Melanesian, Arabian and Indonesian influences have all been cited, and an African influence from the Mozambique coast is at least likely.

THE STUDY OF AFRICAN ART

Art objects from sub-Saharan Africa first arrived in Europe as curiosities for princely cabinets, the oldest mention of a work of art being one of 1470. Islamic art had been known and had exercised some influence on European art long before then. It is not surprising that an awareness of this art developed as the history of art was emerging as a discipline, although the main scholars who studied art were active only after 1900.

By the late nineteenth century, objects from sub-Saharan Africa were acquired and housed by European museum curators as specimens of material culture. Concurrently, curators developed the first methods of cataloguing and labelling artifacts. The looting of Benin by a British expedition in 1897 led to the realization that there was art in Africa. Benin's naturalistic art work in 'bronze' and ivory appealed to European tastes. Some art work found its way to most royal collections in Europe. An early use of the word 'art' in connection with Africa appeared in the title of A. Pitt-Rivers' descriptive book of 1900, *Ancient Works of Art From Benin*. Only L. Frobenius, later a famous culture historian of Africa, had used the term earlier (Frobenius 1896). The Benin boom led to the first art historical study, F. Von Luschan's massive *Benin Antiquities* (3 volumes in the original!) of 1919.

A wider recognition of African arts began in 1905 when European avant-garde artists in France and then in Germany recognized them as such. A wave of almost delirious enthusiasm followed and gave rise to the first private collections and to C. Einstein's *Negerplastik* (Leipzig 1915), which set the tone for a spate of lyrical works that followed. Only artistic form mattered, social context and meaning were irrelevant!

Anthropologists began to redress the balance after 1925. The first field trip specifically directed towards an examination of art dates from 1933 (Bernatzik 1933; Gerbrands 1937:52–65). By 1945 a specialization in 'African art' was beginning to emerge in anthropology. Given the characteristics of the discipline at that time, interest in the history of the arts was unsustained. Then, from 1956 onwards, archaeologists who viewed African art seriously, entered the field. The historical perspectives developed only very slowly until recently. Now the pace has quickened and a commitment to the study of the history of art in Africa is growing.

These developments have been immeasurably affected by the concomitant growth of a market for African art. Even today scholarly studies have insufficiently disengaged themselves from mercantile interests and are partially crippled by them. Meanwhile, for over a half century, large private collections have been assembled, and have saved many art works from destruction. Nevertheless, the proliferation of forgeries, the keeping of precise origins as trade secrets, and the publications, written or directed by dealers, touting their holdings, have certainly blemished the services that the market has rendered.

For much too long an attitude fostered by some entrepreneurs of the market place was that of African art objects as *art trouvé*, 'found art', like pretty pebbles on a beach, and further fed the aesthetic involvement of collectors by titbits of exotic sensationalism. Unfortunately, students of African art were not totally free from such influences and still must beware of them. And so it came to pass that 'African art' was the sculpture of West and Central Africa, and that, until recently, dating it did not matter. Now, however, there are changes in the market; induced perhaps by archaeological successes and the passage of time. Now the greater age of an art object enhances its value and an attribution of date becomes a matter for expertise of authenticity.

CHAPTER TWO

IDENTIFICATION

LABELS, OBJECTS AND DOCUMENTS*

Most visitors to museums or readers often just glance at an object or its reproduction and then look for a label or caption such as 'Ekoi headpiece' or 'Qait bai mosque, Cairo' before they turn to a study of the work. Labels and captions provide identification. They are coordinates in space and time and allow the 'placement' of objects in relation to others, because they form a grid according to which any work of art can be ordered.

Minimal labelling should consist of three items of information: a reference to the object, the name of the artist and a date. Very often, for African art, the name is replaced by an ethnic name and the date is omitted simply due to lack of information or to lack of interest in a date. Omission of the date indicates how much art history in Africa, especially south of the Sahara, still remains in its infancy.

Labels are felt to be essential by most viewers. The art work by itself does not give this information. It must come from other sources. Thus, looking at the Ardra board (Plate 1.1) does not tell us that it came from Ardra in the seventeenth century. We should also know that it is now at Ulm and that seventeenth-century catalogue data exist (Willett 1971:81–2). All of this is documented in writing. And because documentation helps provide identification in space and time, documents play a central role in art history.

But the link between object and document is rarely foolproof. Inscriptions on monuments provide the closest relationship possible, at least if they are contemporary with the making of the object. If so, the link can hardly be faulted. A piece of Fatimid pottery signed 'Sa'ad' (Talbot Rice 1965:92) refers to that pottery, no other. A dated inscribed frieze in a mosque can be a direct indication of the date that mosque was built. In all other cases, documents may refer to other objects than the ones they now are associated with. A sixteenth-century text about a salt cellar in ivory from African cannot automatically be taken to refer to one of the known salt cellars with African features.

The description of objects in such documents becomes quite important. Photography, the perfect description, now used by most museums as part of catalogue records, is a practice no older than a generation or two. Formerly either a drawing or a detailed written description gave the best guarantee that one item would not be mistaken for another. But such notices and drawings were rare. The usual mention of objects was found on ledgers, catalogues or

* F. Graebner, *Methode der Ethnologie*, Heidelberg, 1911, pp. 12–54.

inventories, that is, on lists. Lists do not usually describe items in more than a few words and do not systematically include drawings.

Hence any critique of identification starting from documents must begin by examining the possibility of error. As there are two sources involved – the object itself and the document – they first must be confronted one with the other. Examination of medium, technique and style (and theme to a lesser extent) tends to group objects in sets of similar features. If the documentary attribution runs contrary to these features, it is suspect. An Isis statuette labelled 'southern Zaïre' on the museum record is either evidence of a hitherto unsuspected spread of late small old Egyptian statuary to Zaïre, or the labelling is wrong. In this case, the error in the label could be established, as the collector in Zaïre had stopped over in Cairo on the way home.

The procedure of giving preference to identification by the features of the object itself over its attribution by record can lead to serious error. The typical case is an attribution by document that is not confirmed by an attribution of technique or style, usually because these features in the object are not found on the corpus of known works from the area and of the time. Either the object is a forgery or the document is in error. But the characteristics of 'typical' works are developed out of an examination of an extant corpus and – especially in Africa – there is no guarantee that the corpus used is in fact representative. Thus, an 'atypical' object may be genuine and the attribution correct. A hitherto unknown variant has then come to light. The weakness in the argument to reject the documentary evidence is that it is based on negative evidence, that is, the absence of 'typical' features in the object. In order to stick, the extant corpus must be totally representative, a difficult proof to provide, when innovation is a recurring part of the creative process.

Discrepancies between motif and the object itself for one feature should be tested against others. Is the wood of the carving similar to the wood of the corpus? Is the technique similar? Is the style comparable? Is the theme rendered in the corpus? In the case of fakes or errors several characteristics differ and multiple negative evidence accumulates. Doubt increases.

The proof of the pudding comes when the characteristics of the object quite clearly refer to a body of art works different in place and time to the one referred to by the label. For now there is positive evidence. If in addition we can show how the documentary error could have arisen, the case is clinched. Thus, the so-called Vallisnieri pieces at the Pigorini museum in Rome were said to be Chinese (Plate 2.1). On the base the legend states: 'Idolo de la China'. Further attributions on the bases eventually allowed the pieces to be traced to Central Africa, to the Kina district of the kingdom of Kongo, which confirms the comparison of the objects with other carvings. Detective work among documents not only established in the end where the statuettes came from but how they reached the Pigorini museum (Bassani 1978; Bontinck 1979). The Capuchin missionary, F. da Collevecchio, probably acquired them between 1690 and the close of 1694 in Kina, brought them to Lisbon in 1695, and gave them to the *nunzio* G. Cornari, who carried them to Padua in 1697. Upon his death, A. Vallisnieri acquired them in 1722 and from his collection they went to that of the University of Padua in 1730 from where they were ceded to the Pigorini museum in 1877. The confusion of Kina and China is explained by the

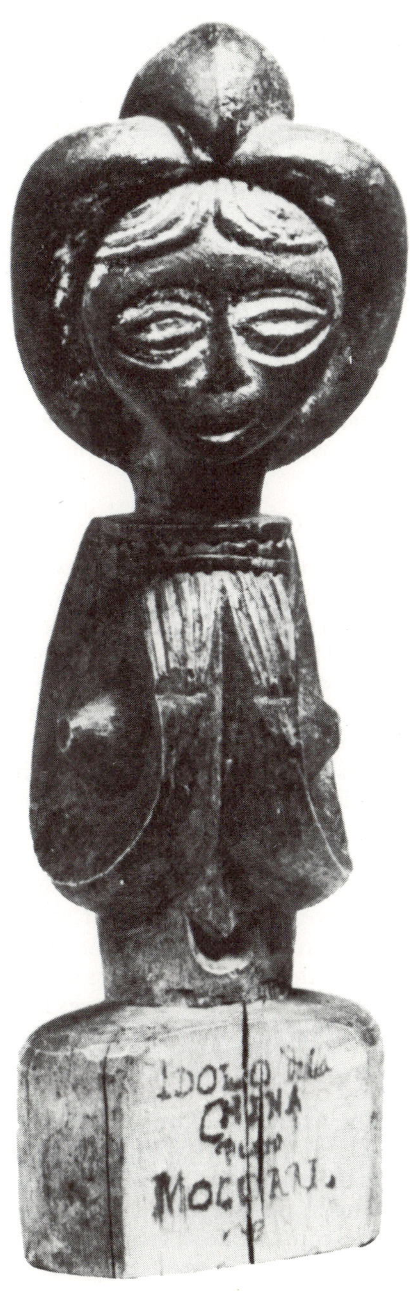

Plate 2.1 *Female Figure. Wood. Use: unknown. Kina (old kingdom Kongo). Museo preistorica ed etnografico, Rome. Height 24·8cm. Before 1694. Known as Vallisnieri Figure. One of a set of two*

identical spelling used in seventeenth-century Italy.

The case above shows clearly how important documents can be. For older moveable objects usually have gone through a history of ownership and this can only be traced through documents, mostly descriptive catalogues, but also other acquisition data. Moreover, documents are even more important for an understanding of the social and cultural background of objects. The mention of desecration in the entry about the Ardra board, for instance, is important. They are nearly as important as the art works themselves. And they should be examined by the ordinary rules of historical evidence, for very often they are vitiated in one or other respect. The catalogue entry for the Ardra board may, for instance, have been written from memory many years after the acquisition and may inaccurately stress some of the sensational details adduced then.

In the following sections the identification of art objects will examine a sequence of questions to be asked: What is the work? Is it authentic or is it a forgery? Who made it and where? When was it made? For if we have answers to these four sets of questions, we have established the position of a work of art in the comparative grid provided by space and time.

THE WORK ITSELF: DESCRIPTION

The first question to ask is: what is a thing and how was it made? Usually there is little difficulty. The Ardra object is a flat board. Common utensils and tools are recognizable as such. But mistakes can occur. What looks like a stool could be a throne and a jewel could be a weight. The first danger for the onlooker is to go beyond the shape of an object and assert a use for it that may be wrong. Exotic looking knives from the Zaïre River are knives, not 'executioners' weapons'! The examination of an object must remain factual. Questions of use are to be dissociated from questions of appearance; these will be examined later. Nevertheless, speculating about use helps in the definition of an object. If we suppose an object to be a mask, we will expect slits for the eyes, edges rounded by use, remnants of cosmetics or perspiration on the inside, ways to slip it over the head or ways to fasten it for carrying. We will wonder about its weight: can it be carried by a dancer or not? If we suspect a ruin to be a mosque, we will be careful to record the orientation, and search for evidence of a *mihrab,* the niche in one of the walls that always should be oriented towards Mecca. So even though an examination of use comes later, suppositions about it help in the physical description of the object by drawing attention to such details.

It is not enough to describe the object as it is seen. The description should establish the medium. The Ardra board we used as an example appears to be made of wood. But what kind of wood? We do not know; no one analyzed it. And unfortunately that is the usual situation in African art – cursory inspection is deemed to be enough, but it is not. Only laboratory analysis will settle such matters. No West African copper-like objects had been analyzed before the 1960s (Shaw 1970a, 1978:182–4). So-called 'bronzes' are now seen to be copper, brass, leaded bronze, less leaded bronze, etc. These raise questions of technologies, attributions to identical or different workshops, problems of supplies of the raw materials and so on. Similarly, iron can be high carbon steel or pig iron. Bricks are never just bricks. They come in standard sizes that differ from age to age and from area to area. The bricks of the great mosque at Qairawan are of a standard of dimensions used in ninth-century Tunisia ruled by the Aghlabids and thus confirm other indications about the age of the mosque (Marçais 1954:42). Wood can be very diverse. To rely on what people say the wood usually used for this or that item is, will not do. The answer is often guesswork and involves the relative prestige of different woods in a society, whereas a laboratory analysis settles the matter (Dechamps 1970/8). The results of analysis, in turn, give insight into which kinds of woods were used (and the number is always restricted), what they were used for, and sometimes we can even find out why such woods were used. The profile in wood use of one community at one time differs from that of other communities and may vary over time.

The description of an object must also include the traces left by the technology used. In buildings, walls can be of brick, bonded or not by one or another type of mortar, and laid in different systems of courses. Walls can be rubble inside, dressed stone outside or stone and wood. A metal object may have been hammered or cast and traces of the casting process used can usually be found. Painting techniques differ and traces of the media and application are quite visible. Patina on wood can be analyzed and the traces of carving by adze or knife or axe are evident as are the traces of polishing by metal file as opposed to sanding by leaves or other materials.

Once the description of the object as it now exists is done, there comes the more difficult examination of whether that was its original appearance, and whether it contains hidden features. The latter is the easiest to discover. When peculiarities in the mass of objects are suspected, X-rays will reveal them. It is not infrequent for sculpture from West or Central Africa to hide features inside. Swords from the Kuba kingdom (Kasai, Zaïre) often bury a tiny *olivancillaria nana* shell in the hilt. Beneath a rather shapeless exterior some western Sudanic (Senufo) sculptures contain a well-carved statuette and some objects from shrines of western Nigeria (Yoruba) contain paired statuettes in metal linked together (Claerhout 1978; Herreman 1978; Neyt 1981:87–9). Such cases tell us that the objects are not what they seem to be to the Western eye. Explanations for such practices must be sought in the cultures of origin.

The most notorious problems of original shape as opposed to the shape now perceived are found in architecture. The great mosque of Qairawan was the most revered in the Maghrib. It was remodelled many times. As we see it now, the minaret is its oldest part and may date from *c*. A.D. 724/728. The basic ground plan also dates from that time or even earlier. The main prayerhall dates from 836 with extensions of 862. Remodelling, and the addition of courtyard galleries, occurred in 1025, and further additions date from 1293 to 1316 and even later. Restorations occurred in every century after that. The mosque has a history of shapes that must be unravelled. As the most prestigious mosque in the Maghrib, it was an object on which successive rulers in Tunisia liked to leave their mark, to aggrandize it or to restore. Additions are detected by a consideration of the present ground plan, the tie-ins of different parts of the masonry, and examination of the different styles of execution, epigraphic evidence and documentary reference. Even in this well-studied case, art historians are still not completely agreed about the sequence of construction (Marçais 1954:9–22; Lezine 1966:12–81; Sebag 1965).

But architecture is not alone in this; a number of carvings or paintings have not retained their original shape as decay or erosion takes its toll. More importantly, many carvings, for example all masks, were only part of a total shape that included feathers, beards, costumes, paint, etc.; the carved parts have been selected out of the whole. Objects should also always be examined with the possibility of restoration or mutilation borne in mind. 'Total restoration' means totally new fabrication, and requires a search for the object which the restorer copied. Moreover, many of the objects that reach collectors and museums are fakes.

FORGERIES AND THEIR ILK

Documents or objects are forged for all sorts of reasons, but by far the main motive is gain. The more flourishing a market in art, the more fakes. Old Egyptian objects were already forged in the last century, while Benin fakes appeared on the European market less than three years after the looting of treasures from that city (Graebner 1911:12–21). Shortly after 1900 a Fang knife (Gabon) with a cuneiform inscription appeared on the market. The knife was authentic, the inscription not (Graebner 1911:18). Fakes have multiplied since then – some are made in Europe, some in Africa by African artists copying older works from the same or from a different area. All of these are forgeries in the sense that they do not correspond to the indications of origin attributed to them (place and date) when offered for sale. Quite apart from out-and-out imitations, some art dealers forge pieces by restoration or, much worse, by destroying genuine pieces to use the parts obtained for several new pieces. Between this and disfigurement of authentic but stolen pieces, the boundary becomes very thin. An extreme case is that of the Chibinda Ilunga hunter's figure of the museum of Belem which was stolen and then mutilated by the removal of small figures on the base (Bastin 1976). Many private collections as well as even major museums harbour fakes and many are unwittingly reproduced in art books. While the owners and curators do not talk much about it, still, some pieces are only exposed as fakes many years after their acquisition.

Careful study of a piece frequently exposes forgery. Examination of the medium can uncover unusual features or even a foreign substance; study of the techniques often yields traces of European tools and signs of haste when the forger has tried to use techniques identical to the original. A forgery crafted with loving care would not afford much of a profit, at least not until recently. The finish often betrays the forger: polishes and patinas are easily analyzed and hard to imitate, artificial ageing by induced corrosion, addition of mud, smoked crusts, even fake insect boreholes, can also be detected rather easily. One should not stop at the examination of one feature, but continue throughout the whole set that can be examined. Style by itself is a lesser indicator because this is the characteristic forgers imitate most. As to theme and motifs, most fakes are faithful copies of some original (which often can be found to be a reproduction in a well-known magazine), but some of the best forgeries are innovative in theme in order to escape detailed stylistic comparison and to attract a higher price as an unusual or a 'unique' piece.

If serious examination can nearly always lead to the exposition of forgeries, why then do museums and collectors not undertake them routinely? Mostly it is a matter of cost, and legal authority (pieces not yet acquired cannot be physically analyzed). Whatever the reasons, there is unfortunately too much laxity over acquisitions. Even in 1980 we saw a major museum acquire a large art work representing a hitherto unknown theme for the area it was supposed to stem from, in an unknown type of composition and accompanied by very slender documentation, without analyzing the wood, the patina, or even attempting to account for several unique and foreign-looking motifs on the piece. Pressure from donors was cited as a reason for the acquisition. The only step taken by the management was to seek certificates of authenticity by consultation with authorities in the field, none of whom actually said in so many words that they believed it to be a forgery. But then, they did not guarantee the authenticity either.

If forgeries occur most frequently among moveable objects for sale, a few have also been reported for Saharan rock paintings (Lajoux), where the motif was a hoax, of a type sometimes played on unwitting archaeologists by members of the public carrying Roman coins (Mauny 1970:79–80). Documents faked to substantiate information about pieces seem much rarer than forgery of objects themselves, and forgery of ethnographic information in general is exceedingly rare, although not wholly unknown (Piskaty 1957). Supporting documentation and unmoveable objects of art should then also be scrutinized carefully for any signs of tampering or forgery.

AUTHOR AND PLACE OF ORIGIN

For any object to be more than an *objet trouvé*, a 'found object' that we can admire but never understand, identification of origin is the first step. For public monuments, wall frescoes and other immovable objets d'art, the question of provenance is straightforward. For movable objects, it can become quite a search as the previously mentioned Vallisnieri statues illustrate. For most of such objects, the indication of origin is reported at the date of acquisition, at least in a public collection. Mention of the name of the artist was exceedingly rare and still remains rare today. Most artists, except for architects, were anonymous and very few works were ever signed; collectors in the field merely noted the place where they had gathered the piece. Unfortunately, even that information is often unclear. At the beginning of the century, the mention of a district or a market town was often enough. Even then, and probably under the influence of the earliest ethnographic museums, the practice was to label a piece by a tribal origin, that is, by the name of the ethnic group where it had been found. Since then, such ethnic names have become the main nomenclature, although some indications of village of origin began to appear in the 1930s and later, but this trend was reversed by the late 1950s. By this time major dealers in the arts of Africa south of the Sahara could send out personnel to buy up or acquire the production of any locality where classical art was still to be found, and scholars, seeing that their lists of villages of origin merely provided guides to buyers, stopped providing such information. The very existence of a flourishing and aggressive market has thus been quite detrimental to the identification of art objects.

Many objects came to Europe or America without any documentation,

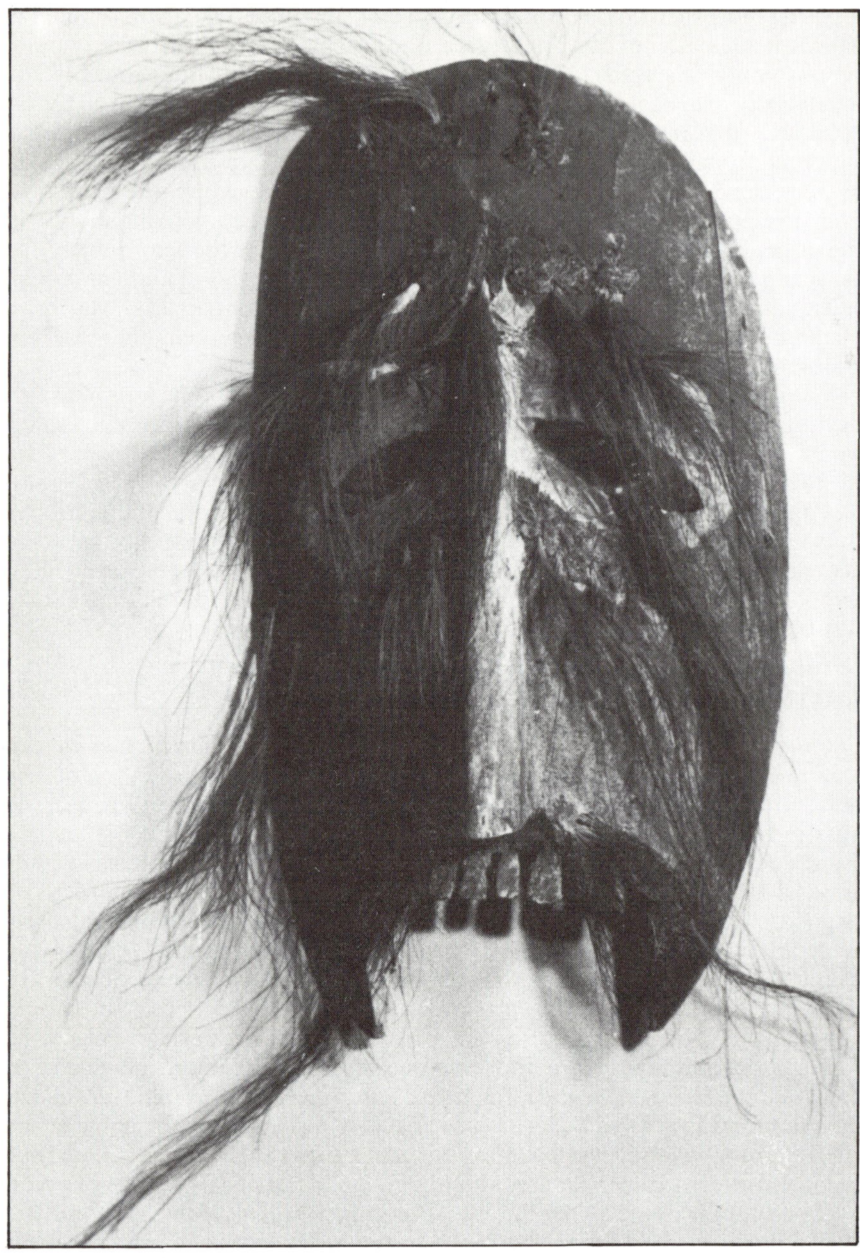

Plate 2.2 *Mask. Wood* (Rhicinodendron Rautanenii Schinz), *hair from dwarf buffalo, eyes from bottle glass. Use unknown. Once ascribed to Eskimo, then Koryak. Via the* question mark *rubric of* African Arts *identified by Linden Museum, Stuttgart, by analogy as from Bukoba, Tanzania. The users may have been the Ziba people* (Vrienden van het Etnografisch Museum, *2 (3/4), 1975, 5). Etnografisch Museum, Antwerp. Height 32cm. Acquired 1955. Probably made before 1914*

and until recently there was a rubric in *African Arts,* asking for identification of objects reproduced there. Identification in such cases is provided by comparison to objects whose provenance is known, usually by overall similarity of the icon and by detailed stylistic comparison. Specialists become so versed in this that they almost unconsciously identify pieces. Thus, even if we did not know that the *ifa* board of Plate 1.1 came from Ardra, we would still place it in western Nigeria (Yoruba) because *ifa* boards from the nineteenth and twentieth centuries (cf. Plate 2.3) are still quite similar in general shape and style. Some over-confident art critics identify workshops in this way, and in some cases artists. 'This work betrays the same hand as the master of the aquiline profile' means that the writer claims that both pieces were made by the same artist. It is also a statement that is usually impossible to check because the maker(s) of any of the works compared remains quite unknown. Such statements should be taken as indicating stylistic groups and presumably close relationship of manufacture, but not providing absolute identities.

Even when places are given by records, they need to be examined carefully. Quite apart from errors as in the Vallisnieri case, the locality in Africa may be that of acquisition, but not of manufacture. Thus, the noted German anthropologist, Frobenius, used to send out helpers to collect objects. An item of his, labelled Bolombo, merely means that it is in that locality on the Sankuru that he acquired the object. His collector might have obtained it up to well over fifty kilometres or so away in a circle all around. In another case a mask was acquired in Tabora, Tanzania before 1898. Yet its style is clearly central-east Luba (see Fig. 2.1). Very likely it came to Tabora along the caravan routes (Frobenius 1898: Fig. 12, Tafel V; Krieger and Kutscher 1960:84, Bild 73, n. 161 and Bild 75, n. 165). As trade and sales of objects were not at all rare in precolonial Africa even south of the Sahara, the latter situation may have been much more common, especially for early objects, than is realized. We know, for instance, that the kings of Mbailundu in Angola had their thrones made to order further east among a people called the Chokwe (Bastin 1968/9:60, ill. 43), and that carvers from the Loango coast, just north of the River Zaïre, operated as far south as Luanda and as far north as the Ogowe river delta in the nineteenth century (Nassau 1904:308–11; Fleuriot de Langle 1876:294–5). In all such cases stylistic identification will usually correct the written entries.

The identification by 'tribe' rested on the ingrained European belief that each then-catalogued ethnic group differed from all others in its customs and especially, apparently, in its visual arts, while all the members of the 'tribe', on the other hand, wrought art objects in the same style. But for more than a generation now, scholars have shown that tribalism is a colonial phenomenon, that ethnic feelings are variable and ethnic identities multiple, overlapping, and generally fuzzy. Nevertheless, this remains the main nomenclature today, and it does lead to inaccuracies and muddles. As a nomenclature the system is sometimes absurd. A huge area in the west African savanna is labelled Bamana (or Bambara), a huge area in the Gabon/Cameroun forest is Fang, but every single town in the Cameroun grasslands is an ethnic unit, such as Bamessing, Bafut, Fontem (Bangwa), etc. We know from experience that several styles are to be found in the one Bamana area but we still label it Bamana. Or we have a

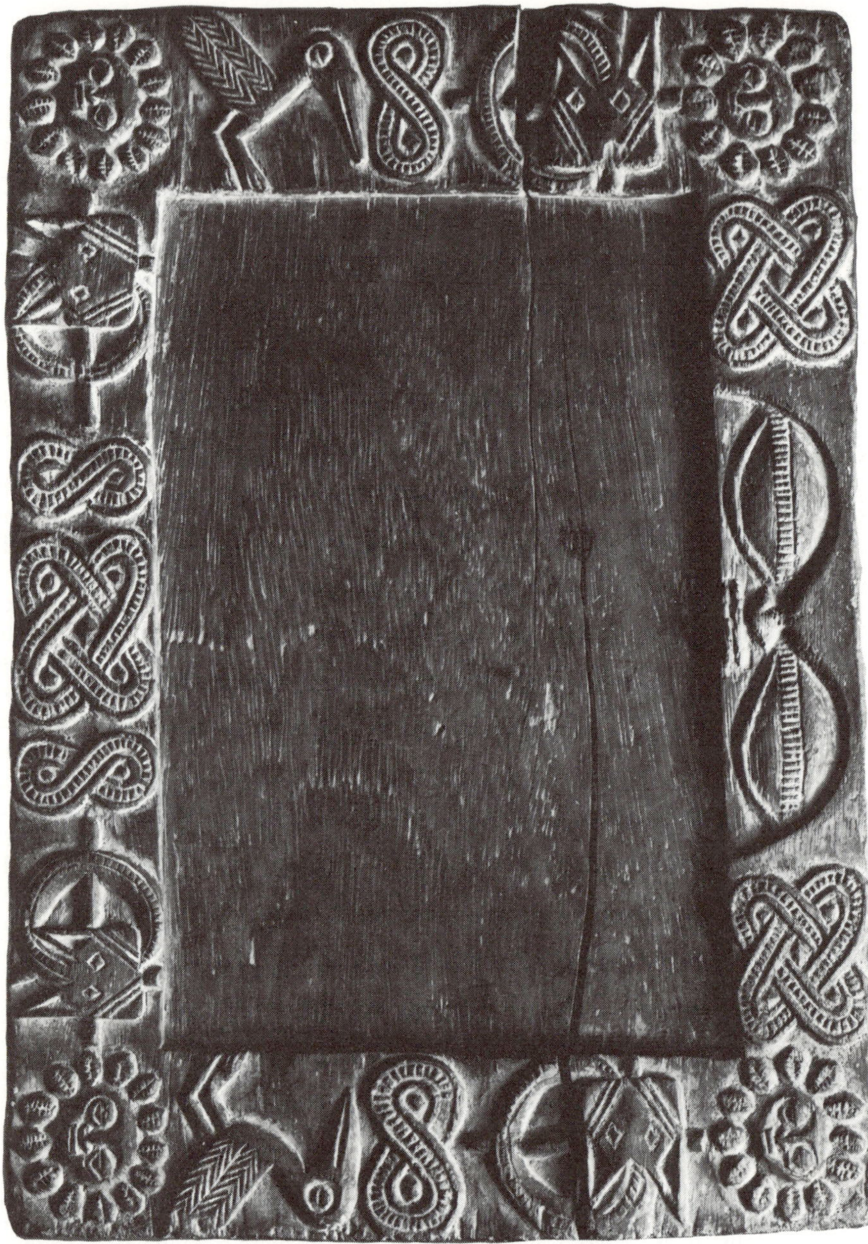

Plate 2.3 *Divination board. Wood. Used in* ifa *divination. Northern Yoruba, western Nigeria. Museum für Völkerkunde Berlin-Dahlem. Width 40·5cm. Before 1910. The face represents the God Eshu/Legba. Compare interlace knots with Fig. 9.4. Probably North African element introduced via decorative pattern on costumes*

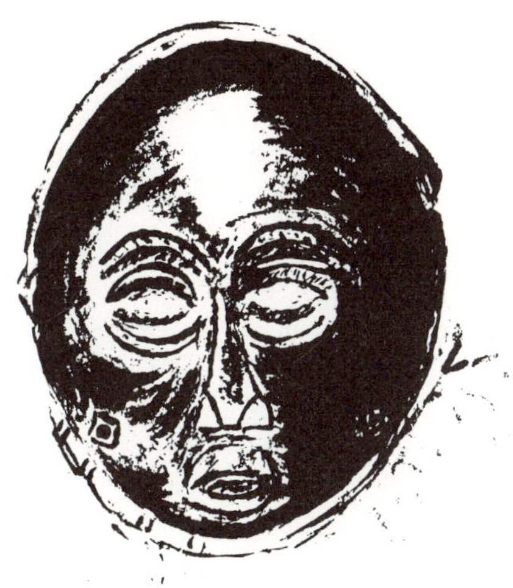

Fig. 2.1 *Luba mask. Acquired at Tabora, Tanzania, from 'Manyema' people in 1890, showing how far objects could be spread by traders. After L. Frobenius 1899, Tafel 2.12a*

label Igbo for eastern Nigeria, where the major characteristic is that style varies greatly from one subgroup to another. In Liberia workshops are known that can work either in the Wee (Gere) manner or in the Dan (Gio) manner, as the client wishes, and these four labels refer to two peoples divided by the Liberian-Ivory Coast boundary (Himmelheber 1960:136–47; Fischer 1978). Contrary to Fagg (1965), there is no necessary link between ethnicity and any form of visual art. True, in many cases features of body decoration, such as scarifications or hairstyles, or features of costume such as distinctive caps or textiles, become badges of identity, but other expressions of visual art rarely become a focus of ethnic pride. Anything can, on occasion, become such a focus: language in the Cameroun grasslands; a certain ritual of female possession among the Tio (Brazzaville); a form of greeting among the Mongo (Zaïre bend); even forms of marriage, so why not on occasions a type of object? Because actual occurrences of such situations seem to be so rare, each case requires proof. The focus of identity should lie on the object, not on the institution of which it is a part, and it should lie on a major formal feature, not on a detail, such as facial scarification that identifies the ethnic group of a statue, for instance. Then one can reasonably apply an ethnic label. The exceptional nature of such cases does not warrant a convention whereby all art is labelled by ethnic group. Why not label it by institution?

An example from Gabon shows how serious distortion can result from such a perspective. A type of reliquary figure, largely two dimensional, made out of wood covered by copper and/or brass strips or wire, was made in eastern Gabon and is known to collectors as *mbulu ngulu,* not quite an accurate name. These are 'Bakota ancestor figures' (see Plate 5.1). A recent study of the different substyles asserts once more that these are Bakota pieces. But the

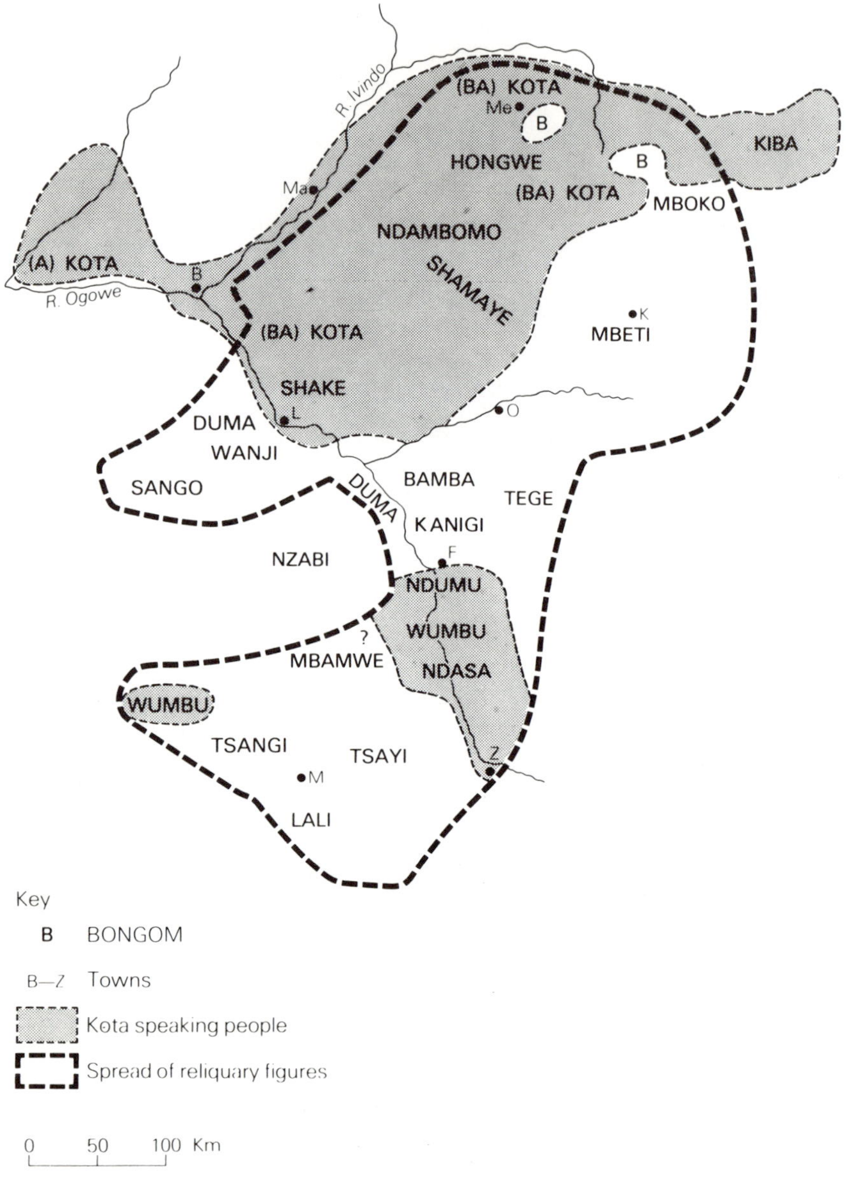

Fig. 2.2 *Kota and reliquary figures. The lack of overlap is evident*

name Bakota or Kota is given to all the peoples who speak similar languages to that of the Bakota proper, a small group East of the Ivindo. It is therefore an artificial name, not a genuine ethnonym. A glance at the distribution map of the reliquaries (Fig. 2.2) shows that two large groups, the Bamba and Mbeti, are included. But they do not speak Bakota languages. They are *not* Bakota. Moreover, while the Bakota proper may have made such reliquaries, their relatives west of the Ivindo, known as the Akota, never did, so the linguistic division does not correspond to a coherent area of manufacture either. There is in fact no relationship between language and the manufacture of reliquaries. The art historians first equated language and culture, then equated culture and aesthetic creation and finally claimed that some groups which had *mbulu ngulu* but were not Kota speakers must be 'Bakota' after all, while omitting the unmistakably Bakota Akota! Having done this, they are still faced with the fact that some Bakota use masks belonging to one tradition, some use masks of another tradition, a third group have their own masks christened Bakota because the Bakota proper, east of the Ivindo, have them and some Bakota may never have made masks at all. Moreover, none of the styles in masks corresponds to the style of the reliquaries. The facts are clear enough by themselves, only the attempt to force them into an ethnic mould clouds the issue (Chaffin 1979; Perrois 1979; Dupré 1980; Siroto 1981).

It is high time to abandon this artificial nomenclature (as against Fagg 1965; Bravmann 1973). Objects should be labelled by village and workshop of origin, if known, otherwise by reference to the institution to which they are associated. In this book I use geographic designations and put ethnonyms in brackets, but I cannot do away with them on penalty of leaving my readers without any points of reference when they consult the literature.

In northern Africa, among the *oikoumenical* traditions, identification of common movable objects such as rugs, textiles, ceramics, works in leather or wood is just as complicated as south of the Sahara. Often identification by style is not as certain a guide here as it is in the regional traditions. Thus almost identical plaster decorations were found at Sadratha and dated to *c.* A.D. 1000, in southeastern Algeria and at Boudenib, dated *c.* 1900 in Morocco. Places of acquisition can be very far indeed from place of manufacture, as a caravan trade or trade by sea carried such objects as far as the East African coast or the northern borders of Akan country in Ghana. On the other hand, monuments are much better documented, often because of inscriptions. Especially in Islamic art, costly textiles, metalwork and some ceramics carried the date of manufacture and sometimes the name of the artist (Hill and Golvin 1976; Atil 1981:51, 148–50; Talbot Rice 1965:92, 148–50, 188). Inscriptions were treasured here and practically all major mosques have older or younger inscriptions relating to their foundation.

DATING

The importance of dating can hardly be overstated. No history without chronology, whether absolute or relative, is possible, and that is as true for art history as for any other branch of the discipline. Unfortunately, very few art historians south of the Sahara have heeded it. In northern Africa and Ethiopia the relative occurrence of dated monuments and of literacy have insured that chronology attracted at least some attention. South of the Sahara the problems were greater and they were ignored. A paper first published by F. Olbrechts in 1941 (Olbrechts 1943) is still the only general discussion of the problem to date, forty years later, the same neglect bewailed by Olbrechts prevails. Yet several means of dating exist, whether by using written and oral documents or by physical means applied to the objects themselves, but clearly the effort involved seems too great for most practitioners. There will, however, be no history of art if there is no chronology.

The written data linked to the object usually include its accession to a collection, sometimes its acquisition in the field, but almost never the date of manufacture. For some objects that date may be the year of acquisition, but sometimes the work may be much older. Objects that have been collected a long time ago, for example, the Vallisnieri pieces, have moved and must be traced down from descriptive catalogue to catalogue and from references in other writings. We have already seen that a major problem here may be to establish with certainty that an object mentioned in a text is the same as the piece we know. Hence the examination of iconographic materials is of unusual value here.

The earliest reference to objects probably of African origin in European collections is contained in the accounts of Charles the Bold (Brussels, Chamber of Accounts No. 1925, f. 348; April 1470): 'To Alvare de Verre, servant of Sir Jehan d'Aulvekerque, Portuguese knight . . . 21 pounds . . . when lately he presented a sword and some figures in wood as idols to him. . . .'.

European archives, repositories and printed documents cannot usually be related to objects now extant, even in curiosity cabinets, but relate to objects seen in Africa, or others brought to Europe and now lost, as in the case of Charles the Bold. But as similar objects still exist, the general conditions of their manufacture, the location and date of manufacture and the general patterns of acquisition and removal to Europe can be known. Thus Portuguese account books and stray references from the 1500s onwards document their acquisition of ivory spoons, forks, salt cellars and horns in Sierra Leone and on the coast near Benin (Ryder 1964; Fagg 1959). Some of these are Afro-Portuguese work because some of the extant objects, as on horns, show inscriptions in Latin and motifs borrowed from Iberian works of art. Others are entirely uninfluenced by this. An occasional detail helps to date actual objects. On the salt cellar now at the Pigorini museum, V. Grottanelli observed that the men wore trousers with a codpiece fashionable in Italy around 1500 and reproduced on Luca Signorelli's Last Judgement at Orvieto (St Brizi Chapel) dated between 1499 and 1502. But codpieces remained fashionable for a long time afterwards. A horn could be dated because it commemorated the marriage in 1500 of a Portuguese king and therefore dates from 1500 or sometime later, and such dates agree with the archival references.

On other pieces, dating by comparison with European drawings of costume or indeed by comparison with extant costumes themselves is possible. In this way a number of Afro-Portuguese ivories can be dated within a decade or two. Late rock art in South Africa can be dated when Europeans or European tools are indicated by the costume or the shape of the tools. In other cases relative dates emerge in similar comparisons. Thus, central Angolan thrones imitate Iberian chairs from the sixteenth century and later, while staffs of chiefs often sport copied rococo motifs, dating them by association to the eighteenth century or later.

Beyond such references, written data and illustrations provide general dating for artistic activity in Africa south of the Sahara. al Bakri (*c.* 1067/8) and Ibn Battutta (*c.* 1352/3) tell about sheet gold and carving in the West African empires of Ghana and Mali. European authors begin to mention art from the

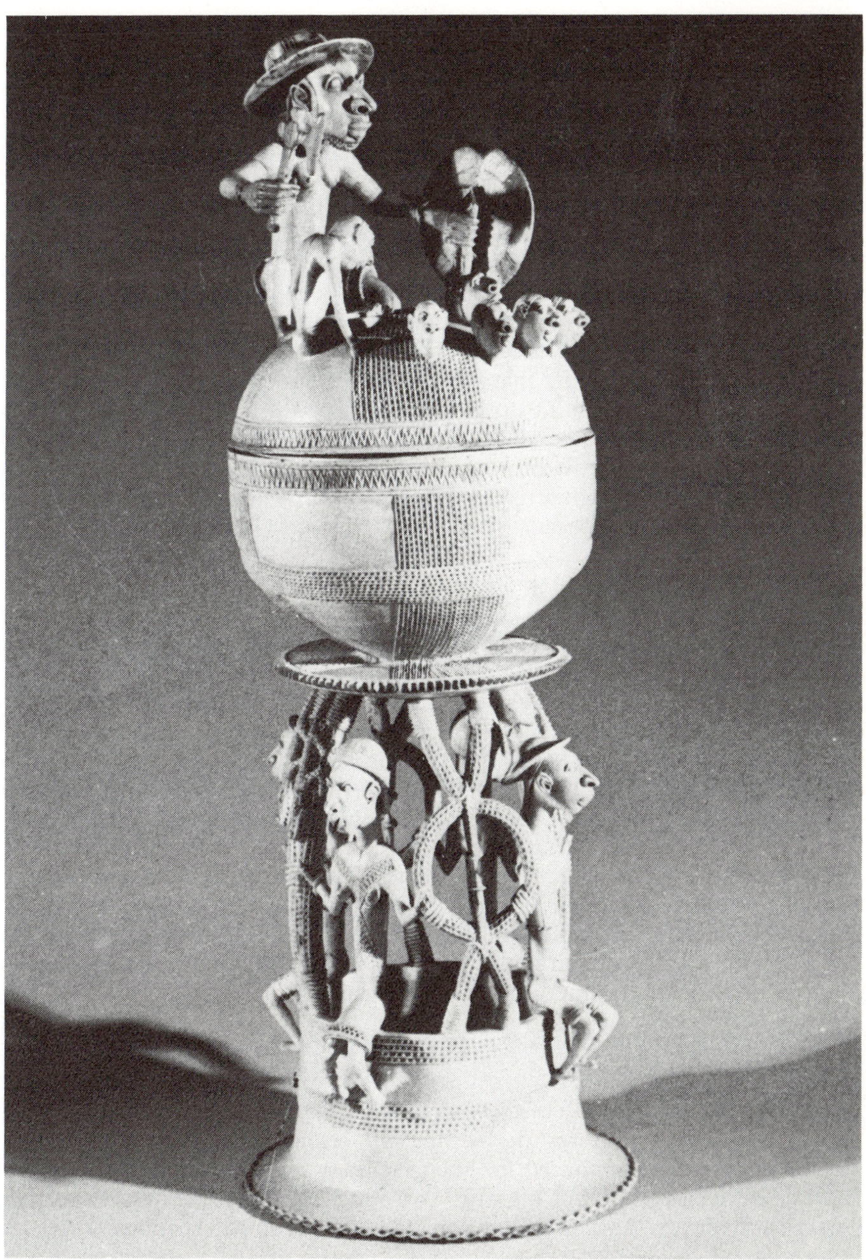

Plate 2.4 *Bowl. Ivory. Used as salt cellar in Europe. Not necessarily made for export, but previous use unknown. Sherbro Peninsula (Bulom), Sierra Leone. Museo preistorico ed etnografico, Rome. Height 43 cm. Probably early 1500s. Restored, and battle axe not authentic. European codpiece and trousers date it post 1499*

mid-fifteenth century onwards, both on the Niger bend and along the coasts and shortly after that African 'idols' are mentioned in Europe itself. Such written sources can be very important, for instance they tell us that curios were made for sale to Europeans on the coasts of Angola and Gabon as early as the 1850s and that by then, and indeed earlier, craftsmen from Loango, north of the mouth of the river Zaïre, were working as far north as Gabon. Except for very early references, and later the best known printed works, art historians have not searched for such sources, yet there is little doubt that written sources should be vigorously explored. From sampling them, I believe that nineteenth and eighteenth-century sources especially have been neglected. Many insights into the arts of sub-Saharan Africa remain to be found there.

Writing and epigraphy date most major monuments in the *oikoumene*, barring only buildings earlier than 1600 in Ethiopia. In Nubia, a chronology of wall paintings has been built up by the combined use of the list of bishops found on a wall in Faras and the superimposition of frescoes found there (Michalowski). Painting in Ethiopia remains undated except for miniatures where the associated manuscripts provide dates and for some wall paintings which can be dated by details of costume or motif (Leroy 1967; Chojnacki 1973).

Oral data can also contribute to chronology, even though traditions are known to be notoriously weak in precisely this regard. The attribution to a particular king of each of the royal Kuba statues (Zaïre) agrees with a stylistic sequence of statues and allows for a dating from *c.* 1750 onwards. In Shaba (Zaïre), the name of one master of the famous Buli style was remembered by the hereditary guardians who kept an ancestral statue he carved for a line of princes. Twelve guardians succeeded each other. The carver may have lived in the early nineteenth century (Neyt 1977:320–1, 444, 464). Oral data in Benin are often cited as hypotheses regarding the sequence in which major art forms were introduced at the court. On the whole, however, the documentary value of such data remains slender. While they are very important as ultimate sources for interpretation or data about use, they rarely deal with chronology. When they do, they most often relate the development of this or that art form and not the history of particular pieces. Nevertheless, oral tradition does provide, from time to time, important information.

PHYSICAL DATING*

Dating the objects themselves mostly relies on physical means of establishing their age and this requires the setting up of laboratories. By and large, archaeologists have clamoured for such facilities and for the development of appropriate techniques, but museum personnel remained passive. Nevertheless, dating can now be securely done on older objects of wood or of terra cotta as

* See Fleming 1977 and Iskander 1980.

Plate 2.5 *Four figures with raised hands in one block. Wood. Use and meaning unknown. Bandiagara cliffs, Mali. L. Wunderman collection. Height 48·5cm. Carbon 14 date with uncorrected half-life and uncalibrated by T. Northern, whom I thank very much: 1305 ± A.D. 90. Range A.D. 1215–1395. Probably 13th–14th c. Dr Northern will publish 30 dates from similar sculpture and discuss their true age, taking into account dendrochronology tables. Such figures are known as* nommo *and labelled 'Tellem'*

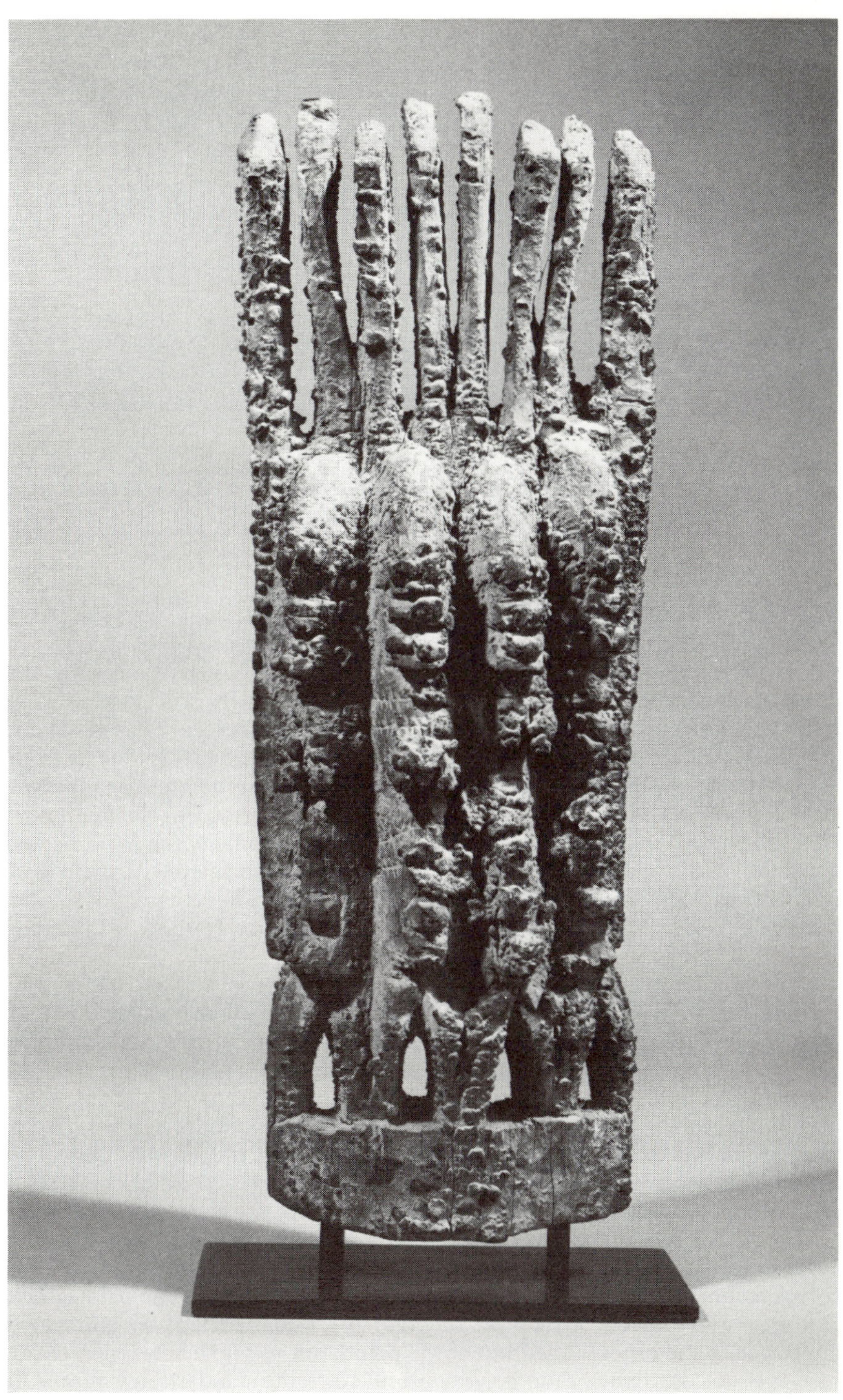

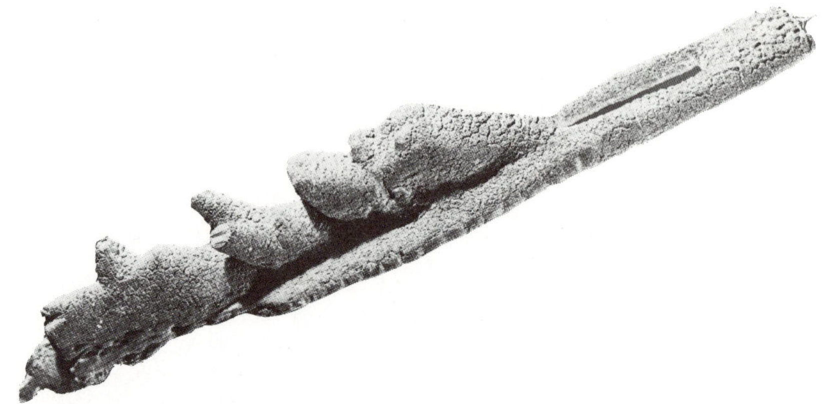

Plate 2.6 *Figure with raised hands. Wood. Use unknown, except traces of sacrificial matter. Bandiagara cliffs, Mali. Koninklijk Instituut voor de Tropen, Amsterdam. Height 48cm. Acquired 1973. Also known as* nommo, *Tellem. The patina is derived from ash, dried animal blood and dried millet gruel or beer. The date of manufacture could be from* c. *A.D. 1000 to 1900. Tellem is used with two meanings: a) for all pieces before* c. *1450 and b) for all pieces, whatever the date, of the style shown by Plates 2.5 and 2.6. Confusion results from a label that defines by time period, whatever the style and genre on the one hand and by genre only on the other. Only dated pieces are best called Tellem*

well as on old iron objects. It may still be possible to date some works in wood one day by the tree-ring method.

The best known of such techniques is carbon 14 dating. It measures the decay of the carbon 14 isotope in organic matter, a decay that occurs at a steady rate. Thus, objects that date from 250 to over 50 000 years back can be dated, provided they were made of organic materials. Apart from test objects from Pharaonic Egypt, only a sample of wooden statues from the Bandiagara caves in Mali (Tellem) have been dated so far (by T. Northern). But the method is very widespread in archaeology and provides the chronology for African sites down to *c.* 1700, and at the same time for art objects associated with them as at Igbo Ukwu. Most iron objects older than *c.* 1700 can also be dated by similar means (Van der Merwe 1969), but the actual technique used to measure amounts of carbon available is still experimental.

Thermoluminescence dating of ceramics relies on the fact that energy accumulates in quartz (sand) grains in the clay as a result of bombardment of particles produced by the radioactive decay of isotopes of uranium, thorium and potassium which are also naturally present in clay. This energy is released in the form of light when the quartz grains in a sample taken from the object are heated, and can be measured in the laboratory. The amount of light emitted is proportional to the time which has elapsed since the object was fired. The method has become quite common during the last few years and has been used to date not only terra cotta from the Middle Niger but also copper alloy artifacts by measuring their clay cores (Stoneham 1980; Fleming 1977:193–200).

A technique now being developed would also allow us to date paint. Rock paintings can now be dated by the rate of rearrangement of aminoacid molecules in the binding medium of the paint. But so far the precision of the results is not great enough to be very useful since the standard deviation still runs to several hundreds of years (Denninger 1971; Iskander 1980: fn. 46; Phillipson 1977:268–9).

All of the extant techniques only yield approximations expressed in numbers and standard deviations. For radiocarbon dates these drawbacks can be overcome by relying on block dating, i.e. obtaining a number of dates (at least three) for closely related material. Particular deviations of results, stemming from variations in the raw materials (pattern of growth in wood, specific properties of shell, bone, etc.) and perhaps the locale (corrective curves proposed for different tropical areas) are often not very significant, but can and often are taken into account to reach greater precision.

So far, then, only items in stone, textiles and non-ferrous metals cannot be dated. It is not impossible, however, that techniques for dating will be found even for them and certainly museum curators should search out possibilities for developing and testing such means. As so much African sculpture, however, is carved out of wood and is presumably younger than 1700, other dating techniques should be developed. Already Olbrechts cited dendrochronology, or the tree-ring count method, which yields precise dates. The method is well established and still expanding for woods in temperate climates. With regard to the tropics, however, quite a controversy rages. Most botanists argue that where tree-rings occur, even in tropical conditions, the method should be applicable (Doutrelepont, personal communication 1980). But banks of comparative natural materials must be set up and quick results cannot be expected, especially since local climatic effects require many control banks rather than just a few for the continent. Opponents claim that it cannot be done, because uncertainties would be too great, because the results would not be worth the effort, and – among museum curators – because works of art should not be mutilated, even by taking fractions out of their core. The issue is far from settled. Given the crucial contribution that tree-ring counts could bring to chronology, certainly in the drier parts of Africa, and even for some species in the equatorial forest, one hopes that efforts will be increased.

So far art historians of sub-Saharan Africa have remained defeatist with regard to dating, especially when it comes to wood. They argue that tropical woods cannot survive for long and that every piece that entered collections after 1900 is practially contemporary with the generation of the sculptor. In the tropics wood decays fast, even if the objects are seemingly cared for. In practice this is very difficult to accept and certainly remains unproven. Some objects were and are kept with great care and might be much older than others. But there is no way of knowing at all unless and until physical means for dating have been perfected to cope with this problem.

Approximate methods of dating by the object in the absence of any outside help consist of relative ranking by style, which will be discussed later, and in dating by context. An example will make the principle clear. A Benin royal head cannot antedate kingship. The presumed royal crown of Loango cannot antedate kingdoms in that area. But one cannot claim the contrary, that is, that this crown dates to the foundation of the kingdom in the fifteenth century or earlier (Volavka 1981b:51). Obviously the crown can have been fashioned later; it only dates to sometime *after* the kingdom was founded. Such reasoning, which depends on use, is always risky, however, because use can change. Thus, in Coptic Egypt, existing *erotes* figures were unchanged but came to mean 'angels', while heathen belly dancers continued to be carved but now carried crosses over their heads.

CATALOGUES

It has been the practice to date pieces by comparison just as they have been assigned places of origin by comparison. In the absence of any other data, this at least is a first step to bringing order into a mass of art objects. To do this well, however, a systematic reference catalogue listing all known objects and all iconographic representations for different periods of time would be necessary. Thus, one could attempt to reproduce all known objects from sub-Saharan Africa in Europe, acquired before 1700, with details about origin in one or more volumes. These would include most of the Afro-Portuguese ivories, but also other ivories, works in wood, textiles, etc. It would, on the other hand, make clear which works were actually dated and which are only dated by association, and how works were dated. Moreover, such a volume could refer to the relevant texts in documents of the period. Standard reference volumes for succeeding periods, up to perhaps 1870 or 1900 could be built up. The result would not only help in placing and dating undocumented objects, but give us a firm basis for a first general framework in art history itself. If this were to be done, one would discover that there are fewer eighteenth-century objects in Europe or America than seventeenth-century objects, that some objects have been crucial for dating many others, even though their own dates are rather vague, but again we could also expect some pleasant surprises.

There is no way that this task can be eschewed if the field is to develop. Perhaps it will not occur in quite this fashion, but rather piecemeal by type of object and medium through series of monographic studies. But an inventory of what was extant in Europe before *c.* 1880 will have to be made. If, in addition, the tree-ring controversy could be solved and physical dating became more routine, the total picture could be transformed. To achieve this end, however, the very first requirement is to revive an awareness of the crucial role of chronology and to have more faith in the potential results of dating techniques. There are encouraging signs that such a revival is underway.

CHAPTER THREE

SOCIETY, THE MOTHER OF ART

Works of art are not symbols only, but objects in the true sense, necessary to the life of social groups

(Francastel 1951:8–9)

OBJECT AND SOCIETY

All social activity uses objects, and not only as symbols but as objects in the true sense necessary to the life of social groups. Hence activities of daily life such as farming, fishing, hunting, cooking, even walking, use objects and not all of these are tools in the narrow sense. Charms for insuring success in any activity, for example, are not tools, but they are utilitarian. All passages from one condition of life to another use objects to mark these occasions and the resulting statuses. Birth, initiation, marriage, and funerals are often surrounded by special objects used in special action. Crises such as war, detection of witchcraft or curing use their own objects. Courts of law, assemblies, spokesmen for communities and rulers all have theirs. Games and entertainment had their own objects. Social status thrives on distinctions of dress, finery, food, furniture, transportation, and housing. Objects not only distinguished between social categories but also between social roles. The headcover of a Muslim judge is not that of the reader of the Quran in the mosque. The emblems of the woodcarver are not those of the smith. Objects were made for use, had social meaning and cultural value. They were almost never made, however, only to be an expression of art for art's sake. As tools and as symbols, objects reflected every facet of the community.

An inventory of all the objects used by a society is a description in filigree of that society itself. Inventories are the material precipitation of social life in all its complexity. This is why archaeologists can attempt to reconstruct long-dead societies and cultures from objects. Art historians are in a similar position if they have access to information relating to use, institutional context, persons and groups involved, and workshops. But their primary task is truly to understand a work of art. An *objet trouvé* without context cannot lead them beyond supposed use. To understand fully a work of art, the social circumstances surrounding its creation, use and function must be known. Society is the crucible in which art is formed. Therefore, aside from aesthetic elements of a general visual and tactile nature, the social context in which it is created is crucial to art history (Brain 1980). In this chapter I will first deal with the use, institutional links and functions of works of art, and then turn to the social matrix of its creation: patronage, workshops and product.

USE

Most objects are used for what they seem to be used for; they are utilitarian. Door locks, heddles, pipes require little by way of explanation as to use; however, one may wonder about their shapes and especially about the differences between ordinary specimens and those that have been made works of art by carving or by decoration. Thus, the lid of a Kuba cooking pot, begrimed with soot, is clearly used to cover the pot, but why would it be plaited in intricate decorative patterns that are quickly obscured by the soot? It took up to three weeks' work to fashion such a lid, and yet soon the charming decoration became invisible. Why then was it decorated? The lid was an indication of status, and reveals that wealthy people could afford the expenditure for labour required to make such a lid.

The actual use of many objects is not self evident and errors of assignment have been made. Thus a copper object, labelled 'fishing basket' in a great museum (Plate 3.1), was later believed to be the crown of the monarchs of Loango (Volavka 1981b)! Other scholars viewing it with the objects associated with it believe that the object was a shrine. Among the hypogee rock-hewn structures at Lalibela in Ethiopia, two that were believed to be churches like the others, were not; they were palaces (Gerster 1968:104–5;

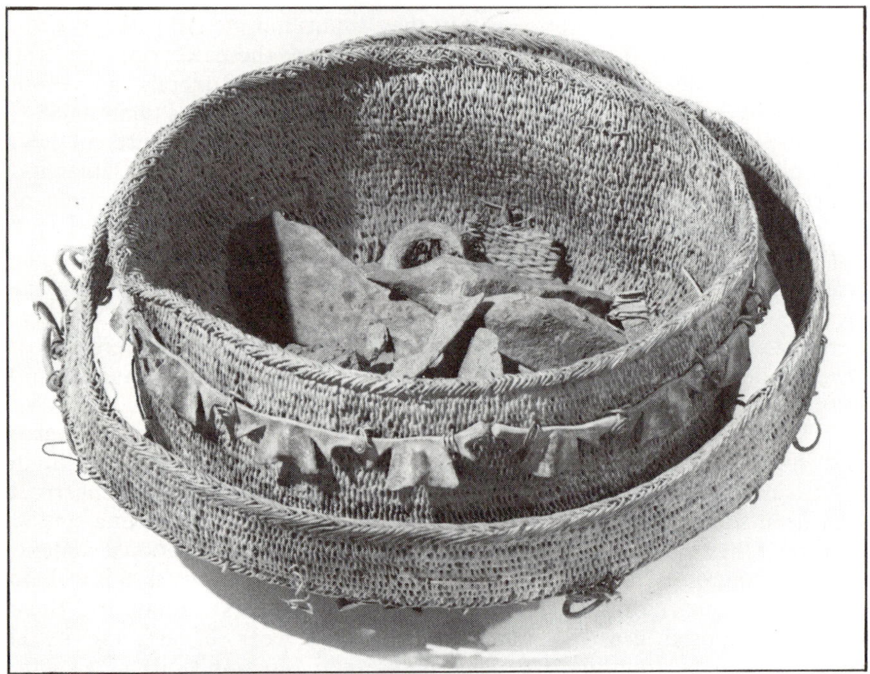

Plate 3.1 *Crown or shrine? Copper thread for the dome shaped object which has a large hole near the apex. Fifteen copper and iron objects with it. Near Kabinda, Angola. Musée de L'homme. Diameter 36·5cm; height 20 cm (double the size of a chief's cap). Before 1933. The museum, after Tastevin, calls it a shrine for Lusunzi, spirit of the fish. The metal objects were strewn around the dome and represented the fish. Volavka (1981b) sees the objects as regalia and the dome as the crown of the old kingdom of Kongo. She dates the dome to the 13th or 14th c. when that kingdom arose. The size of the dome makes it too big for wear. Crowns do not necessarily date from the foundation of kingdoms*

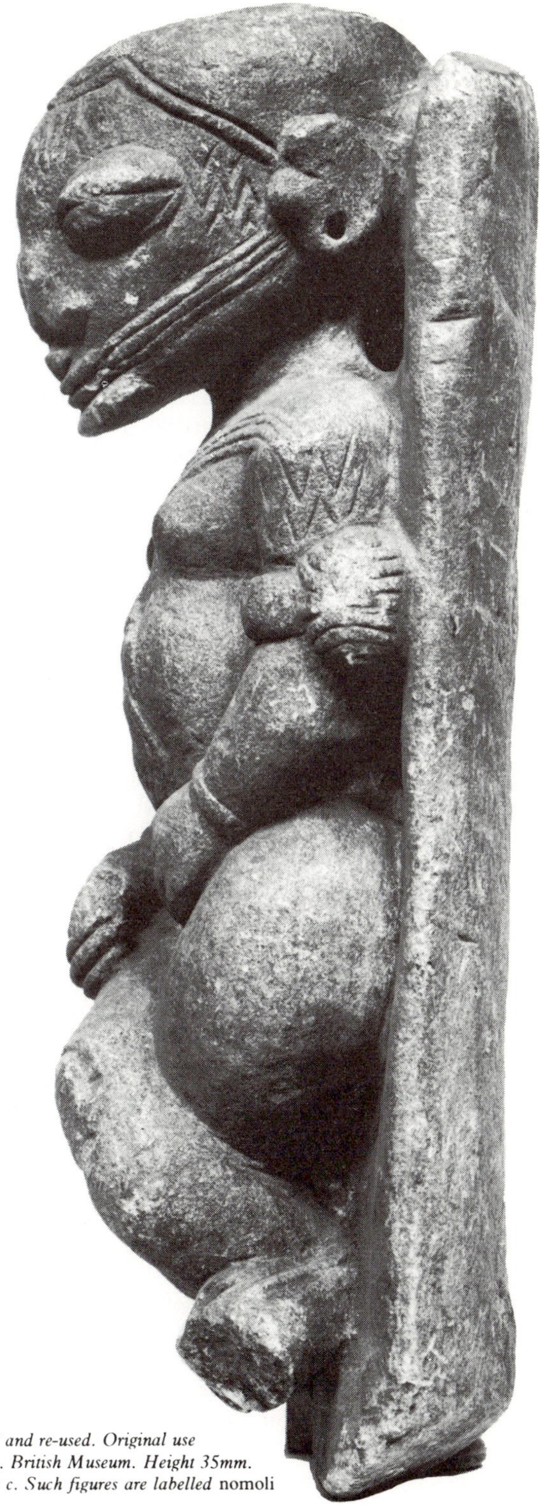

Plate 3.2 *Figure. Soapstone. Found in soil and re-used. Original use unknown. Sherbro Peninsula, Sierra Leone. British Museum. Height 35mm. Acquired 1904. Believed to be 15th or 16th c. Such figures are labelled* nomoli

Leroy 1973:145–6). On postcards a circular-looking building around an open oval in the interior of southern Tunisia and adjacent parts of Libya is labelled 'Berber Palace', whereas such structures, in fact, are granaries.

Moreover, questions of use, when art is involved, can also have complexities. Thus, the *minbar* in north African mosques is a staircase, leading to a platform. Obviously its use is not that of an ordinary staircase and no one ever ascends the highest rungs. The *imam* addresses his congregation on Fridays from one of the lower steps. Consideration of use related to structure raises questions such as: why so many steps? Why the shaping of a platform on top that is never used? Why an entrance gate to some, not to others? Why is the *minbar* on wheels in northwest Africa and not elsewhere (Schacht 1957)? Often a discussion will be couched in language placing so-called functional features in opposition to non-essential features. It should be stressed that 'functional' here refers not to function (the overall impact of the object on the community that keeps it or/and its goal), but to use. We can only know what is 'functional' in an object if we know how it was actually used. That is the first step for any understanding of any object, work of art or not.

Although such an observation may seem banal, it warrants attention because, in many cases, the precise use of an object cannot be determined for lack of information. This obviously is true for many objects found out of context such as the stone figurines in Sierra Leone or Guinée. Local finders put them into fields to raise an abundant harvest and sometimes whipped them when the rains were late (Paulme 1981). But how had the makers used them several centuries earlier? Were they put in shrines and talked to? We do not know. Moreover, use is not a simple concept. Objects such as decorated flywhisks are emblems of authority. They are used by the holder to underline his status when addressing a public or presiding over a court. If in so doing, he swats a fly, that is incidental. The main use, like the main use of drums of office or of thrones, rather than stools, expresses social relationships. Unlike tools or utensils, such objects are not strictly utilitarian. Such a non-utilitarian use has often been called function, but as we shall see that term is better applied in another sense. Function is more than observable use.

PATRONAGE*

Most works of art in Africa were commissioned for individuals or for collective groups. Artists on occasion also worked for themselves to produce art works as utilitarian objects, to advertise their mastery, or in even rarer cases, just for fun or to commemorate privately some person or event near and dear to them. But usually there were patrons and commissions.

The majority of patrons were also the consumers or represented a collectivity of consumers. Individuals often represented collectivities as when commissions came from bishops, *Gadi's*, abbots, sultans, kings, village leaders. The works commissioned were most often destined for their collectivities, although they also served more personal needs of the commissioner, for example, when a palace had to be built. Individual patrons quite often commissioned works for the collectivity as well. This was the case with the

* See particularly Ben Amos 1980b.

successful merchant or general who built a commemorative mosque or the wealthy man who had broken taboos in southern Cameroun who commissioned the *so* initiation ceremonies for the young and the sculptures that were part of it (Laburthe-Tolra 1977: vol. 2 1359–1554). Sometimes the patron did not specify the details of the commission, leaving the decisions to someone else. Thus, in eastern Liberia, the *go* religious master decided who would be entitled to a new mask and what type of mask it should be (Gerbrands 1957:86).

In practice the community of patrons and users expected works to have prescribed iconographies executed in a certain style. Works that were not up to expectation might be refused or, for assurance, patrons might supervise the execution as in the case of buildings. The conception of a work of art thus always involved the community as much as the artist in the same way that an interview is the joint product of interviewer and interviewee. Even when the customer was unknown, the artist was still influenced. Even if he made objects for sale to unknown patrons, he still had to know what they liked (that is, what would sell).

In this sense, then, works of art are truly collective creations. The magnificent frescoes at Faras, for instance, were not conceived exclusively by the artists. Each fresco, each theme, was predetermined for each portion of the wall of the cathedral church, according to rules common to the whole eastern Christian Church. The patron/bishop knew which locations were proper for crucifixions, for the positioning of archangels Michael and Raphael, for various scenes from the liturgical calendar. The local artists at Faras followed convention for centuries in these matters of location, as they did in matters of themes and composition. The artist's freedom in such matters was limited.

On the other hand, while the collective character of works of art is true enough, it has often been misinterpreted by partisans of 'tribal art'. They stressed the dead weight of tradition and claimed that artists were but artisans lacking all creativity. We know that was not true for Pharaonic Egypt or for Eastern Christianity, or for the architects of mosques in the classical style, although traditions certainly were as stringent, and probably more so, than in regional traditions. There were more dynamics in the evolution of taste in collectivities than the partisans of tribal art were willing to acknowledge, probably because they underestimated the complexity of the relationships – practical and aesthetic – between artist and public. In Africa south of the Sahara, as in many instances elsewhere, the public commissioned and the artist could attempt to revise the taste of his public by introducing innovations in the work that was commissioned.

It was rarely true that a given ethnic group was completely wedded to a single style. Often different styles coexisted in the repertoire, being applied to different objects as when in southern Gabon naturalistic masks were made for the same public by the same workshops which crafted highly expressive ancestral figures. The extremes of angular cubism and smooth affected naturalism were turned out by the workshops of eastern Liberia according to the demand. It is incorrect in a case like this to say that they turned out Guere (Wee) masks or Dan (Gio) masks as if Wee patrons asked for one type and Dan patrons for the other. The *same* clientele could ask for one or for the other. In northern Africa, a mosque could sport a Turkish minaret next to a main building in classical style. The expectations of patrons, users and artists did not rule out flexibility and innovation. Within given ethnic groups, different workshops could have different ideas about what form was proper for what object and in some cases form did not matter much at all, provided a very specific meaning was expressed. Initiation baskets of the *Bwami* association (Lega, Eastern Zaïre) contained well-carved ivory and wooden artifacts of great diversity along with buttons, celluloid dolls and natural objects. Whether the thing was an apt metaphor expressing the intended proverb or aphorism mattered here; not its style (Biebuyck 1973:142–57).

And yet specific art forms were related to specific communities, often dominant in a society. Thus, there could be a court art in kingdoms such as Benin, where specific objects with clear stylistic characteristics were reserved for the king or the court and could become items involved in competition for power; and there could be court art as there was among the Kuba, where the most appreciated and imitated works gravitated towards the courts which remained the pace setter of fashion. In such cases, folk art, in the sense of provincial imitation, existed. For example, a small nineteenth-century Moroccan rural fort (*Ksar*) sported an imitation of the celebrated gates at Meknes, while others copied the famous *mihrabs* of the great mosques at Fes, no doubt as an expression of local pride. Folk art in another sense existed where skilled artists could not be afforded by poorer folk, who imitated the better crafted works done for their superiors. Kuba dolls are an outstanding example of this; some are fine carvings, some crude toys.

Artistically, the taste of social classes could differ very much within a given society. In Kongo in the sixteenth and seventeenth centuries, the upper class was Christian and adopted Christian imagery and indigenized variants of Renaissance styles, while most of the population remained faithful to its own art objects and their styles. The East African coast with its division between ruling strata and their Islamized tastes as against the other layers and their 'African' tastes is another case in point (de Vere Allen 1974). The very definition of Coptic art is based on social stratification. At first Copts were Egyptian Christians as opposed to the higher classes who were either devoted to Hellenistic art or to early Christian Imperial fashions. After the Muslim conquest of Egypt, Coptic art was the Christian art of the country, still practised by the lower classes and by isolated monasteries for centuries (Wessel 1965:53–80; Du Bourguet 1967:3–15). The more research has progressed the more such differences between social strata have become apparent. Further examples could not only be adduced from the *oikoumene*, but from places as diverse as the upper Middle Niger, the Akan area of lower Ghana and the peoples of central Angola. Tastes may not have varied as much there, but specific representations and the quality of the work attests to stratified societies.

Clearly ethnicity has been overestimated in the past as a force shaping forms of art and class has been underestimated. But it would also be wrong to see class as a dead hand stifling innovation in the same way as the partisans of tribal art viewed the relationship between ethnic group and artistic expression. The relationship rather revolved around the use of art objects linked to institutions which in turn were themselves linked to class. Thus, in Kongo, East Africa, and among the Copts, religious institutions requisitioned the art made and set the styles. At the Benin or Kuba courts, the taste of the patricians prevailed and expressed itself usually in the formula 'rich is better' and 'more is better' promoting rare media such as ivory or even gold and more lavish decoration.

SPECIFIC SOCIAL CONTEXT

The connection between social institutions and art is the primary one. The following example illustrates the influence on form which institutions exercised. Given a similar basic shape of drum, three drums are compared: a village drum of the Kuba, a royal drum of the Kuba, and a village drum of their western neighbours, the Lele (see Plates 3.3 and 3.4). The difference in execution is striking. The Kuba drum, owned and used by the village, is decorated only with a modest band of decoration. The Lele drum usually shows decorative carving all over in a very fine pattern and exhibits a human face on its side; this rich drum is also only village owned and village used. But Lele villages, unlike the Kuba villages, were sovereign units. They were often larger and always more proud and their drums show it. The Kuba royal drum has deep incised decorative patterns all over and inlays of copper, beads and cowries. It was much richer than the Lele drum and reflected the institution of kingship even though a dynastic drum such as this one was the emblem of one king only, not the drum of kingship itself.

On examination, both the ownership of works of art and the conditions of their use show which objects belong to which institutions and are used on which occasions. In the case of architecture, it is particularly easy to distinguish between communal and private dwellings, to discern what are mosques, churches, shrines, temples for spirit worship, palaces, men's clubs, and so on. In the case of sculpture and painting, textiles, or body arts, the difference between personal belongings, with or without a mark of social class, and collectively owned or used art, as in masks for instance, also becomes evident. It is possible in this way to express a meaningful link between an art object and its social niche.

These links extend to the form of a work of art as well. Usually one type of work of art is found for a defined usage within an institution. This type of statue is an ancestral figure, that type of statue is a charm for healing, this type of mask is used at such and such a stage in initiations, that type at another stage. A one-to-one correspondence between form and use in a given institution, nevertheless, did not always obtain. Masks could be used in other contexts than the primary one for which they had been fashioned. This has been reported for eastern Liberia, where masks of similar appearance could be used together in different ways, within the same general institution, according to the prestige and standing of their owners (Fischer 1978). In other ways masks or other objects could be used outside their primary context among the Kuba where the primary context of some masks was in mimed dances at the capital, although they also appeared on the top of initiation walls. Nevertheless, there rarely exists a problem in identifying the primary context and the relationships between works of art used in a given community or between works of art and other objects there.

Because the tie between institution and work of art can easily be

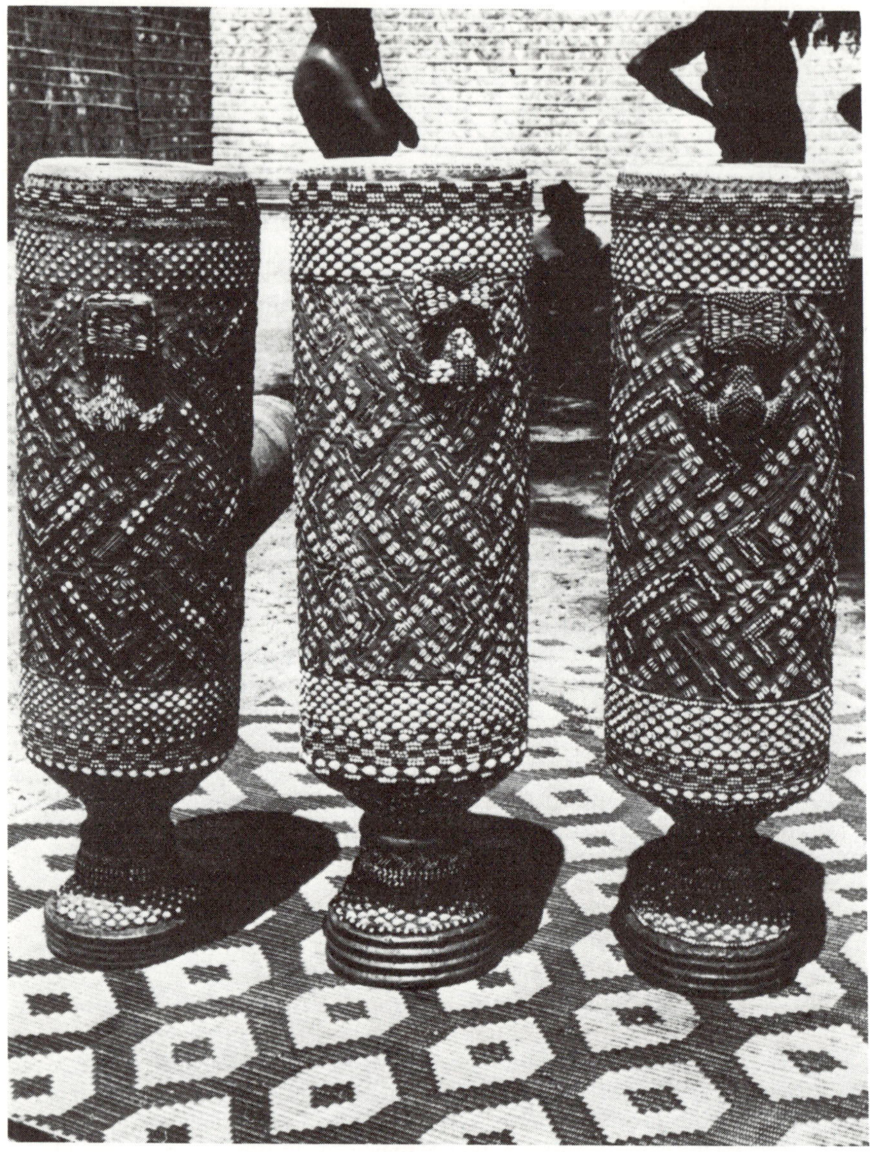

Plate 3.3 *Royal drums*, pel ambish. *Wood, copper, cowries, beads. Nsheng, Kuba kingdom. Now at Institut des musées nationaux du Zaïre. Height 110cm; diameter 30cm. 19th c. The main pattern on each drum identifies the king for whom it was made (one per reign). Rams' heads under the knobs. The richest decorations are the latest drums. 18th c. drums of the same shape and general composition have no beads nor cowries and only a single copper plaque incrustation. Kings associated by oral tradition*

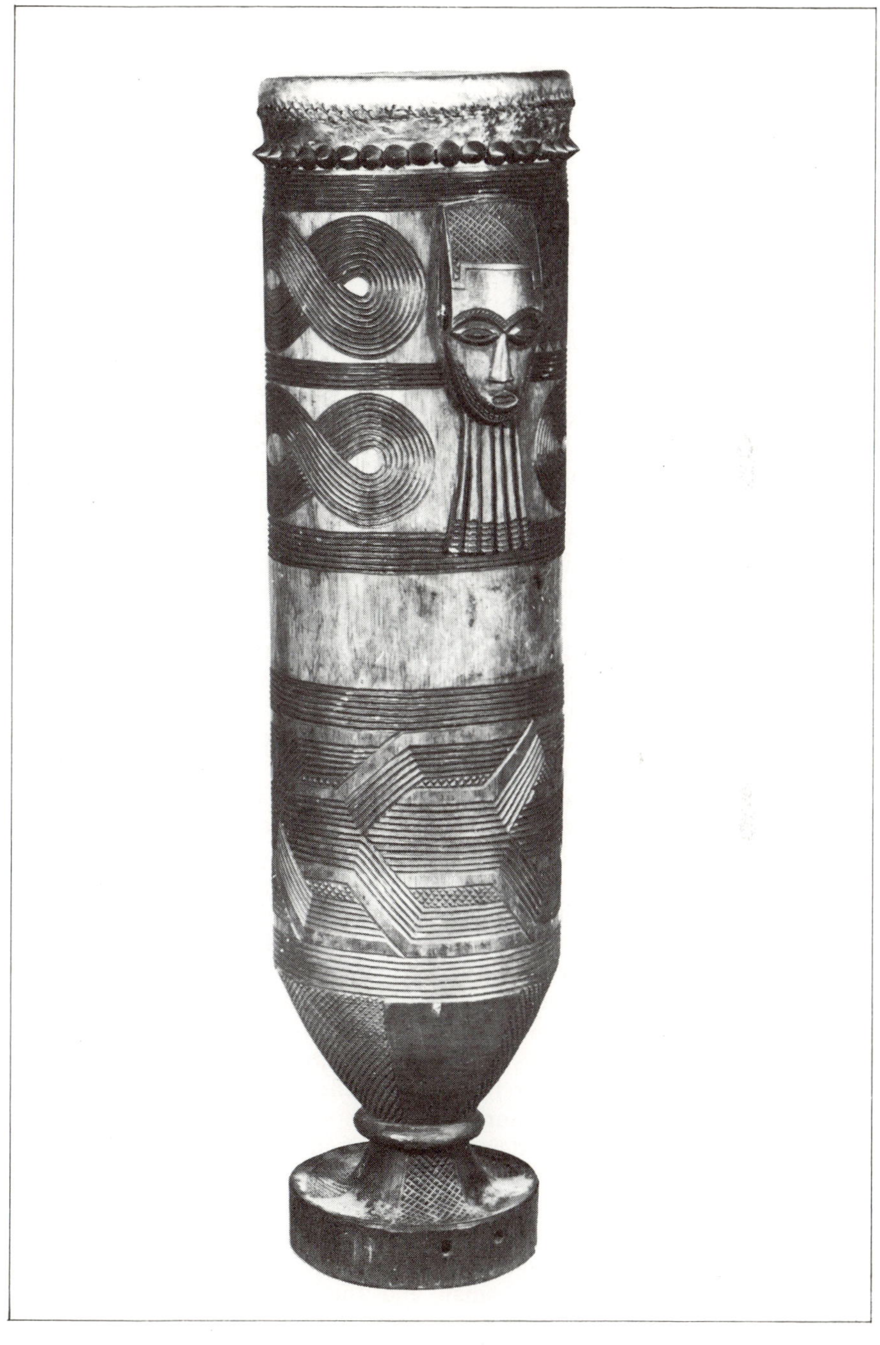

Plate 3.4 *Village drum. Wood. Lele village, Zaïre. Koninklijk Museum voor Midden Afrika, Tervuren. Height 92cm; width 28cm. Date of acquisition: 1924. Probably 20th c. Such drums all have a similar composition with the carved head (a few exceptions are known) and ornament in very low relief*

established, if only by an examination of the ownership and control over use of the work of art, a nomenclature based on the institution to which a work of art is linked, rather than on a simple ethnic name, is much to be preferred. Thus, ancestral figurines of northeastern Gabon should not be labelled 'Kota'. They are figurines to be put on top of bundles or baskets containing the relics of ancestors; a short label would be: 'Ancestral relic figures'. The geographical location should be expressed by village or workshop, where known, or else in general terms as 'northeastern Gabon'. In this way the nomenclature would avoid the false problems that arise out of tying ethnicity to certain objects and certain styles.

ARTISTS AND WORKSHOPS

The institutions in which works of art were produced are the workshops. Even an artist working alone constitutes a workshop. It is there that youngsters learn the craft as apprentices, it is there that the crucial portions of the process of production take place, and it is from there that the finished product is disseminated. Artists were artisans and to the public their skill or specialization was what made them different from other people. As in preindustrial societies, most men and women put their hands to many different tasks. South of the Sahara, wood carving or weaving were known to most men, while most women could fashion pottery for instance. Hence one hears of men crafting dolls for their children or medicine men carving their own charm statues. But skilled work remained the attribute of the specialist, the artist, because he had more practice.

Almost everywhere the division of labour between the sexes left metalworking, building, carving to the men, while pottery was often for women and weaving was man's work south of the Sahara, but woman's work for certain textiles in the north. Often women had something to do with the decoration of woven stuffs. In rare instances women were woodcarvers as well as men. The only reported situation, so far, where they could be equal is in eastern Zaïre, just east of the Upper Zaïre among the Hemba speakers (Neyt 1977). But women as makers of ceramics, mud sculpture, sculptures with paste, decorators on walls or on textiles were not rare. Still there is no denying that those arts which were felt to be important by men were reserved for males almost everywhere (Gardi 1969).

Like all specialists artisans started out as apprentices. Often they were related to the master of the shop by ties of blood, but equally often they were not and had been accepted by unrelated masters on the strength of promise. Beginning with the most menial and crudest of chores, apprentices gradually learned the trade by imitation and they advanced in skill a step at a time. Depending on the media and techniques of the art, this took a shorter or longer time. Thus one became a painter in Ethiopia after a longer period of apprenticeship than an illuminator.

Workshops were large or small and this depended in part on the techniques involved. A building site contained many people, while a carver might work alone or just with one or two apprentices. In some cases artists were grouped in guilds, the most famous instance being that of the ivory and the brass guilds at the court of Benin. They could only work for others with the king's approval and were kept under his watchful eye in the capital (Ben Amos 1980a).

The social status of artists varied from society to society. Where manual labour was despised most, visual artists were despised as well. Thus in western Sudan, Ethiopia and northern Africa, metalworkers, carvers and workers in leather were casted; they could not marry people outside their caste and their calling was strictly hereditary. This did not necessarily mean that individuals were not respected for their skills and their creation, but in the social order their status was low. In Fatimid Egypt, Copts were weavers, woodworkers, masons, potters and architects for minor projects. They came from the lower classes and as such were not prized. Those who had remained Christian but had risen in society dissociated themselves from the artists. Other Copts were monks or attached to monasteries like many artists in Nubia and Ethiopia. Their status as artists was not different from the status monks enjoyed in general.

In portions of Africa some forms of manual labour were highly prized. Smiths enjoyed the highest esteem in west Central Africa so that kings pretended to be descendants of smiths or at least learned how to work iron (de Heusch 1956; de Maret 1980a). Kuba kings all claimed to be carvers and the visual artists in that kingdom were held in high repute, although they did not enjoy special privileges. Chiefs among the Bangwa, a portion of the grasslands of Cameroon, thought so highly of carving that they maintained the fiction that they were the artists, but thought so lowly of carvers that most of these were slaves attached to their household (Brain 1980:135–6). The workshop here produced for the king who then gave away or sold the carvings as his own creation! From the above it appears, then, that no special status or role was set aside for the artist as artist, but that his place in each society was that of the appropriate category of labourers.

Social conventions also moulded the activities of workshops. Some were more specialized than others. Thus in West Africa's Sahel, smiths were also woodcarvers and their wives were potters. The same workshop produced all these products. In Central Africa some smiths were potters but not carvers and their workshops would be different. Most of the smiths' wives, however, would be potters, so that among pottery shops some were thus linked to the smithy and others were not.

The production programme of a workshop could be very varied or very restricted. Thus, in eastern Liberia, where specialization in general was not greatly developed, a carver's workshop made masks, carved stools for boys' initiations, carved spoons, huge display spoons for the wives of leaders, dancing staffs, staffs of office, birds as gable ornaments, little animal figures to be given to the village headmen as a token of respect, wooden statuettes, neck-rests, playing boards for *warri*, pipes, house-posts and a host of implements (Himmelheber 1960:164–81). In the Kuba capital on the other hand the specialization of labour in general was very pronounced by the 1890s. It was natural to find workshops there that did nothing else but carve the heads of pipes and others merely the stems! The production programme was in part the result of technical processes and in part the reflection of the general division of labour.

It is not surprising that when it came to the disposal of the products, the workshops acted like any other production centre. In kingdoms they were taxed on labour or by being given commissions or even on products made for sale. Products were made for sale in many societies, especially when they were unique in some respect, so the art historian must take into account the possibility that some shapes and styles spread simply by trade. It is well known that much of West Africa's decorative arts have been influenced by Islamic models from the north and it is also well attested that many of the examples that were copied moved through the trade of textiles and metal vessels in these areas.

The commercial value of the products should never be forgotten. After all, workshops had costs of production and these had to be met. The value or 'price' of the output was related to them and the greater or lesser commercialization of the societies in which this art appeared established how costs could be calculated and how they could be compensated. In general, smiths were richer than the average person because their wares were in high demand, but carvers were not, especially in societies where leaders were few and the size of the group was small. For some products the specialization was so successful that production ran to an enormous output as with the celebrated Tunisian glazed *zallij* tiles, or the no-less famous Coptic textiles from Egypt. In other cases production had to be small. There were never more than perhaps 150 or so frescoes executed in Christian Nubian churches of the Faras diocese. The scale of the community was small and demand was slow. Whether a permanent workshop could even function there remains unknown, but can be questioned. In turn, raised output could lead to advances in techniques or simply to a faster change in style, whereas the contrary could occur with a very low output. It is therefore important to know of the high outputs of smiths in Ghana who over several centuries turned out millions of goldweights. Enforced idleness never occurred so their skills remained high and the incentive to innovate was strong, if only to escape boredom – at least if the public accepted innovations as they did there.

The economics of production are important in any consideration of art. The volume of output, the size of workshop, the size of the area affected by the product, the possible speed of innovation in form, the relative number of workshops, the relative frequency of skilled artists and even the relative influence of the taste of patrons, all were related to it. Thus there would be few skilled specialists in a rare and costly medium and few commissions. The patrons, affluent leaders, could influence shape more perhaps than in cheap work for large markets. And certainly such rare works set the dominant taste and affected general stylistic evolution as their example trickled down.

FUNCTION

Having sketched out the relationships between works of art and society in general, we can now turn to a consideration of what social scientists call function. Unlike most art historians who mean by this 'use', they apply the term to the effects of use on social relationships. They see art objects as the crystallization of social relationships and a tool in social communication. Art can express power, status, wealth, challenge. Function therefore differs from use or goal as it is the expression of an effect. Thus funerary pole carving in

Mijikenda country behind the Kenyan coast was *used* to mark a grave and its *goal* was to commemorate ancestors (Brown 1980). But its *function* was polyvalent. These carvings helped to assert the authority of elders over youths, to enforce customary norms left by the ancestors over innovations and the like. Through its link with ancestor worship it affected all social relationships in that society.

The fact that expressions of visual art are objects, concrete things, is especially important here. For unlike mere mental propositions, such concrete visual concepts as are expressed in art acquired great reality, as we shall discuss later, and hence their effects were enhanced. This remains true even for ephemeral products such as masks or costumes used as props in performances of dances or festivals.

But the concept of function is treacherous. It implies a double cultural interpretation: that of the community that uses the object and that of the culture of social scientists who interpret the object in terms of institution and social integration. Functions are always deduced, never observed. Because meanings of art objects are often multiple, functions are multiple. Thus mosques represent the community of worshippers, its dependence on God and the rule of its law, but they often also unified a fraction of a community against others who had their own mosques. They could express the importance of wealth, when a benefactor built them. They expressed power in the case of all Friday mosques, because that is where the prayer for the sovereign was recounted on Fridays before the assembly of local government. Similarly, one can say of masks in eastern Liberia that they expressed collective coercion, the power of arbitration, the state of competition, the notions of healing and so on. They were so polyvalent here that they in fact expressed all aspects of social life, and their functional effect was diffuse but generalized.

Art historians should not accept the social scientist's function as a 'fact' but as an interpretation. They should require convincing argumentation and documentation and they should never forget that one function never excludes another. In general, discussions about function often remain loose statements turning around the nature of the most profound ties between art, society and culture. If the documentation is adequate art historians can make up their own minds and marshall their own knowledge to express such relationships.

DOCUMENTATION OF SOCIAL CONTEXT

Crucial as it is, social context is not given by the object but only by descriptive accounts that stem from local authors or foreign observers. Even in northern Africa, where many local writings are extant, much still stems from foreigners, if only perhaps because foreigners were struck by practices, institutions and related works of art that were unremarkable to locals. By far the majority of sources stemmed from men and most foreign accounts were written by professional travellers, businessmen, military officers, civilian administrators, missionaries, physicians, transitory persons such as sailors or Christian slaves in North Africa, or even, from the 1870s onwards, anthropologists (Pechuel Loesche 1907). Local sources were usually chroniclers although a number of letters and accounts can also be found (Djait 1980; Hrbek 1980).

The usual historical critique should be applied to all these sources. First the distinctions between primary and secondary source is highly important. Ibn Battuta (1352–3) did travel to Mali whereas al Bakri (1067/8) relied on merchants' reports. A notice in a museum, or even worse in a general printed work about African art is derivative and its source should be sought.

An example is provided by a Kuba object representing a folded hand (Plate 3.5). This was said to be the emblem of a society of warriors and to represent the hand of a slain enemy in a number of books, all copying one another. Indeed, W. Fagg who had visited Kuba country himself said this in 1958 even for a hand carved on the handle of a drum, quite a usual way of dealing with the handles of a type of village drum (Elisofon and Fagg 1958:211, n.270). I was told that this merely referred to the handle as a visual pun. None of the books gives its source of information, but they obviously copied one another. The first ethnographer of the Kuba, E. Torday, did not mention this in his works, and during my fieldwork (1953–6) it became evident that no such association ever existed and the motif did not represent the cut hand of an enemy. Nor did Frobenius, who collected the earliest such object, give this meaning. He merely called it a ritual object (Krieger 1969 vol. 3:66).

The earliest reference seems to stem from an administrator in the early 1920s and came from a file at the museum of Tervuren (Belgium). No one ever

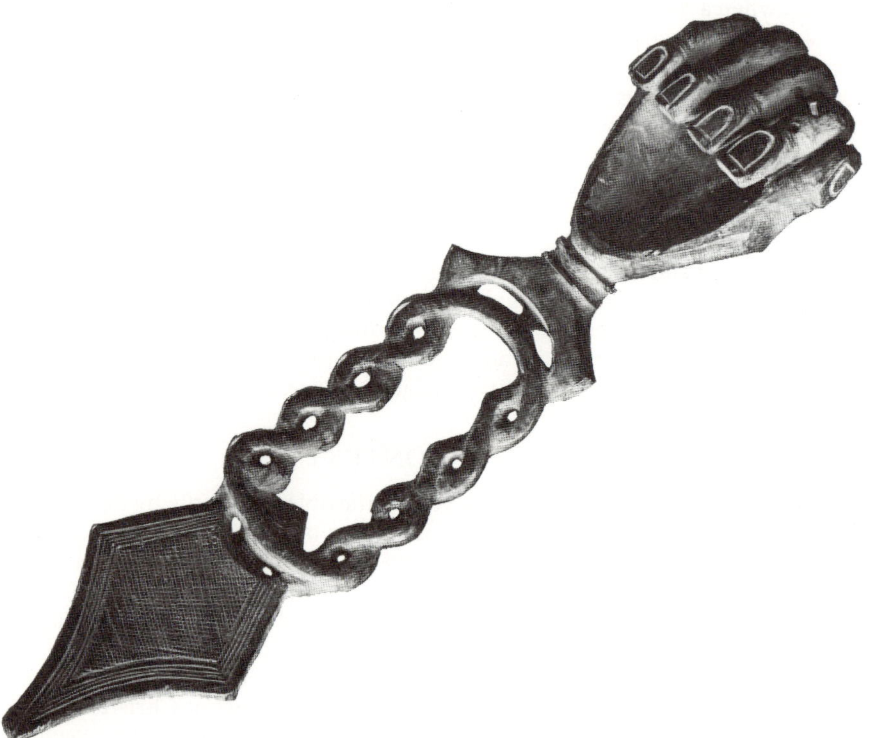

Plate 3.5 *Emblem in shape of hand and forearm. Wood, iron hook at back. Use unknown. Northern Kuba. Museum für Völkerkunde, Berlin-Dahlem. Height 45·5cm. 1906. Probably acquired by Frobenius at Bolombo on the Sankuru river. For his method of acquisition cf. Frobenius 1907: photo 453*

questioned his reliability. The mention of a 'secret society' by Fagg is not very reliable either. His stay was very short, this clearly was an incidental comment and he may have been misled. The cut hand motif does go back to the Independent Congo State and many, in this area, refer to a raid in 1899 by allies of the State on a portion of the kingdom. The eye-witness description of the raiders smoking cut hands over a fire stems from an observer who had been in the country since 1892 and wrote much about the Kuba. The very fact that he did *not* mention any such practice among the Kuba is more significant than negative evidence usually is (Elisofon and Fagg 1958: no. 270, 211; Preys n.d.; Shaloff 1970). The whole attribution is clearly a fabrication in one or more stages. But the prevalence for sensational labels such as 'sacrifical stool', 'executioner's knife' and others, indicates that such inventions have not been unusual at all!

When using documentation it is important not only to establish whether it ultimately stemmed from an eyewitness, but equally to assess the credence to give to such eyewitnesses. With regard to foreigners, obvious points to check are whether they could understand what they saw. Hence the length of stay, the degree of fluency in the local language, the special interests and abilities of the witness, the nature and the extent of his relations with the local population, all are important. The military were better on arms, the trader on trade, the missionary on religion, but the latter was wont to misinterpret matters of religion and certain details could be hidden from him. The military were often waging war against the people they described, whilst the traders were often – in the early days of colonial rule – obtaining goods by force. Anthropologists are not necessarily better sources than others. Their theoretical concerns directed both the selection of their observations and even more the selection of their data for publication, as well as their interpretation of these data.

Internal sources include not only written material, to be examined by the usual rules of evidence, but also oral texts. These can be precious provided they do not refer to a long-past antiquity. Often they refer to the use of objects and yield a fair amount of background about them, whether the narrative in which they are embedded is itself supposed to be truth or fiction. A great deal remains to be learned from such sources, not only narratives, but also proverbs and songs.

Not nearly enough attention has been paid by specialists in the arts south of the Sahara to such questions of documentation. Often even the elementary levels of critique are not attained, and yet historical critique is crucial to establish a sound body of data. To neglect it on the grounds that data from the field are never forged is childish. Some totally faked relations exist and in many cases it is not at all clear exactly how the data set forth were obtained nor how reliable the observations about art actually were. To neglect to apply the rules of evidence on the grounds that this is only a minor by-product of an art historian's main task is myopic. Given the primordial importance of context to any understanding of any work of art, questions about the reliability of the information should rank near the top of any list of concerns to the art historian.

CHAPTER FOUR

MEDIA AND TECHNIQUES

Artists are poets (*poiein:* to make) in the literal sense of the Greek word. They are 'makers', and lovers of art should never forget it. An art work is the transformation of a medium into an artistic form, and each medium has inherent physical properties which, in accordance with the techniques used by the artist, affect the descriptive and aesthetic features of the work of art. They do not merely allow it, or influence it, but they are form inchoate before the work is done, form realized afterwards. Their qualities, shapes and textures differ, so that a work in one medium is unlike the same work in another. A bangle in ivory, decorated or not, differs from a bangle in copper, by the grain, the texture, the colour, the touch, but even more by the hint at the shape of the material: the natural hollowness of the tusk as against the fluidity of metal setting around another hollowness. Visual images like all objects belong to one medium, or to one set of mixed media. A raised tattoo is a form of decoration. It cannot be imagined to have the same effect on any other material than the human skin. Yet objects, even art objects, sometimes are carried out in another medium than the usual one, just as an engraving differs from a drawing. The Kuba imitate decorated calabashes in wood, but the result will never be mistaken for the original. It becomes a new art object on its own, with its own values. This process of translating the form of one medium into another is called skeuomorph development.

Media themselves are often already transformations from inert natural material into man-made materials. The iron ore block is not iron, the raffia palm frond is not the raffia textile, raw clay is not the medium the potter handles. Often technological processes already intrude between raw material and medium, whether or not they are executed by the artist. In this chapter we cannot describe all technologies that transform raw materials into media, because that would be tantamount to surveying the production of all material culture in the whole continent (Gardi 1969). We can only mention the major techniques by which media become works of art, and even that only for the most common resulting arts: architecture, sculpture and major forms of two-dimensional art.

Creative conception, coupled with skilful manipulation of the medium, are necessities if a work of art is to be a fine one. And the concordance of these features marks the work of a superb artist in contrast to an indifferent artisan. Virtuosity is highly appreciated in many African cultures. But south of the Sahara at least, the transformation of a raw material into a very similar medium, as, for example, in the case of metals and sometimes the making of the form out of the medium is not all attributed to skill. The makers must observe rules relating to the 'real invisible' world. The raw material can be guarded by spirits, as is the case for gold in the western Sudan; or it may be either the abode or even the nature of a spirit, as when a tree is propitiated before being cut; or the belief is not explicit but ritual purity is required during the working of the material as when smelters must abstain from sex before they reduce iron. In African cosmogonies raw materials, and the activities of reducing them to media and then to find hidden form, have a place. No 'natural' action alone will produce transformations that are believed to be meaningful. Making is not just prosaic, it involves invisible guidance and inspiration. Especially striking new prime works are often attributed to the revelation of form in dreams by supernatural beings to the artist.

ARCHITECTURE*

The material for building was long-lasting, such as brick, stone, mud brick, cement, or more ephemeral, such as mud, wood, fibres. It could be raw such as undressed stone, but usually was made into a medium by dressing as for stone or wood, baking (brick), puddling (mud cement), plaiting (fibres). Brick and stone were the favourite materials for public buildings in northern Africa, mud in West Africa, undressed stone, later regularly laid, and minimally dressed stone in southeast Africa. Elsewhere wood, thatch, even fibres or leaves were used. The impermanence of many architectural achievements south of the Sahara has led to the popular belief that architecture did not exist there. That is as erroneous as to claim that Japanese pavillions made out of wood and screens are not architecture.

The techniques of architects, influenced by the purposes of the buildings, were dictated by their goals. They were concerned with interior or enclosed space and with the positioning of masses. In northern Africa architectural concepts closely resemble European concepts. There technique coped with the building of walls by taking standardized units such as brick, and by roofing over the inner space by means of beams, arches, or domes. The basic technique was additive. That means that the vision of form could be deployed in space, unconstrained by the size of any block of material in which the form had to be contained. Only one architecture in Africa was subtractive, i.e. hollowing the building out of a mass given in advance. This is the case of the rockhewn, monolithic churches of Ethiopia. The concept there is closer to sculpture than to architecture (Gerster 1968).

The main problems encountered by architects stemmed from stresses caused by the weight of the medium and by roofing resting on load-bearing walls. The construction of openings such as doors and windows affected the total strength of walls. Even blind walls were limited in height by such stresses. As for roofing, both the span of units used to roof and the weight of the roofing are classical problems. Wider spaces could be obtained by the construction of internal supports (posts, columns, pillars, sections of interior wall) while larger open spaces required structures such as arches (both in walls and between walls), vaults and domes. Where the materials were lightweight and less strong, the walls would not carry a heavy roof and interior space usually remained quite constrained in width. Some remarkable achievements were

* See Denyer 1978; Marçais 1954; Creswell 1952–9; Gerster 1968; Badawy 1978.

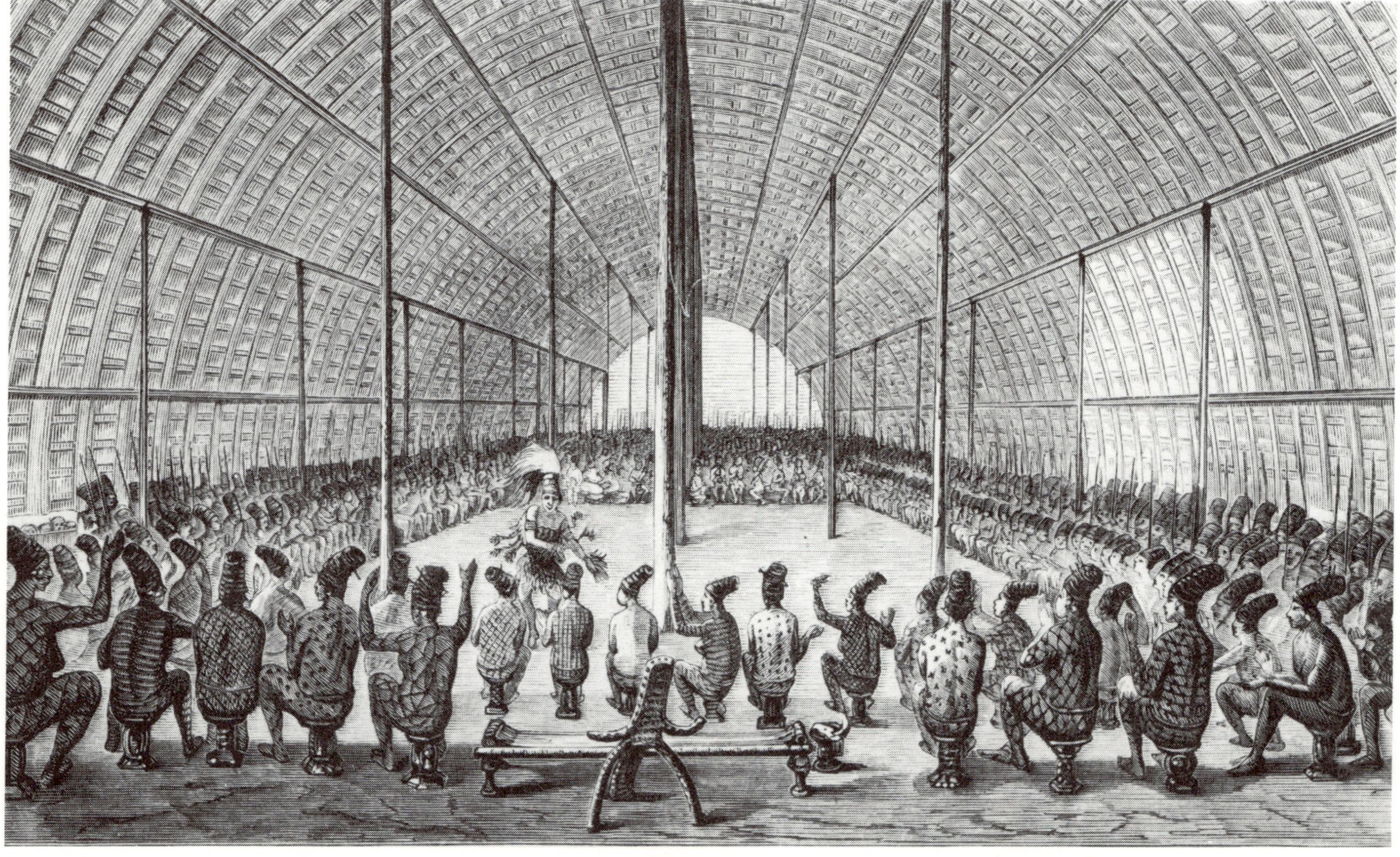

Plate 4.1 *King Munza's reception hall. Wood, raffia stems, leaves, grass. Mangbetu kingdom, Zaïre. Sketch by G. Schweinfurth in March 1870.* (The Heart of Africa, *Sampson, Low, London, 1878, opp. p. 28/5). Dimensions estimated at 100 × 40 × 50 ft (30·5 × 12 × 15m). Built shortly before observation*

nevertheless constructed as in the huge Mangbetu halls of the nineteenth century with 12m wide barrel vaulted roofs or roofs sloping from *c.* 15m height to very low sidewalls, while the front and back wall as well as interior posts supported the armature. The length of such buildings was *c.* 30m and posed no problem. Often architectural constraints were severe, because shifting cultivation forced the people to move their settlements once a decade or more often. The solution consisted in building lightweight walls and roofs in prefabricated form, so a dismantled public building could be re-erected elsewhere. In such circumstances, the architect's interest was not focused much on interior space – most life went on outside anyway – but on relationships of buildings as masses to outside space, enclosed by walls or streets. Thus, although the Kuba capital was not permanent, precise measurements for every street, and for the positioning of every public building in or out of the palace, of every plaza, of every private compound, were kept as a plan by the architects, recreating similar effects wherever the capital went (Vansina 1976).

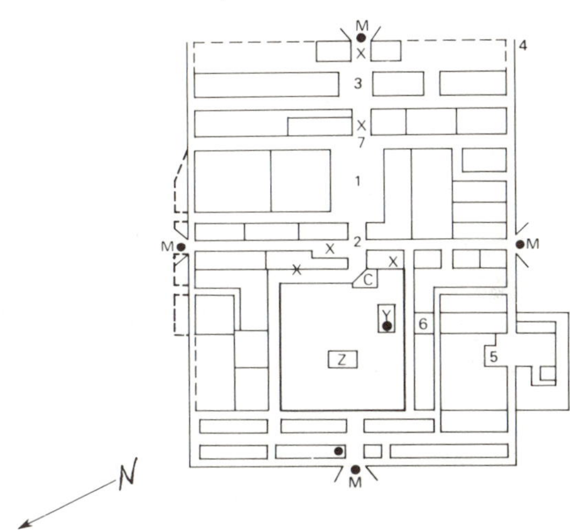

Fig. 4.1 *Plan of the Kuba capital, Nsheng. 1953/6. Kuba right is our left. Upper part upstream, lower part downstream and more prestigious. 1 Great square; 2 Square of the crossroads; 3 Square* mbweengy; *4 Square of the crown council; 5 Square of the royal dynasty; 6 Royal drum: 'the leopard in town'; 7* Yon *drum; M markets; x public buildings; thick line: Palace wall; thin lines: compound walls; dot: trees protecting the town. No details of palace grounds. Note, however, C: daily council square; Y: private council square; Z: Harem square. In 1953* c. *2 000 inhabitants. In the 1890s between 5 000 and 10 000*

Skill in architecture is a complex notion as building involves the collaboration of many people: the architect, usually also the contractor and his unskilled or skilled help. Skilled masons were quite important for stone, brick or mudbrick buildings. The effects of media on the form were obvious and not always perhaps intentional. Intentional effects included *ablak* in Mamluk architecture, the alternation of stones of different hues, also a feature of early Coptic churches in Nubia, or the patterning of bricks and stones as they were laid. Less intentional effects, on the other hand, included the slope of minarets, walls and buttresses in the mud architecture of the Sahel in West

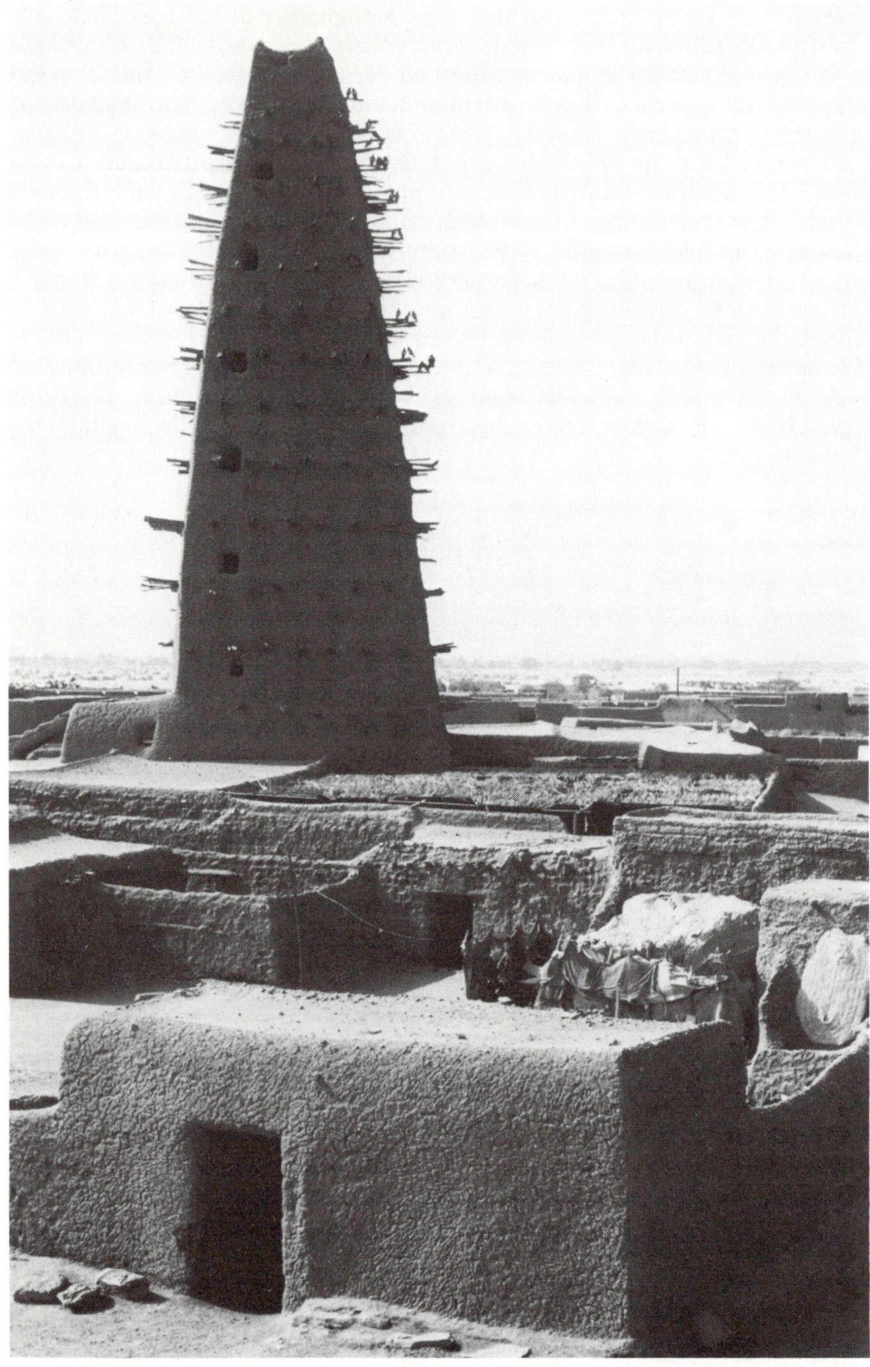

Plate 4.2 *Minaret. Mud and wood. Agadez, Niger. Photo 1968. Reported from the mid 19th c. but real age unknown. Top corners in central Saharan style going back perhaps to 11th c. as a feature*

Africa. The visual effects imposed by the materials were remarkable there. Not only do minarets and walls often look like hedgehogs with beams projecting from them, not only was the impression of mass and horizontality overpowering, but details on big buildings or the whole of smaller buildings such as holy tombs in southern Algeria, looked more like mud sculpture than architecture. Where interior space was quite small, mass turned into volume (see Fig. 7.1). The hedgehog effect resulted from permanent scaffolding for the continual repairs mud walls needed. The sloping effect was a result of coping with weight stresses and the horizontal effects stemmed from the inability to use such materials to build walls up to any great height. Low as the walls of mosques on the Niger were, they still had to be massively buttressed.

ADDITIVE SCULPTURE; METALWORKING

The texture of a medium is extremely important in sculpture, whether in the round or in relief, because just as architecture deals with the closure of space, sculpture is concerned with volume. Like architecture it is a three-dimensional art but volume predominates, while mass in architecture is subsidiary to space. Volume could be either built-up (additive technique) or subtracted (carving proper). The differences in media, techniques and effects are such that we will discuss them separately. Additive media were usually metal, ceramics, or mud. Other materials such as pastes (among the Kuba made of powdered camwood) or even leather, such as in early nineteenth-century dolls from the Cape, were also additive. Additive media were quite pliable and weak when the form was moulded and then hardened or were hardened to achieve some permanence. In its fluid or plastic state, the additive medium allowed the making of almost any shape. The subsequent necessity was to achieve a permanent stable state. Even mud sculpture must dry!

Metals have been used for jewellery and larger sculpture over most of the African continent. The main metals were iron, copper and alloys of copper, gold and imported silver. Lead was sometimes used. Metallurgy requires complex expertise for the reduction of the ores and the preparation of alloys. Basic techniques were known in Africa from two millennia ago (iron in southern Africa) to over five (copper in Northern Africa). The history of developing and varying technologies is still very imperfect, but the technologies existed and produced different media. Thus iron is not just iron; steel, more or less carbonized, has different properties of tensile strength and malleability. Cast iron is a different medium altogether because of its brittleness and lack of elasticity, while wrought iron again differs by its ductility and ease to work. Already in the ninth century the smiths of Igbo Ukwu (Nigeria) knew that copper was better for smithing and chasing while bronze was better for casting. Leaded bronze is more ductile than copper, but copper is more easily hammered, embossed, twisted and engraved (Shaw 1978:119).

The metal was worked either by heating and hammering into shape or by heating it beyond the melting point and pouring it into a mould; that is, by casting. Open casts could be used, in which the mould was formed by a hollow stone, or by hollow ceramic, or even by a prepared hole in the ground. This certainly was the oldest procedure in use. Kongo (lower Zaïre) used these techniques, for example. The other main method was lost-wax casting. It

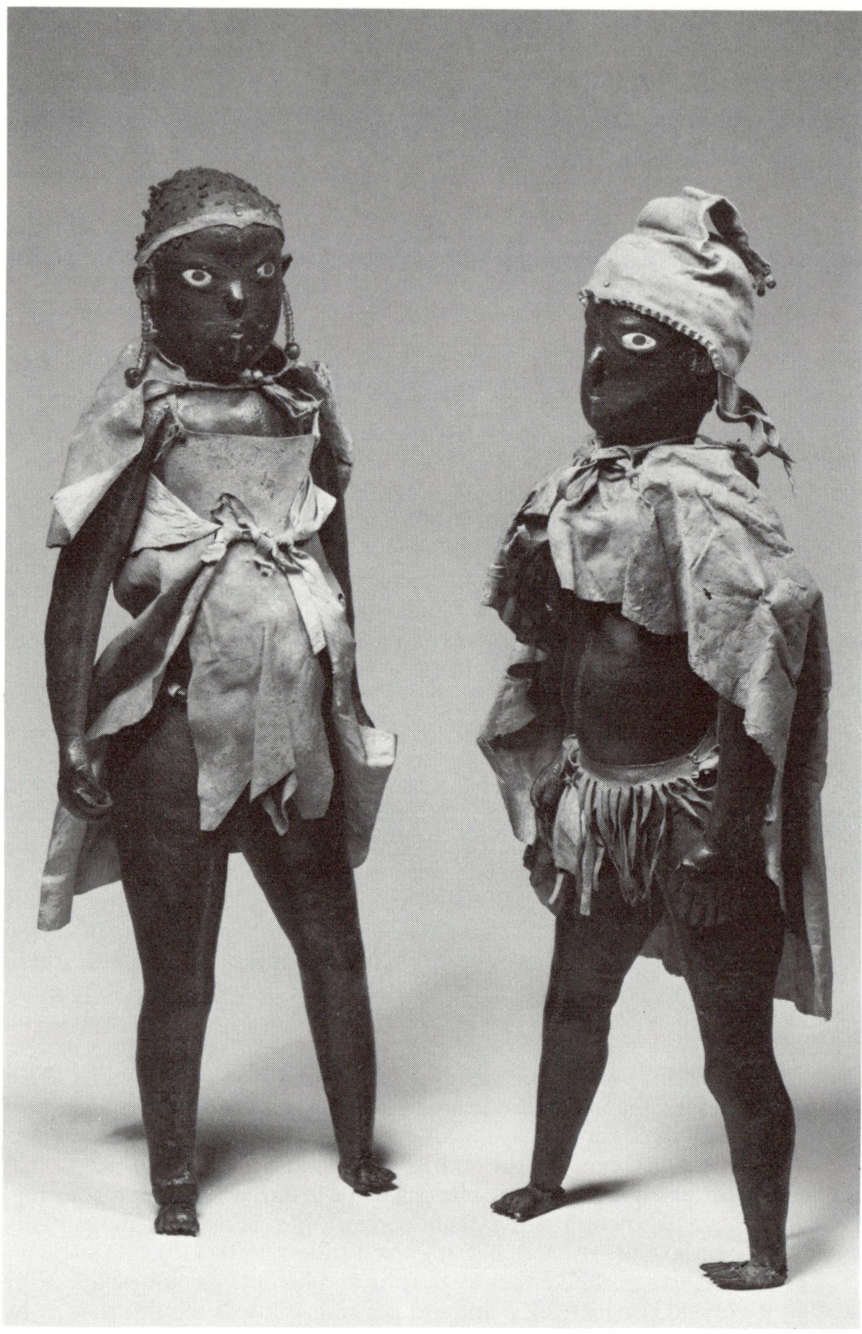

Plate 4.3 *Dolls. Leather stuffed with cotton. Glovelike stitch and material. Use: costume doll for sale. Cape Town. Museum für Völkerkunde, Munich. Height 35cm and 36·5cm. 1815–1830. European or European inspired work. Represents a San couple (man with cap). The tradition lasted at least until the late 1860s. Source for costume of San, Khoi, Khosa and others portrayed, but usual name 'Zulu doll' unjustified*

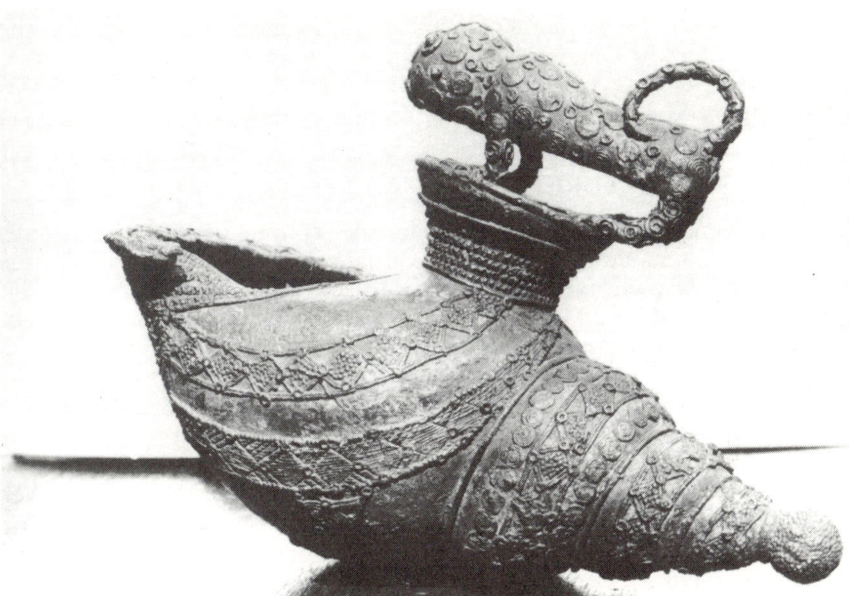

Plate 4.4 *Vessel surmounted by leopard. Leaded bronze with low tin content. Isaiah-Igbo Ukwu. Length 20·1cm; width 9·4cm. Ninth century A.D.. The shell imitates that of a Triton shell. Triton shells are found on the coast 100m away. Note the anti-clockwise (sinistral) winding which is quite unusual. The very fine and dense decoration follows the winding. The object is now at the National Museum, Lagos (Nigeria)*

involved the construction of a ceramic mould, the core, on which the icon to be cast was modelled in wax. The core was then covered with a hollow clay mantle and fixed to it to keep its relative position. The completed structure was then heated up till the wax ran out, leaving an empty space in which the molten metal was then poured. As wax is very pliable, the casting could achieve almost incredible fineness and detail; but the process was complex. For instance, special care had to be taken that the gases of a molten metal would not crack the mould, but could escape through the outer wall, whose porosity was usually increased for this purpose by incorporating organic material or charcoal into the claystuff that made up the wall. These tiny materials burned out and opened the way for the gases. Ducts had to be provided for the wax and excess metal to leave the mould at less visible points and so that the stays that linked the core to the outer mantle should not hamper the flow of metal. Garrard (1980:116–21; Williams 1974:179–213) gives perhaps the most impressive description of this incredibly difficult technique requiring perfect timing, perfect control of temperature and an impressive deftness of hand. The technique had been known in Egypt since Pharaonic times and spread to West Africa before the ninth century A.D.

Hammering and heating techniques also developed with diversified operations such as annealing, hammering, punching, chasing, embossing, filigreeing, and using inlays. Most parts of the continent show ample evidence of a range of techniques for handling metals. Thus art objects are sources for technological history and sometimes can be 'placed' by the techniques used. It is worthy of note that techniques of welding and riveting were not very much developed so that size became a permanent limitation of metal sculpture. The giant iron statues of Dahomey, where such techniques were used, are rare. They can be contrasted to the seated statue of Tada (in the Ife style) which was cast in one piece, an amazing feat.

ADDITIVE SCULPTURE: CLAYS AND RELATED MEDIA*

Ceramic techniques had to be known before metal could be worked as tuyères for smelting and moulds for casting were usually made from clay. Basically the technique involved purifying clay, adding grit and homogenizing the material. It was then shaped, dried and fired, either in the open or in a kiln. In most of Africa, barring the northeast and lower Zaïre after the sixteenth century, the potter's wheel was not used. Bases were moulded on an older ceramic or a natural base such as the bottom of a calabash. Walls were built up by coiling rolls of clay and smoothing the walls to the profile wanted. That is the colombine method. Technical intricacy varied from pottery made over an open fire, to the use of clever kilns where temperatures were reasonably controlled and in which ceramics with glazes, slips, enamels were produced. Such a factory for ceramics was unearthed at Faras and operated in medieval Nubia (Adams 1977:496–8). Ceramic figures were usually made in kilns as well. The products of work with clay were immensely varied from plain crude kitchenware, to earthenware, faience, glazed wares, from plain bricks to the luminous *zallij* (Tunisian and other) tiles, from weights to figures, sometimes life size in the round. The oldest known tradition of sculpture south of the Sahara is the culture of Nok. The range of techniques was vast. Glass manufacturing was closely allied to them. Northern and later western Africa made beads, while small sculptures or vases, bottles, and lamps were made in Egypt. Painting on glass flourished in nineteenth-century Tunisia (Ayoub and Galley 1977).

Clay allowed the greatest versatility of expression of all the media used in sculpture. Ceramics could achieve intricate curved volumes as well as blocked angular ones and could provide the finest detail. Hammered metal could achieve effects of silhouetting: volume reduced to a line or cut-out effects. Ceramics could not achieve this. Perhaps metal was also a better medium to intertwine space and volume. But even metal was not as versatile as ceramics. The only limitation of ceramics was one of size: the size that could be managed by the artist in the firing and the weight that made it moveable. Unlike metal, uneven firing, variation in porosity, and even variation in the composition of the prepared clays could all be exploited for effect.

Mud sculpture required little technical skill beyond the shaping of the volumes on an armature. It was less versatile than ceramics because it was more fragile and had to be protected from humidity which limited it to works which could be contained within a house or which could have a roof built over them. It was also clumsier; volumes had to remain more massive and details much less worked out. Perhaps as a result, the product was often painted, much more so than ceramic sculpture. But mud sculpture was widespread especially in

* See Fagg and Picton 1970; Coart and Hauleville 1907.

sub-Saharan Africa. The best known manifestations may be the *mbari* houses of southeastern Nigeria (Cole 1969a and b, 1975), but tomb figures in the Zaïre river bend (see Plate 8.5), large sculptures in eastern Angola, and initiation statuettes from central and East Africa, all deserve mention. Mud sculpture was however an ephemeral medium. No nineteenth-century products even seem to have survived.

SUBTRACTIVE SCULPTURE: WOOD

In contrast to additive materials, subtractive media imposed more limitations, but on the whole required fewer technical operations. The shape, texture, and size of the product was largely determined by the block to be carved. The most common materials in Africa were stone, wood, ivory and bone.

Techniques for carving wood and the tools used (adze, gouge, knife) were simple but required great skill. A block was hewn out of a tree trunk, a branch, fork or root. It was first proportioned for the main volumes, and then these

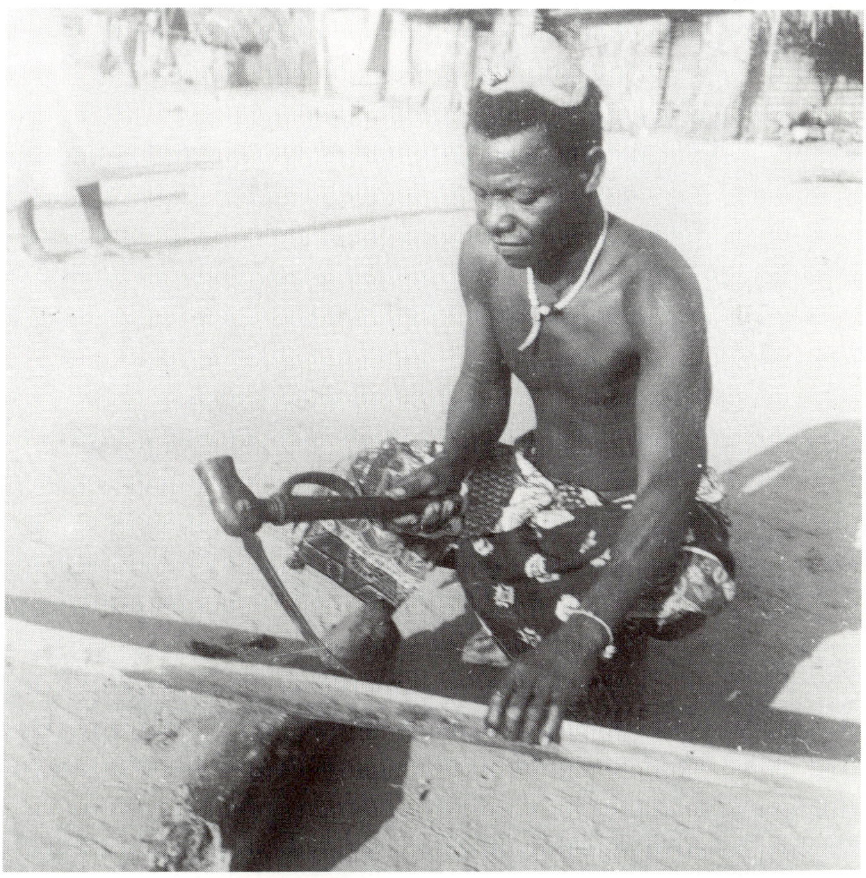

Plate 4.5 *Carver. Bolony, Kuba country, Ngongo group. Photo June 1956. He carves a paddle. Note the adze shaped as a person in the style of some Kuba dolls. Details of costume typical of that period except for the imported cloth*

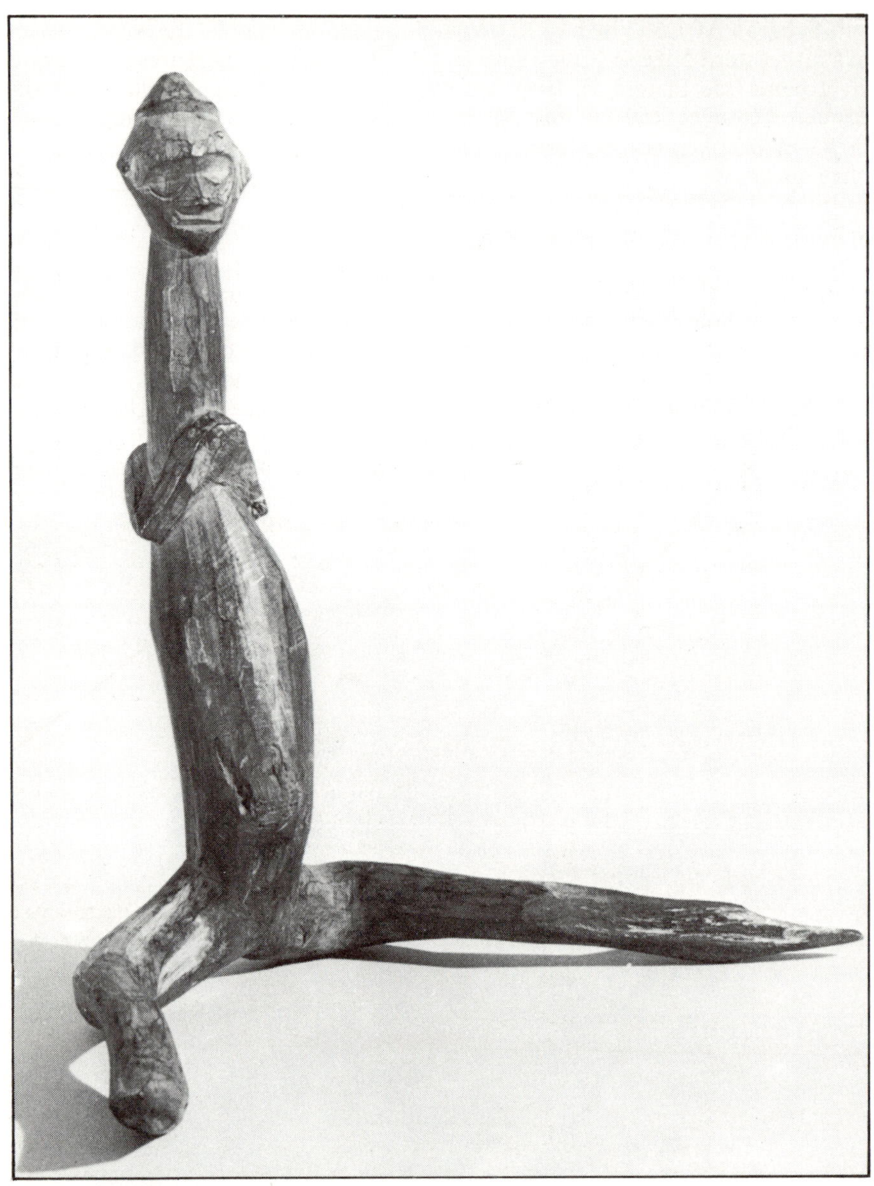

Plate 4.6 *Seated figure. Wood. Use unknown. Kambundi, Lembwa Basuku, Kwango, Zaïre (Suku). Koninklijk Museum voor Midden Afrika, Tervuren. Height 27cm. Acquired 1932. Shape inspired by forked branch used, or branch chosen because the shape could be executed*

were carved. Detail was then worked out, after which the wood was often polished with sandpaper-like substances (often leaves) and could be given a patina (Willett and Picton 1967; Willett 1978; Drewal 1980:9–18). The carver had to choose his block with great care, visualizing the finished form in the block. He had to be very attentive to the possibilities of the grain and often worked patterns of texture into the general effect of the finished product. South of the Sahara the most common block was cylindrical and finished work either emphasized this, producing 'pole-like' sculpture, or, on the contrary, ignored it so that other geometric volumes predominated. Sometimes forked pieces or twisted roots were exploited, as for example in the country of Bandiagara (Mali: Dogon) or on the Middle Kwango (Zaïre: Suku) to produce works in which the suggestive form of the raw material was emphasized. The grain of the wood was an essential factor for the carving itself. Thus Lem (1948) argued that Sahelian styles are angular and tall, with rather scanty detail, because the soft coarse-grained wood required this, while their southern neighbours made compact, rounded sculpture, sometimes with exquisite detail and almost lacquer patina, inspired by the possibilities of very dense and fine-grained wood, which withstood such treatment. The finish, especially on masks, included not only staining or a patina but involved polychroming as well in the coastal lands between Togo and northern Angola.

If the effects of wood sculpture were greatly enhanced by inherent shapes and texture, the size of such pieces was severely limited. Joinery could overcome this handicap, but where joinery is found south of the Sahara, as in the Niger Delta or in nearby Benin, the technique used shows European influence. The relative absence of complex compositions in African wood sculpture may be related to the monoxyle (one block) execution. Large compositions could only be hewn out of very large trunks and were much more difficult to envisage than if joinery had been common.

SUBTRACTIVE SCULPTURE: IVORY, STONE

Ivory, which was also widely in use all over Africa, was constrained by its curved shape and its hollowness. It could be carved much more finely, however, than wood, and was strong enough to be fashioned into a tracery of forms barely tied together if this was the required effect. Most carvers avoided this, however, and emphasized the solid volume of the medium, made the best use of the curvature and stained the product perhaps even more delicately than wood was stained. The fineness of the grain of ivory was thus fully exploited. Joinery was found only in Benin, but may antedate European influence. The best known example is that of the Bini leopards carved out of five pieces of ivory, fitted one into the other.

Stone for sculpture in the round, relief or architectural sculpturing such as on capitals or friezes had been used to perfection in north Africa, where perhaps the highest technical achievements date from predynastic Egypt with its sculptures and vessels in extremely hard stone as well as its translucent alabaster. Working most stone was a matter of chiselling first, polishing later, except for soft stones such as soapstone (steatite) and some graphites which were the favourite material south of the Sahara when stone was used. Such media could be worked like wood and the stone sculpture from Guinea, Sierra Leone, Zaïre and Angola was clearly derivative of techniques used for wood. Ancient Ethiopia, and North Africa before Islam, produced monumental sculpture either out of a single block of material or by bonding several parts together, when the intended size required it.

Sculptors in the north took advantage of every particularity of the medium, whether it be of natural stain, roughness of grain, shine of polish or reflectivity of light (e.g. marble vs. diorite). Their skill in the treatment of hard stone was much greater than sculptors south of the Sahara who used this medium.

MIXED MEDIA

Mixed media were very common in the sculpture of Africa south of the Sahara. The Bini ivory leopards have bronze spots and a Bini ivory mask wears iron strips on its brow. Wooden statues or masks often carried additions of horns, shells, fibre as beards or dress, teeth, claws, bits of glass or of mirror. On the Cross River, some masks were even totally covered with skin, thus hiding the natural medium completely. Such adornments were often a requirement for the use of an object, as the cavities covered by a mirror on charms in lower Zaïre, or the nails stuck in charms of the same area show, but foreign materials were also often used to render eyes (shell, glass) or beards (raffia) and other attributes. What mattered was the total effect. Masks were much more often in mixed media than sculpture because they were only part of a dancing costume – the total effect of a masked dancer had to be theatrical and often gaudy. Thus sometimes the very qualities of the medium were lost when it served as a support or carrier, rather than as the final form of the object in space by itself.

PAINTING AND DRAWING

Because the graphic arts are two-dimensional, they require the feigning of greater illusion than is required for three-dimensional arts: illusions of planes, illusions of volume, illusions of space, illusions of texture, illusions of atmosphere. Apart from the basic techniques, a range of technical skills to create such illusions had to be added here (Gombrich 1960).

Basically, the technology required first the making or preparation of a surface to carry the design or image: rock, wood, plastered wall, canvas, paper, leather, even the skin of the human body. Most surfaces were then covered with a ground for painting. The degree of absorption and the way in which pigments or stains lay on the grain or were absorbed were crucial factors. Pigments had to be manufactured for drawing, painting, or dying thread and a certain amount of chemistry could be involved here. Hues were obtained from organic or mineral products. The binding media that held the bonding agents were mostly organic. Then the lines or paint or dots could be applied with reed, pen, brush, or finger. Preliminary drawings could be executed for paintings or engravings; it was common, for example, for Egyptian painters to outline the composition first by placing red lines with a string dipped in colour. They prepared such a detailed outline that each element could then be quickly outlined and immediately given a ground hue, grey blue in the eighteenth dynasty, later yellow, then white. Then the artist overpainted the flesh, the clothes, the jewellery, the hair, using one or several layers of colouring as required by the effect of opaqueness desired (Mekhitarian 1954:22–35).

The processes varied almost endlessly, not only for the two-dimensional arts such as painting but also for other media such as tiles and potsherd pavements. In painting, binding agents could be as different as encaustic (wax)

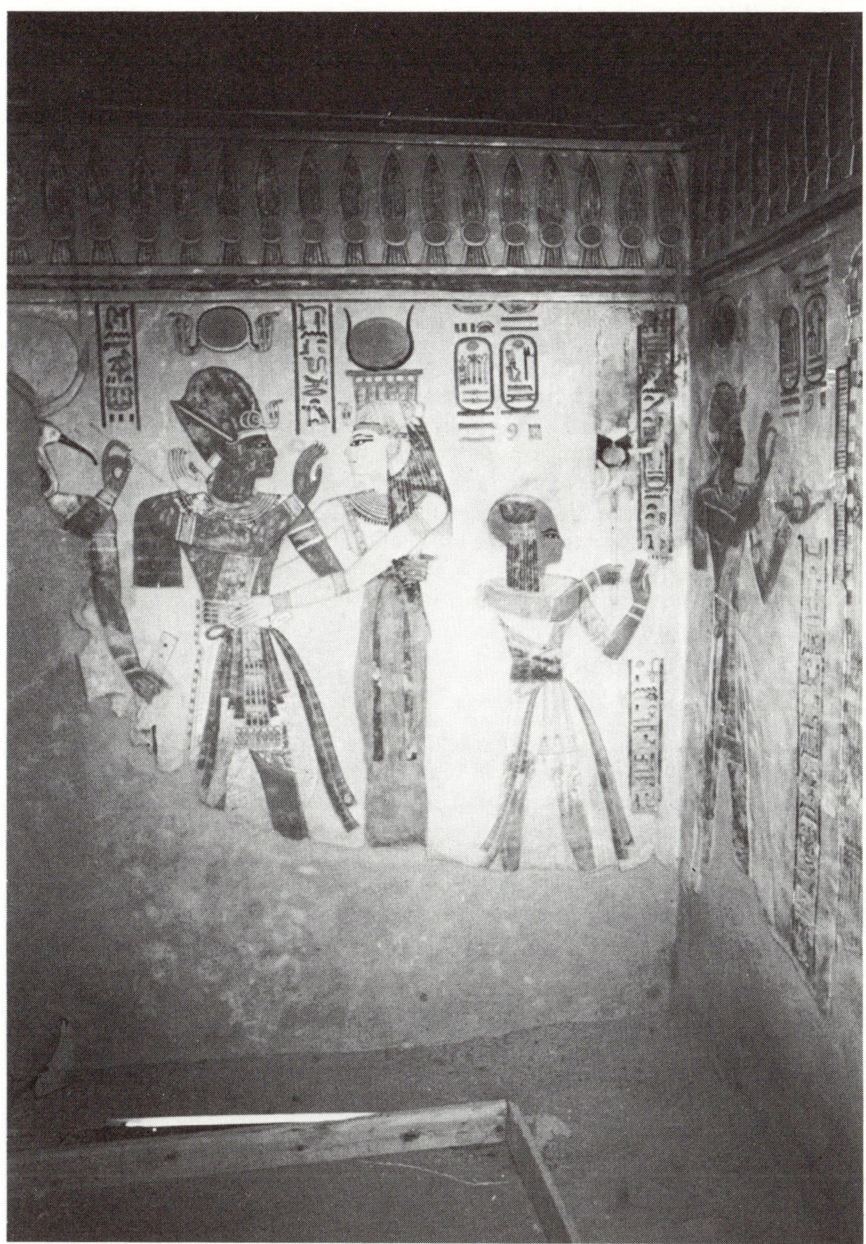

Plate 4.7 *Tomb of Amen Khopshef, Valley of the Queens, Thebes. From left to right: Thoth writing, Ramses III embraced by Isis, Amen Khopshef. Hieroglyphs: above Thoth: 'Thoth records for you the renewal festivals of kingship'; between Ramses and Isis: 'To be said by Isis, the Great Divine Goddess'; to the right: 'Lord of Appearances, Ramses, justified. Lord of the Two Lands Ramses III'; under the Prince: 'Son of the King, of his Body, Whom he loves, Amen Khopshef, justified'. Tomb of Amen Khopshef, royal scribe, Overseer of horses, son of Ramses III, Queen's valley, Thebes no. 55. Wallpainting, west wall, near entrance XXth dynasty* c. *1180* BC. *The painting technique is visible.* Gesso *base on plaster, red basic drawing, dark colours painted first, lighter ones later. Overpainting on the headdress of Isis. Hieroglyphs translated by courtesy of Prof. M. Clagett. Photo Dr T. Webb*

or glue boiled from animal skins and sinews, or the techniques could consist of transferring patterns from a copybook (common in Coptic and Nubian wall paintings) or apparently direct painting without any previous outline as in the rock arts of the Sahara or the San. In other media, scenes obtained by the juxtaposition of prepared tiles and the execution of mosaics were widely used in north Africa at different periods, while potsherd pavements in West Africa reproduced geometrical patterns only.

The techniques of graphic art were more varied than was usual in sculpture because of the special constraints of two-dimensionality. Figures, for instance, could be merely outlined, rendered by areas of colour only, shaded or not to suggest volume, rendered by short strokes, zebra hatching, dots of equal or unequal size, parallel and hatched strokes and so on. All of these techniques are already found on Saharan painting (Lajoux 1977). Planes and depth could be suggested by overlapping, sparing out, positioning on registers or foreshortening. In painting, the application of the paint for the final illusion was frequently as idiosyncratic as a signature is; in drawing, the characteristics of line were the equivalent of a signature. Because such features could be much more individualistic than those in carving, the study of such techniques may be more revealing and rewarding to the art historian. The whole concept of *ateliers* – workshops characteristic of style – and of individual hands, was first developed in the examination of painting and such assignments often remain most convincing for two-dimensional art.

TEXTILES AND OTHER FABRICS

The decoration and painting of textiles, basketry and mats, as well as of other fabrics, such as barkcloth or leather or animal felt, is ubiquitous in Africa, and has been for many centuries. In woven stuff, the art work is crafted in the material itself during the process of weaving. First, the fibres must be made ready from the raw materials such as raffia, cotton, wool or silk. The technologies of spinning for the latter three materials vary, while for the first the raffia strip is extracted directly from the foliole and then cut or carded with a comb into thread. The thread can then be dyed if necessary either completely or tie-dyed (*ikat:* an Indonesian term) by tying threads together so that the dye will not affect the spots where they are tied.

Weaving is done on a loom where the weft threads are inserted over and under the supporting or warp threads. In much of Africa, looms have been the only machines known in the precolonial period, and many, such as the Tio or Kuba weavers I have known, were quite conscious of this. The simplest looms used were single heddle, the heddle being the device by which the threads of the warp which had been separated by a stick (the shed stick) so that the weft thread can be passed, are separated again in reverse order for the next passing of a weft thread. Double heddle looms used two heddles instead of a shed stick and a heddle, linked them together with a rope going over a heddle pulley and allowed the weaver to operate much faster, using a foot pedal connected to both heddles. Single heddled looms were all over the continent, while double-heddled looms are found in the *oikoumene* and beyond in West Africa as well as in northeast Africa. The West African strip cloth loom is a double-heddle loom that weaves narrow strips of cloth. It seems to have come

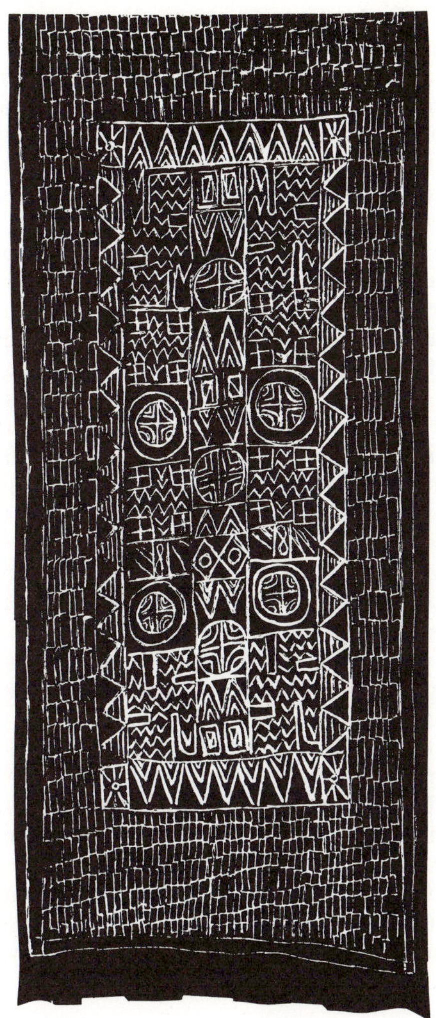

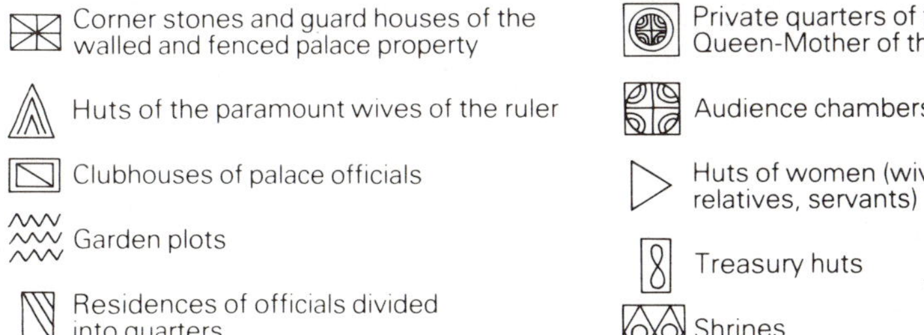

Fig. 4.2 *Plan of the Bamum capital on textile. Cotton strip weave, indigo dyed. Stitch and dye with resistant raffia thread. Width 180cm × length 540cm. Acquired 1936. After P. Gebauer 1979:374, pl. 163.*

from the Nile valley in Sudan (Johnson 1977). Variations in the passing of weft under and over warp threads yield different kinds of weaves from simple plain weaves (once over, once under) or simple floating weaves (twill is twice over, twice under) to complex compound weaves where supplementary wefts were worked into the fabric, either over its whole width or over a part of it, often with supplementary heddles. Different patterns can be created by the alteration of the rules used to pass wefts through warp, and the patterns are much enhanced by the use of coloured thread. The most complex technique ever used in Africa was probably the work done on Coptic medallions and borders, where up to twelve different dyed threads of wool were used.

Once the material is woven, it can be further ornamented by dyeing. The most common technique was resist dye, where the cloth was tied or stitched so that the dye would not affect certain areas. It also was possible to paint freehand or to use a stencil to apply a resisting material to the cloth so that the dye would not affect the parts thus covered. The contrary operation consists in painting the cloth directly with dye, as painters do on a canvas. Patterns were printed by stamps in Akan country (Ghana) and stencilling on woven stuffs or fabrics is known from several areas. Appliqué, a technique found in the West African coastal areas, in Sudan and in northern Nigeria, consisted of sewing further materials on the finished cloth and thus produced figurative patterns, letters or simple geometric effects. Other stuffs such as beads, shells, leather or, in rare cases, metal could also be sewed onto the basic fabric to produce richly ornamented articles of clothing. Quilting and patchwork were less widespread; the former was used only for armour in the regions around Lake Chad and for winter coats in the Maghrib.

Embroidery with long threads was not uncommon and the production of plush-like cloth is best known from central Africa. Here the embroidery thread is passed vertically through the fabric and brought back again, after having been knotted or not, and the ends are then cut off above the surface of the fabric to yield a pile. The Ulm cloth from Angola (Plate 9.1) is an example of this technique. Much rarer and from the same areas is open work, where, as in lace but by different techniques, patterned gaps occur in the finished fabric. The technologies involved have best been described by Picton and Mack (1979), but also by Lamb (1975), Loir (1935), Menzel (1972) and Polakoff (1980).

The history of the technology and decoration of textiles can be reconstructed for the drier areas of the continent from surviving stuffs, especially along the Nile valley. Iconography in European documents helps to recover more data for West and Central Africa, while a few costumes and materials from these areas were brought to Europe from the seventeenth century onwards. But to date a history of textiles still remains to be written, partly because they have not been recognized as art, partly because of the neglect of all technological history.

Techniques for making baskets and mats are similar to simple weaving, but the plaiting is done by hand. Colours can be used here also and often decorative effects were achieved either by plain plaiting or by the use of contrasting colours (Coart 1927; Rossbach 1973).

ORNAMENTING THE BODY: SCARIFICATION AND PAINTING

Scarification of the body or tattooing have been mentioned by many authors, but have in fact been the object of very little study. The technology varies: the skin was cut and dyes could be introduced under it, in which case tattoos resulted. Foreign bodies could also be put under the skin so that welts resulted from the healing process producing keloids, a process usually called scarification (Gebauer 1979:104–5). Cutting and letting the cuts heal without any further operation resulted in cicatrization. All these interventions produced permanent results. The processes were common south of the Sahara, but not nearly as universal as is sometimes believed. Not all scarification, tattooing or cicatrization was intended to be decorative – medicinal or magical purposes and accidents produced scars as well.

Paint can be used to decorate parts of the body, such as hands, feet or the face in a permanent way when the patterns are refreshed until the dye has permeated the skin. Patterns of this type are found among Berber women, but are much rarer than painting with henna or other substances for certain occasions only. Tripolitanian women, for instance, paint their feet when they are brides or attend weddings (C. Herman, personal communication). Painting for initiations, rituals, war or festivals was very common all over sub-Saharan Africa, although it is most often mentioned with regard to eastern Africa. Sometimes the whole body was painted with, for example, camwood or barwood. Often large portions were painted in contrasting colours as decoration, or to frighten enemy warriors. Ritual painting very often covered a limited surface and consisted of painting rings around the eyes or the mouth in the basin of the Zaïre river. The painting of decorative linear patterns was relatively rare, but the best known cases may be those of the country east of the lower Niger and of northeastern Zaïre, where the blue colour extracted from the gardenia plant was used by women. The dyes most used were white or yellow chalk, red from the camwood and barwood trees, and black from vegetal sources, charcoal or soot. Usually these three colours and the painting had a definite religious significance. It is noteworthy that not all dyes could be used for painting the body or scarifying, as some were quite toxic; and that no colour could be painted over too large a surface of skin for too long, as this interferes with the breathing of the pores and can lead to severe illness or even death.

Complex hairstyles, sculpture of hair and other matter, were common in many west, central and east African regions. They have often been illustrated (Paulme and Brosse 1956) but no in-depth study exists, yet they too were an art. If some hairstyles were linked to ethnicity or with social position (as in southern Angola), others were varied and developed mainly for aesthetic purposes only. Some were creations for a few days only, but others lasted for months and must be seen as more permanent art, not associated only with a passing event, and in that they are comparable to masks.

MEDIA, TECHNIQUES AND THE HISTORY OF ART

The first characteristic of interest to the art historian is the relative durability of a medium. Thus ceramics and stone last almost forever, basketry, matting, and mud the least, and many claim that wood under tropical conditions rarely exceeds a century of age. Be that as it may, it is obvious that our knowledge of art forms in the past is heavily influenced by what has survived, and what can still be found in the ground. This means that our chances for arriving at a general history of art objects in metal is good, with the exception of gold which is melted down too often, but for objects in mud, it is worst of all. In sub-Saharan Africa, works of metal, ceramics and ivory, all long-lasting media, are more numerous than was once believed, and the prognosis is good, but can we reconstruct general features even of sculpture from works in ceramics, ivory or stone? Are these media so different from others, especially wood, that we will never be able to trace even the main characteristics of the bulk of sculpture here? Perhaps not, when we consider works in metal and ivory. Certainly, as the comparison between a Kuba work in iron and one in wood shows, there are some resemblances, but the execution is altogether too different. Even ivory, except for small pieces, like masks of Maniema (Zaïre) that do not enhance the natural curve of the medium, may present differences that are too great, but when ceramics, stone and wood are compared, the prospects can be better. After all, clay can exhibit technical features (angularity, flat planes) which are more natural in a wood medium but are also easy to achieve in clay, and stone sculpture in steatite or graphite was worked like wood. So media in clay or soft stone, I believe, can often be compared to wood. Sometimes, however, different media are handled by different conventions. Willett (1971:ill. 176–8) gives a striking example of a naturalistic rendering in pottery, as opposed to stylization in wood, in works from a single society! The reader can easily explore the problems of comparability by examining the body of sculpture in western Nigeria where work in all the media mentioned has coexisted. The transition between the stone figures of Esie and presumably wood sculpture is easy, it is also easy between ceramic heads and brass or bronze work at Ife, but nineteenth century wood sculpture and brass (Ogboni) statuettes are not easily comparable. Work in ivory also differs considerably from comparable objects in wood. On balance, then, reconstructions of the past will never be full due to losses through impermanence, but main traits may be determined to some extent.

A history of drawing and painting will be even more difficult to recover in many parts of the continent than sculpture. Often the supports were in perishable materials such as mud walls of houses, bodies, or clay platforms. For textiles, the conditions of preservation are very good in dry areas but not elsewhere – Nubia may have the longest sequence in the world of preserved textiles. The reader will note that styles of textiles and styles of body decoration are often quite comparable, so that the former can shed some light on the latter.

The next point in the consideration of techniques is that questions as to chronology and even place of manufacture can be much more complex than first imagined. What we see now can be the end product of a very long history, and this is particularly obvious in complex architecture. But even other works made within a workshop pose problems of authorship: was it the same hand that applied patina and that finished the details of a wooden sculpture? Was it that same hand that worked the main volumes by chipping with the adze? Was it that same hand that blocked out the main volumes? Often not, and often a statue is the product of a workshop group rather than of a single master.

Questions about when and where become more complex when the process of the manufacture of the prepared medium is concerned. Questions as to the preparation of the medium itself may not be directly relevant, and fade into a general history of technology, but they cannot be avoided! Where did the iron come from that was used in the Kuba statuette? Where did Benin's copper come from or the alloy used in the Igbo Ukwu bronzes?

Also unavoidable are questions of technological development. How was lost wax actually produced? We learn that it was not indigenous to West Africa but reached Igbo Ukwu perhaps by the ninth century A.D. (Shaw, 1970a, 1970b, 1978:118–19). Its distribution in West Africa is consonant and explicable in relation to trans-Saharan trading routes and other channels for diffusion in the area. Close examination of the use of the technique in southern Nigeria shows that instead of wax, latex from the *euphorbia* was used. But the *euphorbia* does not grow there; it only occurs further north. Details of Igbo Ukwu pieces convincingly show that latex was used there, too. So before the ninth century, lost wax must have been used in northern Nigeria and long enough to allow for the development of the *euphorbia* latex technique (Williams 1974:179–213).

Questions of technology help to link styles together as well as techniques. The fact that goldsmiths in Ghana imitate filigree, proves that earlier foreign filigree work must have fascinated them (Garrard 1980:108). Such work was current in northern Africa. Once we know this and additionally take into account that north African vessels have been found in the area, there is little doubt that comparable decorative work done in filigree or by the Ghanaian

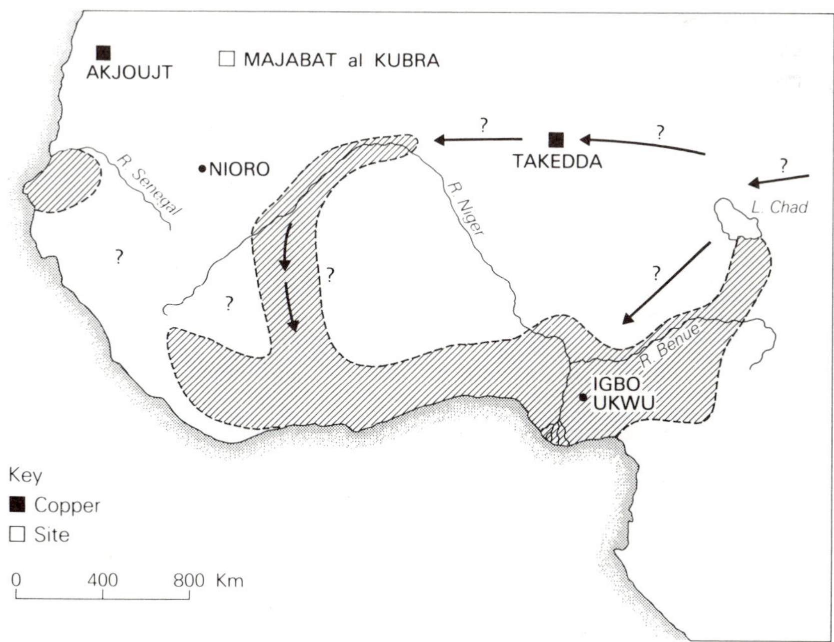

Fig. 4.3 *Lost wax techniques in West Africa*

method is similar because the smiths there copied the result of filigree working.

Skeuomorph tendencies are also historical clues. The hypogee churches of medieval Ethiopia hewn out of the living rock reproduce all the elements of a basilica, all functionally useless here, such as beams, lintels, arches, corbels on columns and domes, even the upper clerestory windows as blind tracery. They prove that basilicas built in the open preceded them. They also raise the question of possible ancestry for an architectural vision able to plan a whole church from a single block by excavation. Was that new or not? In fact it was not. Was it an Indian inspiration as some thought? It was not. The presence in

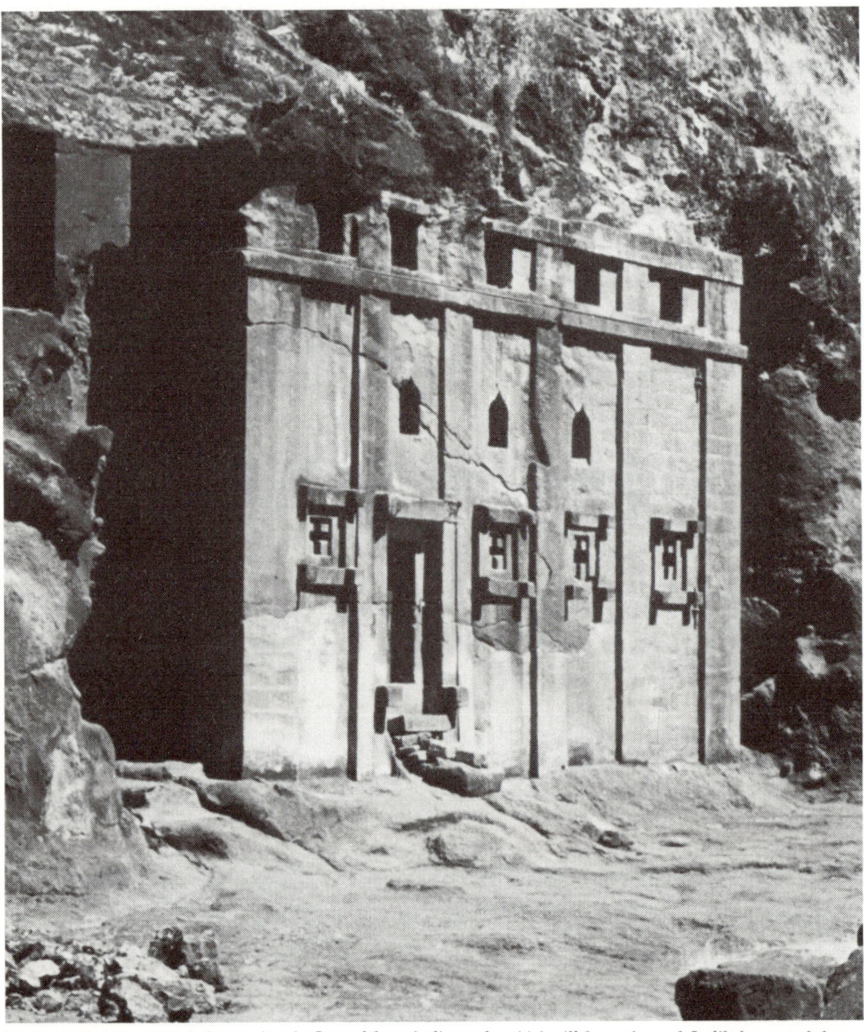

Plate 4.8 *Façade. Abba Lebanos church. Carved from the live rock, which still forms the roof. Lalibela, second cluster. Ethiopia. 9m by 7m by 7m, almost a cube. A.D. 1190–1225. Three nave basilical plan. Axumite elements e.g. in window frames*

Ethiopia of rock hewn catacombs at Axum as well as the carving of rooms underground at Matara in the early centuries of our era, if not before, tell us that. The rockhewn churches were a unique combination of two traditions that had coexisted close to a millennium in Ethiopia. Their fusion produced that astonishing phenomenon: the basilica concept rendered as a piece of sculpture (Gerster 1968; Chittick 1974, 1976).

The examination of the precise medium and the technology used in the production of a work of art is indispensable to the art historian. It may help him or at the least establish possibilities. Lost-wax work in lower Zaïre implies that the technique was either invented there, a remarkable – almost unbelievable – feat, or that it was imported, probably from West Africa (Wannyn 1961). But when and how? It allows historians to place a work in a technological series. Admittedly this is much more common in architecture than for the other arts and then especially with regard to Islamic, Ethiopian or classical architecture. Often technical innovation and new forms go hand in hand. The development of the stalactite (*muqarnas*) from its simplest form in the tenth century Qala'a of the Banu Hammad in Algeria to its triumphant transformation of the surfaces in the honeycombed domes of the almoravid mosque Qarawiyyin in Fes is a story of stylistic evolution as much as one of technical development (Marçais 1954).

Thus the historian is led to ask how or why certain technical innovations take place. Why is the dome so important in North Africa? Did it have a relationship to the domed structures of the Saharan populations, reported since Garamantic times before our era (Daniels 1970:41–2)? Or must we believe those historians who derive all domed forms from the Middle East? Probably both the use of domes in northern Africa, and in the Sahel, as well as Near-Eastern techniques, have been involved.

In their beginnings, most techniques have little to do with art. They were invented or adopted for purely practical purposes. Thus raw materials were transformed into media because cooking pots or iron tools or cloth were needed, not to provide means for the artist. Artists usually adapted what they found. But beyond this, certain techniques, such as the lost-wax process or the construction of domes, were not directly utilitarian. They relate to art and it is to them that the art historian must give his closest attention. Sometimes, and with this example I conclude, both artistic and utilitarian purposes become blurred. The Copts developed a highly sophisticated technology of weaving, allowing them to create inimitable masterpieces of art in textiles (Grigorieva 1980:28–9). The technology was fuelled by the demand for such products in the Roman Empire. Similarly, the Kuba developed more dyes for textiles than any of their neighbours and kept the techniques secret, for their polychrome cut-pile textiles were their major export in the eighteenth century, as they are again today. However, once a medium was available and a technique was developed, artists used these materials and procedures, and so the history of technologies become part of the history of art.

CHAPTER FIVE

STYLE

The study of changes in shape over time is held by many to be the core of art history. Once any object, such as the board from Ardra, has been localized and dated, once its context is known, it can be put in a set of series of similar objects: series of technically similar works, series of objects similar in subject matter and a series by shape or style.

Style refers to the formal properties of works of art (Layton 1981:134; Focillon 1943:11). The concept designates the shapes of each component in a given work of art, as well as the composition of all the elements into one overall visual and tactile design. The term can be applied to the formal properties of a body of art works as well as to a single work. Style, as the summation of design choice, may have different characteristics in the works of each individual artist, in the arts of one locality as compared to another, or as changing tastes in design may occur as period follows period. Therefore studies of the style found in the arts of a place, of a people, and of a period in time, are major means by which an ordering may be established in the history of an art. As style excludes meaning, a stylistic history by itself cannot achieve understanding and hence cannot be art history, even though it is a core component of such a history.

The relationship between art objects and the things they represent is far from simple. Scholars still dispute how exactly a natural thing is related to its representation in art. Gombrich has conclusively shown (1960) that their apparent sameness is an illusion. A representational work of art is a natural object interpreted and simplified. Representation always involves a reduction of all the features of natural reality into a few that are significant to the artist and the community involved. The reduction uses schematic patterns, conventions to realize this reduction. Such stereotypes are the language of form (Layton 1981:144, 161–71). All scholars agree that there are always stereotypes, there is always convention. Style then refers to the sum total of such conventions in a body of works of art or in a single piece. It refers to formal elements common to a series of works by one or several artists and also to formal elements that are uncommon or even unique. For a convention can be unique, as long as it is understood.

CONVENTIONS

Let us look first at an ancient Egyptian painting. Certainly its perspective is arbitrary, registers separate scenes, the sides of a scene are laid open like the lids of an opened box (Ragghianti-Collobi 1968:52). Odd things happen to figures: the perspective is frontal for the shoulders, torso and eye, but in profile for the other parts of the body. The depth of the field and planes are indicated

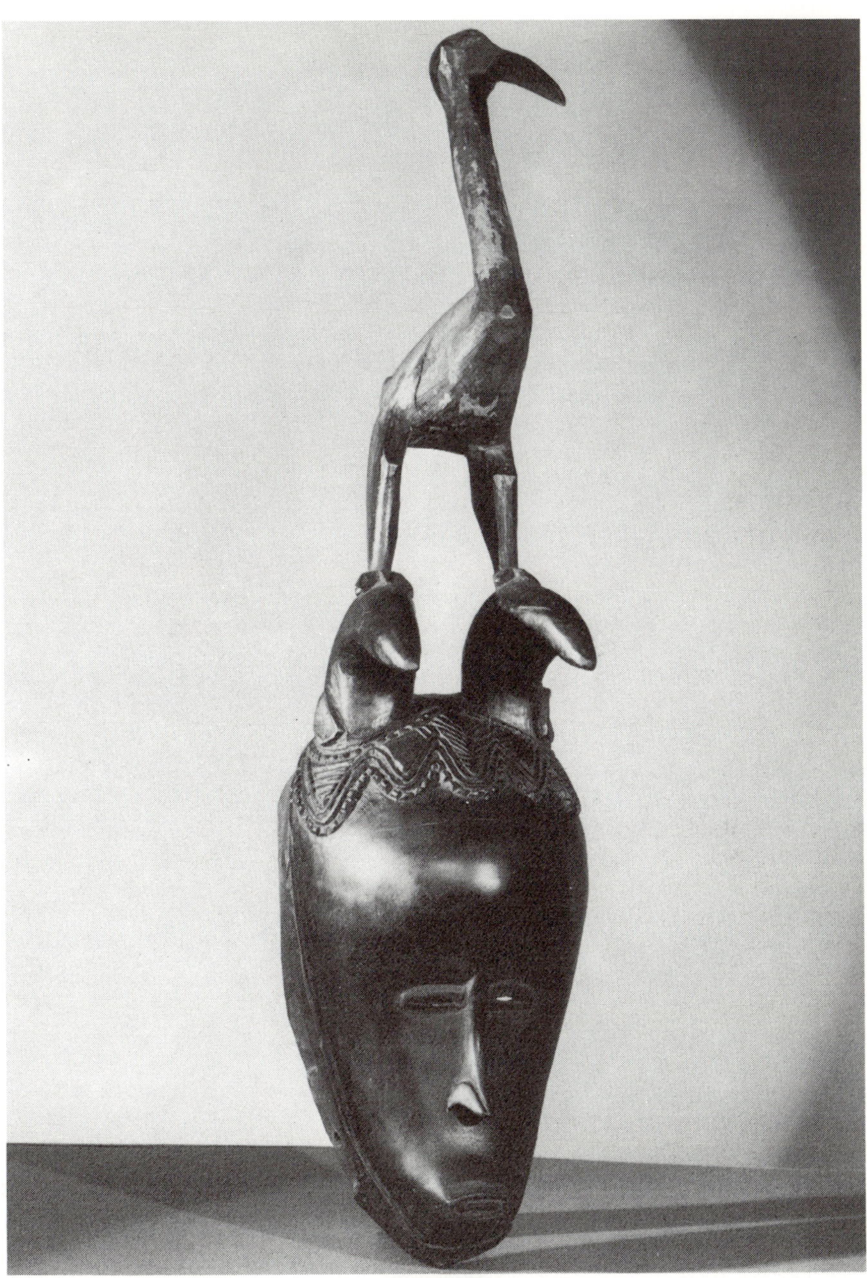

Plate 5.1 *Horned mask, surmounted by heron. Wood. Face black and brilliant patina. Hair, black, white, red. To be held in front of face by teeth of the wearer. Exact use and meaning unknown. Central Ivory Coast (Guro). Museum, University of Pennsylvania. Height 52·6cm. Acquired 1929 from a US collector. Sharp-nosed style; perhaps, hence from Zounoula area*

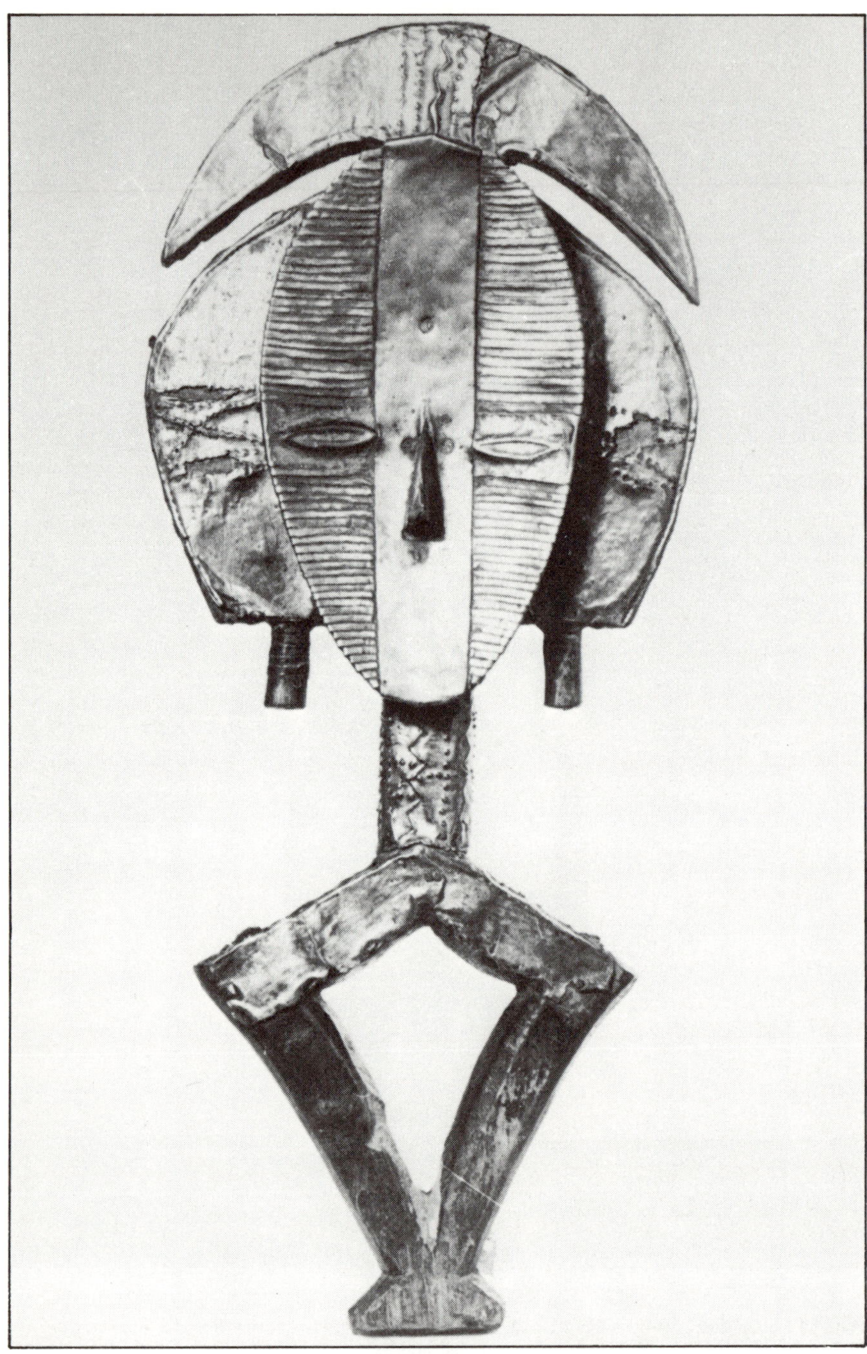

Plate 5.2 *Reliquary figure. Wood, copper, brass. Used on top of the bundle holding ancestral bones. Taki. Museo preistorico ed etnografico, Rome. Height 42·7cm. Bought by A. Pecile, Sept. 11, 1883 from Taki, head of the village near Franceville, then inhabited by Ndumu. See Fig. 5.1*

by overlapping figures, but not by the size of figures; the colours are largely conventional. If we look upon such paintings with an eye trained by post-Renaissance conventions in Europe, all this hurts and we cannot relate to it. Planes are not integrated, perspective is not unified nor is light, foreshortening is unknown or almost unknown, composition is based on the linear, must be read in one direction only, and does not conform to the clever geometric figures in European art. Modelling to render volume by shading of colour is also absent. We come away from the contemplation of an ancient Egyptian painting convinced that all styles are conventional and create illusions of reality by the mutual understanding of how to read images that exist between viewers and makers and that such and such conventions stand for such and such realities (Gombrich 1960).

Representations in two dimensions are more dependent upon synoptic illusion than are three-dimensional representations, while carving, because it is subtractive, may be more in need of stereotype than additive sculpture. But whatever the technique and medium, renderings remain arbitrary to a very large degree. Thus the classical sculptured Greek nose has its counterpart in the upturned nose of one Ivory Coast sub-style (Guro, Plate 5.1), or the single accolade of the eyebrows in the Kwango-Kasai area (Pende). None of these is really close to reality as perceived. It is easier to realize that convention rules in very stylized or expressionistic art than in 'naturalistic' or idealized art; but in fact conventions are almost as strong in one as in the other. The reliquary figures of eastern Gabon whose heads become two-dimensional or almost so and whose bodies are just a lozenge, where torso, arms and legs are caught at a glance, except that there is no torso below the neck and the legs are in fact a simple columnar volume (Plate 5.2), still, we see that these are people and we realize that this type of realization rests on a collective convention. Yet we should also realize it when we look at an extreme in naturalism such as Ife figures or headpieces from the Middle Cross River (Ekoi). The ears, the eyes, the lay of the symmetry, the mouth, cheekbones, etc., are all 'artificial' on

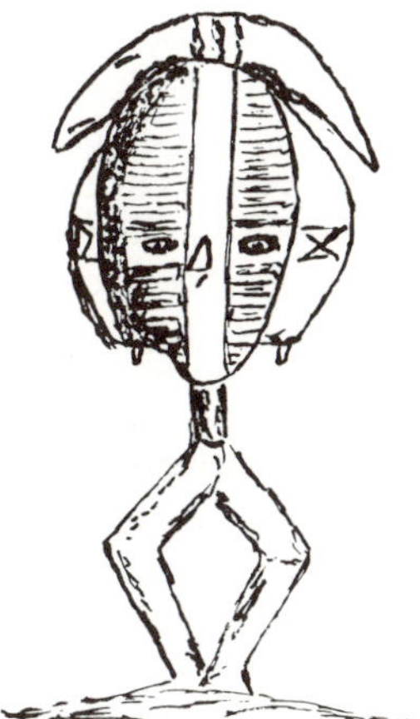

Fig. 5.1 *Reliquary. Taki, near Franceville, Gabon. This is a drawing of the item plate 5.2. Copy of A. Pecile's drawing of 1883 (E. Zorzi,* Al Congo con Brazza, *Rome 1940:312). The drawing establishes the identity of the piece. Note differences in medium between drawing and photography*

closer inspection; they are not like 'real' ears, eyes, mouths, cheeks. The composition is as conventional as the Gabon reliquary.

Even in architecture convention rules. Intended use certainly prescribes the size and sometimes the general plan of a shelter. But the buildings can be high, low, roofed in any of a dozen fashions, wider or narrower. Traditions in the realization are as strong here as in any other art form. The conventions ruling ancient Egyptian temple building lasted for just as long as those pertaining to hieroglyphs. The basilica, an imperial Roman achievement, became the model for Christian churches and remained one of the models for churches over the ages, being virtually unchallenged in Nubia, Egypt and Ethiopia. The basic features of the ground plan of a classical mosque as opposed to later Mamluk, Libyan or Ottoman plans are still alive today and just as arbitrary as any of the other styles of mosques. The round plans of Zimbabwe, the rectangular shapes and their assemblage around quadrangles of palaces in western Nigeria, or the basic features of a palace on the Cameroon grasslands with their mixtures of pointed beehives on square bases, all are equally arbitrary, and equally conventional.

Such stylistic conventions are learned by the eye as objects come to be perceived as visual concepts. A mosque to any Muslim is only one of a few models of buildings. To the Cameroon grasslanders, a palace must have beehive doming on square bases. Artists learn their conventions along with their craft. Apprentices imitate, as we have seen, and this includes all the recipes for rendering all the varieties of reality that are rendered in that workshop. Moreover, conventions do not operate one by one nor are they learned as such. Style is like grammar: everything hangs together to a large extent by common rules, and a copy of a single subject from one style into another becomes a total translation, as Leroy (1967:57) has so beautifully shown by reproducing side by side an engraving by Tempesta (1591) and an Ethiopian replica. The differences in the works do not concern this or that detail – the eyes, for example – but everything. To Europeans the Ethiopian replica looks vaguely like a caricature only because that is the effect of the systematic application of foreign canons of convention.

Style then is everywhere in a given work and in series of works from the same workshop. It is a total phenomenon. Often all works in a given medium exhibit the same basic style for long periods in a given cultural continuum: the Ethiopian style in painting lasted over a millennium. Within that framework there will be stylistic differences just as the speech of one person differs from that of his neighbour, but the language remains the same.

The conventions of style are arbitrary and hence eminently rooted in time and place, but not totally arbitrary, because style is constrained by intended use and even more by the medium and technology available. Thus, a stone house on the coast of Kenya in the eighteenth century had to have its entrance and all other doorways located in such a way in relation to each other that complete intimacy of the inhabitants, especially the women of the house, was preserved (see Fig. 11.1 and De Vere Allen and Wilson 1979:11). Their rooms were long and narrow because the mangrove poles used as beams to span the width are never very long. That characteristic helps to explain a stylistic element unique to those houses: the development of multiple niches in the walls, of varying depth and slant so that the illusion of greater distance was given to the roving eye, than the actual distance. The room looked much roomier and the wall further away than it was.

Such constraints are obvious. Masks have to be carved in light wood as they are worn during dances, and they must have slits somewhere to see through. Charm statues in lower Zaïre or in East Kasai (Songye) must have hollow bellies or horns on top of the head to stuff with medicine. The size of a raffia cloth was set by the length of the fibre extracted from the palm frond. The size of a support determined the size of any two-dimensional work. Frescoes had to be executed very quickly, because of the technique involved, so patterns were prepared in advance and applied to one section of wall after the other, and in turn that led to striking repetitions with minor variations as the same stencil was used over and over. Once patterns were evolved and copied, they could be transferred to work on other surfaces such as the canvas used as support in Ethiopian churches after *c.* A.D. 1400.

As we have seen, techniques changed and with them the constraints of conventions changed. But the constraints imposed by the media remained much more constant. The fluid line of the cast metal could not be achieved in stone or wood, while the special density of angular volumes balanced against each other in wood could not possibly, in Africa at least, be executed in iron. Nevertheless skeuomorphism occurred and involved a partial translation of the style appropriate to one medium into another. The incised calabash imitated in wood keeps its general shape, albeit more regular than most calabashes would be, and the fine incisions turn into deeper and angular engravings. In Ghana, the theme of the mother and child on a chair may have first been made in ceramics, and replicas in wood became much more precise in line and set the volumes in sharper contrast (De Grunne 1980:152, 155).

But the constraints of media never wholly dictated style. The most striking feature about style remains its fundamentally arbitrary character which gives each period and each culture its uniqueness. Labels such as 'cubist' or 'stylized' or 'idealistic' or 'naturalistic' are often appended to different African styles by Europeans for that is what they remind European viewers of, not to mention the use of 'archaic', 'classical' or 'baroque' and indeed 'rococo'. The use of such terms highlights the pitfalls of stylistic assignments. First they are obviously ethnocentric; secondly, quite a number among them imply general theories relating to the change of shape over time whether that be expressed in the series 'archaic' etc., or by more innocent-looking terms such as 'abstract' or 'naturalistic'. Finally, such practices highlight the danger of summing-up stylistic characteristics in essentially holistic and impressionistic terms. Just as one can discover the grammar of a language one can find the components of style in an analytical way. In African art south of the Sahara, this approach has been called morphological analysis.

MORPHOLOGICAL ANALYSIS

The goal of morphological analysis is to establish to what degree a style differs from all neighbouring styles, the main principle being the arbitrary character of any representation. If representations resemble each other in the whole composition as well as in a number of dissociated elements, they must be historically related, usually as replications from a common prime work with or without further borrowing.

F. Olbrechts (1959:29–35) was the first scholar of Africa south of the Sahara to develop the techniques by which styles can be established. Four levels were distinguished: the element of added and decorative detail, the position in space, the proportions, and the sculptural detail. Added detail involves, for instance, representation of hairstyles and tattooing, while sculptural detail deals with the way dissociated elements such as the nose, ear or mouth, have been rendered. Added detail is very useful in localizing objects, since emblems, costume, hairstyles, scarifications, jewellery, reproduce those used locally at a given time. Sculptural detail relates more directly to core conventions. Position in space concerns the linking of different volumes, for instance, the transition between torso and pelvis, the main axis (repetition of volumes, accenting, etc.). Proportions concern well-known canons of sculpture. For instance, the human head is one-third to one-fourth of the total height in many African sculptures south of the Sahara, while the proportion is one to seven or eight in European art.

Depending on the art, a study of position in space or a study of proportions will be dominant. In the analysis of the art of the Bandiagara cliffs (Mali: Dogon) the first is crucial, whilst the latter is important for the ancestral figures of northern Gabon (Fang). In any case, propositions derived from the examination of one of these four categories are much strengthened by the eventual concordance of the results from the examination of the other categories. A study of the art of northern Gabon illustrates the technique. First, L. Perrois (1972) assembled artifacts from a known area (Fang) into a corpus of alike-looking objects. Two to three hundred ancestral statues seem sufficient for an analysis where similarities are great, while a larger number is needed for more variable images such as masks. The numbers must be great enough to achieve statistical significance. So Perrois measured proportions such as the height of the head in relation to the height of the torso and that of the lower limbs. He found that his statues were reduced to four groups only: hyperlongiform (very long – comparing head to torso) torsos, longiform (long) torsos, equiform (equal length) torsos, and breviform (short) torsos. As carvers begin by establishing the relative proportions of the head to the torso to the lower limbs, the measure was objective. He then turned to the position in space, classifying general head shapes and the relationships of volumes. These are obviously in large part determined by the canon of proportions used. Then Perrois turned to the associated detail. He distinguished, for instance, between no fewer than seven types of eyes: mirror applied with resin, coffeebean shape, copper plate, incision, disk shape in relief, rectangular shape in relief and absence of eye indication.

Every single object fell into different groups for differing measurement but the overriding classification – here the proportions – was the one where covariation of the greatest number of features coexisted, showing objectively the greatest internal consistency. Last of all, added detail such as hands holding horns or not, was considered. The final Perrois classification included the following criteria in rank order:

1. General proportions:	torso/whole height head/legs neck/whole height
2. Position in space:	relative concaveness of head frontal/lateral proportions of the head
Style of hairdo	
Position of arms	(attached to sides or not)
Position of legs	
3. Associated details:	types of nose mouth: shape, with or without beard ear: shape (5 types) eyes: shape (7 types) navel: shape (4 types) breasts: (4 male, 4 female types)

Every style could then be described in the relevant terms such as: 'Longiform. Head 20 to 30% of the height, torso 40 to 50% of the height, legs 10 to 30% of the height. The torso is half of the total height. Hands to the belly, with mouth at a level with the chin or hands holding a horn, associated with a bearded mouth'. Only the general shape of the head did not vary along with the other criteria. Ornamentation personalized objects. It made 'portraits' out of the ancestors represented by the treatment of hairstyle, tattoos, jewellery, eventual dress and the objects held in the hand.

The validation of the classification was reinforced by the coincidence of stylistic variation with spatial distribution, linking the stylistic categories to practices in different workshops, although Perrois expressed them in terms of ethnic units. The basic division was between northern hyperlongiform and longiform styles called Ntumu and Ngumba and southern equiform to breviform styles called Fang, sub-divided into Nzaman/Betsi, Okak/Mekeny and the extreme breviform Mvae. From that he could conclude that there had been two centres at first, because there were two styles: one north (Ntumu), one south (Betsi), although it is not evident why he did not also consider the Mvae as a centre, since there is little overlap between them and other southern styles. The ethnic labelling introduced once again an element of fuzziness. For Ngumba do not belong at all to a Fang cultural and especially linguistic grouping and the use of other names begs historical questions, as to ethnic identify, relative position of different groups at different times (the pieces in the corpus are not dated and could vary considerably in age) and so on.

The end result of this example of morphological analysis was firstly the more objective description of the whole corpus. All the works had concave faces, high and swelling foreheads, hairstyles in the shape of a helmet, round body volumes, prominent muscular relief of arms and calves but less so for shoulders, torso and thighs, bottle-shaped torsos and a general stance of immobility. The whole corpus was called Fang. Secondly, the substyles distinguished could be put in a series of variations. The analysis established a stylistic series over areas, which presumably corresponded to a time series and a succession in time of 'prime works', works showing major innovations.

Morphological analysis proceeds differently according to the corpus and its characteristics. Thus, for Liberian masks, the first basic distinction made

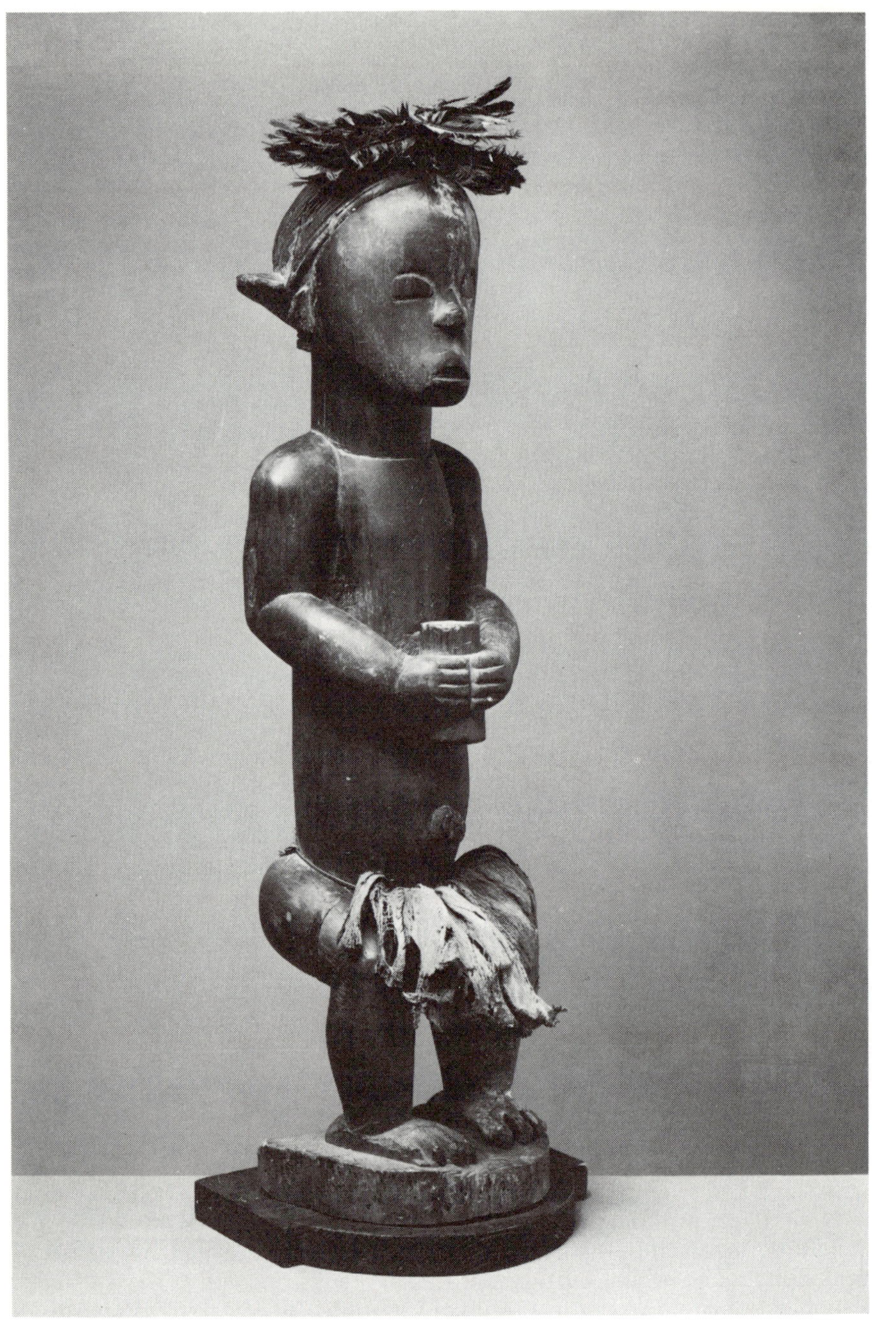

Plate 5.3 *Ancestor figure. Wood, feathers, barkcloth. Left part of face and left leg white, right part of face red. Used on top of a box containing ancestral bones. Northern Gabon (Fang). Museum für Völkerkunde, Berlin-Dahlem. Height 65cm. Acquired 1882. Longiform in Perrois' morphological classification*

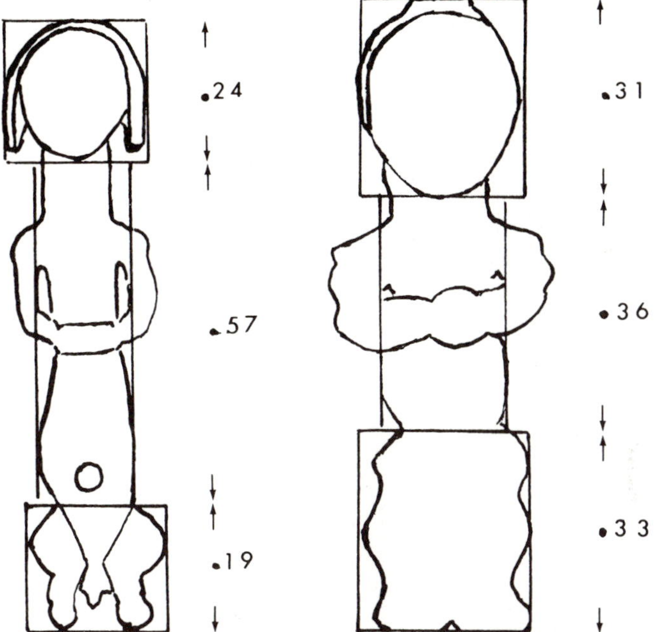

Fig. 5.2 *Morphological analysis of Fang (Gabon) statues, after L. Perrois. Hyperlongiform and breviform according to the length of the torso in proportion to that of head and legs. Hyper-: very long; brevi-: short. After* La sculpture traditionelle du Gabon, *Paris 1977:33*

was between 'expressionism' as opposed to the degree of 'idealistic realism' (Vandenhoute 1948). In F. Neyt's recent exhaustive study (1977: esp. 48–50) of ancestral figures from northeastern Shaba (Hemba), Perrois' strictly statistical approach was used only as a general but perhaps secondary technique. Selections were first made between prime works or prototypes and replications or copies. Neyt distinguished eleven styles and atypical works based on the shapes of heads, eyes, nose, mouth, ears, neck, the plane of the shoulders, the torso from four vantage points, the arms, hands, pelvis, feet and stand. The secondary characteristics of hairstyles, finery, scarification and prestige emblems were added to this. By then considering for each of the styles what the prime works were in relation to the replications and comparing them to those of the other styles, he attempted to establish an hypothesis about historical development. Despite the lesser reliance on statistics, the attempt was in fact stricter than that of Perrois, because it forced the author to consider each step from prime work to replication and from workshop to workshop.

The main danger of morphological analysis and taxonomizing remains subjectivity. The units chosen for measurement must correspond to those that were considered significant by the carvers and their public. Where fieldwork is possible, errors of this sort can be avoided by studying the practice and the aesthetics of workshops and artists. Otherwise, one must make assumptions through analogy. More problematic is the impossibility of measuring everything, including some of the most significant signs of individual signature. The stroke in painting, or the 'attack' of an adze in wood sculpture

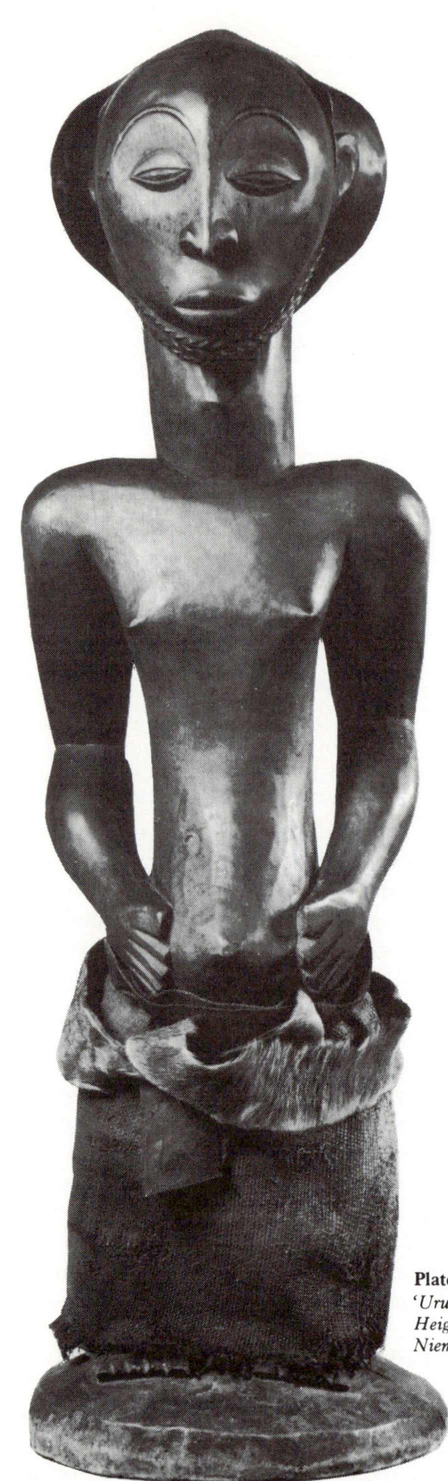

Plate 5.4 *Ancestor figure. Wood, leather belt, raffia skirt. 'Urua' i.e. Hemba (Shaba). Museum Berlin-Dahlem. Height 81cm. Acquired 1897. Neyt 1977: 'classical Niemba style'*

cannot easily be integrated into a system of measurements, nor can more obvious visual clues easily be quantified. Thus, a given line for the bridge of a nose is there, or it is not, or it is 'sort of' there. All that can be done comparatively is to organize such lines into one or several categories and then use them directly as a criterion. Statistics become less valid here than in the case of proportions and the morphological outline tends to become a comparative shorthand description. As long as this is realized and as long as it is also realized that in setting up categories of such phenomena arbitrary decisions necessarily intervene, morphological analysis still has the great advantage of making comparative intuition explicit, and replicable by others. Subjectivity remains but its analytical progress can be traced. Nevertheless, morphological analysis is only an aid to better informed qualitative assessment.

ATELIER AND ATTRIBUTION

The more refined morphological comparisons are, the more styles they disclose – eleven in the previous example for Shaba, an area that was about 100km by 100km. The tiny Suku group in Kwango is credited with four independent styles, their neighbours, the Pende of Kwango and Middle Kasai, with three (Neyt 1977:430). The eleven Hemba styles were crafted in thirteen administratively recognized chiefdoms, grouping ten villages or less, perhaps each style corresponds to a dozen settlements. We are close to the level of the workshop, and so we should be, for clearly styles are transmitted in workshops and workshop traditions should be discernible in their output. We will call them ateliers to draw attention to their role as a unit of tradition in art history. To find the atelier that corresponds to a style is a major discovery.

By the 1930s Olbrechts (1959:71–5) had recognized an atelier in southeastern Zaïre which he named Buli, after the provenance given for some of the wooden statues which shared the stylistic characteristics of the 'long-faced style of Buli'. But the name was an administrative designation. The style, however, was so similar that to this day, some defend the notion that all Buli works were the creations of a single artist, called 'the master of Buli'. Recently one statue was clearly traced to the village of Kankunde, chiefdom Nkuvu, to the northeast of Kongolo in eastern Zaïre (Neyt 1977:321, 442). The statue was so famous there that the genealogy of its keepers was known for four long generations, with several keepers per generation, back to the first forty years of the nineteenth century. The statue was carved by a certain Ngongo ya Chintu, who lived at the village of Kateba, close by. Better known stylistic characteristics of that area allow us to say that the Buli atelier shows evidence of a triple stylistic input; from the area itself, from the southwest (Luba) and from the northwest across the Zaïre river (Kusu). If there was but a single master of the style it was Ngongo ya Chintu. But there were probably several. We still do not know whether the atelier lasted only a single generation, early in the 1800s, or several. Perhaps further inquiry can settle at least the issue of the number of masters involved. The conjunction of historical data and of stylistic analyses has allowed the art historian to account for the style and suggest the general conditions of its appearance.

Because style is linked to an atelier there is a spatial aspect to style classification. One should expect therefore that transitional styles could occur between stylistic centres. This is precisely what happens. Indeed in some cases the transitional style is quite a feat in its own right. Consider the typically central style of Shaba (Luba) all built up in rounded volumes and then the typical style of northeastern Kasai (Songye) with their angular blocked out

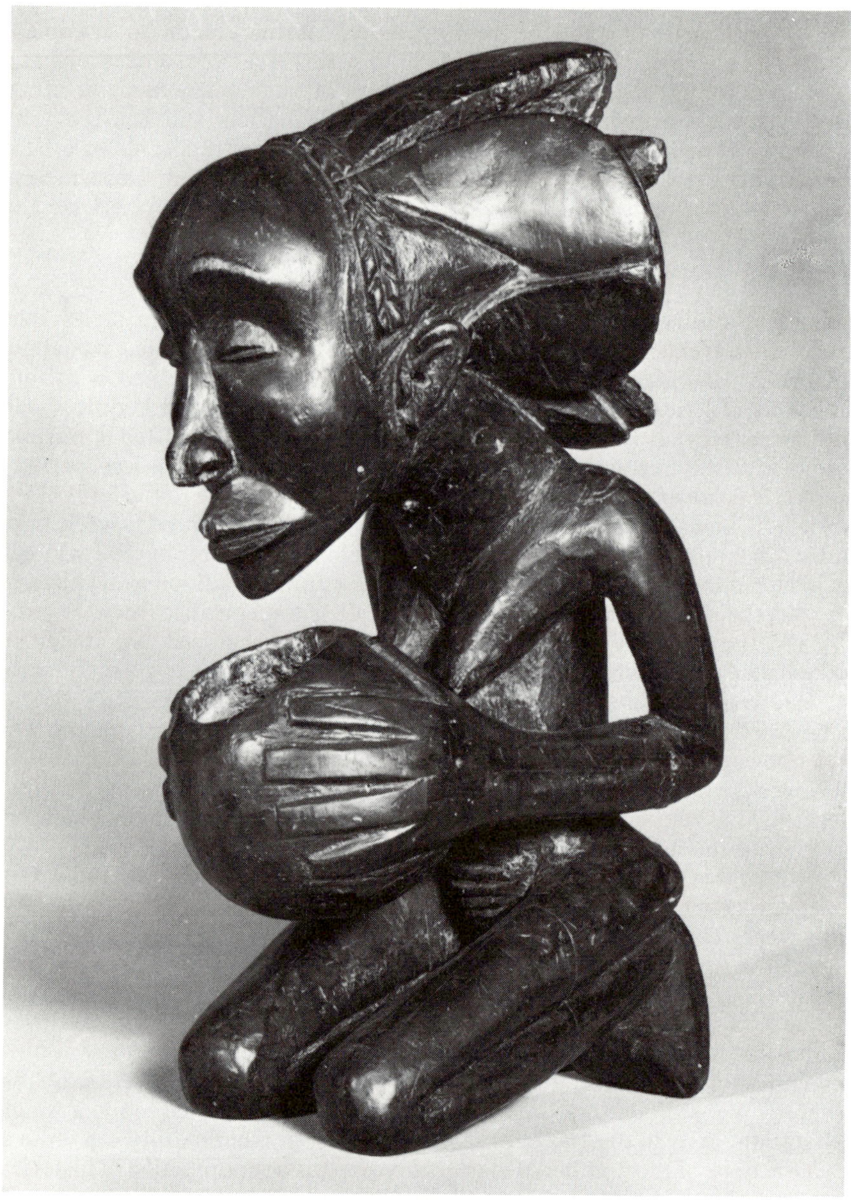

Plate 5.5 Kabila *figure. By Ngongo ya Chintu? (Buli Workshop). Wood. Used by diviners. The bowl may have contained white clay. The woman represents a nature spirit* mutitenta. *Kateba, Shaba, Zaïre. Koninklijk Museum voor Midden Afrika, Tervuren. Height 53·5cm. Before 1840. A product of the 'long face style workshop' of Buli. Ngongo is the only carver of this shop known by name and may have carved all works in this style. Dated by genealogy*

geometrical volumes, almost cubistic. A transitional style is hard to imagine here. And yet it did exist and yielded some very striking masterpieces. Historically we do not know where the ateliers were located, nor when. They must have been somewhere on the border of the Luba empire with the Songye

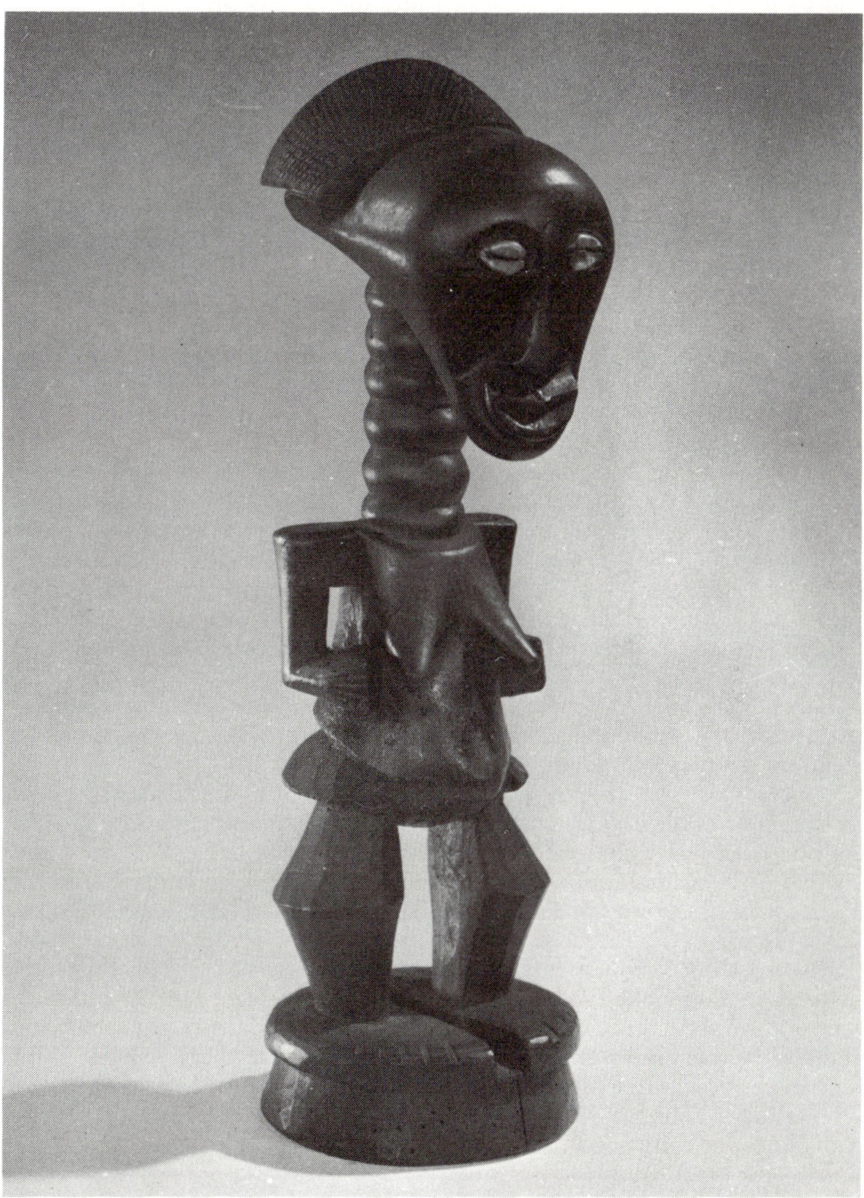

Plate 5.6 *Charm figure. Wood, cowries (eyes), oiled. Use unknown. East Kasai, Zaïre. Etnografish Museum, Antwerpen. Height 40·5cm. Acquired in Belgium 1920. The combination of very angular and rounded style suggests an origin among the southern Songye chiefdoms bordering on the Luba empire*

chiefdoms. But we do know of other strong influences from the Luba empire on certain of these chiefdoms (Fairley 1978). Moreover, the chiefdoms were organized in towns and the numbers of possible localities is restricted. The general area and the general conditions of cultural influence are now known and such transitional styles between Luba and Songye are placed.

Significant distributions of style over space are not limited to sub-Saharan Africa. A striking example is the architecture of domed tombs in the Sahara and its northern fringe from the Atlantic to Libya and its extension into eastern Sudan and the Horn. Thus Marçais (1954:435–7) distinguished five types by area, three of which were found from the Horn to the Atlantic. The two others show Turkish (post-1500) and Andalusian influence. One of the widespread types is linked to the structure of the oldest dome at Qairawan, but we still do not clearly know which came first, the tomb or the mosque! Similarly, so-called pillar tombs of East Africa and Madagascar fall into few styles. T. Wilson enumerates eight main types of East African monumental tombs. The relationship, especially where stepped corners exist, between such tombs and those of northern Africa, is evident, but the whole question, like that of the Saharan tombs itself, still awaits its investigation.

To link style and atelier, indeed even a master, is not equally possible with works in any medium. It should be easiest in painting, for the very notion of atelier developed by studying style and 'hand' in European painting. It is quite possible in carving, especially perhaps in wood, but it is much harder in additive sculpture where the plasticity of terra cotta and metal makes replication much more nearly perfect on the one hand and allows variation in so many directions on the other, that no corpus ever seems to include enough pieces of the same 'style'. Differences in individual works by the same hand tend to be taken as different styles! The technique has not been widely used with regard to northern Africa, yet it should be able to extend our knowledge with regard to such different arts as painting in Ethiopia, the smaller rock churches there, small-scale architecture in northern Africa, works in painted ceramics, textiles and perhaps decorative woodwork.

To achieve the recognition of an atelier or of a single master by the examination of their products is remarkable, but morphological and other stylistic examinations alone can only lead to probabilities. We know well enough from such attempts in European art that while some have stood up against later discoveries of data, others have not. Nevertheless, the attempt to link style and atelier is crucial to the endeavour of the art historian and should not be abandoned. Statements about it must however be capable of objective inspection. To invoke the invidious distinction between those who have the aesthetic eye and can see intuitively that these two works are by the same hand, and those other unfortunates who do not have an aesthetic eye, is simply nonsense, because replication of reasoning and result is essential to scholarship. Thus morphological analysis and other stylistic shorthand techniques for comparison are of the greatest value.

STYLISTIC SERIATION

Morphological analysis usually leads to seriation. This is the practice of placing the objects studied on an imagined continuum of forms, whose poles are the

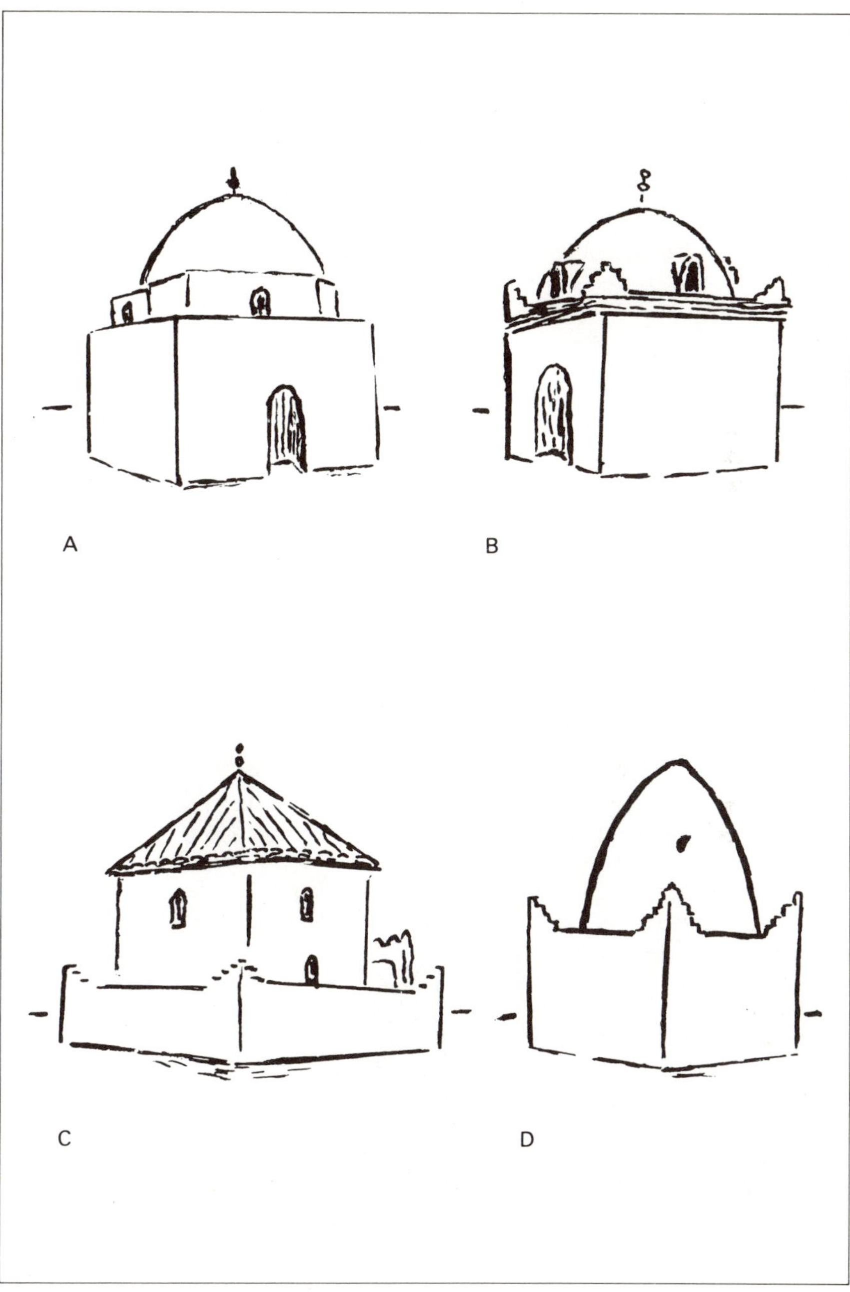

Fig. 5.3 *Tombs of Holy Men. Northern Maghrib. The styles derive from general architectural style and are a good indicator of cultural influences. A Tunisian style since the 9th c.; B Turkish influenced style, Algeria, since the 17th c.; C Andalusian style, Morocco and western Algeria, since the 12th c.; D Algerian plateau, south of the other styles and Nile valley, since* c. *8th c.(?) linked to nomads. The simplest style (not shown) consists of a semidome on a cube, and occurs in eastern Algeria and Tripolitania as well as elsewhere sporadically. Other variants occur in the Sudan and the Horn of Africa*

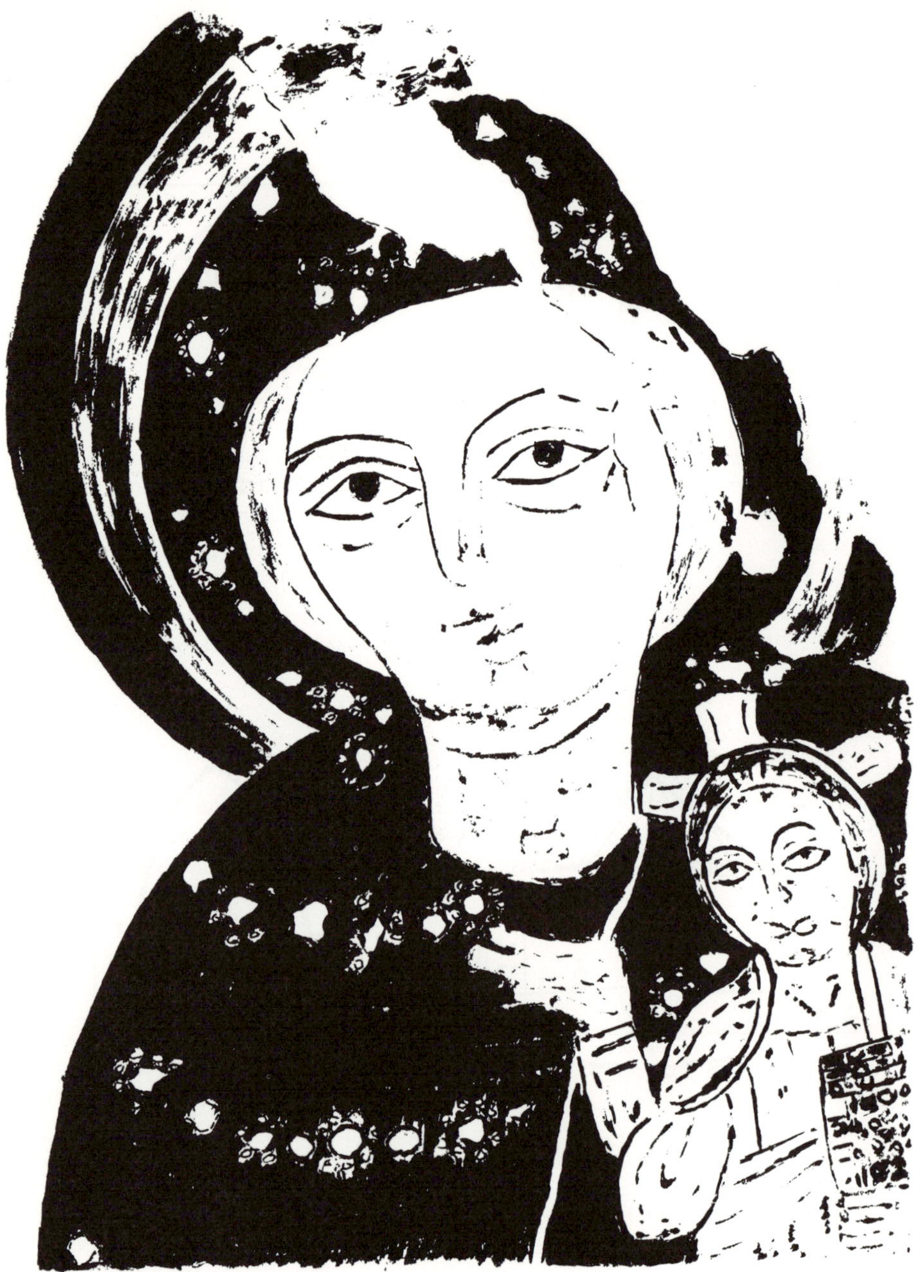

Fig. 5.4 *Madonna. Detail. Fresco 'Bishop Marianos, protected by Madonna and Christchild' in South Chapel, eastern wall, third layer of the Cathedral at Faras, Sudan. Face 18cm high. Polychrome period, after A.D. 1005. The round face of the madonna, her double chin and the treatment of the skinfolds of the neck are typical for the Master of the Madonnas, who was active from this date to almost 1100. Another master painted the Christ figure and yet a third bishop Marianos, a remarkable division of labour*

most extreme variants. Seriation is implied in the Fang corpus or the Hemba's eleven styles. Seriation implies time, either quite consciously and explicitly, as in the Neyt approach, or by the less explicit approach of Perrois.

Style changes over time and stylistic seriation can be described over time. The most famous example in Africa may well be the Cathedral at Faras with its superimposed frescoes (Michalowski 1967). Their sequence and helpful inscriptions allow four successive styles to be identified between *c.* A.D. 700 and A.D. 1200. Labelled by the dominant colours used, they are the violet (700–850), white (850–900), red and yellow (900–1000) and many-hued (1000–1173 at Faras only!) styles. The major ateliers were always at Faras although provincial ateliers following the dominant style of Faras, seat of the bishop, have been identified. Each style evolved locally and characteristic influences from the outside are known, from Coptic at first to Palestinian in the white period, Byzantine in the red/yellow period, and intensified Byzantine in the many-hued period. The problems of style, barring a few details, are solved at Faras.

But this case is uncommon. Usually a series is established, it is known that it must have some antiquity, and then it is classified. The best known example concerns the seriation of Benin copper-alloy works. Traditional data ascribe their origin to a time well before the Portuguese appeared on the coast, and brass heads continued to be made shortly before 1897, when the Benin palace treasures were looted by the British expedition. The first stylistic classification of von Luschan (1919) was replaced by one which W. Fagg and his school elaborated from *c.* 1950 onwards (Elisofon and Fagg 1958:57–8, 64–6; Dark 1975), and which gained wide acceptance. In its mature form, five periods were distinguished for the heads. The fourteenth to fifteenth centuries knew very thin brasses of very high technical quality with high collars under the chin. By the first half of the sixteenth century the collars were rolled; by the late sixteenth and seventeenth centuries high collars reached over the chin. The eighteenth century saw the addition of a base flange to the heads and the metal work had become much thicker. By the late nineteenth century the cap acquired wings. All through this evolution the faces became more and more stereotyped and occupied a smaller and smaller portion of the whole. The typical Benin plaques were believed to have been made between the 1550s and 1700. Dark divided them into three stages, according to background and relief. The chronology was based in part on oral tradition, in part on passing references by authors.

From the 1970s onwards the scheme has been challenged on various grounds (Shaw 1978:172–84 for a summary; Tunis 1981; Fraser 1980, 1981a). The more naturalistic heads were assigned to the onset of the sequence because traditionally it was claimed that the art came from Ife which had a naturalistic tradition. But the Ife connection is evidently much less direct, if there actually was one, than had been assumed. The sequences for plaques and their terminal dates have also been questioned and even been turned completely around by some scholars. Features such as flanges may have appeared side by side with flangeless works for quite a while and early heads or rolled collar types might be variants referring to certain situations or belonging in the beginning perhaps to a rival workshop (there was one at Udo according to tradition). In short, convincing proof of Fagg's scheme is lacking. Many more pieces must be dated by thermoluminescence of the clay cores before the matter will be settled. Today we know that in the thirteenth century tin bronze arm or leg rings (manilla) were manufactured in Benin and that established nineteenth-century works were in leaded brass. The heads are all brass. Some supposedly sixteenth-century items have been dated to that century but items that present particularly close similarities to Ife have not always turned out to be of early dates, some perhaps even being from the seventeenth century. Traditions tell us that one king ordered a stool to be fashioned as a replica of one made two hundred years earlier. Thus revivals of older forms in plaques or heads are not to be excluded either. The whole sequence will certainly be more

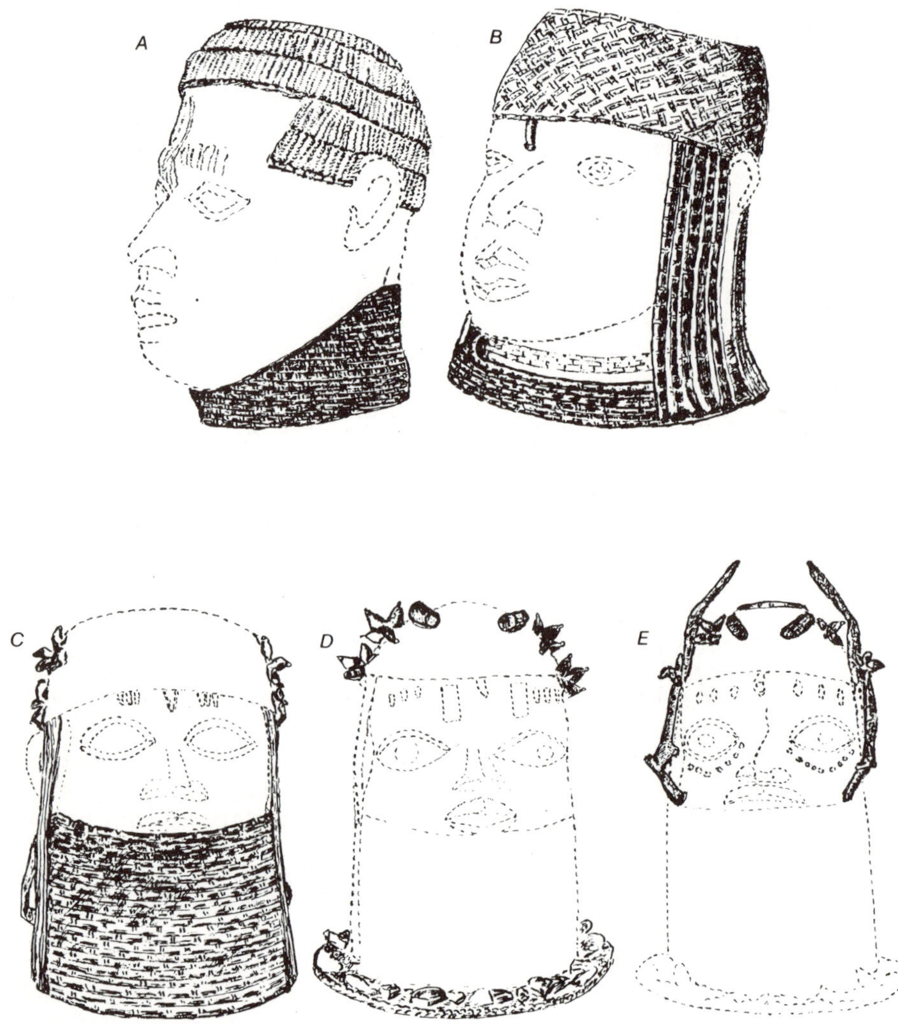

Fig. 5.5 *Seriation of Benin brass heads, as proposed by W. Fagg and P. Dark. The appearance of new distinctive elements, full lines. Progression from A to E spans perhaps four centuries*

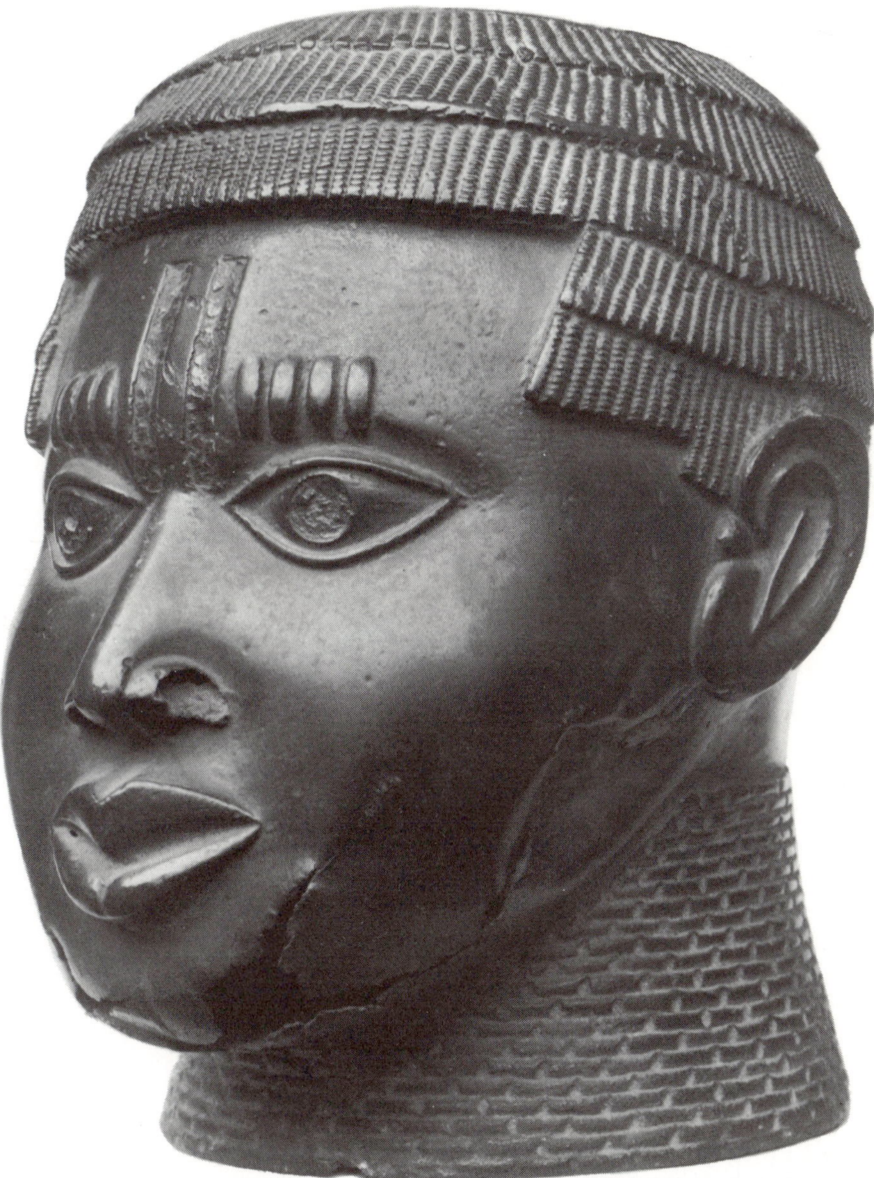

Plate 5.7 *Head. Brass. Use unclear, perhaps on ancestral shrine. Benin, Nigeria. British Museum. Height 21cm. Supposedly 'Early Style'. Hence 15th or 16th c. But the four marks and hairstyle indicate a foreigner. Hence this is a trophy head. Two such heads in Benin are linked to kings living* c. *1500 and just before 1800, respectively (cf.* Ben Amos *1980:18). Date unknown*

complex, when unravelled, if it ever is, than the logical sequence posited by style seriation alone suggest.

Seriation can be applied to the other arts just as it is to painting or sculpture. Dated series of the portals of congregational mosques in the Fatimid

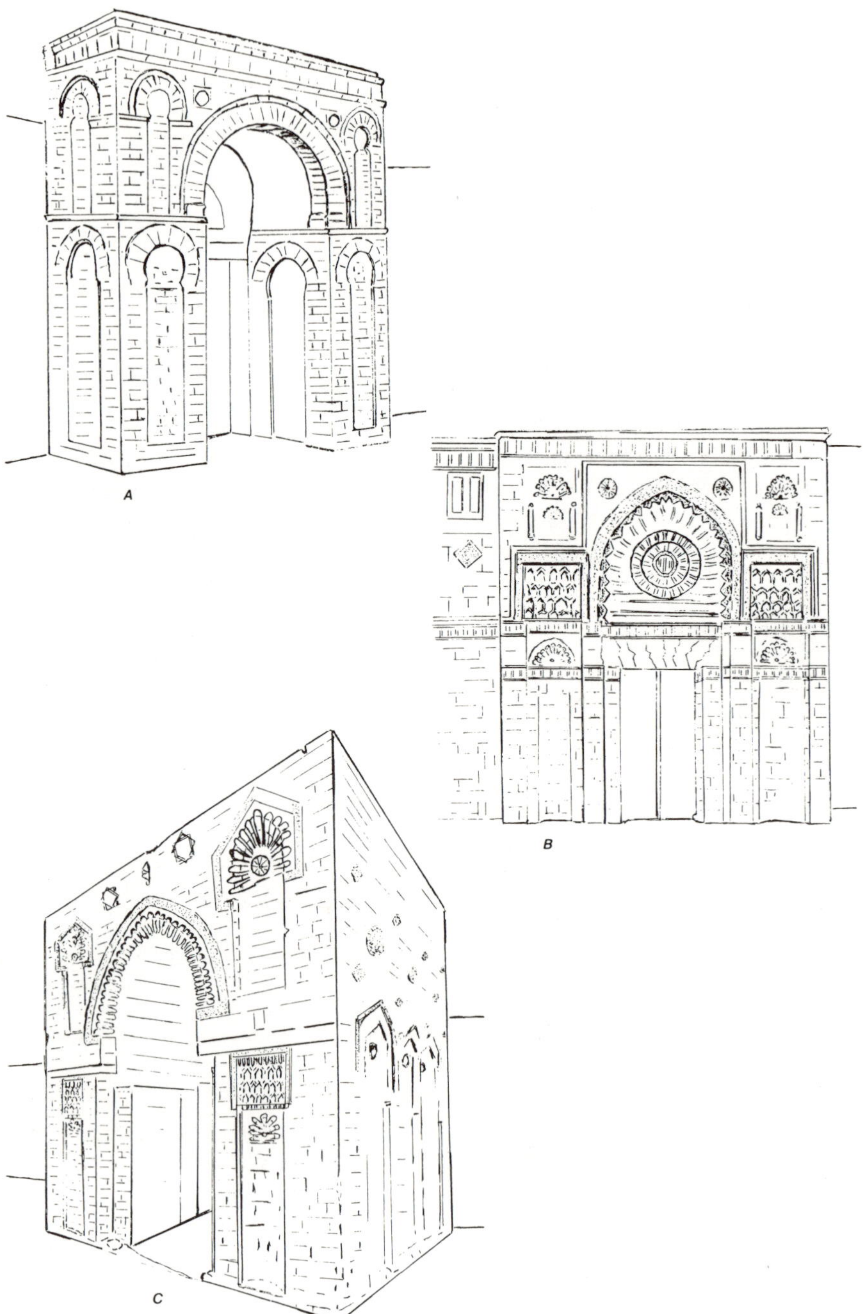

Fig. 5.6 *Fatimid portals. All stone masonry. A Mahdiya, Tunisia 913; B al Aqmar, Cairo 1125; C Baibars, Cairo 1267/9. All portals for congregational mosques. The portal is flatter at al Aqmar because it had to be integrated in a façade on the street (the first in Cairo) and it is deeper at Baibar's mosque where it supported a minaret. The continuity of the basic design is remarkable*

period show the appearance of a portal first at Mahdiya in Tunisia *c.* 916, its development in the al Hakim mosque *c.* 991 in Cairo, its incorporation in the first true street façade at al Aqmar in 1125 (Cairo), and its final elaboration in the sanctuary built by Baibars I, the first Mamluk ruler and dated to A.D. 1267. The original portal may have been inspired by a Roman triumphal arch. This structure at Mahdiya not only led to the sequence in Cairo, but also to the composition of the minaret of the Banu Hammad at their Qal'a in Algeria. By the onset of the Mamluk period the rulers began to build madrasa and tomb complexes rather than mosques. The portals of these new types of building are strikingly different, as, for example, in Sultan Hasan's complex of 1356. Apparently the model for these is the portal of the Gök Medrasa at Sivas (Anatolia), a creation of the Seljuk Turks. But the *notion* of having a portal in front of a religious complex was familiar in Cairo from the Fatimid congregational mosques, even if the *shape* of the new portals was Anatolian.

It is significant that the Fatimid portal series was linked to congregational mosques. The madrasa/tomb complexes were very different in overall conception as well as intended use and had come to Egypt from the Middle East. Thus there was no replacement of one type of portal by another, but the replacement of one type of building by another as the object of the ruler's attention (Sourdel-Thomine and Spuler 1973: ill. 162, 163, 168, 176, 288, 295; text:244, 249, 329).

The stylistic series for Fatimid portals is convincing, because the series is dated, organically linked to one type of building and to the preferences of one dynasty. Without dates the series might have been arranged quite differently, Mahdiya might then have been seen as a provincial copy of Baibars' portal, for instance, and been last in a series rather than first. Such possibilities of arranging undated elements in other equally convincing series recalls the puzzle from Benin and highlights the dangers of using the fact of a stylistic series as a real historical chronology. A stylistic series always represents an hypothesis of sequence over time. It is a logical device, much used by archaeologists, for instance, in the seriation of pottery or types of tombs. The simpler the shapes, and the denser the series, the greater the chances that the sequence has some historical validity. But seriations should never be confused with proven chronology. To the contrary, they should be tested by every known device in an effort to falsify or confirm the hypothesis.

SHAPE IN TIME

The study of style will always remain subjective, but the degree of objectivity can be considerably increased by a clear exposition of an author's reasoning, either by the use of a highly formal technique of analysis such as morphological analysis or by a clear exposé as to why some works are seen as prime works and others as their replications. The reasoning can then be checked for circular elements, low probability (as when a supposed replicate could well be the original or vice versa), inconsistency and implications from the point of view of spatial distributions and known historical developments in the area studied. It will then be easier to see just where research stands on a given stylistic problem. A typical example is the stylistic sequence sketched out for the sculpture of a small coastal group, west of the Cross River, called the Eket.

Neyt (1979:24–6) studied one collection and distinguished between archaic forms and later derivative forms. Archaic sculpture was characterized by such features as the heart-shaped form of the face and often by ray-shaped appendages around it. The classical form following showed a more definite precision both in the cutting of volumes and in their assembly, while its polychromy has a 'delicateness of tone and an equilibrium of colours' used as slip and as highlights that is absent from later works. Later work, from the present century, simply lacks the perfection of classical work, both in the carving and in the painting. The rationale for the archaic end of the sequence was that such archetypes were common to the Eket and all the neighbouring groups sharing in the same general culture.

The main specialist for the Cross River area, Nicklin (1980), approved of Neyt's stylistic approach, and so we have a consensus of two. Presumably he understood just what 'delicateness of tone', 'equilibrium of colour', meant as any reader could by comparing classical and late works. Nevertheless, more specific statements about muting or not of colour and about colour oppositions and complementarities would help.

How is one to go beyond such a consensus on a local sequence? In this case, diligent study of a larger corpus and morphological analysis would render the argument more specific. A detailed search into the historical conditions of the Eket and their neighbours can be made from the late eighteenth century onwards and should not make the proposed sequence improbable, but rather strengthen it or bolster an alternative. In the end, this local sequence must be placed in a much wider West African framework. Such problems are beyond the stage of style seriation. They are discussed in Chapter 10.

CHAPTER SIX

THE INTERPRETATION OF ICONS

ICON AND CONCEPT

A study of medium, technique and style has still not considered the gist of an art object. Art objects are physical images which are the materialization of mental images associated with definite meanings, i.e., icons. Whenever I want to stress the link between the object and the visual concept underlying it, I will use the term icon. Because of their meaning, art objects are understood, decorated or handled in a special way. The Ardra board (Plate 1.1) is not just a board: it is a board for *ifa* divination. It has an effigy of Legba or Eshu, the trickster god of Chance and Fate. It carries symbols of divination, and is used for divination. Most of the images around its rims refer to meanings now lost to us. We see only gesturing men and women, animals and a few objects such as tusks – the latter representing wealth – but we cannot make sense of the whole. The user in the seventeenth century could, and probably all these meanings are connected with Fate.

While the quality of image is evident in the case of the Ardra board, it is not so self-evident in the case of household objects such as a wooden milkpot from the Great Lakes area (Sieber 1980:ill. 277). Yet that, too, is an image that stems from and leads to concrete visual concepts. When the people of this area think about a milkpot, it always has a particular shape familiar to them and not that, say, of the calabashes in which West African pastoralists store their milk. The mental image of the object exists before the object itself, an idea that guided the maker. In turn, the object made impresses itself as an icon on the mind of the viewer. It is known that visual concepts are more powerful than auditive stimuli because the memory codes them twice, once as a memory of sound and once as a memory of image. They are more immediate than most other types of memory because of their concreteness. Visual concepts of this type also persist more over time, because the object created lasts and acquires its own independent life, independent from any mind, unlike auditory stimuli which are *only* preserved in the mind. Hence visual images, icons, can have a great impact on concept formation (Ohnuki Tierney 1981).

A Kuba man once described his unexpected encounter with a nature spirit near the river in the early morning mists. He described it in detail. But the account from which this episode stems goes on to explain that it was the trickster, who had donned the costume and the *bwoom* mask that represent nature spirits. To the Kuba, the idea of a nature spirit looks like a *bwoom* dancer. The concept is visual and because it is, it becomes concrete. No one doubts the existence of nature spirits, because people know what they look like. This is no different from the popular conception of the devil in the West. We know what he looks like, with his pitchfork, tail and hooves, nimble as can be, matching black and red hues. The concept is real because it is visual. Its concrete character saw to it that its reality was rarely questioned. Yet there was a time in the first centuries A.D. when this stereotype did not exist, and devils were portrayed as refulgent angels. Similarly, we know what dragons look like, although there never was a dragon. So it is natural that a nature spirit among the Kuba is perceived as given by experience. A little further reflection shows many natural items to be seen, not as they are, but as they are portrayed. Gombrich and others have shown that we perceive the world as it had been portrayed. The visual arts therefore carry great weight in any culture.

The existing icon is a link in a chain of images running from the artist's mental image, over the icon, to the visual image it inspires in the viewer and the artist alike, who later commission or execute just such a work as inspired by the icon. The icon becomes the source for an artist's mental image. The whole process is shared by the community of patrons and artists. The visual concept is a 'collective representation'. In this sense, works of art are collective products, cultural products, and this sense is very real. It is not therefore wise to argue that art in Africa or medieval art in Europe is communal whilst modern Western art is not. At the most, one can say that expectations of visual concepts are less defined now than they were before in practically any art anywhere at any time. Industrialization has allowed us to make more and more perfect, but banal, copies. Hence the dissociation between a unique art object and some other thing which is mass produced.

Visual concepts such as the Ardra board or a *bwoom* mask are also statements. Even though the tray's visual impact is immediate, it is composed of motifs, associated with the divination. Chance (the circle) is there, Fate (the top figure of Eshu/Legba), the World (carvings around the board). As a statement, visual objects represent a theme or a subject. This sculpture represents a hunter, that painting a nativity. The theme is made up of details,

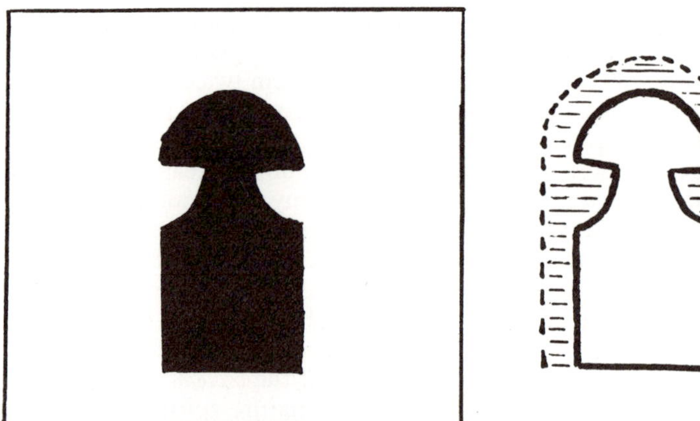

Fig. 6.1 *Keyhole window, Lalibela. Ethiopia.* c. *1190–1225. This represents the window opening created by an arch on capitals and cornices, supported by columns or pillars. Those structural elements are, however, omitted. The ability to see voids was essential for Ethiopian architects who carved churches out of live rock*

the motifs, which are visual units often isolated in space, as in this case, but not necessarily so. Decorative borders as a whole outline space, but within them, the motif often forms a pervasive repetitive pattern.

Isolated motifs clearly are the 'words' of the statement, which is the icon. Isolated visual units pose no problem here, but patterned ones do. For they must be the units seen by the artists and their public, not the units stemming from the visual habits of the scholar. Sometimes there are obvious problems here. The keyhole windows in monolithic Ethiopian churches make no immediate sense to the Western eye, yet they represent the opening of an arched window with pediment and corbelling. The Ethiopians did not 'see' the arches, corbels, pillars and bases around the window, but they saw the space delimited by them as a unit. To Western viewers, the effect is rather as if the background had become the motif, and the real motifs the background. In the rock-hewn churches, the shape of space was reproduced: that is, the keyhole shape.

THEME AND MOTIF

The cumulative effect of the parts yields the overall visual concept of the icon. Often motifs and their compositional arrangement are all part of the conventional composition rendering the theme, 'the' visual concept. Consider the Central Angolan (Chokwe) statue of the ancestral hunter Chibinda Ilunga in Plate 6.1. He stands holding his gun in one hand, his staff of a wanderer in the other. His hat tells us he is a chief, and the horns or figures on the hat show his control of supernatural powers. The horns are filled with magical substance, the figurines are his invisible spirit, familiars. His shoulder bag identifies him as a hunter and not as a warrior. The size of his hands and feet tells us of physical strength and endurance. The stare, the flaring nostrils, the wide, thin mouth, and even the ears, tell us of power also to be feared. More of this can be understood as the theme of Chibinda Ilunga becomes known. The name refers to the supposed founder of the civilized world, a hunter appearing from the East who united with the then-ruling woman to found a mighty empire. Even if we know this, we still cannot infer from the statue alone what the details mean, not even by comparison with the other Chokwe works. Local informants have to tell us about the meaning of the facial features and hands. All the motifs here are fused into a single composition, rendering a single theme and they can be found with little variance on other such statues. A glance tells Chokwe they all represent Chibinda Ilunga (Bastin 1965). On the other hand, there is absolutely nothing in any subject or theme that requires it to be rendered in a particular way. The relationship between the concept and the rendition is almost as arbitrary as that which exists between sound and the meaning of a word. In the Lower Niger the hunter figure was represented as striding in movement with a kill over his shoulders, in other sculptures he trails his dog. But the variance can be much greater than this. We imagine that a mask of a person should at least represent a face, but this is not necessarily so. Just west of the Cross River, along the coast, among the group known as Eket, one series of masks looks like a huge sandwich board decorated with gay floral-like patterns (Neyt 1979). Yet the mask represents a person. It is important to stress this point because the relative, arbitrary, character of a

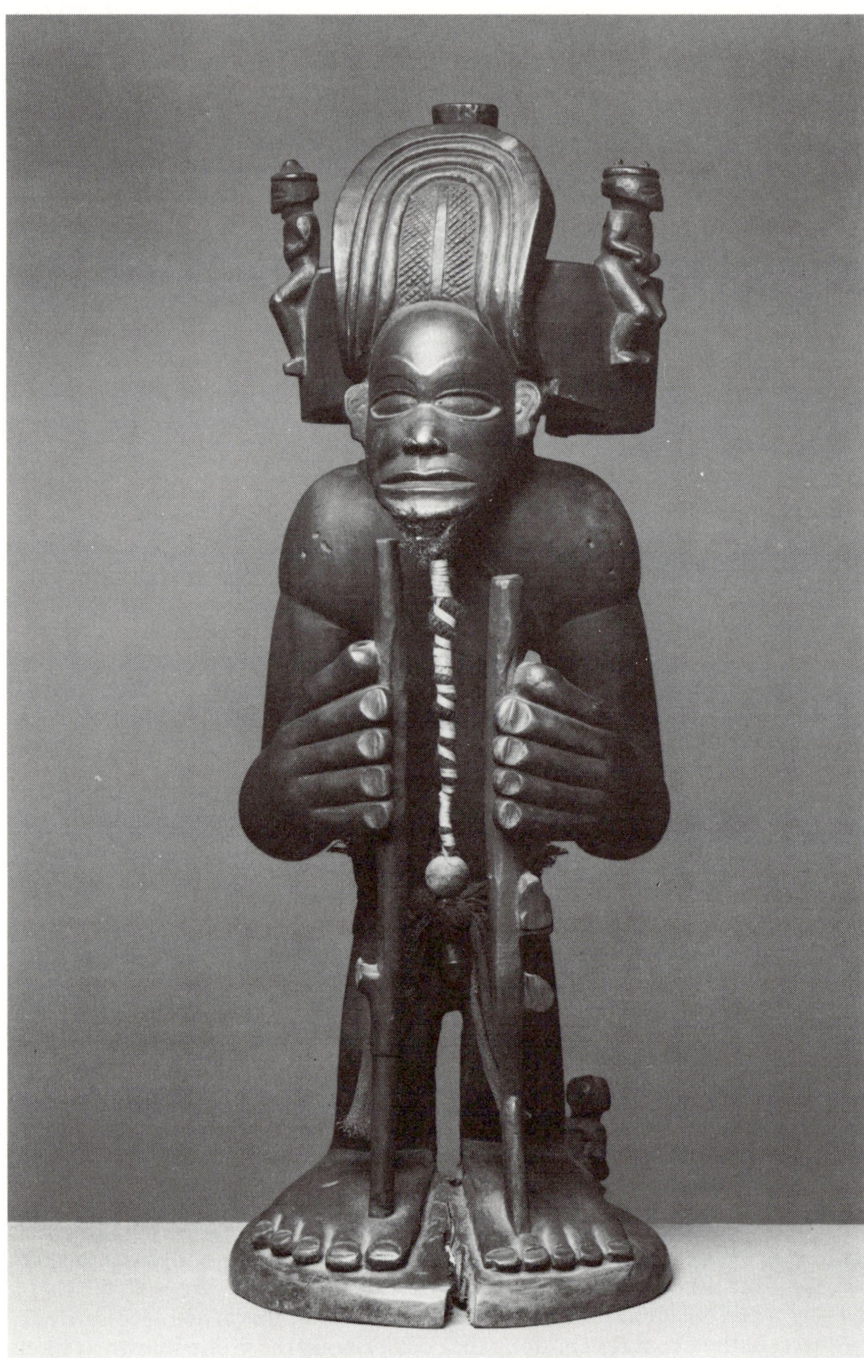

Plate 6.1 *Chibinda Ilunga. Figure. Wood, cotton belt, natural hair, fibre, yellow bead (bard). Use unknown. Chibinda Ilunga is the mythical hunter who married Rweej and thus founded the Lunda empire. North central Angola (Chokwe). Museum für Völkerkunde, Berlin-Dahlem. Height 39cm. Acquired 1879*

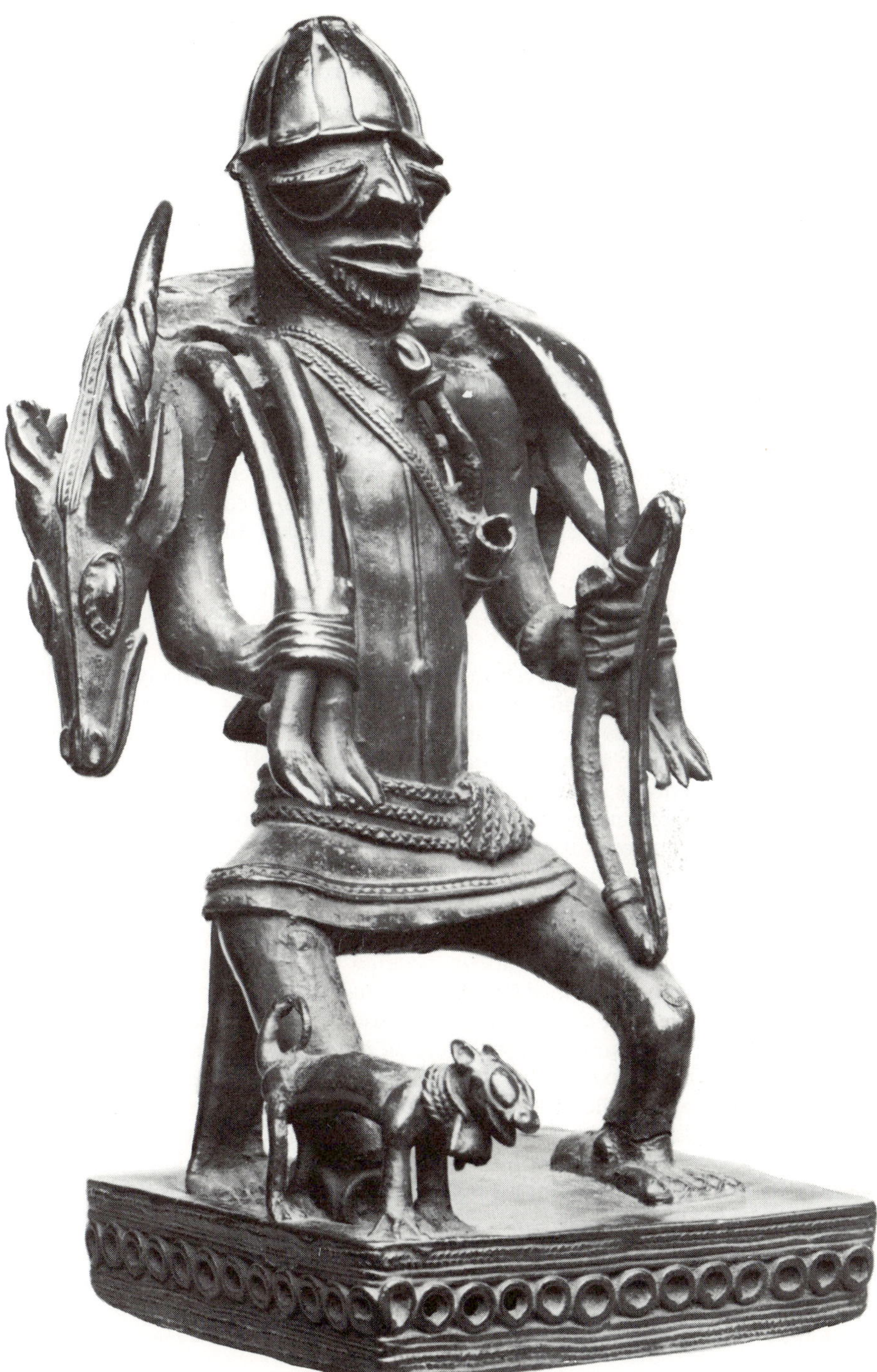

Plate 6.2 *Hunter figure. Copper alloy. Use unknown. Found at Benin 1897. British Museum. Height 21cm. The style is totally unlike any other Benin work. Date of manufacture unknown, could be 15th to 19th c.*

representation means that when several representations of the same theme are quite similar, they must have an historical connection.

As visual units, motifs can occur in other compositions than the one where they first originated. Women with their hands on their bellies and men with raised arms occur on the Ardra board. But they are quite common in nineteenth- and twentieth-century Yoruba sculpture of the same general area as well. The royal hat of Chibinda Ilunga is the main element of one of the Chokwe initiation masks and occurs on the upper back rung of thrones. Motifs then are real visual units, and yet the term is also used, perhaps unfortunately, in a vague sense. An arm is raised and one can talk about the 'raised arm' motif. The motif is no longer self-contained. It may not have been a visual unit to the artist, to be separated from the figure to which the arm belongs. It is a motif within a motif. The problem is not that motifs may be internally complex, but that the term is used to designate compositional particularities which may not have been visual units at all to the makers. Thus, a sentence referring to the motif of repeated volumes is very different from one identifying a hat as a motif. In the first sense, the term refers to an analysis of composition, in the second to a demonstrably separate motif. The confusion introduces us to the problem of interpretation.

INTERPRETATION

Meaning is never self evident, even though it often seems clear enough – this is a mosque, that is a crucifixion, that again is the statue of an ancestor – but it is clear only because it has become familiar and we have been told what these buildings, paintings or sculptures meant. The icon has become part of our culture. Apart from the culture, the meaning is as opaque as anthracite coal. The first step in dealing with interpretation, then, is to give an objective description of the object, not refer to meaning. 'Kneeling woman with a bowl' is an objective description of a *kabila* figure of Shaba (see Plate 5.5). 'Beggar woman' is perhaps compelling but it is totally wrong (Maes 1938:78; Olbrechts 1959:71, 106–7). 'Monkey with bowl' is correct for a figure from the southern Ivory Coast (Baule), 'Trained baboon begging' is wrong. Interpretation is therefore often dependent on data not contained in the art object itself and poses critical problems. Figurative representations pose especially formidable problems of interpretation, unfortunately all too often overlooked.

The Saharan rock paintings (5000 B.C. and later) illustrate the question. At first, scenes were labelled with imaginative names such as the 'tooth puller', 'martians' (a whole category of faceless representations), and even 'Josephine sold by her sisters'. The description accompanying this composition tells how a woman was sold by her sisters to strangers while all we see are four figures! The inspiration for this particular fancy seems to have been a mix between Joseph in Egypt and thoughts about African bridewealth (Lajoux 1977:110–11). Later scholars tended to be more circumspect but still accepted the interpretation of

Plate 6.4 *Rockpainting. Family scene in and near a shelter. Inside a child plays under a stand for a bowl. Other bowls, gourds, pots hang from the wall or lie on the floor. A person rests in the shelter. In front, near a fire(?) a woman and child. Below them another woman addresses a child in front of another shelter. Sefar, Algeria. Earlier than 2 000 B.C. Pastoral neolithic. The periodization is very approximative. The styles of Plates 6.4 and 6.3 vary not as a succession of a single style over time, but as different styles in both time and space. Note the various perspectives used* →

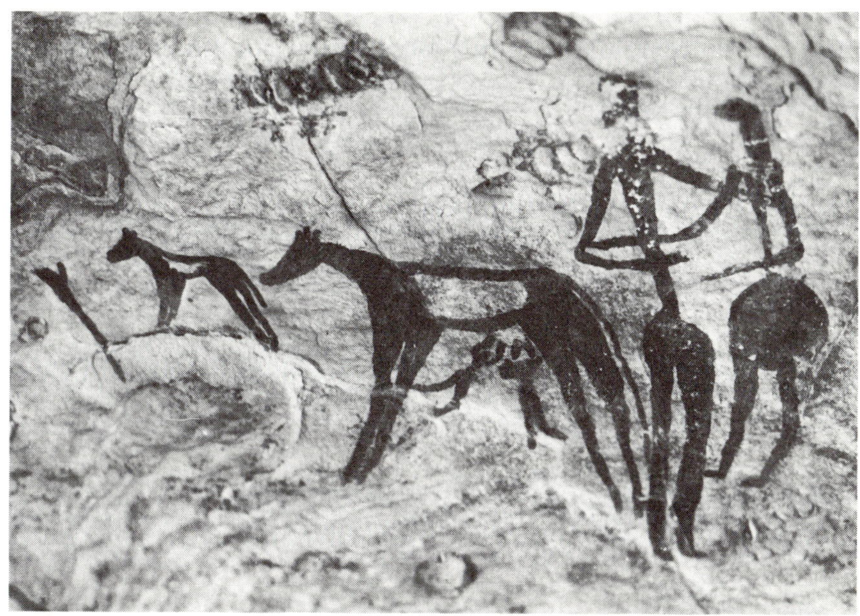

Plate 6.3 *Rockpainting. Family scene: man, woman, two children sucking, a cow, and its tethered calf. The cow needs to see the calf in order to give milk. Karkur Talh, Jebel Uwainat, Libya. Pastoral neolithic. Earlier than 2 500* B.C. *Compare with Plate 6.4*

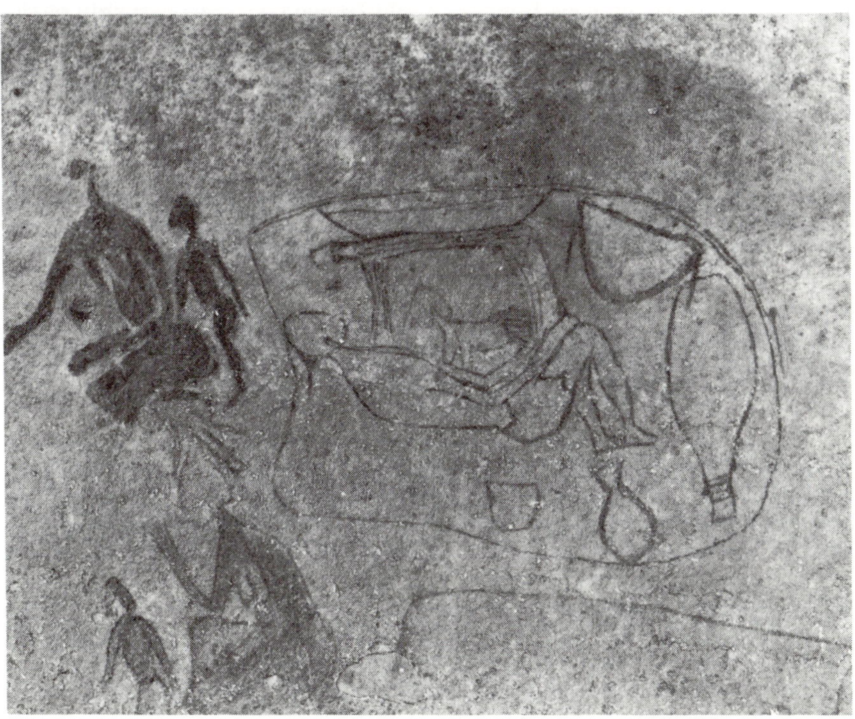

certain scenes as episodes from an initiation myth, because they were so understood by a Fulani scholar, who thought he recognized episodes of the Fulani initiation myth in them. But so many centuries separate the Fulani of *c.* A.D. 1900 from the scenes dating earlier than 2000 B.C. that the one cannot shed light on the other (Lajoux 1977:106). We must therefore restrain our labels and commentary to unmistakable objective elements: 'a hut with a man, a child, a bowl, a calabash and another object'. It means that historians will learn less from Saharan paintings than they once hoped for, but at least will not mislead others.

In some cases the interpretation was linked to much wider issues. In the Brandberg area of Namibia exists a famous rock painting, labelled 'the White Lady from Brandberg' by the inventor Maack and later Abbé Breuil, a famous French prehistorian (Breuil 1955; Jacobson 1980). Breuil had seen reproductions of it in 1929 and 1942. In 1947, Field Marshal Smuts helped him to visit the site. On his return, he gave a lecture at Windhoek* and 'confirmed' that the 'white lady' was of a European or Mediterranean type, perhaps Cretan. That he had already seen from the photographs and told to Smuts before going to the site. He now concluded:

> Allied with the grey and extraordinary figures in the Brandberg arises the question of the origin of a certain number of figures of strangers of different races, painted in Southern Rhodesia and the South East of the Union.
>
> The trade winds: Monsoons, Sofala civilization of Ur. Sumer 3000 B.C. The Fort Victoria frescoes. Chibi Impey [sic] cave certainly of the same style as the Brandberg and point to influence coming from that region.
>
> The spiritual landscape of Africa.

A glance at any illustration of the figure shows it to be male and black (Willett 1971). Its datation by amino acid counting makes it 1 200 to 1 800 years old – nowhere near 3000 B.C. – and this is no surprise, as Breuil mentioned shards of pottery on the site (Iskander 1980:218). There is no close relation to Zimbabwean rock paintings at all. The illustrious archaeologist was so blinded by racial prejudices that he apparently could not even see what the representation showed. His error was demonstrably monumental. But was it that much greater than those of the scholars who labelled the Saharan paintings, or of all those who attribute awe, fear, mystery and such like emotions to African sculpture?

The difficulties of interpretation cannot be over-stressed. In Old Egyptian paintings a typical composition shows a larger sized person surrounded by smaller people occupied with activities of daily life; these are all tomb scenes (see Plate 6.5). Is the larger figure the deceased supervising work on an estate of sorts, or is the scene merely recording the theme of a daily round of life and divorced from the larger figure? We often do not know (Gombrich

* Breuil papers f A461. Notes by Abbé Breuil for his lecture, Windhoek 1947. From the Department of Historical Papers. University of the Witwatersrand Library, Johannesburg. I thank Dr H. Scheub for the text.

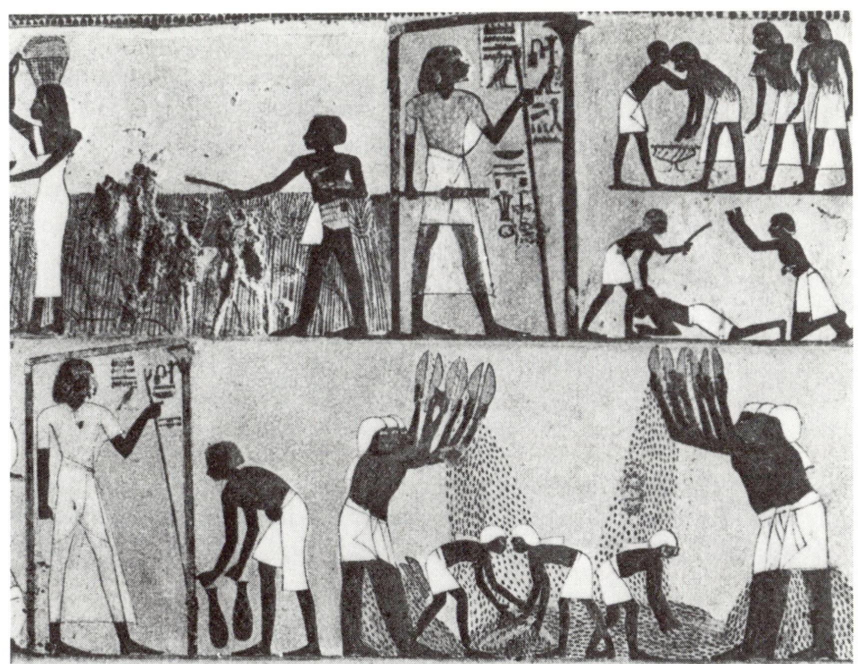

Plate 6.5 *Tomb of Menna. Shaikh 'Abd al Qurnah, Thebes. Scenes from farm life are shown with figures of Menna under a canopy. Upper right two registers show managers from his estates arriving with produce required (not shown on this photograph). The upper group is honoured because their remittances are satisfactory. Those of the lower group are not and they are being beaten or will be. Different authors explain these scenes differently, the managers being servants or guests and the person pleading pleads for himself, for the person being beaten or is a servant praising Menna. The inscription in the top canopy reads: 'The Scribe of the fields of the Master of the two lands, North and South: Menna'. It is unclear whether all the scenes must be read together or not. Is Menna supervising the arrival of the managers and the threshing? Is the person carrying vessels bringing them to Menna or putting them on the side of the field? Is Menna shown in his role as an overseer, actually on the estate? Or is his canopied figure something to be seen completely apart, a representation of the deceased? Tomb no. 69, southeast wall, detail of wallpainting. XVIIIth dynasty,* c. *1420* B.C.

1960:122–3). Frescoes in churches such as at Faras do not depict scenes from the life of Christ, although we designate them as such. They depict highlights of the liturgical calendar. The location in the church and the choice of episodes proves it. If we relate the motifs of the Ardra board to Chance, Fate and the World, we do it because such boards are still made (see Plate 2.3). Fieldwork has shown them to be part of the tools of the *ifa* diviner and to have such meanings, but as we saw, we cannot thereby still interpret all the details of the Ardra board; we might be anachronistic. If we interpret ivory as wealth it is because we know that ivory was exported from there at that time as a valued product of trade. Our interpretation of the whole board, however, will probably always remain fragmentary.

How does an outsider reach a valid interpretation? The ideal would be to know the total sum of local interpretations, which may vary from person to person, but revolve around a common intellectual and emotional core, the 'collective representation'. No ethnographic report is that detailed. At best we have hermeneutic exegesis by an insider. Thus, among the Dogon people of Mali, Ogotemelli, a blind sage, thought and talked a great deal about his culture and interpreted myths, themes, motifs for M. Griaule (1948) and his colleagues. In turn, they expanded these and checked them with other inhabitants of Ogotemelli's settlement. The interpretation of Dogon sculpture certainly is more authentic than outside guesses but it is a personal statement which required careful checking with other Dogon. Ogotemelli's views certainly cannot be extrapolated to interpret other works of art in other areas as has sometimes been done. They do not allow in the name of symbolic equivalence, for instance, to equate 144 holes on a vessel with 87 or so, as some researchers have done. The *visual* evidence remains the most important!

Often we do not have much ethnographic information, or it deals only with usage and not with a detailed reading of the iconic statement. Moreover, for many older objects, we can only speculate by analogy, with all the dangers inherent in that procedure. Here there exists in fact a deep difference between the literate cultures of the *oikoumene* and the regional traditions. Christianity, Islam, classical antiquity, Pharaonic Egypt, have left us a treasure house of texts by which we can venture to interpret icons, if they do not, in detail. This is especially true for all religious works. Elsewhere the researcher will always be faced with difficult choices of interpretation and it behoves him to make the grounds of the interpretation quite clear.

ART LANGUAGE

Icons make all sorts of statements. They can be narrative, signs of identification, comments. But all icons need not make statements. Some motifs do not. Moreover, icons always evoke emotional appeal. In narrative compositions the motif becomes an element in telling a story. The Faras painting of the Nativity tells of the shepherds aroused by angels, the holy family at the manger, and the visit of the kings. A few brass plaques of Benin may represent historical scenes such as 'return of the Igala war' and their juxtaposition may well have evoked narratives, now completely lost (Ben Amos 1980a:23, ill. 21). Sometimes narrative becomes mere anecdote as in the Kuba cup portraying a man holding a cup which relates to an individual who was known for his propensity to imbibe. On the whole, narratives were rare outside Christian art. Compositions were not very frequent on a larger scale and usually the representation of a single person or animal was to carry the whole message.

Statements indicated by signs, usually signs of identification, were by far the most common. Thus, attributes of Christian saints identify them: St Andrew carried his cross and had tousled hair (Wessel 1965:166–7). Differences in hairstyle, beards, sideburns identify different saints in Coptic painting. The attributes of the Chokwe figure of Chibinda Ilunga identify him as such by his gun, bag, staff, hat, figurines or horn, hands and feet. In toto, they are a statement explaining who Chibinda Ilunga was and what the concept represents. This is similar to the statements made by Chokwe chairs where every rung may be carved. Scenes of initiation, fights over women, daily preparation of food, trade, caravan life and sex are common. Each of these groups of icons seems to tell a separate anecdote, but the scenes can all be related to the concept of the chief as the upholder of ordered social life (Kauenhoven Janzen 1981). The great difficulty in interpreting such icons is the complexity of the statements made. Each scene is deciphered easily enough, but the relationship among them is not evident. Usually the scholar's tendency is to link all the details to the statement of the theme, but that need not be the case. The interpretation tends to remain hypothetical as long as actual informants living at the time and near the place of fabrication are not available. Yet stronger grounds for linking parts to the whole can be obtained by comparison. For instance, if different Chokwe chairs show the same limited number of subjects – as they do – the chances that all are related to the theme of kingship are higher. At the level of cultural analysis a link of all these statements to the central theme of kingship is valid. Yet it may not be valid at the level of the intentions of each artist, his intended composition of a particular chair. A scene invented by one carver, appreciated by others and by the public, could become a favourite theme in later chairs even though its connection with the concept 'kingship' was rather tangential to begin with. The accumulation of scenes may not reflect kingship, but only the special character of a throne as an object of prestige or merely the mastery of the carver. Eventually the very existence of the chairs would lead to a visual association of the scenes they portrayed with the notion of kingship although it is likely that many scenes on the rungs were not intended from the beginning to be portions of a detailed and purposeful statement about the nature of kingship.

Motifs as signs often led to identifications that became portraits. A tattoo, a style of hair, a horn in hand, a piece of jewellery or clothing, placed a statue in a social group and a type of social role as clearly as any attribute identified a Coptic saint. Beyond these general identifications, portraits of individuals could be meant. They were never made from nature, but they carried signs which identified them as such for the *cognoscenti.* A Kuba (ngongo) statue of a pregnant woman was the portrait of the daughter of the carver who made it and who died in childbirth (see Plate 6.6). The sign of pregnancy was the only indication of this visible to outsiders. The sculptor himself claimed to have rendered the features of the face, conventional though it looked to others. Kuba royal statues refer to individuals by impersonal signs. The founder king was identified by his rows of emblems, which later kings lacked in quite such profusion (see Plate 8.4). But essentially it was the emblem placed in front of each statue that identified it, rather like a label. A game board, an anvil, a woman, drums with different decorative motifs for different kings, all identified the statue. Physical differences barely appeared, one only in the set shows more than the ordinary obesity (an ideal of Kuba kings) by a slight indication of rolls of fat in the neck. But in general the physical representation merely refers to an ideal, just as rolls of fat in the neck of masks of the Sierra Leonian Sande Society refer to the ideal of feminine beauty and well-being there, while their small mouths denote wisdom. Portraits thus existed but not lifelike portraits. Perhaps the representations of Ife heads may have been lifelike. If so, they were the great exception. This is also true of northern African arts in general where identification occurred by general signs and by inscription of a name. Only Roman portraits and the painted effigies of mummies in the first centuries A.D. were really intended to be lifelike.

The use of icons as incidental comments detached from the main statement, or the main theme, was not unknown. A Coptic painting of David

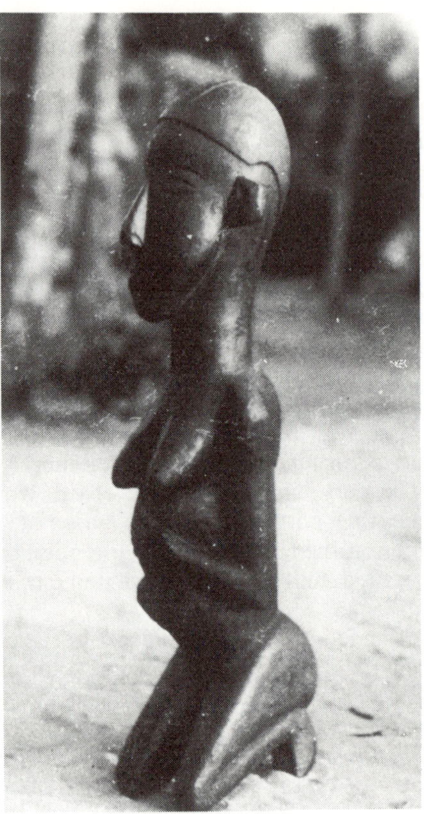

Plate 6.6 *Figure of a pregnant woman. Wood. Used as a memento. Keenge, northeastern Kuba kingdom (Ngeende village in Ngongo and Mbeengi area). Photo: June 1956. Portrait of the daughter of the carver who died in childbirth. Unlike any other style in the area, this piece is unique*

and Goliath shows Goliath, the bad man with an Arab beard and clad in Persian armour (du Bourguet 1967:170). A strident comment is the Ethiopian painting of the prophet Muhammad, bound to a horse and led away by Satan, a scene sandwiched in between the usual themes at Debra Berhan Sellassie near Gondar (Leroy 1967:35).

South of the Sahara, such statements are known from the performing arts, but have not been reported in the visual arts, probably because the allusion remained esoteric and not because it did not occur.

THE COMPLEXITY OF MEANING

The full meaning of icons can be quite complex because of the situation in which they appear. The well-known juxtaposition of proverbs with depictions on goldweights in Ghana or potlids in Cabinda typify this (Appiah 1979; Cornet 1980). The concrete meaning of the icon was apparent only in its use. To send a goldweight of the two friends shaking hands to one chief in one circumstance meant one thing; to send it to another at another time meant another. A potlid sent by a woman to her husband in one circumstance could carry a message different from its use in another circumstance. To decipher interpretations it is therefore not enough to find the main field of meaning, but it also becomes necessary to review the circumstances of use.

Juxtaposing several icons produces even more complex statements in which each icon acts as if it were a motif of the larger ensemble. The wall Kuba built on the occasion of boys' initiations illustrates this occurrence (Fig. 6.2). On it many icons were displayed together and the whole wall formed one unit. Such a wall consisted really of a scaffolding of poles from different kinds of wood, all symbolically significant, covered with raffia fibres. The wall was shaped like a screen with three triangular peaks, well over nine metres in height, the whole being sixty metres long and more. In front of the wall near its centre a round armature covered with raffia fibre encircled an almost life-size female figure and, in 1953, when I saw such a wall, two small figures were planted just outside the enclosure surrounding the woman. In brief, the wall represented the journey the boys to be initiated were to undergo once they passed it. It all represented the mythical journey of Woot, the Adam of the Kuba. The triangles represented hills; the mask on top of the central hill represented Woot; the female statue was his sister, the primordial woman; her seclusion was the icon for the prohibition of incest, while the tears on her cheeks told of the grief of woman, forever separated from her kin. Masks on top of the right and left hills were, taken in isolation, those of the king and of the nature spirit, taken in conjunction they represented the king and the common man. At the capital, that is precisely what they meant in mimes. Here they also stood for the headmen of the right and left sides of the village, the village itself being a symbol for society. When all three masks were considered together, the central mask was the king, the right hand mask was the aristocrat, and the left hand one the commoner. More than a dozen other carved objects representing persons, birds, animals and a palm tree climber all had multiple meanings, one in isolation and one in conjunction. Thus, some birds in a tree were the icon of

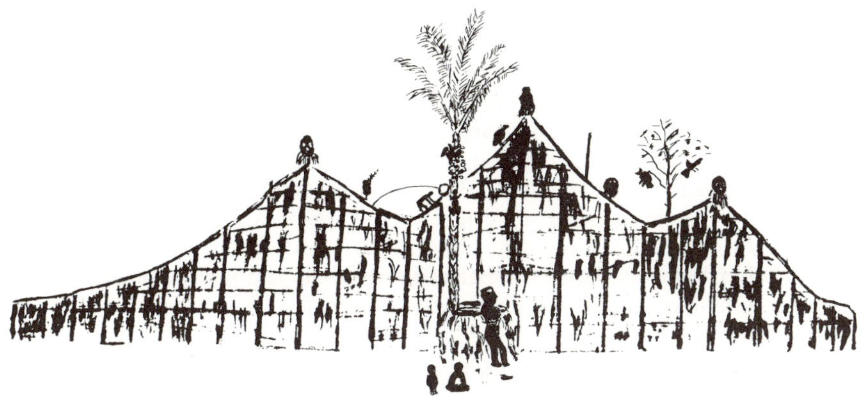

Fig. 6.2 *Kuba initiation wall, Mapey, Zaïre. Height* c. *9m. 1953. On the wall display of masks, pole heads and other icons some in composition (e.g. on and near the palmtree). In front female figure (see Pl. 11.3) and two charms,* ishak ndweemy, *functionally similar to Pl. 11.4, but in very different style. The wall was a symbolic discourse, down to details such as the three 'hills' and the different woods used in the scaffolding. It was a major teaching device during the boys' initiation*

the rain and the moon taken separately, but jointly here represented the boys to be initiated (Vansina 1955).

Among the various purposes of this wall, the main one was teaching symbolic reasoning to the boys. At the same time, the children's perception of the canons of Kuba art were reinforced by such an exhibition at a time of heightened emotions in the context of their passage from childhood to manhood. Furthermore, the icons expressed complex relationships and abstract concepts in a concrete way at a glance, thereby instilling visual images which had much more lasting impact than a verbal explanation only would have had, for reasons explained at the beginning of this chapter.

This thumbnail sketch must suffice to illustrate the complex nature of meaning in art. It is almost always wrong to attribute just a single meaning to an icon, as if it were a sign, like a giant letter standing always for the same sound or better, as a hieroglyph. The meaning changed with circumstance and equally important, the emotional impact of the concept changed with the situation in which the icon was displayed, the number of times a person saw it, and idiosyncratically as well. The icon was perceived as a unit and no one differentiated between its aesthetic, emotional and conceptual appeals. In this icons played a role very similar to ritual. Communities all participated in the same ritual but, in the absence of the dogma put down in a holy writ, all were free to experience it differently. Hence the full meaning of an icon should not be confused with the intention of its maker only. In Niger Delta (Ijo) art, masks such as the familiar hippopotamus or shark masks were carved as representations of the spirits, but were not to be seen by the viewers. As they were worn facing the sky, viewers rarely saw them in full face. When studying such masks, it is very useful to know this: they were carved as concepts, not as objects to be seen (Horton 1965a). But this does not suffice. The context of apparition, the iconic attribution of one mask in relation to other icons, the range of variation allowed in the carving of such masks, and the range of experience evoked in the beholders, are all equally important in assessing the full meaning of such objects.

If the primary interpretation of representations is already so difficult to establish, it is even more difficult to acquire valid information on the full range of meaning in varying circumstances, and these facets of arts in Africa have so far rarely been studied in depth. The situation is better in literate environments, but even for major features of the monuments of Islam it is hard to explain the overwhelming appeal of some forms such as domes *(qubbat)*; the sickle of the half moon *(hilal)* or the appeal of chandeliers in mosques, an appeal quite equal to that of church bells for Christians. Bells are an abomination to Muslims; only the human voice can call the faithful to prayer, and so, when they captured the bells of Gibraltar, the people of Fes turned them into chandeliers for their Qarawiyyin mosque (Terrasse 1968).

DECORATION: ART WITHOUT A STATEMENT

Not all motifs make statements. A famous example is the *mappula* or handkerchief of Ethiopian madonnas of the seventeenth and eighteenth centuries. The handkerchief in the hand of the virgin meant nothing in particular. The motif had come to Ethiopia when reproductions of the famous

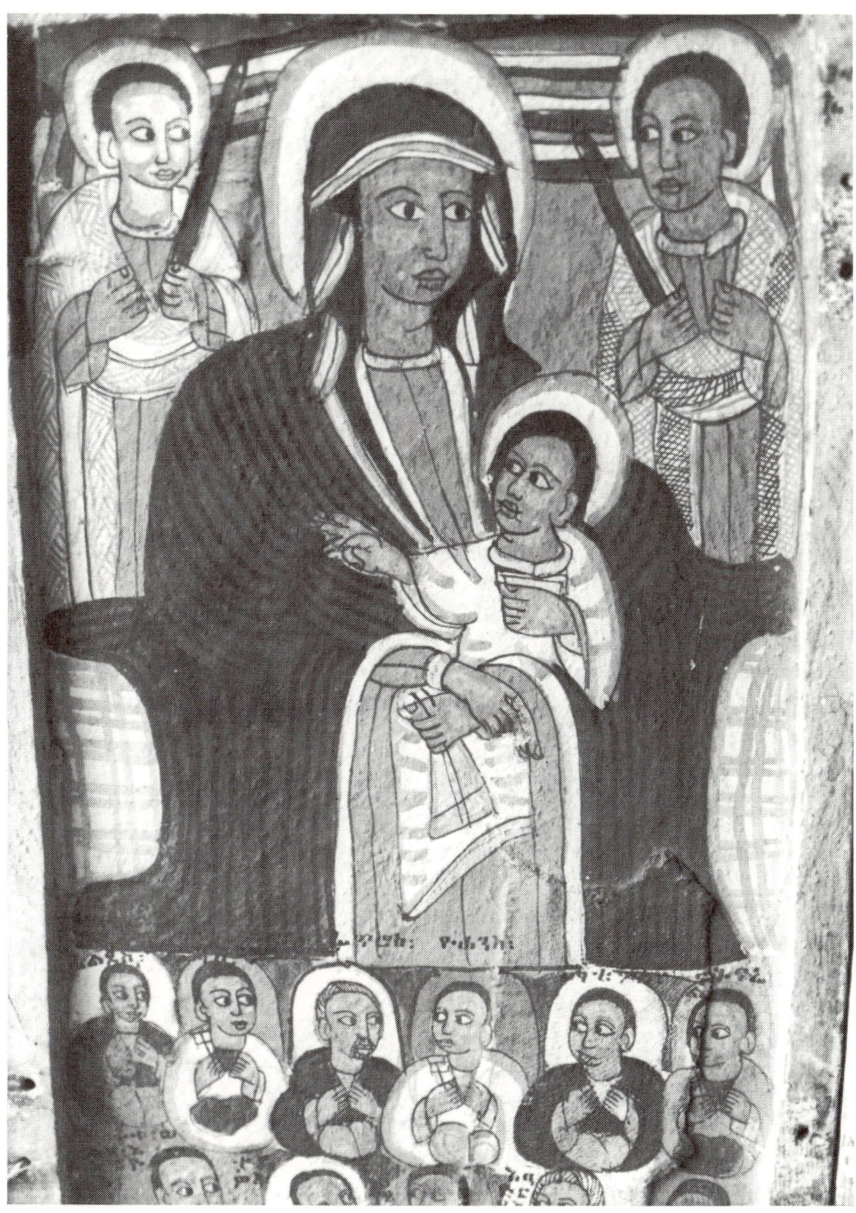

Plate 6.7 *Madonna Hodegithria. By Anorewos? Painting on cloth fixed on wood* (Hagenia abyssinica). *Central panel of an icon. Northern Ethiopia. Mss. 81–301364 Museum für Völkerkunde, Münich. Height 36·5cm; width 21·3cm. Gondar first period, 1700–1750. The handkerchief* (mappula) *and the folds of the headcloth correspond to the ultimate model, the madonna of Santa Maria Maggiore, Rome. Unlike others in this style no star occurs on the veil or on the shoulder. The madonna guarded by two angels with apostles at her feet, is a standard composition (cf. S. Chojnacki 1977:44–7, 56–61)*

Byzantine icon at Santa Maria Maggiore in Rome, so highly venerated by Catholics at the time, were brought to the country. Ethiopian artists copied it, gradually rendered it into a local setting and introduced local motifs. But the *mappula* remained. It became smaller and smaller, but the madonna could no longer be visualized without it, so it stayed (Chojnacki 1977:46).

Some decorative art may have developed in similar ways. Decorative art, usually, but not always non-representational, has no meaning. It is there for design reasons only, it enhances. Decoration was used to provide a frame to enclose a space, or to separate spaces as in architecture. Decoration could also organize space, either by covering it with a patterned web, giving repetitive or geometric meaning to space, or by using isolated motifs as focal points regularly distributed over otherwise empty space, to suggest space as a presence rather than as an absence. Decorative art is universal. All African cultures used it from the rim of potteries, to the most varied surfaces such as shields, bags, baskets, bodies, walls, pediments, ceilings. Decorative motifs were made in all media by any means that could produce a line, a dot, a point. It reached its summit in Africa as arabesques or sequences of geometrical figures, with interlace (rinceaux) originally stylized leaves, stems and fruits and arabic script. These were used in isolation or in combination and allowed an aesthetic expression of form as refined as any other and as linked to technical and stylistic skill. Unlike figurative art, arabesques, writing apart, had no specific meaning, and their aesthetic was completely different, acting only as linear, textured or spatial design. But it was no less a great art. North African decorative patterns profoundly influenced some decorative patterns of West Africa, and all those of the coasts of eastern Africa.

Decorative art was meant to embellish or to convey emotion, not to express statements. Even if patterns were named, the names formed no statements. The Kuba have some two hundred named patterns but the names refer to analogies between the shape of the design and some natural shape such as the track of an iguana or refer to the name of the inventor. A very few indicate that perhaps once the pattern had a meaning. Thus one is called 'the house of Woot'.

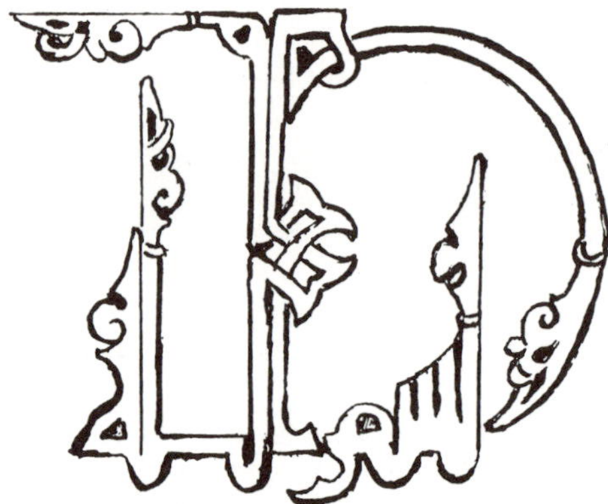

Fig. 6.3 *Kufic script as ornament. Plaster on the wall of Sidi bel Hasan mosque, Tlemcen, Algeria. It reads:* Bismillah: *'In the name of God'. 1296. After G. Marçais 1954: fig. 221*

Sometimes motifs could be used, not for their decorative effect, but for their name. A Kuba motif of an insect called 'god' was found under a rendition of a crucifixion where it obviously was to be read as 'God'. This rebus-like use was unique there. Several authors have claimed, however, that decorative patterns isolated in space and juxtaposed, really formed a rebus or a script, but the most detailed claims for both goldweights and Bini patterns, mainly on tusks, have not been substantiated (Hau 1959, 1964; Dark 1981; Thompson and Cornet 1981). Still, Egyptian hieroglyphs developed in this fashion and in a reversal Arabic, especially Kufic, script became a major element in the arabesques. The reversal was not total, for Arabic script kept its meaning and such decorations are in fact inscriptions.

We have seen that on occasions a motif, even a figurative one such as the handkerchief, can have lost its original meaning, and that decorative patterns usually contain no statements, and yet there are isolated cases where a pattern functioned as a sign and is a statement. Like many other peoples in Africa, the Kuba use a free-standing pattern of guilloche (interlace) in double knot form on a square, called the *imbol*. When it is used on the back of a certain type of mask, however, it indicates a relationship to the king. In other contexts it has no specific meaning. Free-standing designs on Masai shields, some tattoos in central Africa, and Mamluk crests indicated group affiliations. Full decorative patterns on cloth indicated position and rank as in the Akan states or in Dahomey. Such occurrences should warn the student not to dismiss decorative art too readily without further enquiry.

THEME AND MOTIF IN HISTORY

Themes and motifs are the product of historical change. They often develop and vary independently from each other, while constellations of motifs will sometimes stay together for amazing lengths of time and spread over great distances. As for themes, they live as images and as tales. An instructive case is the Coptic icon representing an equestrian figure slaying a crocodile (Plate 6.8). The figure in imperial garb was supposed to be Horus, the crocodile Sebk. As an icon it belongs to a series of martial equestrian figures that developed in Sassanid Iran and in Egypt itself. Later, with Christianity, Horus became St George and Sebk the dragon or a snake. The icon became the theme for the legend of St George saving the maiden and both legend and image are found far and wide over Christendom, from Russia to Ireland, from Egypt to Ethiopia and Scandinavia. But the tale spread further even without the icon. The same tale explains the foundation of Daura, the oldest Hausa city-state in northern Nigeria, the first foundation of the empire of Ghana as told about Wagadu in Mali, the beginning of kingship in Taqali in the Nuba mountains of the Sudan (De Grunne 1980:27–34; J. Ewald, personal communication). The tale can be found across the Sahel and the Sahara from the Nile to the Atlantic. It spread to Europe with the associated icon, and without it south of the Sahara.

The history of the fish-legged figure in southwestern Nigeria (Yoruba and Benin) tells the story of a complex motif (Fig. 6.4). In Benin it appeared on over a hundred objects in ivory or brass, on bells, on wearing apparel, on bronze plaques and in Yorubaland almost as great a range of settings for this

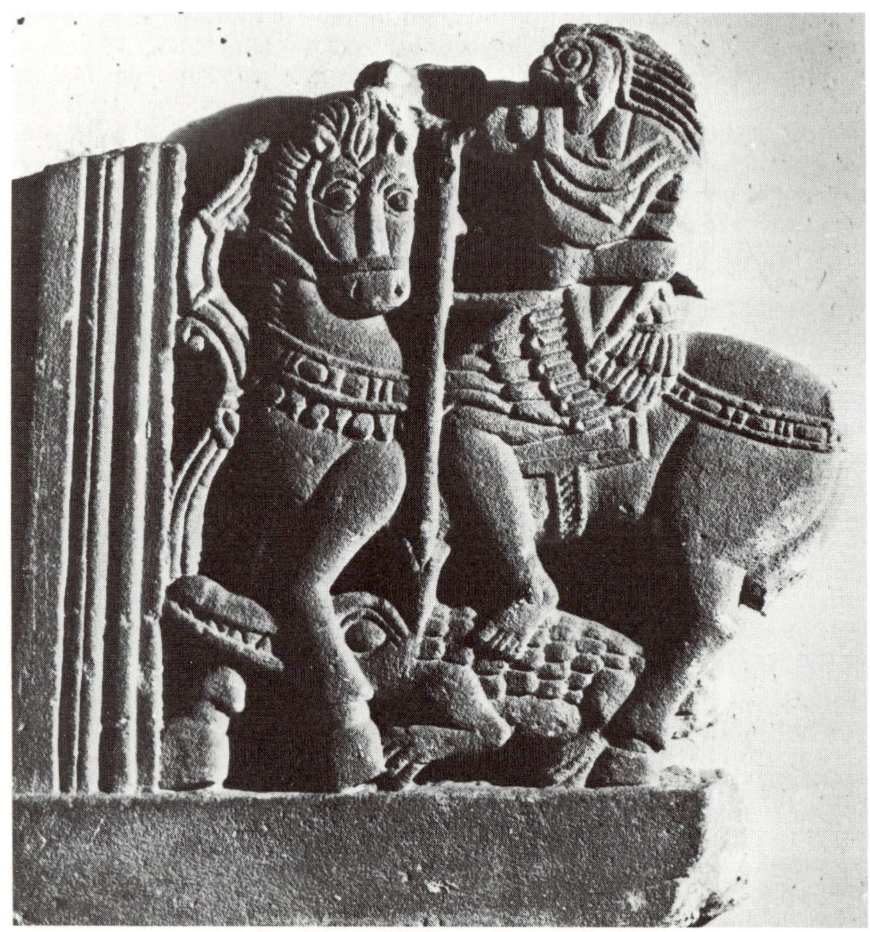

Plate 6.8 *Horus and Sebk. Sandstone. Coptic. Musée du Louvre. Height 49cm; length 32cm; width 7·8cm. Fourth century. Horus in the pose of a Roman emperor spears the crocodile, an allegory for Good triumphing over Evil. This is a forerunner of the iconography of St George*

motif can be found. It was already to be seen on Yoruba ivories that reached Europe in the seventeenth century. In Benin, the central position of the figure indicates that it represents either a king or a god. It wears crossed baldrics, crisscross straps – signs of high rank – and its skirt ends in undulations, rendered by the Yoruba as scallops. Some Bini take it that the figure represents their Neptune, Olokun, others take it to be an old king who became paralyzed in connection with Olokun. In any case, the interpretation is uncertain and shows all the signs of being speculation about the figure rather than an inspiration behind the realization of this motif. In Yorubaland as well, interpretations seem speculative.

Fish-legged figures, sirens for instance, were very common in both European and West African art, but fish-legged figures grasping their own legs with their hands were rarer. Only the Yoruba have this variant, Benin does not

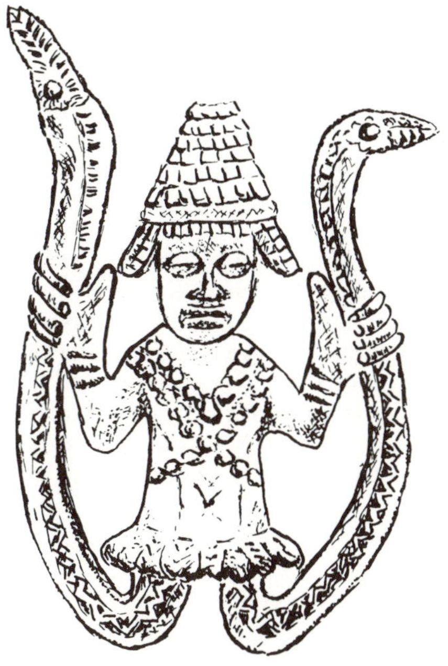

Fig. 6.4 *Fish-legged person grasping its own legs. Ivory armband (detail), western Nigerian, perhaps from Owo. British Museum. Date unknown. Here the legs are not fish but reptilian. The whole motif derives from the Hellenistic eastern Mediterranean. The conclusion is valid because of the unusual subject and a variety of elements remaining stable in the composition: (a) self-grasping fish or reptilian legs; (b) baldric; (c) deep navel; (d) scalloped skirt. On other pieces the complex includes further waistbands and segmented necklaces. The motif was common in southern Nigeria generally and is attested before 1674. Such similarities cannot occur by chance. This motif as well as five others link southern Nigeria to the Hellenistic world*

know it. D. Fraser (1972, 1981b), who studied this case, showed that such a figure was known in medieval Europe from the twelfth century onwards, where it was called Melusine, or, more recently, Neptune. By 1674, the motif was in use on ivories in western Nigeria. A link with Renaissance motifs is possible, but the European legs do not terminate in fish heads, nor are there baldrics or deep navels, as in the African examples. The full similarities occur, however, in the art of the eastern Roman empire from 100 B.C. to *c.* A.D. 300. A figure from Begram in Afghanistan was shown to be the most similar. The prototypes were probably current in the heartlands of the eastern Empire and radiated by trade to Afghanistan, India and ultimately perhaps Nigeria. It is not a wild thought since Coptic lamp imitations of not much later date have been found in northern Ghana. In fact, alternative explanations do not really account for the similarities. Independent inventions did not invent fish-legged figures, grasping their legs, with baldrics, deep navels, scalloped skirts and even segmented necklaces! The motif travelled with all of these features, over these great distances and kept them over such astonishing lengths of time. The case is especially convincing on two counts. The icon is even more arbitrary than is usual – who ever saw a fish-legged person grasping his own legs? Parts of the icon were quite common in the eastern Mediterranean, including Egypt at that time. Baldrics, scalloped skirts and deep navels were normal iconographic attire for high military officials, even for the emperor. Self-grasping was a theme in that area since hoary antiquity, and the link between persons and fish (at least dolphins) was quite common at the time. The fish-legged hero grasping his legs could have arisen easily in this milieu.

We have seen that icons represent visual concepts that are often statements involving complex meanings, statements such as those that are revealed in poems, with their emotional appeal and layers of meaning, rather than those that are common in prose. Cases show that meanings, themes, and motifs associated in any icon at a given time are unstable. They can change independently of each other and have their own histories. Historians should never reduce meaning to a gloss nor consider a composition of motifs, a theme, as a once-and-for-all creation. Such an association lies deeply embedded in the whole culture that produced the work of art and the pursuit of the full ramifications by which the composition came into being becomes cultural history. For culture is not, as society is, the context of art. Art is an integral part of culture and can only be fully understood as such.

CHAPTER SEVEN

CULTURE AND ART

Culture is not the context of art, nor a matrix for art. Art is an integral part of the culture which it expresses and thereby communicates to others. Visual art works are the visual realization of visual concepts held in a community and realized by the artist. The concepts are visual, just as visual memory exists. The icon then feeds back into the community's visual concept. This explains why the seventeenth-century Ardra board is so similar to Ifa boards from the same area, even after 1900 (see Plates 1.1 and 2.3). The visual concept was alive over all that time and it was collective.

Culture is the sum total of the ideas, aspirations, values and beliefs in the mind of the people living in a given community (Spradley and McCurdy 1975:3–41). It includes not only ideas or even beliefs but emotional stance as well. *Most* of this can be rendered by the expression 'collective representation' and people's patterned reactions to them. For most of what is in people's minds is held in common by them, just as visual concepts are, and just as language is. There is nothing surprising in this, as the furniture of the mind is gradually put in place even from birth onwards. Babies not only acquire language, but grammars and worldviews as well. They not only learn to see, but they learn to see what is significant and to see in patterned ways. They not only learn to remember, but to remember by a master code common to the community.

Arts are called expressive culture because they express the world of the mind either by performance or through the creation of objects. Like language, they are a mode of communication, but unlike most speech, their statements involve an expression in terms of forms linked to metaphor. Among the arts, there are those which, like language, are statements over time: the performing arts such as dance, music, oral art. And there are arts that once created are statements at one moment of time. These are the visual and tactile arts.

The relationship between art and culture is discussed here in several steps. First, the relationship of one art to the others, then the relationships to the whole of the culture. The specific relationship of culture to the human group in which it is examined falls beyond the scope of this study. The reader will note, however, that culture is a relative concept because it presupposes the recognition of a given human community. Since on the one hand every mind contains some idiosyncracies, every person's culture can be examined. But since a portion of the commonly held representations can extend over many societies, culture can be applied to very large groups of people as well. Thus an *oikoumenical* tradition where everyone accepts the basic tenets of Christianity or Islam can extend over large portions of the globe, even while such tenets are perceived and certainly expressed in very local terms.

THE VISUAL ARTS COMPARED

In previous chapters we have already compared art objects in order to set up stylistic series and to discuss style in general. Here we examine the mutual relationships among the visual arts. Architecture, sculpture and the two-dimensional arts are differently related in different cultures. Thus, architecture occupied pride of place in all of northern Africa; in Islam as in Christianity, as in Pharaonic Egypt, as in pagan Rome, as in Ethiopia, monuments came first. Sculpture, furniture and painting complemented architecture whenever these different arts were used together. Muslim sculpture included the non-representative forms of capitals, conchs, friezes. In Ethiopia, most sculpture consisted of reliefs in churches and palaces. Similarly, non-representative painting in Islam was used only to decorate. In Ethiopia or in the Christian art of Nubia, as in Pharaonic Egypt, wall painting was the most common form and was strictly integrated in the architecture, for instance, particular scenes from the liturgical year had to be painted on predetermined portions of wall within the churches.

This contrasts markedly with sub-Saharan Africa. In most regional arts there was less of an organic hierarchy. One cannot really speak of the dominance of any art, even though the literature often gives the impression that sculpture dominated in West or Central Africa. This neglects non-representational, two-dimensional art and wall or rock painting. In most cases, sculpture was not as subservient to architecture as in the *oikoumene*, and in a few instances one can see how the conception of architecture, i.e. a set of masses and interior space, was translated into a set of volumes. Figure 7.1,

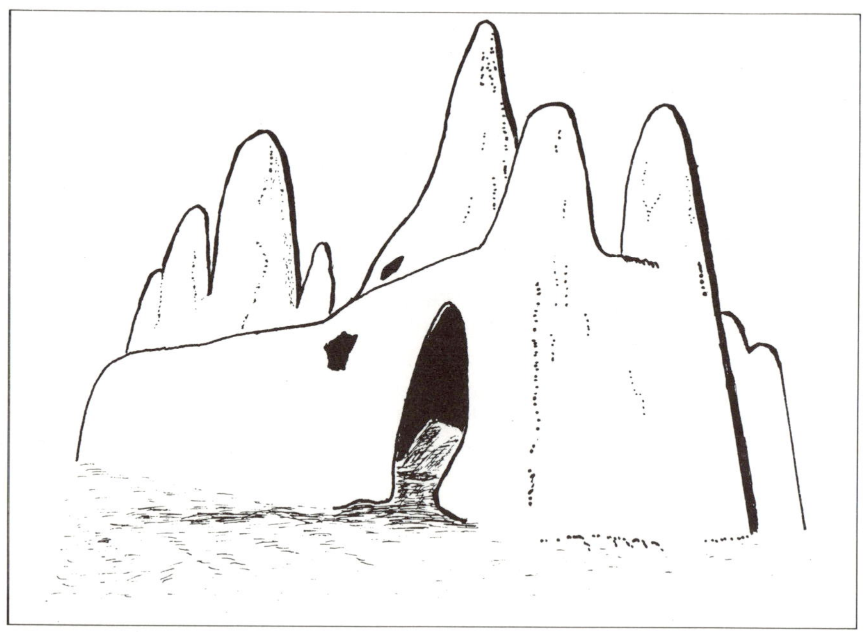

Fig. 7.1 *Tomb of Sidi Aissa. Melika le Haut, Sahara. Algeria. Dried mud. Date unknown. Compare with Fig. 5.3. Sculptural handling of architecture*

showing a tomb at Melika in southern Algeria, strikingly illustrates how a northern Sahara tomb building became a tomb sculpture. Studies of mosques in West Africa (Prussin 1968) document the tendency for such buildings to become smaller and more shrine-like in the southern parts of the Sahel, while the latent sculptural qualities of mud architecture were more and more exploited.

Public buildings in Gabon and Congo, such as the Bwiti temples of southern Gabon (Tsogo) or the men's houses near the Sangha River, were simple constructions. Only the fact that they housed the carved posts and figures really distinguished them from other dwellings (Bruel 1910; Gollnhofer and Sillans 1963). In some regional traditions, however, architecture did come into its own. In part of the Cameroons grasslands (Bamileke), for instance, the sculpture of the posts of palaces was subordinate to the total architectural effect (Lecocq 1953). Sculpture in ancient Zimbabwe also seems to have been partly subservient to architecture insofar as it was destined to decorate the top of the walls. Sculptures as posts in courtyards could also be found along the West African coast, from Dahomey to Yorubaland, and to Benin, even though most sculpture here was certainly not tied to architecture.

Painting, especially non-representational painting in West and Central Africa, remained more important than is usually believed. It can be seen as a subordinate technique to decorate the walls of houses, panels, posts, or to be the polychrome decoration of sculpture. But it came fully unto its own in personal art and on textiles. Painting, like architecture or body art, is only beginning to be studied, and it would be rash at this stage to claim that it was unimportant.

It is also abundantly clear for West and Central Africa that decorative, schematic design was highly developed in all media as for example on textiles or on ceramics. Just as in the European tradition, such arts were judged to be of minor value to Africans south of the Sahara, and have therefore been less studied, but they can be crucial in some regional arts. Among the Kuba, for instance, design is the essence of artistic activity; there is no Kuba term for 'art', but there is one for 'design' *(bwiin)*, and it seems crucial to their aesthetics. Decorative design was the most discussed, the most practised, the most developed with regard to the solution of formal problems (Crowe 1971) of all Kuba art forms. Even though architecture and sculpture were fully developed, was decorative art the dominant art? It was often integrated as part of buildings or sculptures. The notion of a dominant visual art simply does not apply to such situations where a hierarchy of either values or commissions has not been developed, unlike the situation in the *oikoumene*.

The relationships between all the visual arts have often not been explored properly. Thus body decoration, a spectacular art not only in eastern Africa but in West and Central Africa as well, has not been related to textile arts, masking or painting, which seem to be quite closely related (Paulme and Brosse 1956). In part, this is due to the fact that in Europe, this was never, until very recently, recognized as an art. To a larger extent, such situations have been influenced, often implicitly, by European notions of major and minor arts. Those concepts have been transferred from Europe to Africa. But such distinctions are entirely ethnocentric. Calligraphy, a minor art in Europe, is highly valued as a major art form in the Muslim world for instance, whereas in the case of figurative painting, the reverse is true for most periods of Islamic art. Such ethnocentric distinctions between major and minor arts merely express the hierarchy of art forms in a particular culture at a given time. The concepts are value judgements and useless for a comparative perspective. Whether major or minor arts exist at a given time in a given place and what they eventually are, are matters for investigation into the convictions of the community that produces these arts. Meanwhile, a study of the relationships of the visual arts in given regional traditions needs to be developed on objective bases as well.

Basic stylistic characteristics were usually similar across the arts, as the same stylistic norms ran through all the visual arts. Given their basic character as a grammar of form, this could be expected. And yet sometimes significant discrepancies occurred between different media even in the same art form. Willett has shown that Zande (Zaïre-Sudan) ceramics were more naturalistic than Zande wood sculpture (Willett 1971:186). Skeuomorphism also must be kept in mind. Thus, the patterns of brick decoration in Tozeur (Tunisia) and nearby Algerian oases are clearly related to those of local rugs. Given the geometry and angularity of the patterns, the wall decoration may derive from textile patterns. Conversely, the architectural composition of the *mihrab* niche and arch appears on textiles, in miniatures and even on scholars' slates. The craving for innovations in arch design, so typical for the Maghrib, was related to the decorative prestige of ever more sophisticated arabesques. The link is so close that the arabesque decoration of the great Maghrebi minarets was expressed as a series of intersecting arches with blind arches of the most varied and fancy designs surrounding windows and even doors.

The use of architectural compositions to frame miniatures was quite common in Ethiopia. South of the Sahara such mutual influences among the visual arts have been far too little studied. Yet they are important, if only

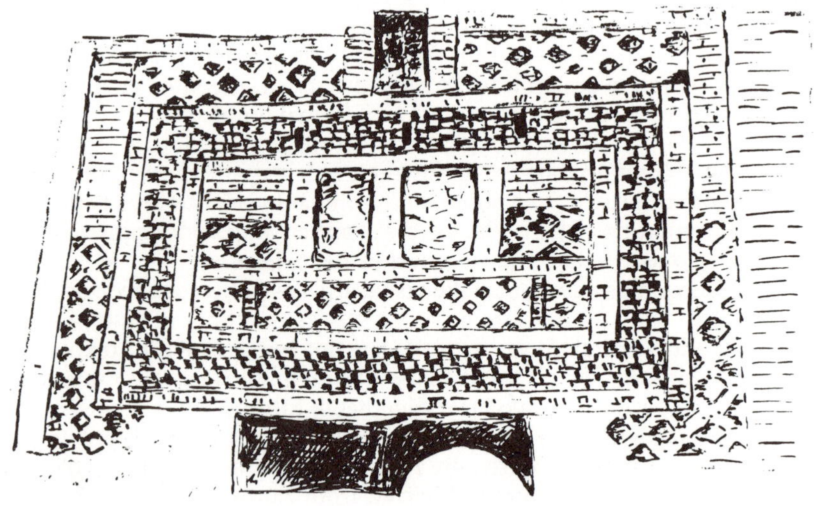

Fig. 7.2 *Façade. Tamelhat, eastern oases, Algeria. Brick decoration, similar to those of the houses at Tozeur, Tunisia. Decor directly (Berber carpets) or indirectly derived from textiles. After D. Hill and L. Golvin 1976:251*

because they show how diverse was the common inspiration for further innovation in the arts.

With regard to themes and motifs, the repertoire in a given culture was normally quite consistent whatever the art form. But the distributions of

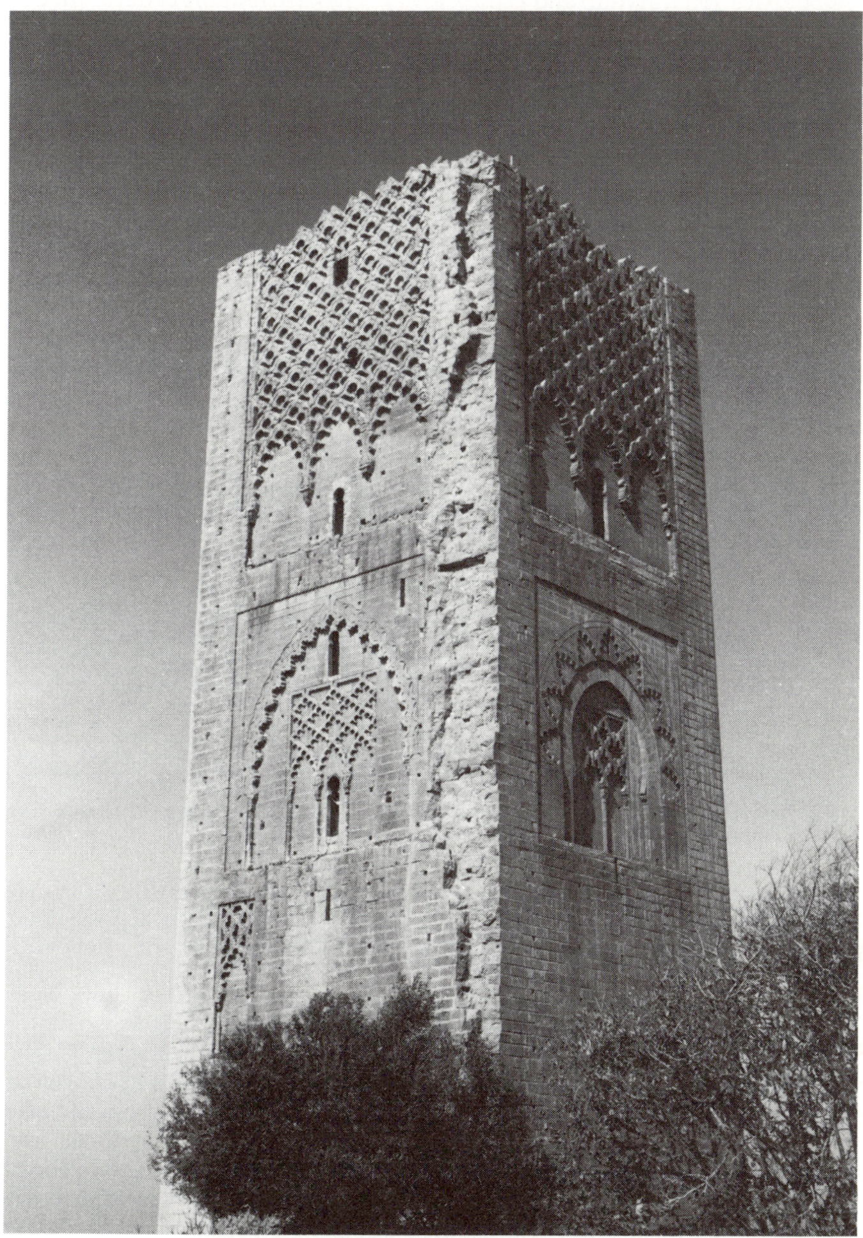

Plate 7.1 *Minaret. Stone masonry. Hasan mosque, Rabat, Morocco. Height 30m. 1196, Almohad period. Decor differs on each face of the tower. Compare with Plate 8.1, possibly by same architect*

themes and motifs over the different art forms could be significant. Thus, figurative painting was outlawed in North African mosques but not on ceramics or metalware, nor at certain times as frescoes in bath houses, as heraldic emblems and even as painting on glass for use at home (Atil 1981; Talbot Rice 1965; Ayoub and Galley 1977). The distribution of decorative art within the Kuba corpus of art is intriguing. Two different ensembles of patterns existed, one of which was reserved for the tattooing of women, the decoration of a certain type of female skirt, and as decoration on the drinking cups made out of buffalo horns, or their imitations in wood. The other set was used in all the other contexts from wall decorations to mats, to ornamentation of wooden objects, even jewellery and most textiles. Cases where the two ensembles were mixed are extremely rare. Why this is so was no longer evident by the 1950s to the Kuba themselves. Examination of the distribution of the repertoire over the arts does in fact usually show restrictions of given themes or even motifs to one art form or another. Such situations are not only of cultural significance, but may also hold traces of historical development.

Fig. 7.3 *Kuba decorative styles. Embroidered textile left, pile cloth right. All Kuba decor belongs to two types only: the geometrical repetitive patterns as on the right (this one is called 'rock') and a juxtaposition of individual elements (all named) on the left. The latter type of decor is limited to women's scarifications, some women's skirts and buffalo horn vessels. Left: after Museum Tervuren 27401; right: after* African Arts, *1978, 12 (1): 27*

VISUAL AND PERFORMING ARTS

The relationship between visual and performing arts was often quite close (Thompson 1974; Drewal 1980:18–20). Masks were usually designed for display while dancing, as part of the decor for the performance. Public buildings were designed for communal action, either praying as in church or mosque, or for other purposes. The elaborately decorated niche walls of a Swahili house, for example, were the backdrop to wedding rituals and designed as such (de Vere Allen 1974b:16–17). Plazas were made for meetings and performance of singers, dancers, sometimes theatrical groups. The Ardra board designed for use in *Ifa* divination implies the performance of the *ifa* diviner.

Such relationships can in fact be so close as to become confusing. The important difference between a mask and the costume with which it came, the poems or songs chanted when the mask was donned, and the dancing itself, is the relationship to time. Performing arts need time. Their paradigmatic and syntagmatic characteristics are separated. But visual arts were seen 'at once', all their paradigmatic and syntagmatic relationships together. Yet ephemeral visual art such as the body paint put on for one performance or even the mask used during one initiation only, just as a complex hairstyle may last a season, come close to being merely props for performing art. They differed from statues in durable media. But even here clay statuettes or mud sculpture were sometimes also designed to last for only one initiation (Cole 1969a, b, c). The student of art must consider the temporal characteristics of the objects studied. Were the objects designed to last? How long? Yet, even with the most ephemeral visual creation, one must remember that they could be complex expressions carefully crafted for an impact 'at once'. The affective impact of the visual arts remains quite distinct from that of the performing arts.

Stylistic principles, or motifs common to both visual and performing arts, were often hard to find. Themes were a common link often referring to myth or other oral art such as the Chibinda Ilunga example or St George's story. In a famous case, M. C. Dupré (1968, 1979; personal communication) showed that the style of a two-dimensional round Tsayi mask characterized by almost total symmetry around a horizontal equator as well as around the usual vertical axis, was directly inspired by the dance it was made for. In performance it was to be worn by a cart-wheeling dancer, so that it should be the same upside down, right side up, left and right. Moreover, she was able to link both dance and mask to the upheavals of the 1870s, when the mask was created, and fortunes seemed to revolve unpredictably. But this can still be explained as a feature of use yet a use linked to performance itself.

To go further can be dangerous. Can one reasonably claim, for instance, that the fioritures in Maghrebi vocal music corresponded to those in the tracery of the lambrequin arches? Perhaps, but how does one prove it? As the basic codes of musical and visual expression differ, what does such a statement in fact mean? Ornamentation by deviation from the main development of basic proportions? If that was meant, it could be tested both for musical and visual styles. Were members of the community conscious of such analogies? If the parallel works out, it then relates to secondary features of expression that could be translated from one code of expression to another. Such parallels may reflect reality by similarity of use, or, more usually, reflect a common approach towards the perception of reality itself. But they are very difficult to prove. It will not do, for instance, simply to note correlations between the use of different styles of masks and different styles of dancing or music associated with their appearance. One must, as Dupré did, show stylistic features of the music or dance to correspond to similar features on the mask.

The complementarity of the different arts with regard to themes and motifs in a given culture should be pursued in each case. The repertoires could overlap or complement. Thus, while the graven image of man in Islam was frowned upon and forbidden outright in places of worship, yet in poetry, especially in love poetry, it was the main theme. The conception of man as a grain of sand in God's universe was one extreme here, the other being man's hubris in search of fame, power or love.

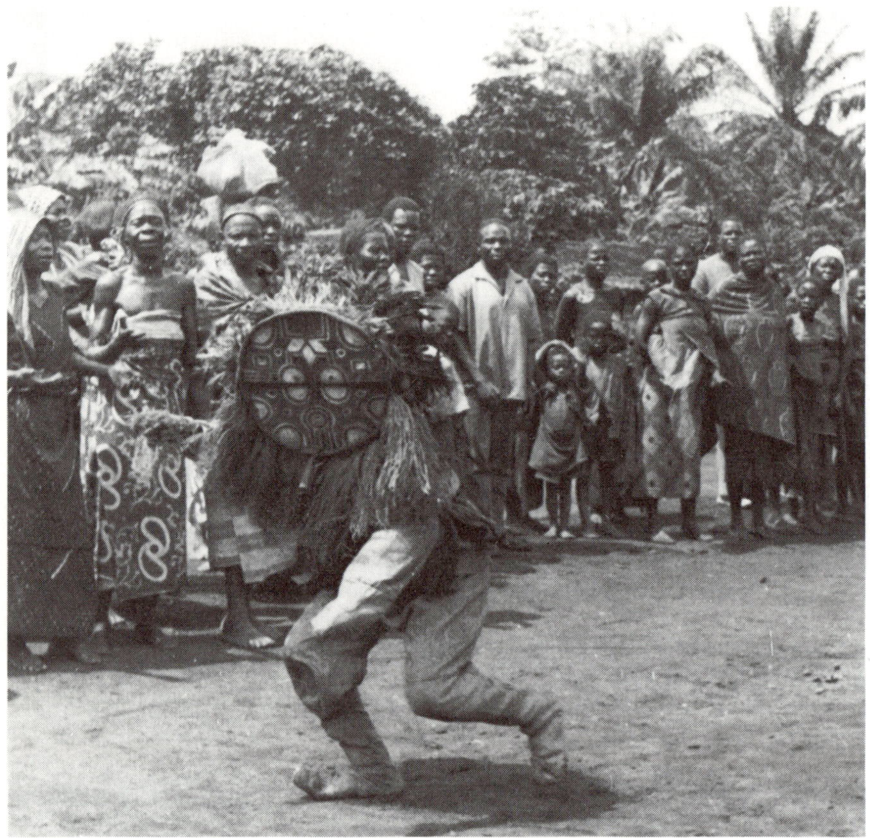

Plate 7.2 *Maskers cartwheeling. Mask, wood, raffia, red, black, white colours. Dances now for fun. Likana, Congo. Photo 1969. The mask, a disc, is symmetrical around vertical and horizontal axes. The designs around the face have symbolic meaning. The mask was invented for the cartwheeling dance* c. *1870*

One can raise questions related to the dominance of any art form in a given culture as well. It would be tempting to claim that the extraordinary development of epics in the forest areas of Central Africa 'compensated' for a relative paucity of sculpture, but if this may appear to be true for portions of the area, it was certainly not so for the western portions or the southeast of that area, where both epics and sculpture flourished. It is difficult to state flatly that Kuba sculpture, or architecture, or music or dance was dominant. All showed similar sophistication and they were all linked to each other. Here epics were clearly not developed but short lyrical poems had been brought to a high degree of perfection. Can this be tied-in to a perception of the world also visible in other arts? It is evident that nearby, in the cultures east of Lake Mayi Ndombe, the main form of artistic expression was the ballet, from *c.* 1900 onwards. One can show there that villages invested great efforts in labour and training to excel in that field. Such questions of interrelationship very quickly force the inquirer to broaden the perspective to the whole field of culture.

REPERTOIRE AND CULTURE

As art expresses culture, so style, theme, motif are intimately linked to the perceptions and the representations which are a common cultural good. In general, the themes expressed in art are those dominant in a culture. Art portrays only a tiny minority of shapes and objects perceived. South of the Sahara for instance the repertoire in sculpture consists first of people but includes also some animal representation and almost no plant life, while some plants are the foundation of a whole stream of arabesques north of the Sahara. The absence of animals could be linked to notions of inert life as opposed to moving life, were it not that only very few species of animals were usually portrayed. A few favourites such as elephants, buffaloes, leopards, spiders, lizards, crocodiles, come to mind. In studying an animal repertoire, the first error is to assume that the classification of animals is the one we are familiar with. Zoological classification had nothing to do with representation. The animals portrayed were all important symbols in the culture (Ben Amos 1976). They were 'good to think and to feel', apt metaphors to express profound thoughts. Not all crucial animal symbols were necessarily represented either. Thus, owls and similar birds were considered in wide portions of Africa to be omens or symbols of witchcraft. They rarely occur in art. An inventory of representations should be established first for a given culture, then the significance of its content can be established with regard to the whole culture drawing not only on performing arts or oral expressions but on ritual, daily life and so on. The whole texture of culture can be brought into play, to reach a full understanding of the collective representations that were expressed in art.

Themes could not only be selected but rejected. We cited Islam's ban on the graven image as an expression of idolatry. It was almost totally effective in places of worship and most strictly enforced with regard to sculpture, but elsewhere the ban was not total. Bravmann has shown that masks which once had religious connotations continued in use among Muslims of northern Ghana or in Nupe (northern Nigeria). Indeed, masks for fun were still to be found in nineteenth-century Tlemcen (Algeria). South of the Sahara we cited the common avoidance of portraying owls. Witchcraft and misfortune were generally not to be represented at all, so no witches or diseased persons, no slaves to be traded appear in most arts south of the Sahara. There were exceptions: in the arts of Ife and along the Cross River (Ibibio) as well as along the Middle Niger before A.D. 1500, diseases were shown on masks or statues, probably to illustrate the powers of the entities that caused them. Unfortunates, slaves and prisoners appear in the art of Ife (Eyo and Willett 1980; Willett 1967).

Evil and the effects of evil are rarely represented. The Lega who had an aesthetic of the ugly associated with evil are an exception (Biebuyck 1973: ill. 66–7). Witches were apparently never portrayed as persons. Perhaps representations of these aspects of life were suppressed because images become real and power might emanate from them. That is the reason given in Ethiopian painting for the convention always to represent Judas with averted eyes; his gaze, the evil eye, could hurt the beholder. In many cases, however, the identification between beauty and the moral good coupled with idealism in art explains the situation sufficiently.

The repertoire gives a profile of the dominant positive ideas, ideals, beliefs, values, gods, spirits, ancestors, mystical forces, whether they be religious or not. Some representations also reflected poetic but anecdotal scenes. Sometimes depictions of sacred history appear, as on the walls of Faras or as on Dogon (Mali) sculpture, sometimes allusions as in the representation of the thunderbolt of the Yoruba (Nigeria) god Shango, that appears in the shape of a double axe. The frequency of the appearance of a theme and the type of object also tells a tale. Richly decorated utensils stem from courts, or denote special significance in other cultures. The only artistically treated objects among the Aka pygmy hunters of northern Congo are their honey adze, the shafts of spears, the back pack and bark boxes. Honey is the most desired food, and once a year the search for honey broke up camps and led to a different pattern of life. The other objects are equally important (Demesse 1980:113–15). Decorated granary poles, doors or locks in the Sahel emphasized the importance of storage even if, among the Dogon, they also expressed the meaning of the granary as the ark of humanity. Thus the inventory of the visual arts in any culture tells us what its main concerns are, barring those that it was forbidden to depict. Even tourist art, when not wholly imposed on the producer, expressed cultural and social concerns. Nineteenth-century Loango tusks depicting the procession of a caravan, the settlement of a court case, the carriers of fish, the local lords in their finery, the foreign traders with their barrels, chests and padlocks, are microcosms of what the carver perceived Loango to be. Many a scene could not really be understood by the European buyer, yet they were carved as part of the statement about Loango. Now they are reminders of the customs and the times.

AESTHETICS

Western aesthetic criticism of African art is largely irrelevant because it is an expression of Western culture about what to them are *objets trouvés*. Yet Western analysis of form can correspond to the analysis made by the artists who created these works. In that case the art historian still needs to be informed about the aesthetics of the culture that created the objects. The agreement between Western aesthetes and their local colleagues may be a coincidence of taste or the mutual recognition of explicit formal values. Pronouncements about 'good art' and 'bad art' reflect Western preferences to the extent that some anthropologists have claimed that 'African art' does not exist at all. It is but the study of Western sensitivity towards African objects (Maquet 1979). To the extent that aesthetic analyses are simply this, they are indeed spurious. So the very first requirement for any study of aesthetics is to know what the aesthetic criteria of appreciation were in the cultures from which the works emanate.

Until quite recently, however, such studies were almost non-existent, and some do not survive a critical reading of the ethnographic information. To claim that objects were made for 'art's sake' in places where tourist trade for colonial officers and traders was common is spurious. To claim that criteria can be deduced merely from a few interviews with random viewers asked to rank objects by 'beauty' is unconvincing. First, such beauty contests did not often

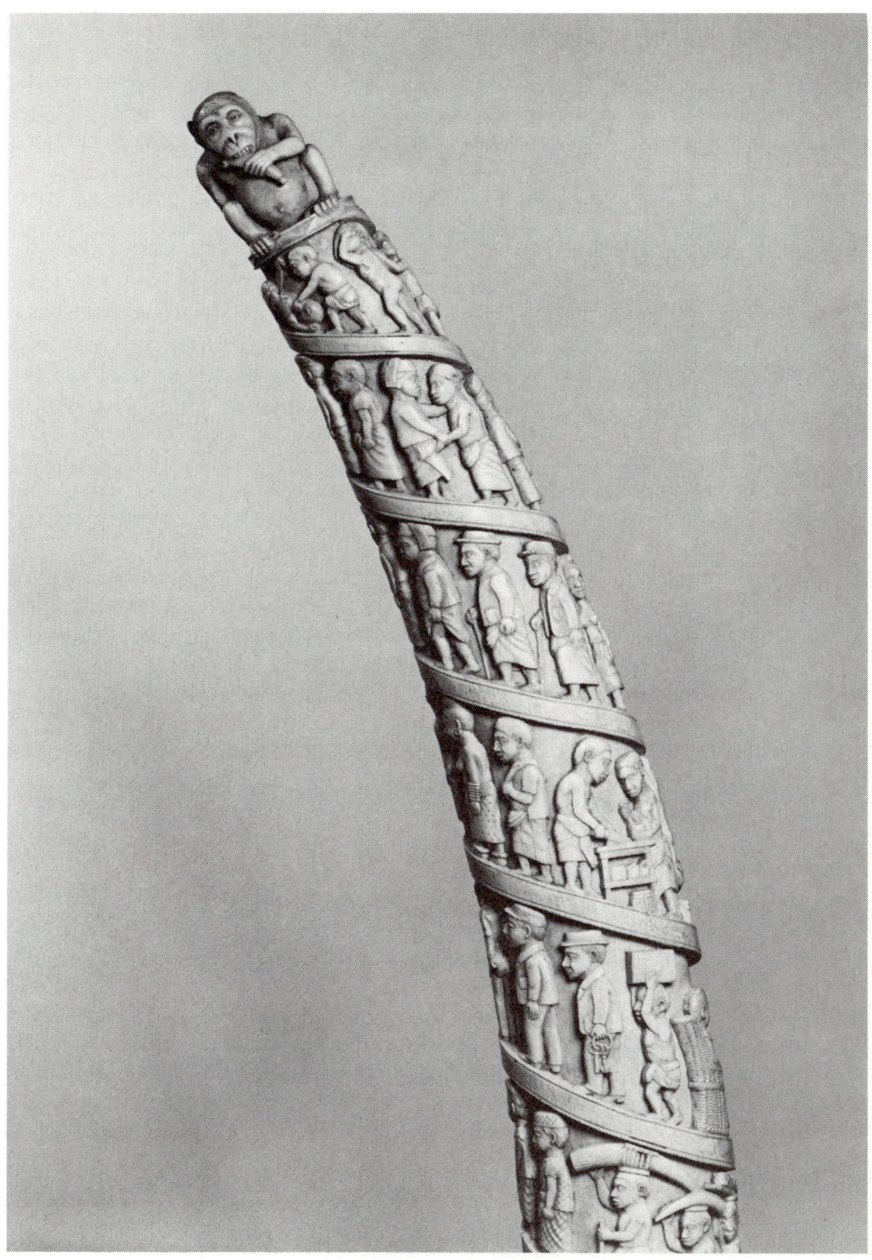

Plate 7.3 *Carved tusk. Use: sale to tourists. Loango coast, Congo/Angola. Walters Art Gallery, Baltimore. Height 110cm. 1850s. Such tusks were carved from the 1830s or 1840s to* c. *1900. The practice spread from Loango north as far as Duala and south to beyond Luanda. Scenes represented on the photo: caravan, European traders, sale, African notables, men and women, execution, ape. Other scenes of the tusk show war, capture of slaves, fishermen, a carpenter working at a table and again the ape motif at the bottom. A slave caravan is also depicted. The composition is European inspired, but the execution and the interpretation of each theme is local, and carries perhaps implied symbolism. We see the mid 19th c. through Vili eyes*

explain why one item was thought to be better than another, nor did they distinguish between the public at large and the creators of art. Only statements by the latter would really be detailed enough to allow us to understand the principles of aesthetic criticism involved, and finally some contests did not even make a distinction between works foreign to the critic and works crafted by him. Any 'beauty contest' should take great care over the sample of persons interviewed and include artists, while the relationship of object to critic (maker, owner, user ...) should also be clearly specified (Gerbrands 1957:75–8, 89–90).

There is no doubt that art objects were first appreciated for their emotional appeal, at least by the general public. That appeal derived from their use, meaning and place in the social matrix. Thus, a type of Cameroon (Bangwa) mask was seen as terrifyingly beautiful because the members of the 'night' society wore it. This was the chiefdom's secret council holding power of life and death over all. Its members secretly executed the condemned. The mask type represented terror (Brain 1980:147–51; Harter 1972), and its aesthetic success depended therefore on its expressionistic power to evoke that feeling. The type complemented that of the 'gong' society which expressed the protective aspects of the chieftaincy.

When comparison starts with icons of the same type, it becomes evident first that aesthetic criteria indeed existed. By working with carvers from the westernmost Ivory Coast (mainly Dan), Vandenhoute was able to specify the following criteria: symmetry according to vertical axis was consciously sought and strictly maintained, but there also had to be balance, rhythm and harmony between the various volumes, surfaces and lines in the mask. Such concepts seem vague, but in fact are not and can be measured. Apart from such formal criteria, finish (polishing and staining) was taken into account as well as criteria of actual use such as the comfort of the wearer of the mask (Gerbrands 1957:91). R. Thompson's (1973) study of Yoruba artistic criticism found eighteen criteria of sculptural excellence, each being named abstractions, for the Yoruba use a technical vocabulary of aesthetic criticism. Most of these were formal and once the criteria were known it was easy for the Western art critic to evaluate sculptures in a way similar to the Yoruba. However, they also all related to larger cultural values, to a system of ethics. Hallen (1979:303–7) shows that Thompson's claims are exaggerated, but, equally important, basically the criteria exist, even though some are inarticulate. It is to be deplored that we still have only a handful of valid studies and none dealing with the arts of northern Africa. To a certain extent aesthetics can be deduced here from writing, but field studies would no doubt enrich the understanding of such aesthetics. Even if in future such studies become available in larger numbers, they will still be lacking with regard to all the art forms that have now died out. One can only hope that it will become more and more apparent that formal criteria deducible from the works themselves will in fact turn out to be the intended criteria by which they were made. If this were a general rule – common sense would claim that it is so, but common sense is often common prejudice – then formal study could, at least to some extent, palliate our total lack of information about older art.

In many cultures 'beautiful' was rendered as 'good'. We saw that the link was so strong in some cultures that 'bad things' could not be expressed in art.

But the notion of 'goodness' or 'beauty' or 'quality' varied from culture to culture: it denotes 'approval'. The cultural conditions in North Africa drove aesthetic expression to the line, to arabesques. Artistic sensitivities ignored the sensual attraction imparted by volume but revelled in the mathematical elegance of intersecting lines and in the play of light and shadow while prisms of colour, if any, merely accented the subtlety of the play of lines. In contrast most art south of the Sahara expressed volume and the sensual, the solid rather than the evanescence of light. Some here were attracted by the clash of angular volumes as in eastern Kasai (Songye) (Plate 5.6) or in eastern Liberia (Guere/Wee), some prized smooth transition above all, deriving compositions from the smooth sphere as in Shaba (Luba) (Plate 5.4) or from elliptical volumes, swelling rhythmically as in northern Gabon (Fang) (Plate 5.3). Some relished rich decoration, glossy lacquer-like finish, while others liked the stark simplicity of the unadulterated medium.

Can one then posit links between the specific aesthetic expressions and other cultural values? Would smoothness correspond to gentle behaviour and clashing volume with martial sentiment? Are the lovers of arabesques and light, rational analysts or deep mystics? Is hieratic art the expression of religious awe or of an appreciation for authority, dignity, tradition? Such broad links are always false guides. One would not expect everyone in a given community to be gentle, martial, authoritarian or docile, pompous or affected. Styles are no better indicators of the overall tenor of a culture than languages are. Sweet Italian and harsh Russian, like sweet Swahili and guttural Arabic, are but stereotypical prejudice. Styles are partly autonomous from the rest of culture insofar as they are arbitrary systems, learned like language in childhood. If links between beauty and the tenor of a culture are to be explored fruitfully, they must expressly be found probably through the analysis of aesthetic criteria and their link to ethical criteria in a given community.

DYNAMICS OF ART AND CULTURE

If style and convention were so important in art, how could change occur? In the same way as culture as a whole changed and in the way language changes. People in a village speak a dialect, but each person has his or her favourite expressions, words and turns of syntax – each person speaks an idiolect. In the same way, concepts, visual concepts, the perception of style, were generally held in common, but each person has variants of his own. Artists, more conscious of their visual heritage than others, were bound to explore it more, just as poets use the language differently from ordinary people. Such idiosyncrasies allow new expressions of art when innovation was required by social or cultural change outside of art.

In most cultures adherence to norms was appreciated as the familiar, but at the same time it was not enough. Within the general framework of tradition, innovation was called for. New variants on the same theme in the same manner were highly appreciated in all the arts. As long as the new creations did not deviate so much from the current canons that the strain of understanding the icon was more unpleasant than the appeal of novelty, innovation was encouraged. Artists thus educated their public by finding new variations on old themes, old volumes, old lines, old colours, old motifs. The only surviving record of these processes are the art works themselves and the change recorded in them for the last century and more.

The distinction between *oikoumenical* and regional tradition relates also to the whole culture and the way that changed. *Oikoumenical* visual concepts were widespread. Everyone in the *oikoumene* did not share everything but most persons everywhere shared common cosmologies, common rituals, some common institutions and common values. Literate persons shared much more than that with other literate persons elsewhere, but not necessarily with their illiterate neighbours (Goody 1968:1–68). Culture was more diverse and stratified in the *oikoumene,* and so was art. Thus we have architecture in Morocco that reflected general Muslim tastes with a local accent, and yet find rural carpets there that were not replicated anywhere else. The ceramic art of Kabylia in the nineteenth century was really unique, whilst the oratories there were commonplace.

Regional traditions usually lacked such great differences between the culture of different strata. Because literacy was absent, they lacked overarching institutions and world views. As a result, their arts were less open to mutual influence and did not coalesce into a larger stream, but from time to time institutions and the associated values and ideas spread and art spread with them. For example, Cross River styles were carried by the Ekpe association along with trade almost to the full length and width of the valley (Eyo 1978).

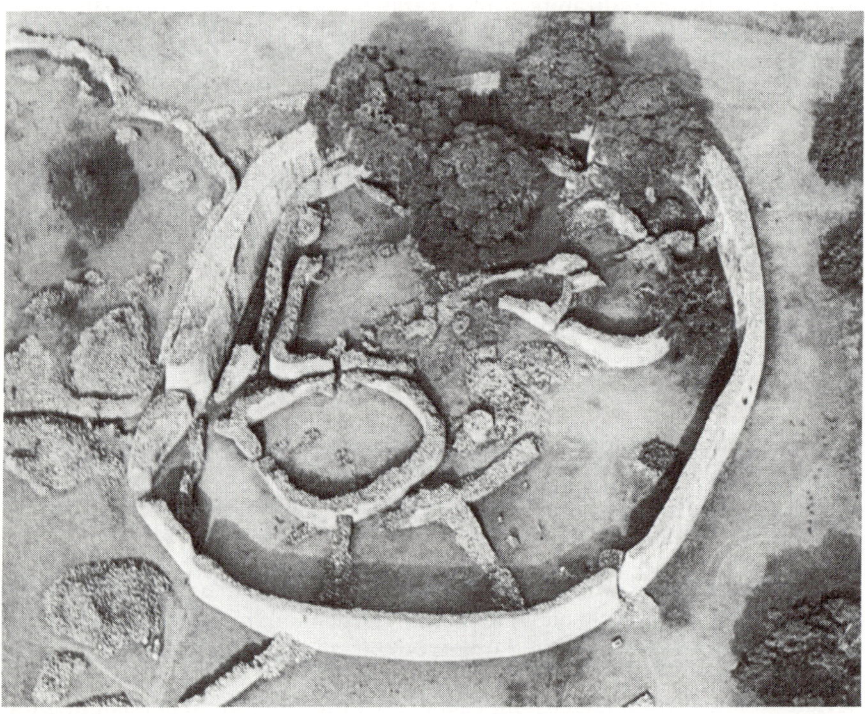

Plate 7.4 *Main enclosure from the air, Zimbabwe. Stone masonry without mortar. Diameter 135m. Outer wall 14th or early 15th c. Centre of the Zimbabwe state. An example of stone architecture in southeastern Africa, which developed from perhaps 1000 to c. 1830s*

Naturalistic Loango styles spread to southern Gabon along, no doubt, with the expansion of the kingdom. Royal architecture in stone at Zimbabwe spread over the whole country of Zimbabwe and remained quite different from most local architecture between *c.* 1200 and *c.* 1450 (Garlake 1973). The river of style out of which Zimbabwe grew may well have begun further south on the Limpopo. But once it became a dominant court style associated with court culture, it remained a hallmark of kingship in Zimbabwe to the eighteenth century. Meanwhile, further south, in the high veld, architecture in stone developed in different directions and, under the influence of cultures that diverged more and more, it too diverged so that a so-called Tswana plan of the eighteenth century was very different from plans in the eastern Transvaal or Orange Free State (Inskeep 1979:135–41).

It is not difficult to give other examples both of the expansion or diversification, or contraction of art styles linked to similar general movements in the cultures these arts expressed. Art is an important and direct signal of culture change and hence of general cultural history. This is evident even in such seemingly minor changes as the dominant colours of frescoes at Faras. They reflect renewed influence from different quarters and changes in the pulse of cultural life at the cathedral. More Palestinian influence in art also meant more Palestinian influence in reading matter, and theological orientation. More Byzantine influence implied more use of Greek again, more attention paid to Byzantine church fathers and their theology (Michalowski 1967; Dinkler 1970). Any historian of culture must therefore be alert for telltale signs in art, because they may indicate the possibility of less visible change.

Sources for the history of culture are available through writing. Those that spurned this medium of expression left little record of cultural change. It is ironic that we know more about cultural changes in the New Kingdom of the Pharaos than we do about eighteenth-century Kuba cultural change, three thousand years and more later. Perhaps the greatest weakness of precolonial African history south of the Sahara is the lack of data and study of cultural matters. I still do not know whether we will ever be able to trace even the main outlines of a history of cultures in the sense in which the term was used in this chapter. If this can be done, works of visual art will be the most direct evidence we have, and it should be given the most careful attention. In the end, a study of art history might therefore well lead us to a better understanding of cultural history in general.

CHAPTER EIGHT

THE CREATIVE PROCESS

THE ARTIST AS CREATOR

Having examined questions of authenticity, identification, context, technique, style, iconography and meaning, we now ask how an icon comes into being, what were the sources from which it sprang and how original is the work itself. The creative process starts both with perception and cognition. Perception of an artefact, a person, a natural object or scene, is probably common to all people everywhere, although Gombrich doubts even this. Cognition through mental predispositions of space, volume, number and time is common to all people in a culture. So are common expectations and interpretations of perceived phenomena. In addition, artists have further developed interpretations linked to the task of translating an object into a new work of art. Artists know from practice. They have learned how to translate perceptions into works of art or can see the problems involved in so doing, especially when they see icons in media and techniques which are their own. Apart from such technical predispositions, however, most cognitive factors were shared by artists and non-artists alike in the whole community. There existed, for instance, an almost universal measure of agreement as to what was worthy of observation and transmutation into an icon.

Perception and cognition were conditions of observation. Motivation – the will to create – was the essential ingredient for action. A mental image of the icon related to one or more material images to be made had to be present in the mind of the artist and his patrons. The mental image of the artist then purposively directed his skilled hands at every step of the crafting (Drewal 1980:9–10). Once the icon emerged, it escaped from the artist's control. As a reality in its own right it started a life of its own.

Motivation itself cannot be proved in the absence of express statements by artists or patrons. Even so, motivations are always mixed: practical reasons accompany and vie with more aesthetic urges. But the product clearly bears witness to the mental vision of its maker, especially when the artist made replications, copied or attempted to perfect or adapt existing works of art. Even when new icons were created, the product remained within the range of earlier techniques, styles, themes and motifs known to the artist.

The creative process turned around three main pivots: the patron, the artist, and the products. However important the influence of the mental images of patron and public were, they only set limitations or requirements on the creation of acceptable art. The artist was the person who turned a mental image into matter. That is why his vision was crucial. In most cultures this was more or less recognized. Creativity was attributed in most cultures south of the

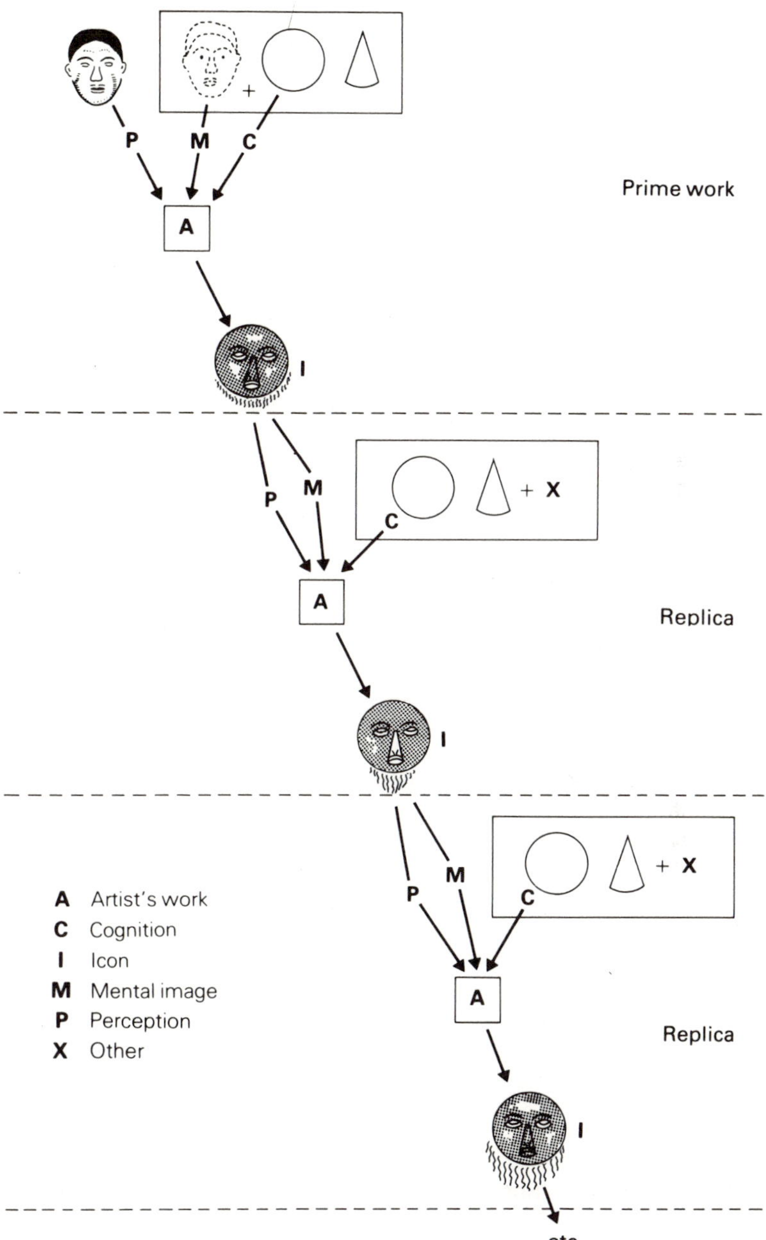

Fig. 8.1 *The creative process*

Sahara to supernatural forces which made visible out of invisible matter. Prayers or sacrifice to media, such as metal, wood or stone, to the artist's tools, to the processes, have been reported. Ritual conditions to be observed by the artist, especially when making objects which were to hold an invisible life of their own as supports or even images of spirits, were fairly common (Drewal 1980:10–11). Skill alone was not a sufficient explanation for creativity. There was nothing surprising about this since skill in anything was linked to the supernatural, often unfavourably: people suspected that any outstanding skill was acquired through witchcraft or sorcery. In many societies inspiration itself was claimed to stem from dreams by patrons about commissions specifying the icon desired. Such an exotic picture of creativity can and has been overdone in ethnographies. Just as not all African art is inspired by religion, neither was all creativity inspired by prophetic vision nor was it totally attributed to it. But creativity was understood in a framework of the dominant cosmology as a matter of course, and this is equally true in Christian or Islamic countries. Muslims not only heeded taboos about representations, but like Christians attributed creativity to a condition of special grace *(baraka)* and not just to skill. Religious commissions were more common in Ethiopia than elsewhere in Africa. Most of the painting and building there were the work of monks, while only a small portion of carving south of the Sahara was done by religious specialists. What matters more than such rather invidious comparisons is the realization that motivations for making works of art, and attributing responsibility for both mental images and success in their material crafting, were embedded in cosmology, but did not exclude appreciation of the individual input of the artists.

Individuality was recognized everywhere but was not easily visible to the historian, because works were seldom signed, even where writing existed. For every few Coptic or Muslim potters who signed the scenes they painted on Fatimid bowls, there are legions who did not. Patrons are mentioned on inscriptions on Muslim monuments, but seldom architects. Western Liberian (Gola) patrons were also remembered, not the artists. In our age we have deduced that this means that both the public and probably the artists saw such realizations either as communal work or saw no special merit in crafting them. But this is not altogether true. For some names of painters in Ethiopia or architects in northern Africa were remembered in writing.

South of the Sahara the situation may have been similar. Signatures do not exist even where marks do, and we must remember that marks were signs of ownership, not of manufacture. In some societies, such as among the Kuba or the Yoruba, innovation was prized. The invention of a new decorative motif among the Kuba was rewarded by calling it by the name of the maker. Thus, the motif Mabiinc, later quite common on mats, bears the name of the woman who invented it. In most communities, artists could tell from the manner of execution who had shaped this or that piece, and among some, as in western Nigeria (Yoruba), even the public knew who had crafted what were thought to be significant works. The particular mix of attribution to inspirations by supernatural forces and inspiration by the artist varied from society to society and certainly varied over time, but individuality was never denied, certainly not by artists. But the conditions of collection have been such that most of this information was never recorded.

The artist was not just considered to be a hand or a tool. In most societies he enjoyed consideration, if not status. Among the social castes of artists of West Africa, for instance, creative skill was ambiguously received. Consideration could be expressed in twisted ways. Thus, in western

Cameroon, good artists were eagerly traded from chief to chief as slaves, and in the Bangwa chiefdom there, they worked around the chief's palace and ceded their products to him. He sold or distributed them and claimed the credit for the inspiration! The chief was the official artist (Brain 1980:135). Artists appear very rarely as heroes in oral literature; only among the Kuba do I know of a tradition glorifying a member of the royal house as the creator of later lost art works of great size in iron. But appreciation for artists has been preserved in many societies by the characteristics attributed to demiurges, who 'invented' arts and crafts.

Creativity in artists was recognized in most, perhaps all societies. Did this recognition involve the attribution of special roles and peculiar behaviour patterns to artists? Was there an 'artistic temperament'? Bohemian ways of life and unconventional behaviour have been reported for musicians in eastern Kasai, but not for visual artists there (Merriam 1973). While in our societies this feature is linked to the notion of artistic freedom, a right derived from the creed of art for art's sake, it could exist in societies where creativity was linked to supernatural inspiration and artists could be likened to mediums, healers or mystics. There are African societies in which those people behaved differently either during a given period of their life, when the vocation called them, or in seances. Artists were expected to play special roles in some societies, roles quite similar to those of inspired persons like mediums. In such cases it was believed that a special bond existed between the artist and a supernatural being by which he was possessed. d'Azevedo (1973a) says of Liberian (Gola) woodcarvers that a tutelary spirit was held to be the source of their creative ideas. Already in childhood deviant behaviour could be detected. Signs of strong spiritual connections, unusual food and preferences, early attempts to master skills, were all signs of calling as a woodcarver. Their behaviour in later life was seen as strange, a mixture of the irresponsible and the strongly committed to goals that were not important to others. But there also are African societies in which artists learned their crafts just as farmers learned to farm, hunters to hunt, or weavers to weave.

Few studies have focused on actual temperaments as opposed to roles. They could be expected to vary as much as the range of temperaments in the whole of their community. Thus, among the Kuba, we found one well-known carver to be an advisor and tax collector for the king, a careful person who budgeted his time and calculated his output, a consultant to the local art school. Another, living early in this century, was driven by ambition, highly talented, frightening to others and competitive. He was killed around 1904, framed by jealous competitors or villagers convinced of his evil powers. He did not survive a witchcraft poison ordeal. A third carver I knew in the 1950s was the perfect trader. He carved a statue, went to town to sell it, calculating quite nicely how much it would bring for how much work, and how long the money would last. Yet his work was not shoddy. Another man of cheerful disposition was engaged, when I met him, in displaying a new variation on an old theme to his fellow villagers. Carving was common among the Kuba but an artistic temperament was unknown, and in this they obviously differed from the Gola. Clearly, variations of role, expected and actually played, vary widely from culture to culture.

The degree of freedom enjoyed by artists in creating is linked to the role they played, the behaviour expected of them. Thus, the Christian monk who painted murals from a pattern of a copy book on set themes and in specific places of a church had very little freedom. But the question of the freedom of the artist is partly spurious. Few artists ever perceived limitations on their creative freedom of expression, as they themselves were embedded in the collective representations that produced icons and were usually inspired by signs and motivations common to all. However the question is partly genuine. The monk painting frescoes had less freedom than a carver replicating existing icons, and yet, as the record shows, innovation occurred. From time to time, startling departures from conventional work did occur, always of course within the world of forms known to the artists, not the larger world of possible forms. When discussing artistic freedom it must be remembered that the contemporary artist has access through illustrations and museums to forms shaped the world over and at all periods, quite a different experience from the usual situation in the cultures of Africa.

The creative urge as a motivation is a vague phrase. It includes motivations such as boredom, the wish to find a better solution to a problem of form, the desire to record permanently, the desire to make a statement. Evidence from series of similar icons often shows minor variations that may well represent the urge to escape from the boredom of executing the same icon once again. In a few cases variation may be motivated by the desire to resolve a formal problem better. This was a major source of innovation in European graphic art and architecture. The treatment of the wall behind and over the mihrab in Moroccan mosques is an example of an architectural conundrum. Different solutions were tried in different mosques until a very satisfying solution was found at Tin Mal (Marçais 1954:238–42). That became standard practice thereafter. But given the lack of expressed motivation by artists we cannot often be certain that this incentive was at work. Clear cases of such solutions found after various trials are practically non-existent because dating is so poor and stylistic series often tend to put the best integrated work first in a series, as its prototype, whereas less perfect works may have preceded them as trial pieces. The desire to put on record is clear when portraits were crafted, especially portraits of those who were near and dear to the artist. Examples – all of the twentieth century, however – are known from various parts of West and Central Africa. As to the desire to make a statement, such as Picasso's in Guernica, the evidence is ambiguous at best, in the absence of literary indications. As we know from oral art, there must have been cases when this was the motivating force, but we cannot detect them.

When artists departed from current work they claimed credit for the virtuosity of execution, and for the thought involved in turning new mental images into reality. Existing ethnographic reports often stress the claims that thinking was the hardest part of the job and execution the easiest (Gerbrands 1957:124). Equally, often both works and reports stress virtuosity for skill's sake. The latter incentive led to the creation of *bravura* pieces, usually non-commissioned, which were one of the major means of innovation in the arts, and, at least among the Kuba, an accepted form of advertisement for the artist (Plate 8.5).

ORIGINALITY

A question to be asked of every object, as of every document, is its degree of originality. Objects may be perfectly genuine – that is, not pretend to be anything else than what they are, but they may still not be original. Authentic pieces can be copies just as they can be prime works. The notion of copy in art depends first on the techniques used. Several items from the same mould, several prints from the same block, are true copies. If the same pattern is used to trace the outlines of a figure for a fresco, as was probably common in Nubian and Ethiopian art, we have copies, but not total copies. Such mechanical copies presuppose a different original: a mould, a block, a pattern book. The technical means to reproduce copies should be well known. Unfortunately, very few if any of the moulds and no blocks or pattern books seem to have

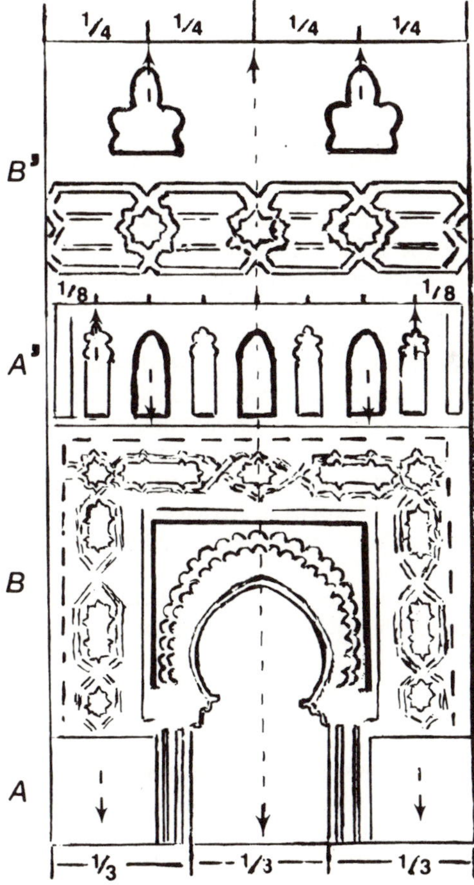

Fig. 8.2 Mihrab *wall. Tin Mal, Morocco. Stone masonry. 1153 (Almohad period). The horizontal tripartite division at floor-level passes into a bipartite one on the top of the wall. The main transition area counts seven units. Vertically a division in two with each half subdivided differently, the upper part in equal thirds, the lower half one-third to two. A^2 corresponds to A; B^2 to B. All dimensions are related to that of the diameter of the arch. The composition developed here became standard in many mosques thereafter*

survived in Africa. Pots can be copies in yet another sense. Where the pottery wheel did not exist the bottom of an old pot often served to mould the bottom of the new one, so that the size of the new pot and most of its shape (given the colombine method) were dependent on the model.

Often the term 'copy' is used in a different sense altogether. It means replication. A pattern, a design, a sculpture, a building, were crafted in conscious imitation of an existing model. A marabout's tomb in northern Africa resembles similar tombs to the point that one talks of a copy. One statue looks very much like another one, as anyone who has seen collections of twin figures from southwestern Nigeria (Yoruba *ibeji*) or stocks of tourist art with Masai warriors wielding spears knows. But such replications are not total. They vary slightly in size, in technique, in the grain of the medium, in a detail (very common in painting and architecture) or they are composite copies, using one figure for part of the composition and another for the other part. The many St Georges and St Michaels with varying dragons and fallen angels in eastern Christian art illustrate this well enough.

Nearly complete handmade imitations were the rule in preindustrial material cultures, for example in textiles, utensils in wood, metal or pottery, in house building. The confidence archaeologists have in determining cultures by their pottery or their house plans underlines the point. Would art objects then be those that differ from run-of-the-mill production? Or perhaps just the prototype? Obviously such a criterion leads us into a quagmire. The art historian merely places the object he studies from the point of view of its form in relation to all others. Series of replications do not rule out that there is a work of art here. Most African masks are taken to be works of art, even though hundreds of replications exist for many of them.

Originality can also be interpreted in a third sense, referring to creative filiation. A sequence of works established by consideration of their similarities yields a time series. Some works are then labelled as archaic, some as copies, crafted by imitators who aimed at emulation or even improvement. The use of such terms presupposes a whole hypothesis about artistic development. Given the often undated character of works in Africa and the unproven assumptions of a wish better to solve technical problems posed by one's predecessors, such terms as 'archaic' or 'epigones' are best eschewed. Classical is used then for all art before *c.* 1900. A terminology using 'replication' and 'prime work' is adequate and less loaded (Neyt 1979:24–6; Flam 1971).

REPLICATIONS

Creative processes led either to replications or prime works. Most works of art are replications. Existing works were strong models. They were imitated through a mental screen, the image of the icon to be imitated. Familiar motor habits and usual skills crafted the object.

Working from nature was as rare in Africa as it was in Europe before the Renaissance (Gombrich 1960:74–83, 148–52); not only unusual, but distinctly odd. Hence counterfeits, exact reproductions of existing objects, were rare, if the techniques did not provide for counterfeiting. Exact reproductions required continual inspection of the model and imitation detail by detail from the model to the new product. Such exercises were totally foreign to the training of African artists, who learned by imitating the actions of their mentors until they gradually mastered the whole sequence of operations and motor habits required to fashion the products of the workshop to which they were apprenticed. Practising artists might keep some objects in their atelier, either because they were not yet finished, or not sold, or were rejects or in order to serve their memory. Some were mementoes to great occasions in the artist's life, some works he liked so much he would not be separated from them. I knew one Kuba carver who held on to perhaps a dozen objects but I cannot say that even one of them served as a model. Given these conditions working from memory never led to lifeless creation or total imitation. There was always room for innovation.

The ability to distinguish between those features in a work that are copied and those that are original is crucial in art history. The determination of ateliers, personal styles, filiation of art works, all depend on the skill with which the origin and derivative qualities of replications can be analyzed, and replications differ between major art forms.

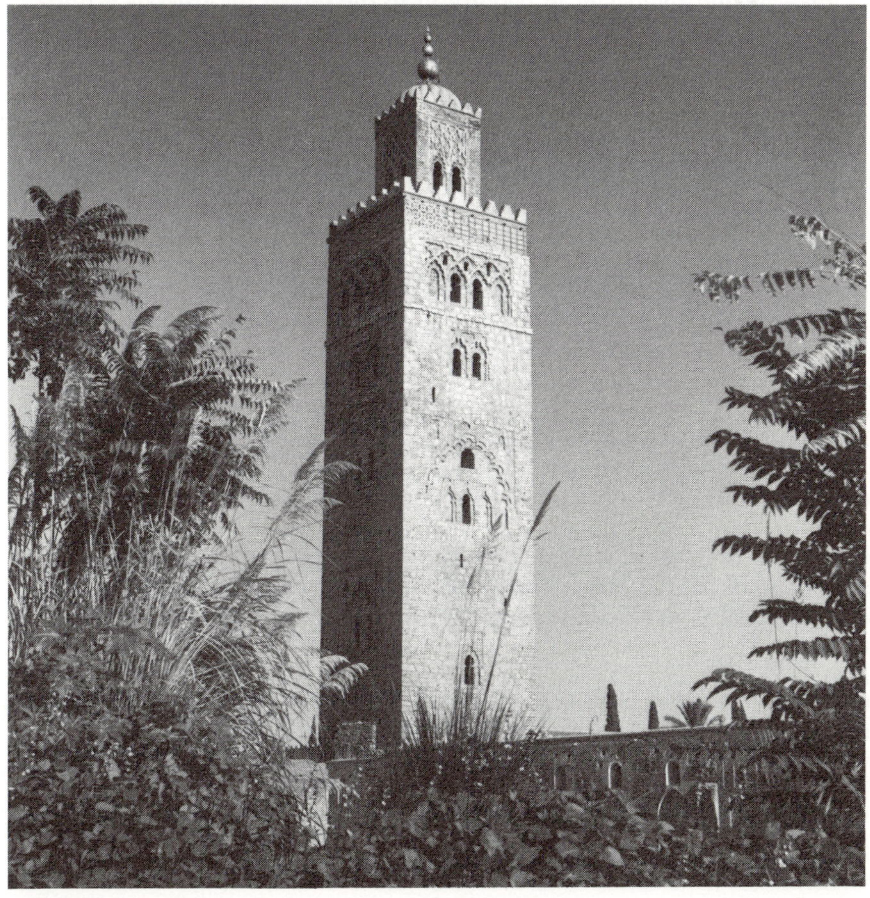

Plate 8.1 *Minaret. Stone masonry. Quttubiya mosque, Marrakush, Morocco. Height 77m. 1146–1196, Almohad period. Compare with Plate 7.1. Decor is here more functional, but less logical than on the Hasan minaret*

In architecture, circumstances usually made it impossible to work with the same plans on the same scale. Replication meant to use the same principles for plans and elevations, the same techniques, the same standardized materials. A famous example of three minarets replicating each other, built reputedly by the same architect in Seville, Rabat and Marrakush, illustrates the point (cf. Plates 8.1 and 7.1). They all varied slightly in dimensions, but not in the method of construction. Interior ramps, not staircases, were used, and there was no central pier supporting the whole tower. Each level constituted a room. The three towers finished in 1196, 1196 and 1198 all differed from previous minarets in this feature. They all shared the fact that each of their four façades was decorated differently. They all stand as a single group different from earlier minarets and were models for later towers (Marçais 1954:209–11). Within the group further differences were the repartition of the decor at Rabat which was less functional than the decor at Marrakush and the variations in the slope of the ramp at Seville allowing a better alignment of outside windows. The delicate balance between the desire to innovate and the desire to be faithful to the model the patrons wanted is evident here. So is the architect's experimentation with technical solutions of decor and interior ramp. One of the main differences between these minarets and earlier ones was the technical innovation that allowed suppression of the central pier.

Additive techniques in sculpture showed fewer limitations in obtaining a close imitation than carving. The material was more homogenous. Even with new moulds or with any of the other techniques used, the imitations could be quite close because the building-up process allowed greater precision. Use could also further imitation. The need to control weights in the manufacture of jewellery and goldweights led to closer imitation of size than in other arts for instance (Garrard 1980). Standard sizes of painted tiles had much the same effect. However, because it was possible to imitate so well, individual hands are much harder to detect in ceramics or in metal work, and variations between one work and another by the same hand were often greater than variation between replications by different hands.

Subtractive techniques led to lesser replication. The shape and features of the initial block, the techniques of carving prevented very close imitation. The use of adzes, chisels and knives preserved more traces of the hands of individual carvers and thus enables identification of products from the same atelier and by the same artist, but polishing and finishing with the knife could erase so many of these individual traces that it becomes impossible to recognize the hand. Hence, arguments of originality in subtractive sculpture need to be realistically assessed in relation to the objects involved. As a rule of thumb, the more finished the work, the less convincing such arguments are, the rougher the sculpture, the more plausible.

With two-dimensional arts, especially painting, other questions arise. Tracing apart, differences are found in execution. The examination of 'signatures' is certainly fruitful here. For just as graphologists recognize different hands, the art historian finds the individual characteristics of how the paint was put on (see Fig. 5.4). Tracing did not occur for illumination nor for the painting on wood, freehand imitation preserved all the characteristics of the atelier and the master. But copying illuminations was often quite literal, just as copying a manuscript is. It leads us to think that while *scriptoria* (ateliers) are easy to identify, the detection of the individual hand may be more difficult than in painting on wood or canvas (but see Leroy 1968:65–6).

Similarly, the production of other art forms, such as textiles or work on leather implies greater or lesser imitability. Decorative art was often easier to copy from memory than figurative work was, and hence it is harder to examine individual characteristics. Any historical critique of originality must carefully take such factors into account.

DRIFT

Because replications were never total copies, replications of replications tended to drift away from the first original that served as a real or mental model. Further, in time this drift could lead to stylistic change. Drift could be random or not, and random drift was very common. Small mosques in the Sahara, for instance, differ in the distance between arches, their actual heights, the execution of the roofing, and the internal proportions of the ground plan. That, however, did not lead to definite change over time, as the variations were considered to be unimportant, occurred in various ways, and tended to cancel each other out. Random drift in other arts is equally common. Drift became significant and is of major concern to art history when it was directional. The history of arabesques developing from the garlands of vines, fruits and leaves in Hellenistic decoration through a gradual stylization leading to geometry is one of drift. Arabic script of the Kufic style began as a monumental austere script, but later sprouted leaves and became flowery Kufic. It became less stylized in the same workshops where the rinceaux became more stylized at the same time. The example shows that there are no laws involved in drift. It was strongly believed at one time that decorative arts simplify and go from more lifelike representation to simplified forms, presumably to speed up execution and to bring out the essential characteristic of line in the representation. But, as flowery Kufic shows, a reverse trend was just as plausible. Later on, further development of Kufic turned it into such an angular style of decoration that it looks like clusters of little blocks. Over a period of almost a millennium in duration, the full evolution shows a movement away from simplified line to more lifelike representation and then back to a very abstract play with surface.

Directional drift occurs when artists develop a personal style, when they seek to improve on existing icons, when they want to produce similar icons faster and when taste changes. Individual styles have been documented, if only by documenting the hand of a painter or carver, or when works from different stages in a career are compared (Thompson 1969:120–82). There is always an interaction between patrons and producers in this process. The attempt formally to improve is evident in architecture and we cited the case of Tin Mal as an instance. Change in order to speed up production is proved by shoddy work and best known by modern replication of classical icons to be sold to tourists, but this factor may have played a greater role than is usually acknowledged. Certainly this is true in the development of hieroglyphic script, and we suspect it in many other cases of simplification of decorative motifs. By and large, change in taste however accounted for most drift. A replication was deemed to be superior to the original in some detail that had changed more or less by accident. The next patron expected the next icon to display this alteration more prominently and gradually the whole composition or style changed, sometimes quite considerably. Thus, the Ethiopian keyhole window was the endpoint of a drift starting with a window flanked by colonettes on a base supporting an arch on a corbel. A series of Tyi wara masks from Mali (Bambara) shows all the transitions between a flowing mane over a majestically arched neck to a flamelike shape in which no mane could ever be recognized.

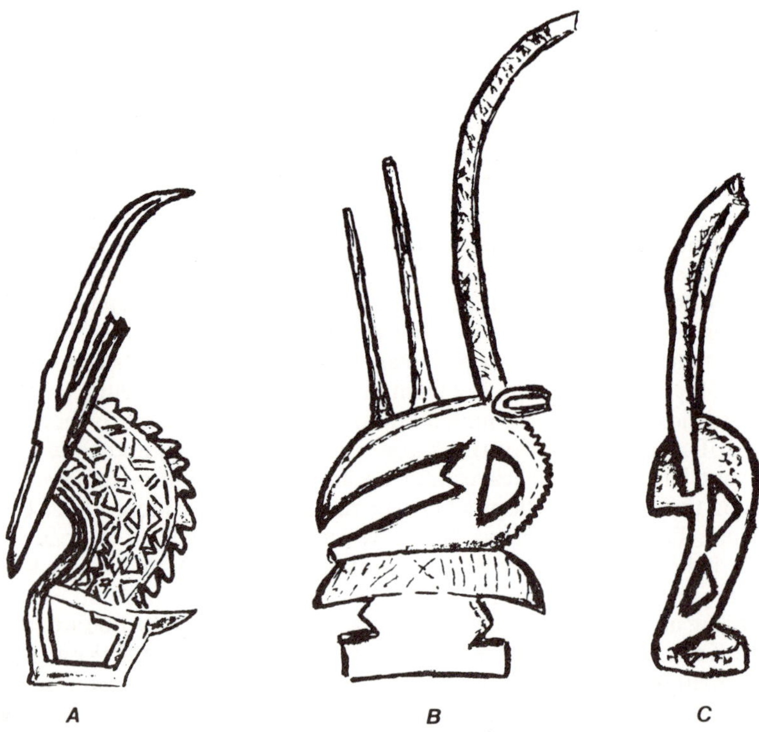

Fig. 8.3 Tyi wara *masks worn on top of the head. Wood. Bambara/Bamana, Mali. Recent. The objects all represent male antelopes. The styles vary by region and over time. C consists only of the horns and mane of form A. A Bamako region: height 40cm and the best known variant; B Suguni region: height 55cm; C unspecified: height 42·2cm. After A. Claerhout,* Afrikaanse Kunst, *Utrecht 1971: pl. 54, 56, 57*

Over the long term, whole art styles show the effect of major drifts, major changes in taste. Coptic art began as a variant on Hellenistic art in Egypt, originally being at the start close to an extreme naturalism. Gradually, the icons were stylized to extremes. Themes and motifs of Hellenistic origins remained, but in abbreviated stylized form. The idea was still there, but the representation was no longer as full. Thus, a textile showing the head of the goddess Earth in the beginning of the sequence with its intricate use of colour for modelling and shading should be compared to late Coptic textiles where women's faces, still held in a medallion, have become rectangular and suggest the natural angles produced in woven stuffs more than the natural angles of a human head. This progressive stylization is evident in all branches of Coptic

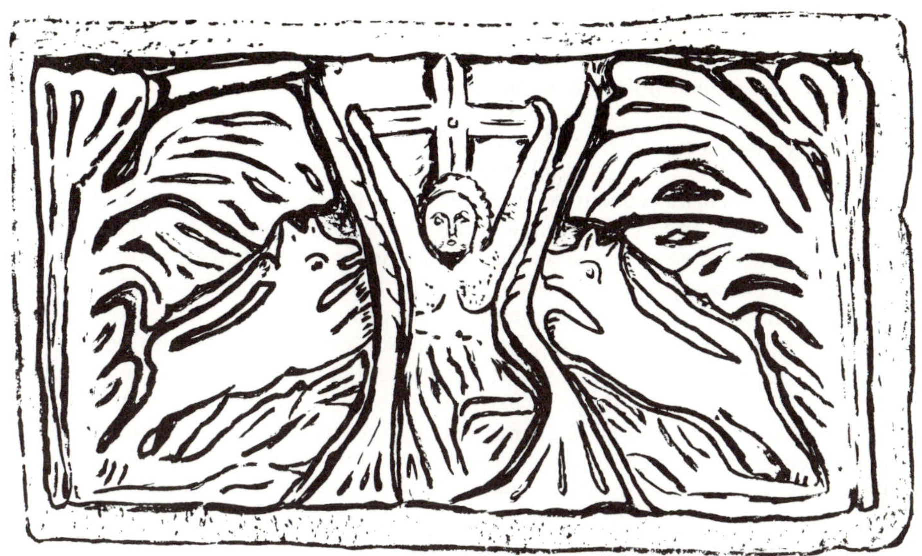

Fig. 8.4 *The martyrdom of St Thecla. Limestone relief. Brooklyn Museum, New York. Height 53·5cm; length 58·3cm. 9th c. St Thecla is about to be burned and devoured by hounds. Coptic. By this period the relief is reduced to two planes, stylization is complete, a horror of the void (filled by flames and vegetation) is apparent and the effect becomes decorative. After K. Wessel 1965:59, pl. 62*

art, sculpture, decorative art, textiles, even painting. Taste changed continually. Was this due to an effect of Christianity with its emphasis on the inner life rather than on earthly pleasures? Who could prove it? The fact is simply that major stylistic drift occurred (du Bourguet 1967; Wessel 1965; Badawy 1978).

In several sequences of styles, one can follow the rise of decorative elements until they swamp all empty space and even push back the figurative parts of the icon. This is evident in the Benin series of heads and in the treatment of walls in the madrasa of Morocco. Kuba art also shows a growing tendency to avoid a *horror vacui,* i.e., to leave blank space. Such similarities in development have been attributed to changes in taste stressing wealth, rather than aesthetics and are commonly associated with centralized systems and courts. This is certainly not a universal rule in art, but several parallels can be found in or out of Africa, just as parallels for stylization in Coptic art can be found. What such cases show is the inherent power of form and shape to develop its own logic. The logic of geometrical decorative motifs is to expand; the logic of an art that reaches extreme lifelike representation is to reverse the trend. Parallel sequences merely show that the given styles logically only have a few major possibilities for evolution. They can remain stable overall as, for example, in the Faras sequence; they can move slightly back and forth from their inherent norms as in ancient Egyptian arts, or they can move decidedly in one of a very few directions such as towards or away from simplification. Having given examples of simplification, we should consider a contrary case: the goldweights in Ghana. They started out as purely simple geometric shapes and styles. They ended in the nineteenth century at the extreme of complexity in line, volume and figure, often having become much more intricate than their use would have warranted (Garrard 1980:274–315; see Plate 11.2). As in the Coptic case, we can only guess the reason.

PRIME WORKS

Change does not always occur by sheer drift. Quite often a new type of icon was suddenly created and became a new fountainhead for replication. Such works are called prototypes or prime works. Such works constitute a clear break in a tradition. The mosque at Qairawan provides a good example, involving only moderate innovation and yet leading to a new prototype. Its plan derives from the plan of the Madina mosque, its mihrab was not the first one to be built, minarets of some form had existed before and it was not the first domed mosque. But the overall shape of its minaret, the oldest now extant in Islam, became the prototype of all later minarets in northwest Africa. Its innovation in the creation of a central nave, the execution of its arches and beamed roofs, the choice and execution of the main dome in front of the mihrab (Lezine 1966:62), were all perceived as so new and so perfect that these features were not only imitated quite rapidly in the main mosque at Tunis, but further inspired developments at Cordoba and in Morocco. Its influence lasted for many centuries.

Sometimes the break was radical. The appearance of round *kidumu* masks (see Plate 7.2) among the Tsayi *c.* 1870 is such a case (Dupré 1968). The mask and the dance for which it was made were invented then, representing perhaps the turmoil of 'new times', but we do not know where its inspiration could stem from. There was nothing like it anywhere in the area. Masks were known, colours were used in other works and on masks, some of the decorative patterns can be found on objects of a different tradition, but not the round flat shape of the mask, not the strict double horizontal and vertical symmetry, not the extreme abstraction of the face. Someone invented a prime work out of nowhere. The apparition of such prime works in sculpture was usually almost as radical as this, but in architecture or in Christian painting such radical innovations have been much rarer.

The greater the break the more difficult it becomes to trace the sources of inspiration. A typical case would be the explanation of the origin of the ancestral statues north of the Sankuru in Zaïre. They are attributed to the Ndengese people and seem to descend from a nineteenth-century prototype, the date being guessed at by the relative rarity of the extant pieces (Cornet 1976). The heads were very similar to those of the cephalomorph cups of their southern neighbours in the settlements on the banks of the Sankuru and further south. The statues have no legs but a broad base around the genitals. That feature recalls the clay statues made by their northern neighbours (Hulstaert 1931), as do the overall proportions of torso and head. The pattern of scarification of the bodies and the caps were probably locally inspired. The idea of ancestral statues for some great persons stemmed either from the north or from the Kuba kingdom to their south, where the royal statues of the Kuba were created in the eighteenth century (Vansina 1978:212–15; Rosenwald 1974). There is enough evidence of social intercourse between the Ndengese, their northern and southern neighbours, to allow for such influences.

But why did the Ndengese feel the need for such works? In the nineteenth century they had no chiefs but were governed by an association of the wealthy, the *etoci*. Yet the statues were not intended to represent all the *etoci*. There are far too few works of art for that to be true. Was there then a further principle of

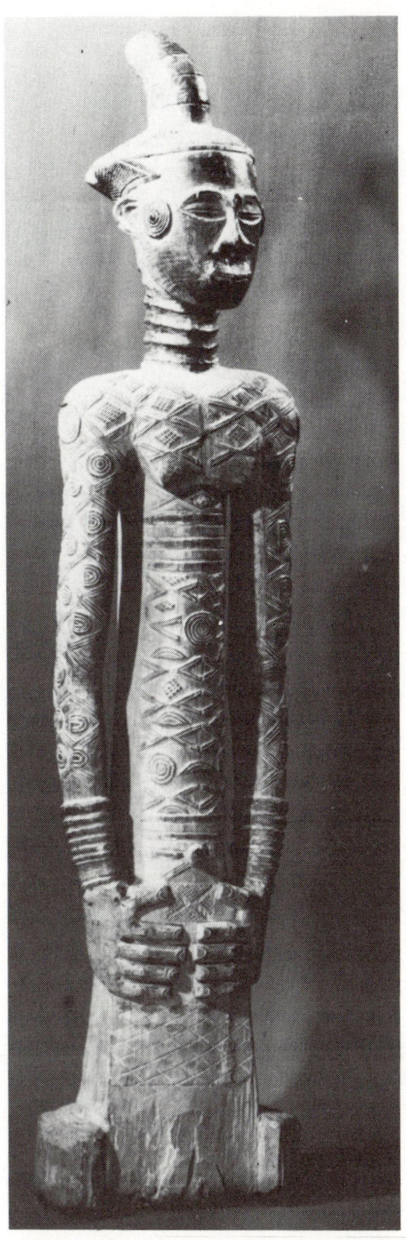

Plate 8.2 *Statue. Wood. Use unknown, perhaps commemorative for leaders, perhaps for a community cult. Near Dekese, Middle Lokenye, Zaïre. Thought to be work of the Ndengese people. Koninklijk Museum voor Midden Afrika, Tervuren. Height 139cm. Acquired 1912*

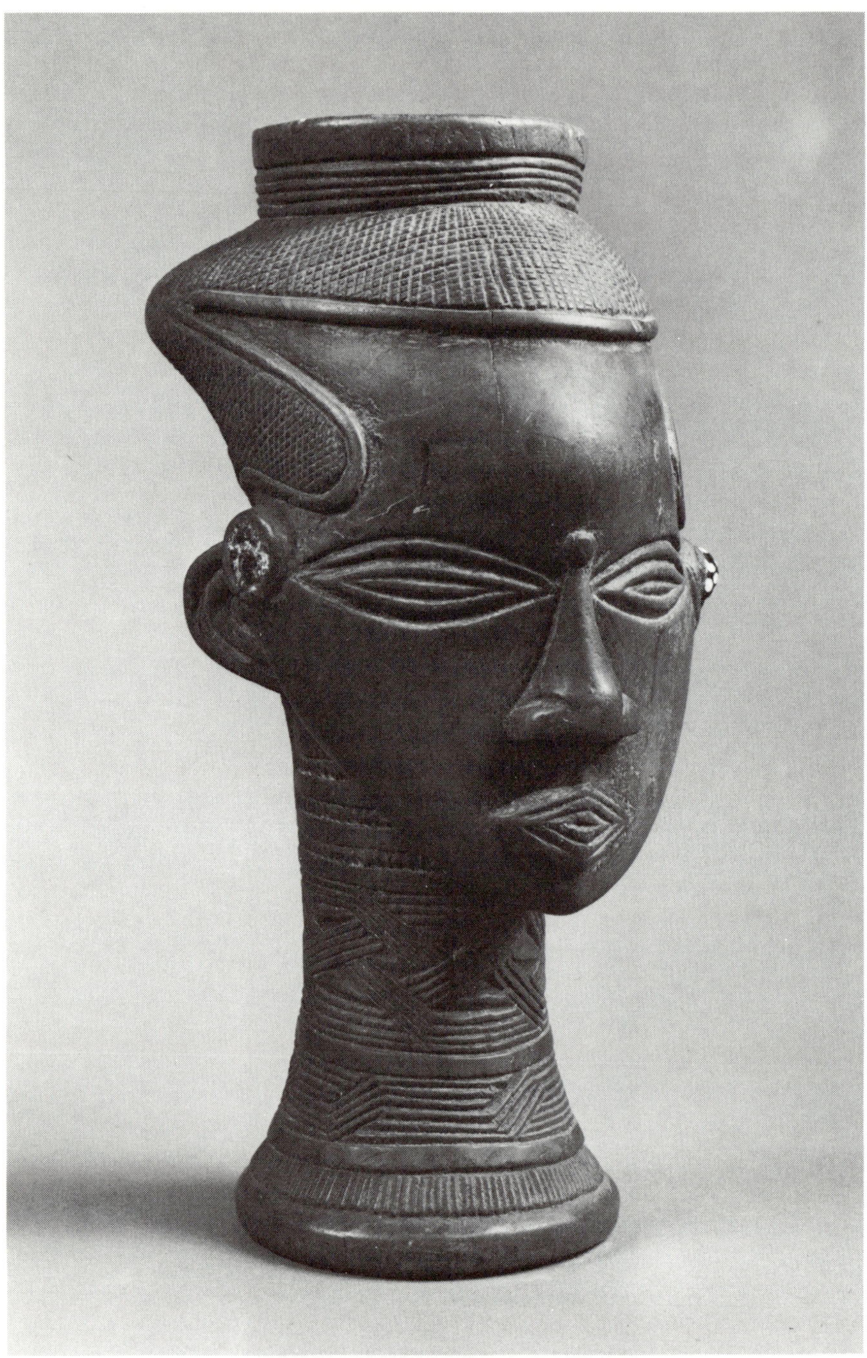

Plate 8.3 *Cephalomorph cup. Wood and a bead in front of each ear. Used as a household cup for patricians. Kuba kingdom. Museum für Völkerkunde, Berlin-Dahlem. Height 23cm. Acquired 1906. The detail (keloid tattoo, top, eyes) favours an attribution to the northern Kuba near the Sankuru*

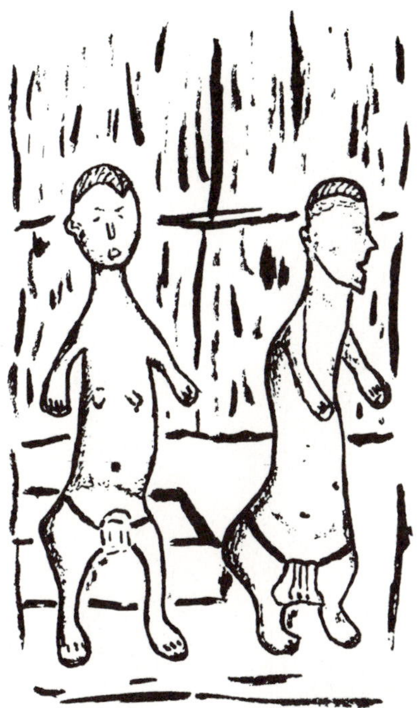

Fig. 8.5 *Shrine figures. Mud. Wagania village near Befale, Zaïre. Height unknown. 1913. The Nsongo people (Mongo group) built such shrines at the entrance of the villages. The figures were placed on a hardened mud floor in a shelter open to one side. They were surrounded by a mud leopard and a mud dog. Shield, basket, hat, cloth and a bedframe against the back wall. Other peoples further south such as the Mbole north of the Ndengese made similar figures. After a drawing by Grégoire in* Revue Congolaise, *1913/14, 4: 181*

selection? Or was it a single workshop or a few workshops in adjacent villages that produced them? Fieldwork can perhaps still yield clues to answer these questions.

How did such prime works come into being? As commissions? Very unlikely, since they had never been seen before. One suspects that the creation of masterworks was responsible. Carvers among the Kuba used to make extraordinary icons as bravura pieces, to attract fame and business, or merely out of fun, or for some pious reason, as in the case of the man who carved a statue of his pregnant daughter, a type of icon hitherto unknown (see Plate 6.6). Cups in the shape of equestrian figures astride antelopes or a dish supported by the lower half of a female torso with three persons kneeling on its rim are obvious bravura pieces, destined to make the sculptor known. The antelope horn in wood which imitated the spiralling line neither of one type of antelope, nor of another but a line in between was a piece made for fun by a carver who would exhibit it and ask which antelope's horn it represented! Such isolated bravura type works can be found almost everywhere. So perhaps they were the seminal inspiration for prime works. If so, the early attempts to create prototypes were destroyed by the carvers until they were satisfied with the new prime work.

But prime works became prime works only if they were copied. Why

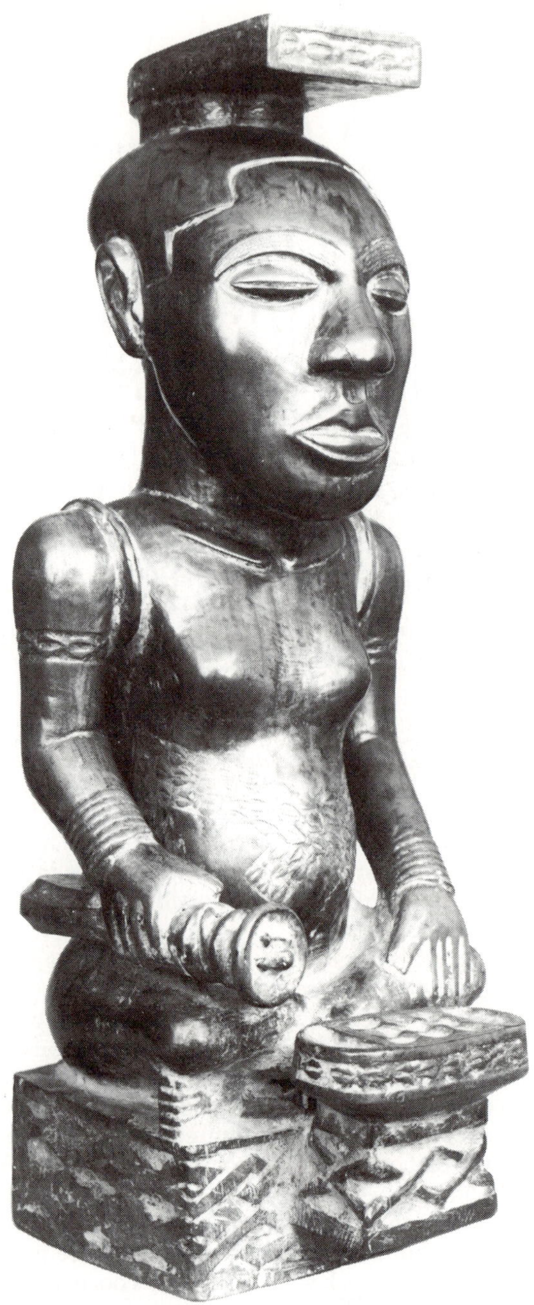

Plate 8.4 *Statue of king Shyaam aMbul aNgoong. Wood. Used as a commemorative statue on display in the palace. Also possibly as a charm to facilitate childbirth in the royal harem and as a receptacle for the breath of the dying king. British Museum.* c. *1750. This is one of the earliest carvings in a set of* ndop, *as they are called*

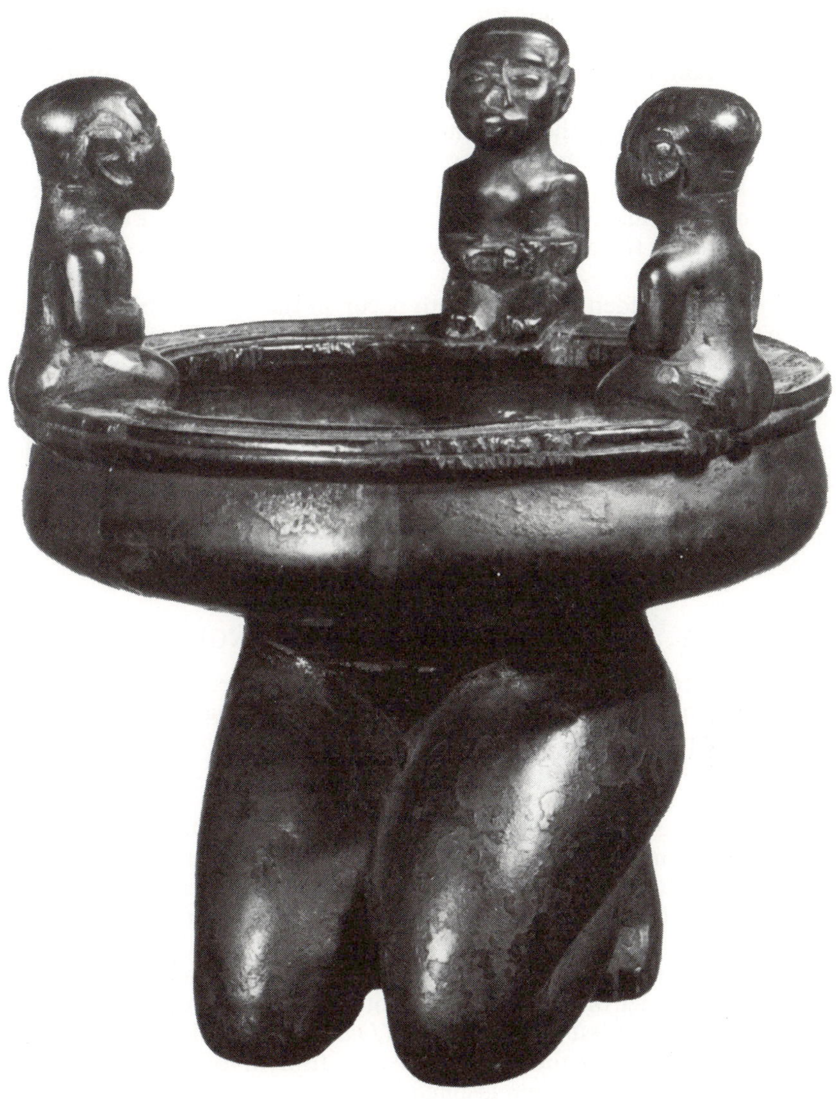

Plate 8.5 *Vessel. Wood. Used as a household object for patricians. Kuba kingdom. Yale University Art Gallery. Height 18cm. Acquired in Africa 1906. Northern Kuba near Sankuru. This is the vessel in Frobenius 1907: pl. p. 233. Note that part of the rim and one figure have been 'totally restored', i.e. added. We are not certain that there were originally three figures nor, if so, whether the third one was similar to the two others. Meaning, probably not symbolic. Possibly a pun*

would masterpieces be adopted? Often the acceptance of a new prototype was linked to the appearance of a new institution or to the fact that it perfectly exemplified a concept relating to a major institution. Thus, the rise of Kuba royal statues is to be linked with the decline of regional cults and the rise of a cult for the king as 'nature spirit'. The statues were a step in this evolution. We will never know if a king thought of them and commissioned them, or if a bravura piece brought the idea into a king's head. The *edan* bronzes of the Ogboni cult, the single most important organ of government in many cities of western Nigeria, must be linked to the very development of the cult (Drewal 1980; Morton Williams 1960; Williams 1964). The intended use of any class of icons is therefore the only clue we have as to why masterpieces could become prime works.

Drift and sudden mutation both occur in the visual arts. To a certain degree, every icon is both a replica and an innovation, never wholly original, rarely a totally slavish copy. Comparisons determine what are unique items: masterpieces never imitated, or prime works, and what are replications. The ability to find the relationships between different works in such terms is crucial to art history. One must assess not only innovation, but the magnitude of change as well. For change in art is bound up with other cultural and concomitant social changes. Not only the nature, but also the magnitude of change in art can be clues to the nature and magnitude of concomitant change in society and culture as well.

CREATIVITY, SOCIAL AND CULTURAL CHANGE

Society, culture and the arts are in reality so closely intertwined that it seems evident that change in one must be accompanied by change in the other. Art is an integral part of culture and individuals participate in social life through the medium of culture (Layton 1981:187). Moreover, visual art is often directly tied to specific institutions, which use art objects as their tools. So the axiom that change in art reflects sociocultural change seems well founded.

A good example of these relationships is the case of the Fatimid portals discussed in Chapter 5, pages 97–9 (Sourdel-Thomine and Spuler 1973; Hrbek 1977). After the conquest of Tunisia in 909, the Fatimid ruler did not settle in pre-existing capitals for long. He built his own city, Mahdiya, so called because he claimed to be the Mahdi, the Messiah who announced the end of the times. As the leader of the Shi'i branch of Islam, he was considered to be a divinely inspired, almost God-like leader *(Imam)*, a sacred king. In this city he built his mosque and the first portal appears in front of the mosque (A.D. 916). The portal may well have been inspired by Roman triumphal arches nearby as Lezine (1966) argues. That would be fitting for the almost-divine king. The founding of a new capital itself was not an innovation. Early Abassid Caliphs and their representatives in Tunisia, the Aghlabids, had done the same. When the Fatimids conquered Egypt (969), they founded a walled town nearby other such foundations and called it al-Qahira, 'The victorious', which became Cairo. There, too, they built congregational mosques and the portal reappears. The portal became a constituent part of any congregational mosque officially commissioned by a ruler until well after the fall of the Fatimid caliphate, the last known one being built by Baibars, the first Mamluk Sultan in 1267–69.

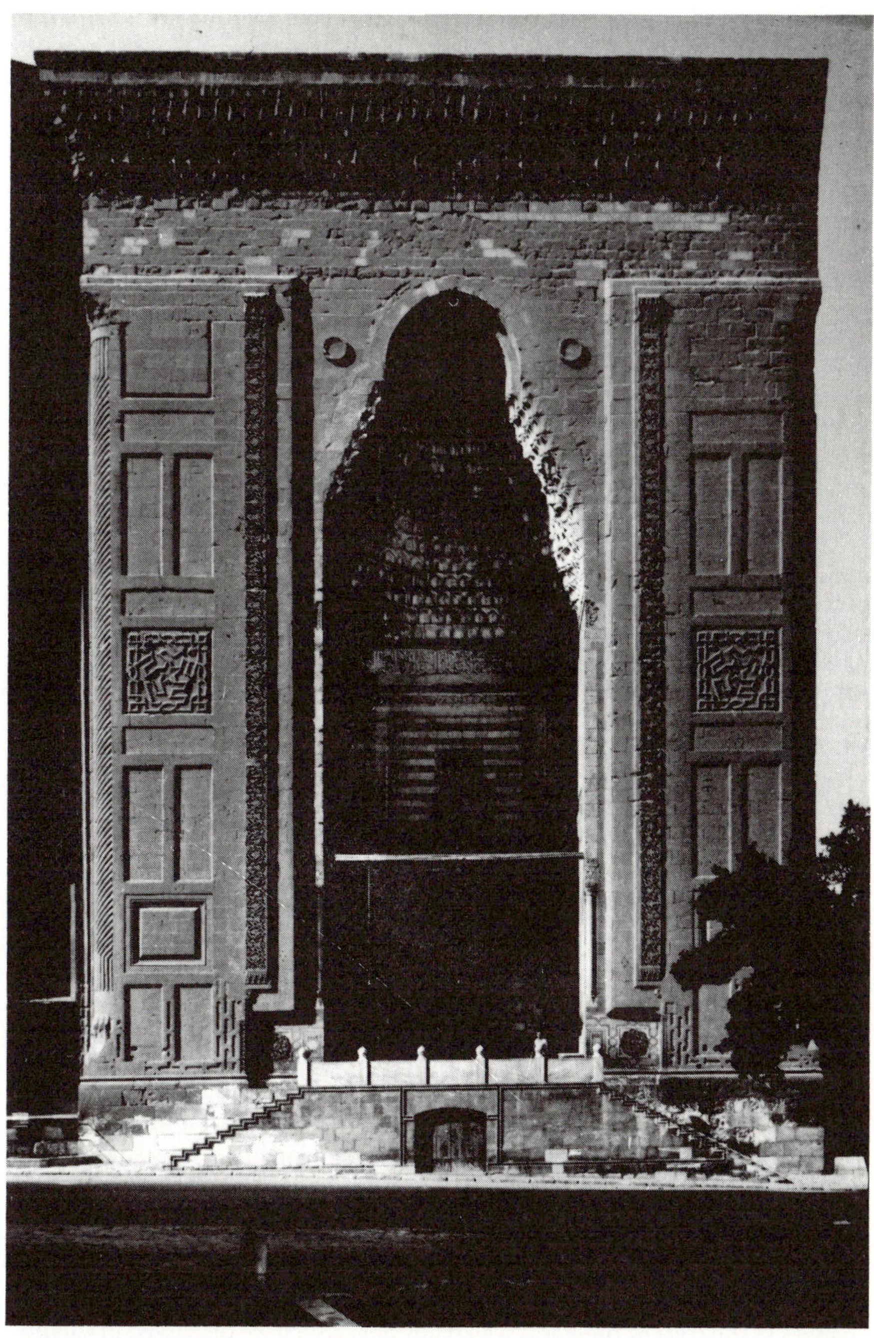

Plate 8.6 *Main portal. Sultan Hassan Madrasa and Tomb Complex. Small semidome with stalactite* (muqarnas) *vault. Stone masonry. Cairo. Height 34·5m. The arch is 20m high. 1361. Shape of portal introduced by Baibars for his madrasa 1262/3*

Later rulers no longer commissioned congregational mosques and the portal does not reappear. It has been suggested that this was due to the lack of space in or nearby the city within reach of a congregation. But other reasons are more compelling. For Mamluk sultans greatly favoured large complexes of tombs and madrasa, which had been introduced in Egypt just after the ousting of the Fatimids by Saladin (1171). As a good Sunni – the name designates the other major branch of Islam – he fought the Shi'i heresy by introducing the madrasa, schools of higher learning where theology, law and the Arabic disciplines were taught. The madrasa complex in architecture had first been developed in Iraq to house the institution. Coming from Syria, Saladin knew about it. Soon domed tombs for royal patrons were attached to the complex. The Mamluk domed tombs of Cairo derive architecturally from the Turkish regions whence they came and the name for such a tomb, *turbe,* is Turkish. The whole complex then is not a mere reaction against Shi'i doctrine, but reflects the cultural origins of the Mamluk.

The madrasa complexes came to develop a portal of their own from *c.* 1262/3 onwards, the most famous being the portal of Sultan Hasan's complex (finished 1361). It greatly differs from the Fatimid model. Madrasa portals derive from façades in the Konya area of Turkey and, like the tombs, reflect the cultural origins of the Mamluk rulers. But both Fatimid and Mamluk portals were built in front of major religious buildings, commissioned by the ruler. In that sense the Mamluk portal was the successor to the Fatimid structure and the people of Cairo were certainly aware of the continuity, which left a trace in the structure. The Mamluk portals seem deeper than their prototypes in Turkey (Sourdel-Thomine and Spuler 1973; Hrbek 1977:10–69). From these brief indications, the reader can see the interplay between large-scale soccial change, large-scale change in culture (religious ideas), and the evolution of portals. The art form followed socio-cultural change and expressed it. In this case, art was an epiphenomenon.

But does change in art always reflect prior change in culture and society? It can be argued that drift is autonomous. Layton (1981:178) lists among his sources of creativity the act required to give an idea tangible form – even a copy is not identical to its model. He also mentions elements of design that are not culturally significant and where free variation is allowed as well as the expression of fresh metaphors. It might be accepted that the appearance of new prime works, i.e., masterworks that are adopted by the public and therefore copied, are different from cases of drift. The latter could be autonomous developments. Thus, when the Kuba adopt a variant on an earlier pattern and recognize it as a new design, by giving it a name, this need not reflect any change elsewhere. Nevertheless, even here the practice is related to the encouragement of innovation in design, itself related to the growth of the patrician class, its need for novelty to offset itself from others and to fuel rivalry between the patricians themselves, and, in turn, this is related to the growth of the Kuba bureaucracy from the eighteenth century onwards (Vansina 1978). The invention is autonomous but it reflects a climate of historical change. The changes in the style of the Faras wall paintings, which we discussed in Chapter 5, page 95, clearly reflect wider – and prior – cultural change. They are linked to the variable influence of Coptic monasteries as against the ordinary hierarchy of the bishopric, the political and ecclesiastical variations in relationships with Muslim and Coptic Egypt, access to Jerusalem and Syria for pilgrimages, and contacts with Byzantium. Stylistic change, moreover, was accompanied by changes in the languages used at Faras (Greek, Coptic, Nubian and Greek/Coptic alphabets), and the appearance of new themes, mostly the depiction of new saints. Coptic saints appear in periods of Coptic influence, Syrian saints in periods of Syrian influence, and Byzantine saints when Byzantine influence became important (Michalowski 1967). Arguments have been developed around the graphic signs on the paintings that allow us to deduce changing over from Monophysite (Christ has one nature) to Melchite (Christ has two natures) beliefs. These are detected in the varying depictions of the madonna. No doubt changes in styles at Faras also reflect wider and prior changes in culture and society.

The adoption of new themes or new prime works means the adoption of new icons, new metaphors, which indicate in turn either the creation or the development of new ideas. Very often this points to institutional development, as most works of art are linked to institutions. In this regard, even masquerades are institutions, and the appearance around 1870 of the round Tsayi mask (Plate 7.2) reflects social change. The masquerade was then created to express the insecurity of the times. Before that time, the Tsayi had been prosperous, mainly in the slave and ivory trade. From that time onwards, they began to be bypassed and beset with competitors, not only for their trade, but also for their land (Dupré 1968).

The autonomy of art lies in its formal evolution. It was perhaps a necessity for Kuba kings in the eighteenth century to develop royal statues to commemorate former kings, and to express an evolution in convictions by which kings were now seen not merely as priests of nature spirits, but as powerful nature spirits themselves. Hence the reason for the adoption of the practice to commission one commemorative statue per reign (Rosenwald 1974). But the work of art itself, the form of representation of the ruler, was an autonomous invention, deriving from earlier forms such as tiny statuettes used in a portion of the Kuba territory near the border to represent nature spirits and by larger statues that probably existed – as they do now – in component chiefdoms to honour an ancestress of a chiefly line. We do not know exactly what the sources were for the new icon, but we can be almost certain that they were local works.

Even Kuba bravura pieces, which best exemplify the autonomy of formal creation, are still linked to a climate where innovation is prized. They embody the competition between carvers and the dynamics of competition between the patricians. They bought such works as a sign of prestige or power, and they encouraged artists to produce new icons, to be used as counters in their own competition for the display of influence. That could only happen in a kingdom whose bureaucracy was constantly expanding.

Lastly, one may wonder whether the visual arts themselves ever led to change. Is art always a passive epiphenomenon? As new metaphors were created, new tools became available for social or cultural use. For instance, every development in body art, textiles, costume or household goods, could be used to stress differences between social strata, and innovation was encouraged when the urge was felt to express such increased differences. Art works as concrete symbols could crystallize unfocused ideas and mobilize people. There are very few records of such an evolution, however. Perhaps the most sensational is the use of existing statues of St Anthony in the former kingdom of Kongo, where the common people adopted them as a symbol of their understanding of Christianity as a truly African and not European church, in turn linked to their opposition against the ruling class and against the lawlessness and insecurity produced by internecine conflicts led by this class. St Anthony had previously been a favourite saint of the European missionaries and had been especially invoked by the Portuguese for lost causes and for the downtrodden. He now became the most important saint in heaven; he was seen in the statues as a black person carrying the child Jesus (Randles 1968:149–51, 157–60; Balandier 1968:263). But even this example is not conclusive. The new conception was a development of the old, and it did not occur before the ideology of 'Antonionism' developed, but concurrently with the larger cultural reinterpretation. It is a good example because it shows an interaction between art and culture that is the answer to our question. Art as a crystallizer of metaphors in tangible form could lead to change by focusing ideas and by mobilizing support. But art could only do this as part of a wider cultural system, as a reaction to some action outside, which art then in turn influenced. Art is an epiphenomenon but epiphenomena can sometimes take the lead by the effects they produce.

CHAPTER NINE

THE CREATIVE PROCESS: FOREIGN INPUTS

DIFFUSION: THE MEANS

Creative processes can be an internal process only (Kroeber 1948, 1953; Sapir 1916; Graebner 1911; Vansina 1968), as we saw in the previous chapter, or they can be induced, at least in part, by external stimuli. Foreign objects, techniques, stylistic characteristics, themes or motifs could influence the taste of the public and set artists thinking. Quite often such influences enriched the local repertoire, and in art as in other fields they were quite important. If the *oikoumene* had such a varied output, it was largely due to the fact that its artists had access to a larger storehouse of forms and concepts from which to choose. The notion of regional tradition itself implies that mutual exchange between neighbouring styles did not reach very far and isolation prevailed. Hence, considerable originality was preserved, but a major voice for inspiration, external stimuli, remained mute.

Historians have shown over the last generation that the much-touted isolation of African communities was largely illusory. There were always relations between communities and societies, stretching like a web over most of the continent and of a more intensive and longer lasting nature than is realized even today. If this is so, mutual borrowing must have played a much more substantial role in art than has appeared hitherto. On the one hand traditions might be less local than they seemed to be at first sight; on the other, the persistence of great originality of expression in neighbouring and communicating communities needs to be explained.

Borrowing of foreign objects certainly occurred. A ewer of brass of Richard II of England (1377–99) was found in coastal Ghana, no doubt having arrived there by the caravan trade from North Africa (see Shinnie 1965: ill. 88; Fagg 1970:51). Foreign objects were also copied. Two copies of Coptic lamps have been found near the northern fringe of the Akan speaking area in Ghana (Arkell 1950). The originals, probably made between A.D. 300 and 700 also no doubt found their way by caravan trade. Chinese celadon abounded at one time on the East African coast, and there are reports of the export of textiles from Benin on the Loango coast (Martin 1972:63). Knives from the Ubangi bend area (Fig. 9.1) were used as insignia just north of the Malebo Pool more than 500km downstream. Such cases can be multiplied. Foreign objects were both imported and copied.

The process of borrowing involves first the means to acquire foreign stimuli, usually objects, and secondly the demand for their imitation or new features inspired by them, a demand that was always internal. Trade was the most powerful mechanism for spreading foreign objects. Intercontinental

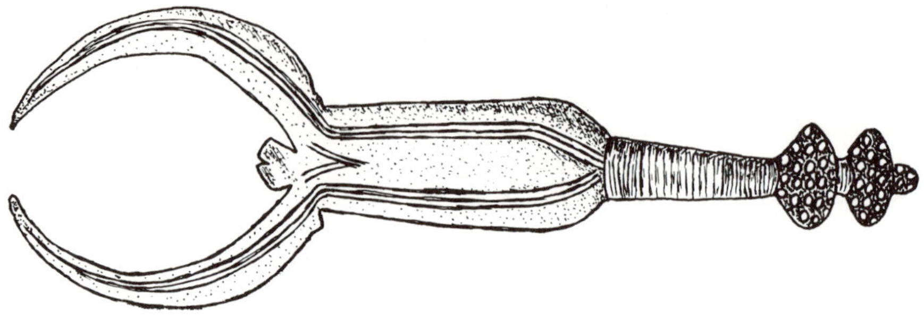

Fig. 9.1 *Ubangi knife. Iron, handle in copper and brass. Ngabe, Congo. Height 49·5cm; width 15·5cm. Drawing in field 1964. The Tio near Brazzaville acquired such knives of honour from the Ubangi river as a byproduct of trade. The original symbolism (female sex) is lost in transit*

trade, for instance, is responsible for the wide diffusion of cowrie shells from the Indian ocean over very large parts of the continent. Already in Roman times the shells were traded from the Maldive Islands to North Africa. Later they became the currency in interior West Africa and seeped inland in portions of eastern Central Africa. It was only in southernmost Africa that the cowrie did not penetrate. Trade was the artery binding the countries of the intercommunicating zone, the *oikoumene,* together. Between this region and other parts of Africa, important channels of trade existed from early times. In the Indian ocean, trade between East Africa and the Red Sea is reported by the first centuries A.D. Trade from the Sahara and beyond created the wealth of Leptis Magna, on the coast of Libya, during the same centuries. After the Arab conquest of northern Africa, a trans-Saharan trade, fuelled by the demand for gold, developed on a large scale and ultimately brought the whole of West Africa into contact with the *oikoumene.* In East Africa intercontinental trade was first limited to the coast but ultimately, as interior trading networks developed, by *c.* A.D. 900 affected central Africa (Zambia and Shaba) as well as Zimbabwe and even the Limpopo area. In Equatorial Africa the interior network of trade along the Zaïre grew under the stimulus of the expanding slave trade after *c.* 1530.

But other means for the dissemination of foreign objects were also common. In northern Africa pilgrimages were very important: Christian pilgrimages to Jerusalem, as well as Muslim *hajj* to Mecca, not to mention minor but favourite sites of pilgrimage such as the shrine of St Menas (before A.D. 400), Egypt's national saint, west of Alexandria from where typical bottles were exported to as far away as Tunisia and even to Europe (du Bourguet 1967:81, 90). Pilgrimage explains why the battle standard in seventeenth-century Ethiopia was an icon of Christ with the thorn crown, brought from Jerusalem (Doresse 1972:15, 85, 117, 216). Legend has a ruler of Mali bringing an Andalusian architect back to the Niger from his *hajj.* South of the Sahara, however, pilgrimages, where they existed, were much more localized. Other religious concerns could lead to dissemination here. Thus, in the 1870s, a Loango healer visited the area near Cape Lopez and carved statues in his own style to serve as protective charms. Later they were moved to near the Gabon estuary (Nassau 1904:308–11). In 1902 a Kuba king commissioned a similar charm from a renowned medicine man of eastern Kasai (Songye) and his statue was displayed for years at the very hub of the Kuba capital (Vansina 1969b:19–20).

Besides trade and religion, occasionally other mechanisms were responsible for the diffusion of alien objects. Travelling entertainers ranked high among these at certain periods, and introduced both dances and masks to places that had not known them, with or without cults. Olbrechts (1959:26) noted such dynamics as early as the 1950s. Another of these occasional mechanisms was state expansion, and the concomitant spread of its dominant culture. In Shaba, this is clearly responsible for the spread of so-called Luba styles, themes or motifs and especially the caryatid thrones, as the Luba empire grew in the eighteenth century. An oddity in the same area is the case of the Lunda empire where certain objects such as swords spread as it expanded, but where no Lunda art developed at the centre (Crine-Mavar 1968; Neyt 1981:219). Rather, the dominant group relied on the import of art from their western reaches, from central Angola. The larger empires elsewhere in Africa must also have acted as disseminators of art. In the case of Benin, this accounts for the occasional use of Benin objects in shrines all over the Niger Delta beyond Benin's realm proper (Horton 1965b; Alagoa 1972: index 'bronze' map 186). In southeast Africa, Zimbabwe-type buildings in the provinces of the country are witnesses to the same mechanisms (Garlake 1973).

One mechanism which was once often invoked must be rejected: the effect of migrations, which were believed to have transplanted whole material cultures in a short time over huge distances. Such spectacular changes have been very few in Africa. Migrations may have killed more artistic traditions than they inspired novel ones. Thus Sape sculptural traditions were ended by the Mane invasion in Sierra Leone (Fage 1977:508–9). The clearest case where immigrants implanted a truly novel material culture was in Madagascar.

DEMAND FOR FOREIGN WORKS OF ART

Once foreign objects were in a community, and there must have been some in all African communities, they could be imitated but that would occur only if there were a demand for them. Typically, some were rare prestige items, linked to ruling groups in states or to big-man status elsewhere, for example the shells of the Indian Ocean conus that were rare, costly and visible signs of prestige in the interlacustrine area and as far west as Lake Mayi Ndombe in Zaïre. Foreign objects, such as a 1785 ship's bell in the nineteenth-century treasure of a Gabonese king, or European crowns in the hands of big men on the Gabon River, and the monarch of the Ogowe Delta, are as typical as the use of a Benin mask by the nineteenth-century ruler of Igala on the lower Niger (H. Bucher, personal communication; Ben Amos 1980a:20–1). The equivalent of European curiosity cabinets existed in some African courts as among the Kuba.

Such prestige items, where possible, could be copied. The case of the double bell, an emblem linked to political and military authority, is striking. The item was first made along the West African coast somewhere between the Ivory Coast (its probable point of origin) and Benin. But it spread across the forest all the way to great Zimbabwe, where it was in use before A.D. 1450. It

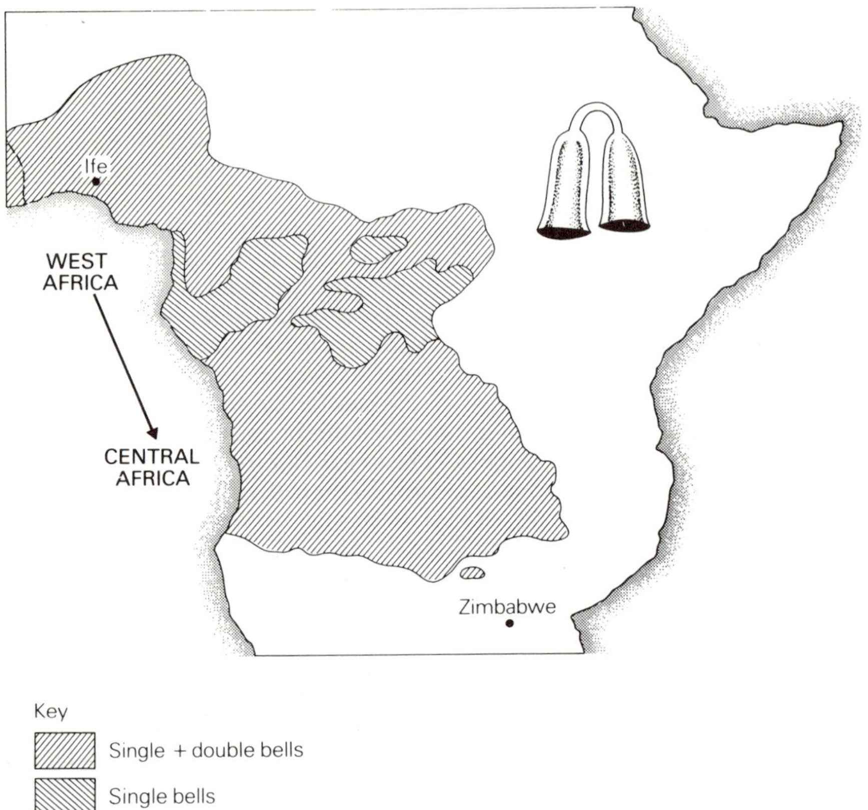

Fig. 9.2 *Distribution of double bells in Central Africa*

was imitated by local smiths everywhere as far south as the Zambezi, but Zimbabwe imported its bells apparently north from the river. In the Ubangi bend, the production became large enough so that double bells began to function as a currency (Vansina 1969a and Fig. 9.2).

Local workshops copied a whole item or a technique, motifs or a theme according to local demand. Thus, lamps in ceramics from North Africa, probably from Kabylia first, reached northern Nigeria with the trade, and local populations as far south as the Middle Benue adopted such lamps. They did not exactly copy the North African models, but it is still easy to recognize the kinship between a Hausa lamp or one of the Middle Benue (Jukun, Ibi) and its North African prototypes, by general appearance, perhaps by the use of the colours common in North African lamps but also common in Nigeria, but especially by some of their shapes and motifs (Krieger 1965–69: vol. 2; ill. 207–9, 219–20). In this case, no emblems were desired, but a new utensil was widely spread. Nevertheless, it is more than likely that it first spread among the dominant groups.

Goldweights had to be borrowed by Akan traders in gold, if they were not to be cheated. They borrowed from the middle Niger and borrowed shapes and motifs with them. Later, however, they rendered European objects and motifs in brass goldweights and in gold ornaments as well. Thus some weights occur in the shape of Dutch teapots. Indeed, the Akan lion developed out of English lions (Ross 1977).

Copies were rarely perfect and did not need to be; if utilitarian objects were practical, they would do. Prestige objects or objects for entertainment would conform to local taste except that the prized foreign features would be retained, as in the case of the Nigerian lamps or of arabesque forms of decoration in West Africa. Here the decoration, as on the nineteenth-century walls of Akan palaces is recognizably inspired by North Africa, but nevertheless quite different (Denyer 1978:79–81; Prussin 1980: esp. 71).

Demand for utilitarian objects and for prestige items was supplemented in some cases by religious demand as well. Converts needed mosques or churches and built them after the pattern of those who converted them. Thus, Schacht (1954) was able to show Ibadi Muslim influence in West Africa, because Fulani mosques there lacked a minbar, the staircase/pulpit, a typical Ibadi feature, even though today Fulani are Sunni Muslims and have been so for centuries.

The importance of a demand is highlighted when the existence of factors blocking diffusion, despite extensive contacts, is recognized. Diffusion and borrowing are not automatic processes at all. The presence of Catholic art forms in Mozambique and even in Zimbabwe during the seventeenth century did not lead to a diffusion of Christian iconography nor even of Christian principles of sculpture. In lower Zaïre, the Christian art of the upper classes did not influence the popular arts, but the reverse occurred probably after 1665 and the collapse of the old kingdom. The relationship between Islamic art and other arts in West Africa, where there has been intensive contact for nearly a millennium, is even more striking. Apart from decorative art and some architectural designs, Islamic artistic influences on the main arts south of the Muslim frontier have been slight. In turn, West African sculpture did not influence northern Africa at all. Even in architecture it is much easier to see that the great city gates from northern Nigeria were not copied further south than to find positive links between architectural plans. Those that are found in western Nigeria may be more closely compared to the classical *impluvia* houses of northern Roman Africa (Ojo)! The main reason is that Muslim tradition condemns idols, and that western African peoples prized representational sculpture and used 'idols' profusely in their religions. West African sculpture and Islam could coexist, as Bravmann (1974) has shown for the middle belt of Nigeria (Nupe) and for northern Ghana, and as can be seen from toys near Lake Chad and in the Middle Niger belt. Nevertheless, as Islam gained, sculptural traditions receded, probably because the traditional religions receded.

Moreover, Islamic architecture in West Africa did not slavishly follow Northern African Saharan practices. Wherever, as in the Middle Niger belt, an autochtonous technique (mud architecture) and tradition of architecture had existed before the arrival of Islam (Gruner 1977; Prussin 1968), Muslim features were translated into the traditional medium and even traditional shapes were often conserved. There was no perceived need literally to copy all the features of North African building. In reverse, West African dome construction and mud architecture *may* conceivably have influenced northern African styles, either in Roman times as seen by Roman concrete construction or even as late as the ninth and tenth centuries, when it is conceivable that the filletted dome, first used in Tunisia, was in fact borrowed from the Sahel. This type of dome has been ascribed Iranian origins but the chronology is unsound (Lezine 1966:79–88). No known West African architectural influences travelled north later. Not only were the inhabitants of northern Africa Muslims, but they felt so superior to West Africans in other respects, that they had no desire to copy anything, except in the realm of music and dance.

A similar barrier is evident in Ethiopia. Muslim and Christian antagonism here minimized artistic interchange. It occurred but was restricted to minor features such as the decorative margins of manuscripts or embellishments in buildings. Christians copied arabesques, *hareg* (Leroy 1967, 1968, 1973; Chojnacki 1973) and eleventh-century Fatimid embellishments found their way around some windows of Lalibela churches, where keel arches, beloved by Fatimids, are occasionally found as well. On the whole, the refusal to borrow, however, is the striking conclusion.

In most instances one should not attribute lack of borrowing between different regional traditions to lack of contact, but rather to active cultural – often religious – barriers. Conversely, where borrowing occurred, its explanation requires a consideration of the reasons why it occurred. Just an inherent belief in automatic diffusion will not do.

DISTRIBUTIONS*

Claims for borrowing are arguments based on the presence of distributions that exceed the range in which the products of a workshop or a set of workshops are used. In the past, distributions have been established mainly when it was suspected that the range or a feature of an icon exceeded the range of an ethnic group. But ranges coextensive with the claimed extent of an ethnic group should not be postulated as freely as they usually are. The situations are much more dynamic than that. Thus, in the Kuba kingdom, the distribution of cephalomorph pipes belongs to the central and eastern parts and is found outside the kingdom in the east. The use of double-headed cups is restricted to the west of the kingdom and beyond its borders between Loange and Kasai. It occurs far to the south in another 'area' that of the Pende (Himmelheber 1960:733, 383–4; De Sousberghe 1959:15, 140; see Fig. 9.3). Ideally, the unit to examine is the workshop or the village only. Lack of data forces us, in practice, to consider whole ethnic groups.

The first point to examine must be the criteria by which distributions are plotted (Vansina 1968). These are always selective. They include features of style, theme and motif, usually in relationship to whole works of art. Use alone is not a valid criterion because it does not necessarily relate to a given object, thus, 'emblems of leadership' are a meaningless category for comparison. Use tied to some formal criteria is valid, such as 'adzes as emblems of chieftainship'. But the main relevance of use is to show that certain features of the objects compared are or are not arbitrary. Slits to see through in masks destined to be worn are not arbitrary. They are essential for the wearer of the mask. But, say, an elliptic shape of the mask is arbitrary and hence valid for comparison.

* See Schmitz 1967.

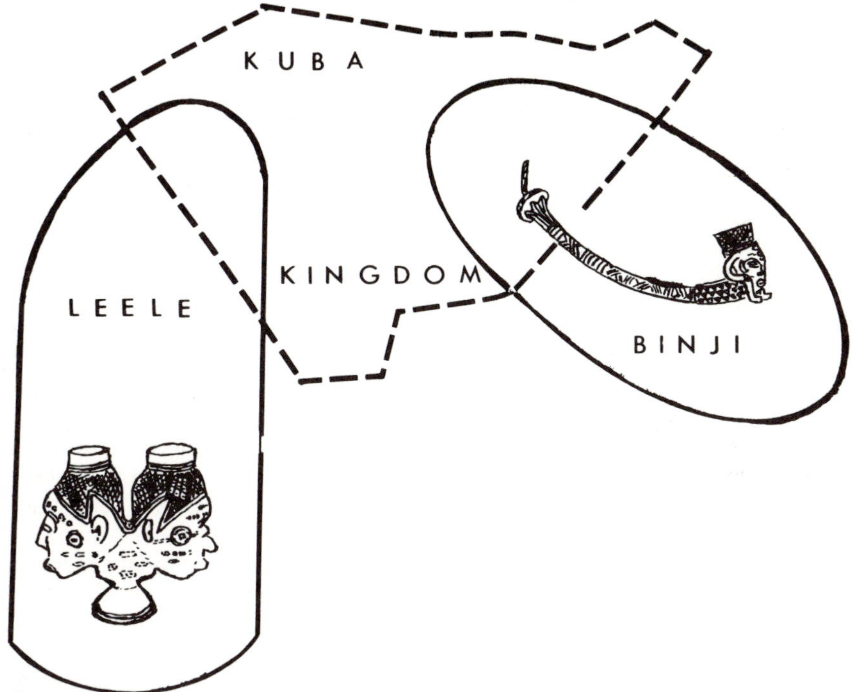

Fig. 9.3 *Topogram of the distribution of doubleheaded cups and cephalomorph pipes in and around the Kuba kingdom. 'Kuba' can designate the kingdom or a wider area. 'Kuba' objects are not homogeneously distributed over either area*

Distributions will only reflect borrowing, if the features compared are arbitrary, and the more arbitrary they are, the stronger the proof. The fundamental criterion for a valid distribution is the criterion of quality. It refers to several independent arbitrary features in the artefacts compared. One such feature may be due to chance, just as a concept may by chance be rendered by the same word in two entirely unrelated languages, but several common features cannot be attributed to chance. An example commonly given is that of the game of chess. The number of squares used, the types of pieces used, the rules by which they move, are all arbitrary. To find the game in Iran and in Europe cannot be accidental (Kroeber 1948). Similarly, if all the characteristics of two churches correspond: from orientation, to cruciform shape, to presence of an apse in the same position on the plan, to the details of clerestory windows, and so on, then the churches must be related. If two pieces of sculpture correspond in general position in space, in proportion, in the carving of major detail and in small detail, especially 'irrelevant' detail, they must correspond. Here the major criterion for establishing affinity is the one used in morphological analysis and to establish stylistic series.

Another criterion, the criterion of quantity, is useful after the criterion of quality has been established, but it can never be used alone. This criterion states that if several different artefacts, or techniques, or non-material features are found, each individually quite similar through arbitrary features to artefacts, techniques or non-material features in another locale, then all these objects, techniques or intangible features are related. In fact, the criterion either strengthens the case for borrowing for a single type of object, or builds a circumstantial case for intensive connections between the places where the objects were found. An example of the first situation is the comparison of Kuba velvet cloth of the nineteenth century with velvet cloth from the Zaïre coast dating from the seventeenth century. The patterns correspond (cf. Plate 9.1 and Fig. 7.3), the techniques correspond, and the term to designate such objects corresponds (Vansina 1978:220). The linguistic evidence, quite independent, yet tied to the object, is decisive. An example of the second situation is the town of Begho (Nsoko) in Ghana when compared to the Upper Middle Niger *c*. 1400 and later. Not only were similar shards of pottery found, but similar ceramic goldweights occur, foreign objects from North Africa occur near Begho, techniques for weaving cotton were apparently similar, and filigree techniques from the Niger were imitated at Begho. The evidence adds up to an impressive set of similarities in unrelated items, not easily invented independently. It points to intensive contacts, and these indeed existed from perhaps 1350 onwards. Gold from Ghana moved through Begho to Jenne on the middle Niger and did so until late in the nineteenth century (Posnansky 1979).

Sometimes it is quite difficult to establish that borrowing must explain the distribution as independent invention could be equally likely. A widespread decorative design known as the Hausa knot in West Africa consists of a plaited

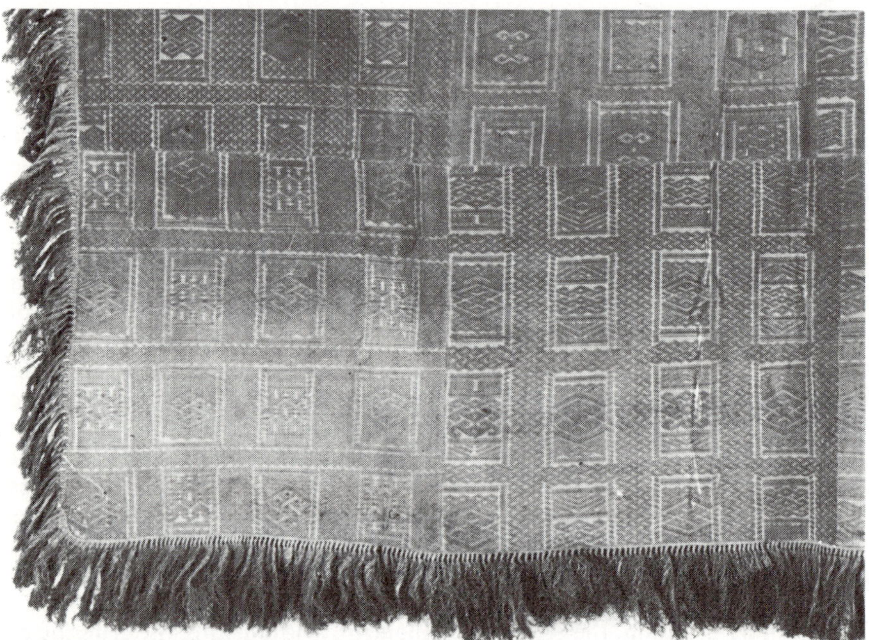

Plate 9.1 *Cloth. Raffia. Pile work, with dyed thread. Used as cloth for aristocracy. Lower Zaïre, former kingdom Kongo. Ulmer Museum. 219 × 175cm. Before 1659. The patterns recall those current* c. *1900 in Mayombe (northern Kongo) as well as some on ivory horns* c. *1552. Technique as in modern Kuba work, which derives from this type of work. Kuba patterns are also geometric but not identical with these.*

set of guilloche patterns often on an angular background. These are known in northern Nigeria, Somalia, the Kuba country (*imbol* design) and North Africa, from Byzantine mosaics onwards (Fig. 9.4). Even though the design looks complicated, in fact it is not. It also occurs on early Iroquois pottery. Yet along

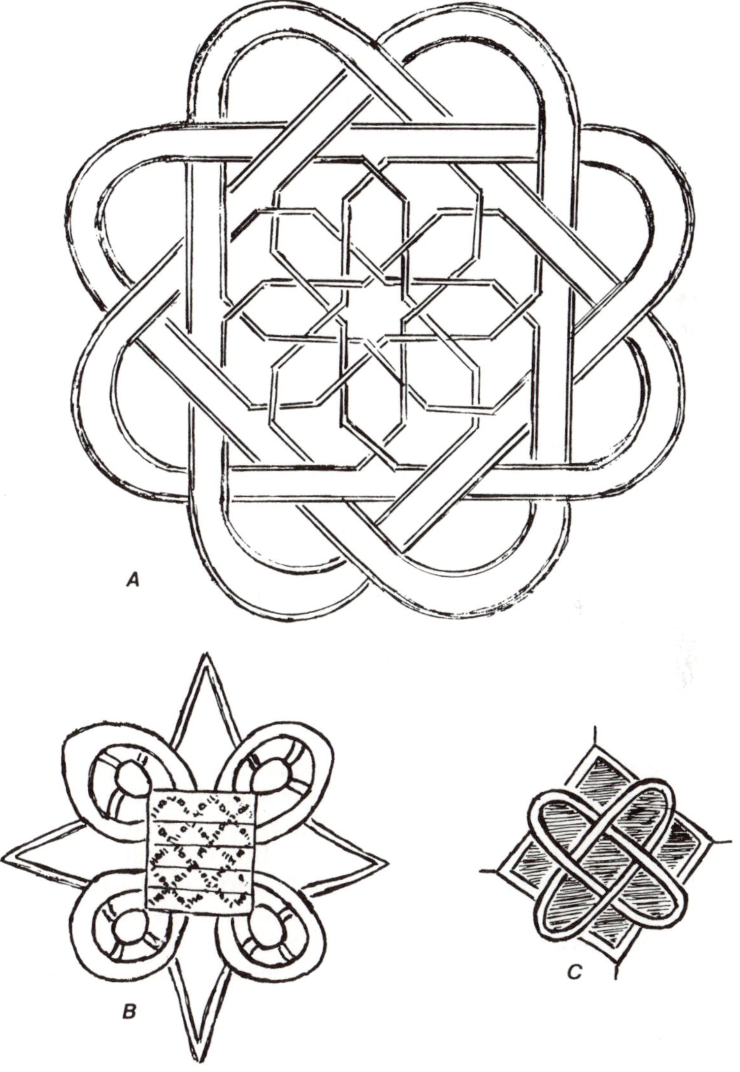

Fig. 9.4 *Interlace knots. A Moroccan, miniature in book, 19th* c.*; B Akan embroidery with muslim magic square, 20th* c.*; C appliqué and embroidery on man's robe, Kano, Nigeria, 20th* c. *For a northern Yoruba instance see Plate 2.3. These knots in West Africa probably stem from North Africa, whence they came as decorative patterns on textiles. In North Africa they derive from such knots on mosaics and pottery since Byzantine and Roman times. Elsewhere in Africa (East, Central) and Asia (India, Tibet, Indonesia) the motif may be independent – it is a simple pattern – although Muslim influence in some areas also may be relevant. In North America (Iroquois pottery) the motif was probably independent. A after G. Vidalenc,* l'Art Marocain, *Paris 1925: pl. XIV. B after Picton and Mack 1979:156 (acquired 1951). C after R. Sieber,* African Textiles and Decorative Arts, *New York 1972:38 (acquired 1948)*

with other similar motifs it is hard not to consider that the continuous distribution throughout northern Africa into Somalia on the one hand and Nigeria on the other is just due to chance. In such a case the means for borrowing must be carefully considered. Trade and especially the presence of these motifs on clothes and leather belongings makes it quite likely that indeed all the patterns from the Mediterranean to the Gulf of Guinea are related, but not the isolated Kuba instance. There – until further notice – we must accept independent invention. Guilloche was quite common in Kuba decoration, whether in angular or rounded form and so was plaited guilloche. It was easy for a Kuba inventor to consider turning the design into a self-contained unit in space. When one knows that the Kuba topologically did in fact invent most of the possible geometric combinations of patterns, the explanation becomes convincing.

The arbitrary character, the possibility of independent invention and, in an accessory way, the presence of unrelated similarities in other objects, are the main criteria by which distributions should be evaluated and hence the main criteria by which they should be established.

RECONSTRUCTING DIFFUSION

Once a distribution indicates the likelihood of borrowing, the researcher must then establish its date, direction, and mechanisms. He must provide a hypothesis that will adequately and economically describe the borrowing process. To provide all these elements is often quite difficult, and distributions themselves must normally be complemented by other data. Thus, direction of borrowing can sometimes be found by a consideration of related distributions. When I am considering one particular type of throwing knife, very similar in two places, one below the equatorial African forest and one north of it, and even strengthen my case by showing similarity in the terminology, I still do not know in which direction the knife spread. But in considering that it is but one of many similar shapes in the north and the only one in the south, one can argue that the feature was older in the north. It has had time there to agree more with local style in other matters and especially to have flourished to the point that all these other forms of throwing knives exist. The direction then would be north to south (McNaughton 1970, Cordell 1973). But the argument is easily reversed. Perhaps the item travelled south to north, but acquired a new significance in the north which led to an efflorescence of derived forms. Given a respectable age, this could have happened. In this case we can be reasonably certain of the north to south movement because the distribution ultimately includes the throwing sticks seen on ancient Egyptian paintings and similar objects on rock art. The distributions of various forms fall into two general groups, an f-shaped knife and others, and the total distributions involved most of the forest people (who cannot throw such knives!) as well as some groups on its southern fringe. North of it the distribution was quite solid. A consideration of the use of the weapon (in open land, especially in short grass steppes) together with the archaeological data, makes it certain that the spread was old and from north to south. The weapon may be Egyptian in origin or Nubian or Saharan and it was first made in wood. When it diffused into the forest, the data on use make it clear that it became a prestige item, linked to big men and

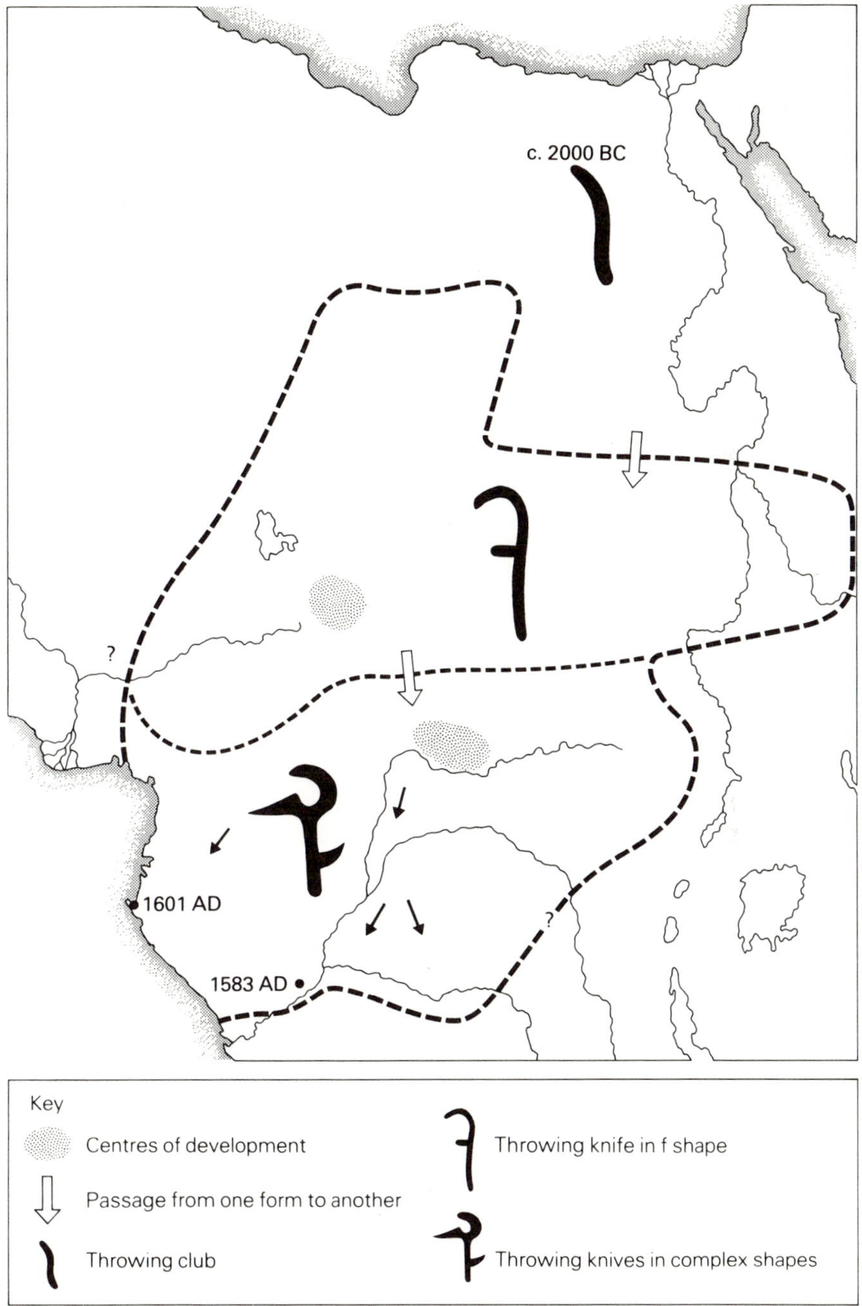

Fig. 9.5 *Distribution of throwing knives. The original form was probably the throwing stick of the Middle Kingdom. Total spread before the 17th c. crossing the forest where such objects acquired new uses. After D. Cordell, 'Throwing knives in Equatorial Africa',* Ba Shiru, *5 (1), p. 95 and own data. Also after P. McNaughton,* African Throwing Knives, *MA thesis, University of California, Santa Barbara, 1971*

even south of the forest it did not turn again into a widespread weapon (Fig. 9.5).

The circumstances of use, the 'core' quality of the object in a society and culture, the shape of the distribution, the shape of related distributions and archaeological data all have some bearing on the previous illustration.

ASSESSING THE EVIDENCE

A few recipes for dealing with distributions as evidence, especially for dating and origins exist (Wissler 1926; Hodgen 1942; Kroeber 1953). Thus a very large distribution, well integrated, *can* be a sign of great age. Broken distributions, that were never unified, must result from independent invention. The distribution of two related variants where variant A either encircles variant B completely or where the distribution of A is broken by B into two or more parts, indicates that A is older. Overlapping patterns of several related variants can be ordered in time sequence by treating them as successive breaks of once-unbroken distributions, especially when other criteria show that the tentative sequence forms a stylistic or technological series. Distributions in the shape of a thread or as a sequence of spots in linear pattern show by which route it took place and often give a clue as to the carriers, such as traders, fishermen, pilgrims and so on (Fig. 9.6).

But none of these arguments, or less often used arguments taken from distributions, is foolproof. Situations are known in general anthropology, linguistics and archaeology where similar shapes of distribution occur and yet have been shown not always to indicate the correct older, younger variants, sequences of variants, origins and dispersal routes. On the whole, such indications are often correct, but not always. They can be used to elaborate a hypothesis, but need to be backed-up by other evidence, either direct or drawn from linguistic evidence about the names used for the objects in the cultures and societies involved.

Any hypothesis of diffusion must ultimately be tested by an attempt at falsification by assessing the likelihood of contrary or variant hypotheses. If a particular explanation is only as likely as another or is only the most plausible one of three or more likely possibilities, it must be discarded. It follows from this rule that the more facets one considers in a reconstruction of borrowing, the more elements enter into play and the more difficult it becomes to arrive at different hypotheses that are equally valid. Hence, the hypothesis that fits all the data becomes much more convincing, and it becomes all the more convincing the more simple it remains. Elegance in hypotheses is not only a logical virtue, but carries conviction.

Conversely, it is easy to show that proposed borrowings are false or unproven if any improbability in dating, distance, mechanism of transmission, circumstance of use, or reason for borrowing appears. Thus Baumann (1969:57) sought parallels between statues from eastern Shaba (Zaïre: Hemba) and Sabaean statuary. The time difference of almost two thousand years, the lack of direct communication between the east coast and eastern Shaba before the nineteenth century, the lack of comparable objects in the whole intervening area, as well as the great length of the indirect route via the Zambezi that could have been used after *c.* A.D. 1000, rule the comparison out.

Moreover, it does not give any reason for borrowing and is based on too few points of genuine resemblance.

In this it differs greatly from the imitation Coptic lamps in the shape of a bird found in Ghana at Tarkwa. True, the distance to Egypt is great, but since

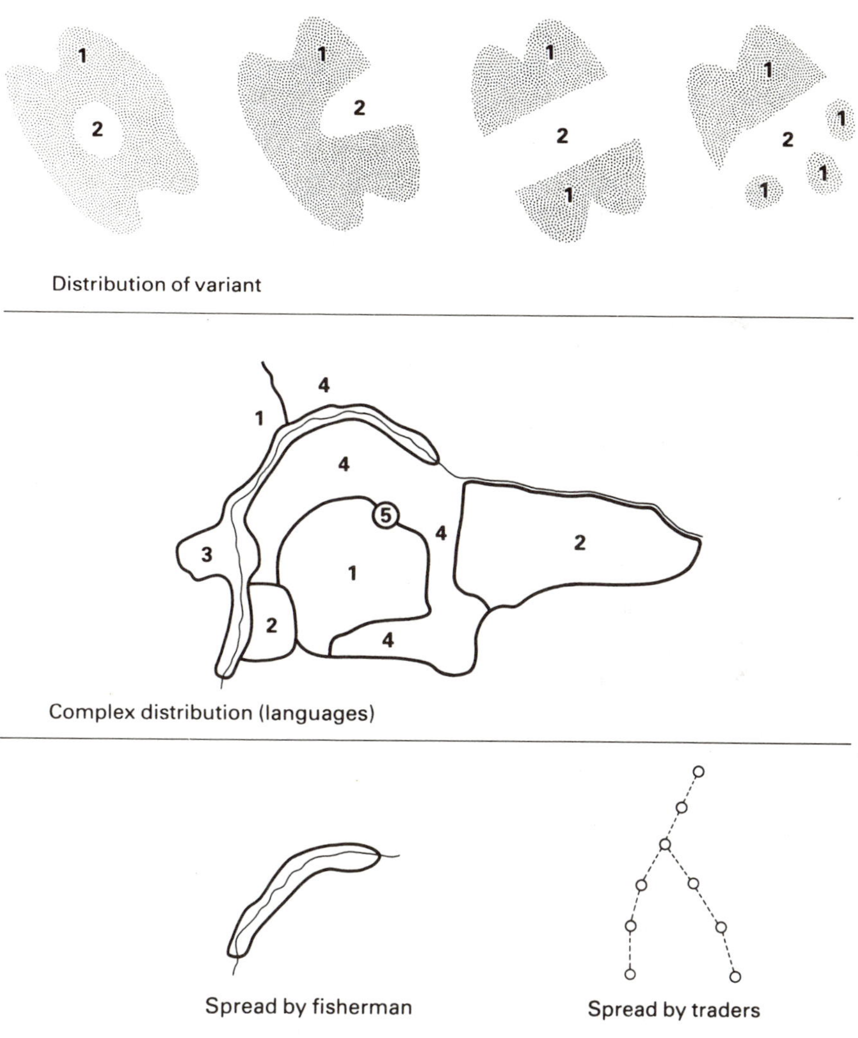

Fig. 9.6 *Distribution patterns as indicators of age and manner of distribution. The case 'complex distributions' shows the distribution of languages in the great Ubangi bend*

the eighth century A.D., and perhaps earlier, communications existed with the Middle Niger and later (A.D. 1300+) to Ghana itself. The object fits in well with evidence that all oil lamps in western Africa derive from North African models. The Ghanaian examples in copper alloy, cast in lost wax, were found in this century but may be centuries old, or their prototypes may be. Moreover, both Ghanaian lamps are of very different type (one hanging, one on a stand), and both can be matched by Coptic examples. In addition, in the Ghanaian copy of one lamp, the functional hinges and support of the original type of lamp were misunderstood and miscopied, a clear sign that the Tarkwa lamp is a copy and that the direction of diffusion was from Egypt to Ghana. It also shows that the Ghanaian object was not intended to be used as a lamp. The lost-wax technique, also found in the originals, would indicate that the Ghanaian lamps were not made before either the fourteenth century, when trade links to the Middle Niger developed, or at the earliest before the ninth century or so, when the first archaeological evidence for lost wax in West Africa appears – in Nigeria. We also do not know for which use the copies were intended. The alternative hypothesis is European introduction of both types of Coptic lamp into Ghana. They were then copied in the twentieth or in the late nineteenth century. But this is much less likely than the hypothesis of borrowing. Because of the remaining gaps in the evidence, the Tarkwa finds should not be given undue weight, however. One cannot, for instance, use it as 'proof' for direct Egyptian-Ghanaian links before Islam, but an historical connection cannot be denied.

Suspicious distributions should first of all be checked for authenticity. The Ghanaian lamps were brought from a certain Kwabena Bonda in Tarkwa on 7 April 1936. He said they came from old graves at Attabubu in Brong country, precisely the area where influence from the Upper Middle Niger was strongest (Arkell 1950). It is a pity, of course, that the site of discovery was not checked out, since dating might have been possible if the objects had been found in situ in the grave.

Not so likely is the provenance of two late Isis statuettes found in Shaba. Undoubtedly of Pharaonic times, even though late, their being found on the Lualaba Lakes is surprising. A check reveals that their finder stopped off in Cairo on his way to Belgium. The hypothesis that he acquired them in Cairo and mixed them with objects from Shaba is far more plausible than the notion that he found them in Shaba, saw nothing unusual in them, and added them to potsherds he was going to bring to Belgium (P. de Maret: personal communication). Such cases occur more frequently than is often realized. At least one other case where data from Kasai and Rwanda-Burundi were mixed has also been discovered (de Maret 1980b).

As we shall see in the next chapter, complex distributions are a feature of all major hypotheses in art. The more complex or the larger they become, the more they tend in fact to rely on fewer criteria. The data sometimes simply cannot carry the weight of evidence that is deduced from them. Thus, one scholar attempted to bring all concave, heart-shaped faces in western and central African wood sculpture into a single distribution, surrounded by other forms (Lavachery 1954). First the distribution is not as continuous as he claims it to be; it is dangerous to claim that the heart-shaped faces must be younger than the other forms, because they are surrounded by them, because the area of distribution is too vast and too irregular. The fatal flaw, however, is that the feature chosen is too simple. One can, after all, only carve concave, convex or on the plane! And concave carving, while sparing a nose and forehead, yields a heart-shaped face. The effect has therefore probably been invented many times over. The whole hypothesis must be rejected out of hand.

CHAPTER TEN

WIDER PERSPECTIVES

FORMAL FRAMEWORKS

Having examined the properties of art works, including their creation, the next task is to discuss the formation of complex hypotheses by which one moves from an understanding of the history of individual or small groups of works to a valid history of art for large regions. The core of such hypotheses is to be an account of the succession of styles, for art history is above all a history of shapes. Many hold that shapes have their own dynamic and point to impressive long-lasting drifts of whole styles to prove it. Once the correct stylistic sequence is found, technological and iconographical questions can be woven within it, just as changing social circumstances of use and meaning should be. Most scholars in the field have attempted to develop coherent frameworks based on similarities of form, either over space or over time, extending the techniques of stylistic seriation discussed in Chapter 5. In this chapter I shall first examine such attempts and propose an alternate model of presenting formal change over time, then I shall argue that stylistic sequences by themselves do not lead to a history of art. It is not merely a question of placing such sequences in the context of technology, iconography or general history. Rather, a general historical sequence must be the fundamental framework, the point of departure for any history of art, a history in which formal development is only one of the elements, however essential, along with technological and iconographical development.

FRAMEWORK BY ART AREA

A dated object in sub-Saharan art is as rare as a crock of gold at the end of the rainbow, and chronological arrays have therefore been impossible to set up. The situation is so pronounced that all handbooks of 'African art' had to be content with the description of typical icons and stylistic characteristics in one area after another, implicitly all at the same temporal level. Conventionally, they begin with the West African Sahel and end with eastern and southern Africa, perhaps, I suspect, because we read from left to right, from top to bottom! The classification obtained is entirely artificial, however useful it may be for the tentative identification of objects from unknown provenance, a major concern to museums, dealers, collectors and scholars. Because styles and types of objects differ greatly from one regional tradition to the next, the system works well enough, but no genuine art historical hypotheses were developed at all. Ordering in time was not considered; ordering in space took its place.

The system works. It may be unavoidable but it breeds disaster. In the end it fails to allow for the erection of larger frameworks of generalization because complex historical hypotheses are lacking. More immediately, its major drawback is the ethnic and spatial implications it carries as hidden baggage. I have already dwelled on the vague and often false assumptions of equating style and ethnic group (*contra* Fagg 1965), the problem raised by replications found in several ethnic groups but deriving from a single prime work, the disparity of styles within a given ethnic group, especially with regard to different classes of objects, for example, statues and masks, and on the fluidity of ethnic concepts over time. Here I focus on the equation of ethnicity and space, to the exclusion of time.

Students of sculpture imagine the map of West and Central Africa to be the juxtaposition of ethnic territories. Some areas are large, such as that of the Bambara or the Senufo in the Sahel. Some are tiny, such as those of the 'grasslands' of the Cameroons, where every single town is a separate unit. Typically, art historical maps either provide separate enlargements for the grasslands or just list all the names. Some areas correspond to states such as the Asante empire or the Kuba kingdom, some refer to a wider meaning of ethnicity as when Akan appears on the map and Asante is left out. In some cases purely geographical criteria become ethnic labels. The 'grasslands of Cameroon' are an obvious instance. The use of linguistic criteria makes sense only when the languages grouped together are dialects, that is, mutually understandable, for in that case the situation attests to frequent social intercourse. Beyond this, linguistic criteria are unconvincing because they refer to a common cultural heritage too far back in the past to be of use.

The spatial units compared vary, but more insidious than this is the conviction that ethnic territory is homogeneous. All the workshops of a given ethnic unit must make the same sort of icons, the same replications from the prime works accepted in that unit. The corollary is that different ethnic groups must have different styles and different prime works. None of these assumptions needs to be true. Usually they are not. Lastly, by some sleight of hand, it is assumed that all visual arts of an ethnic group partake of the same features. This is not true, as a comparison between a Kuba mask and a royal statue (Plate 8.4) shows, and this is only in the realm of sculpture. Style is closely tied to genre and genre in turn to the institution that commissions and uses the works.

Thus we have maps of stylistic areas. The style of each ethnic group is characterized by the style of a 'typical' icon only. In West and Central Africa this was almost always a statue or a mask carved in wood, 'typical' because well known from collections and illustrations. The earliest objects stemming from 'Tribe X' became the gauge by which all later objects were evaluated, for these earliest objects became the visual concepts associated by scholars with 'Tribe X'. Objects acquired later were dubbed atypical if they did not conform to the gauge, even though perhaps acquired half a century after the first gauge had been set, the atypical works greatly outnumbered the typical ones! Such 'typical' works were then held to have been made all over the associated ethnic area at all precolonial times and to represent a tribal style valid for *all* objects in *all* media made in that area, as a shorthand expressing the genius of the ethnic group inhabiting that area. Possibilities for confusion and error are staggering.

Even the most rigorous art historians did not altogether escape the consequences. Professor F. Olbrechts (1959:29–31) is rightly remembered for his objective approach towards the determination of stylistic criteria. In his attempt to establish the stylistic areas of Zaïre during the 1930s, he grouped the sculpture from known ethnic provenance together, using both stylistic criteria such as proportions and treatment of detail and the simultaneous occurrence of replications from different prime works in the ethnic area. His greatest success was the discovery of the Buli long head style, which must stem from one workshop, or even from one hand (see Plate 5.4). One of his failures in the same general body of data was to see that he had a large subset of typical icons and a simultaneous occurrence of these which set that body apart from the general mass of works included under the ethnic name 'Luba'. It was not until the 1970s that F. Neyt (1977) disentangled this and using Olbrechts' own methods set up a Hemba style. Neyt was himself still entrapped by ethnicity. Typically enough, he starts his account by claiming that the Hemba were not Luba, nor Luba-Hemba, but a separate ethnic group. That is irrelevant! What matters is that in a series of geographically contiguous workshops, art work was produced that differed stylistically from all other artwork. A set of interrelated styles in the sculpture of ancestor figures was shown to exist. The same workshops also produced some other works, such as a distinct type of mask, not found elsewhere. But it is not at all certain that in all sculpture or in architecture these places differed in fact from others surrounding them. The 'area' holds only for ancestor figures and to a certain extent two or three other traditions of replication for wood sculpture. These figures may well be 'typical' for the area, but they cannot stand as a shorthand for all sculpture or all visual art there.

Areas are best thought of in relation to one type of object at a time. Failure to do this erases the spatial imprint left by the dynamic evolution of art. To present a Kuba area, including the Kuba kingdom, or – as is now usual – add to it some neighbouring territories and then to describe Kuba 'visual art' is an unwarranted generalization. We saw that the distribution of double-headed cups differs from that of cephalomorph pipes (they barely overlap!) and the distribution of ceramics, types of masks made out of plaiting, divination instruments and so on, all vary. Anthropologists have learned, a generation ago, to forget about culture areas (Kuper and Van Leynseele 1978). Art historians should also realize that such mapped areas are reifications, spurious concrete-looking realia, which evaporate under scrutiny.

Alternatively, areas of art can be thought of in relation to a reference group that has historical validity. Thus, the Asante capital, Cairo, Fes, etc., were central locations that set tastes and exercised a wide influence around them. The total assemblage of art objects in such capitals would be the corpus of reference and the art area then represents the area over which works were influenced by elements of this corpus. Such art areas need not be exclusively thought of in political terms. In medieval European architecture, there was a Scheldt, a Meuse and a Rhine style, that is, styles by river valleys which served as arteries for trade and for the transmission of art. Art areas in this sense have for the most part not been established yet south of the Sahara. In many cases, the poles of artistic attraction were not dominant enough to create obvious areas around them. Art areas are problems to be studied realistically in relation to societies over time, and not shorthand means to provide a classification of objects.

It is tempting to claim that stylistic areas of the classificatory type are useful to orientate novices in the field. But even this may well be illusory. The massive reductions of reality are too great. Thus, students introduced to a Dogon (Mali) art area may never realize that much of the architecture should not be seen in Dogon confines only, but as a variant of a body of mud architecture typical for the whole upper Middle Niger. They can be baffled by some statues which look as Senufo as Dogon or other works that can be confused with products from the southeast of Dogon country. These can be distinguished but sometimes the distinction is finer than other distinctions even within the Dogon or within the Senufo styles. Any advantage of the system as an introductory guide is soon lost.

Classifying by art area has led to the inability to produce any wider framework for the arts of sub-Saharan Africa, even though the need for such a larger framework has been felt almost from the onset of svstematic inquiry. Various attempts were made to enlarge areas, to group several or many of them in larger units, but the reductionism invoked in this led to failure. Some authors speculated on the basic distinction between pole-like sculpture and rounded styles. The first respected the geometrical form dictated by the tree trunk, the other broke away from it. Gradually the round style came to be seen as naturalistic and the pole style abstract. Some sculpture that was not pole-like at all came to be lumped with the latter because it was perceived as abstract. In 1960, Leuzinger's book even charted the two types. Lavachery (1954) attempted to replace the pole/rounded opposition by one featuring concave or convex faces, and Baumann (1929), a culture historian, attempted to link the 'round' styles to political centralization, but none of these attempts succeeded. There were too many cases such as the case of Ife where both pole-like (or schematic) and round (or naturalistic) works coexisted (Willett 1967). None of the distribution maps showed convincing distribution areas. Textbookwriters were not convinced, and continued to subsume ethnic style areas into practical units such as 'coastal peoples of Guinea', 'Gabon' or 'East Africa' (Bascom 1973; Vogel 1981).

TREE MODELS: NIGERIA FROM NOK TO YORUBA

The spatial criterion writ large implied the refusal to hazard any art historical hypothesis. But such hypotheses could be attempted and frameworks constructed larger than the consideration of a single style sequence. One paradigm imagines an art form as developing from a single point of departure whereupon drift and mutation yielded various branches that further developed in their own right. The 'tree model' is often used in historical linguistics. A model of this type has been elaborated for some Nigerian styles. According to this model, the ceramic art of Nok (before 500 B.C.–A.D. 200) was the common trunk. After transitional terra cotta sculpture found at Yelwa (A.D. 200–700), the next chronological body of sculpture, both ceramics and copper alloys, is a body of art from the city of Ife (*c.* A.D. 100–*c.* 1500). Ife, the model claims, grew out of the experience of Nok. Later works of Ife coming closer to modern

Yoruba sculpture are thought to date from between 1500 and 1700. By then Yoruba sculpture was established, that is, sculpture in wood, copper alloys, ivory and fired clay practised in the cities of western Nigeria inhabited by Yoruba speakers. From *c.* 1600 onwards, a large state, the Oyo Empire, ruled much of this area. A body of art from the city of Owo was seen as an offshoot of the art of Ife. It probably flourished in the fifteenth and sixteenth centuries. Owo ceramic figures also show relationships to another body of art: the copper alloy heads of Benin (Plate 5.7 and Fig. 5.5). We saw in Chapter 5 how a stylistic sequence for the brass heads and the plaques of Benin was established by which the earliest works were those that seemed most similar in technique and in style to those of Ife (pp. 95–7). Because Benin traditions claim that the technique was imported from Ife, the whole sequence was then seen as derived from Ife, from *c.* A.D. 1400 onwards. The art continued to flourish at the court there until our own day. Thus, from the single trunk of Ife art branches arose that became Yoruba and Benin art. Within Yoruba art many lines can be distinguished, Owo being one of the most prominent. Over the years stylistic similarities were found and used as evidence to back up the proposed sequence, and further evidence is still being marshalled to strengthen the framework. The latest work by Eyo and Willett (1980) presents it clearly. Figure 10.1 graphically represents the hypothesis as it now stands.

WESTERN NIGERIAN STYLE RELATIONSHIPS*

Over the years circumstantial evidence such as the discovery of Owo art seemed to strengthen this hypothesis more and more. But archaeology also recovered another body of sculptures in the general area, at Igbo Ukwu, that is totally different from any of the arts described, moreover, that is dated to *c.* A.D. 800–1000 (Plate 4.4; Shaw 1970b). There is no tie between Igbo Ukwu and Nok sculpture either. So it is now evident that the tree model is inadequate to explain the evolution of all sculpture in ceramics and copper alloys for Nigeria. Once this is acknowledged, other troublesome facts must be brought up. First, there exists a body of so-called Lower Niger bronzes, which do not belong to either the Benin or Ife traditions (see Plate 6.2). Some have tentatively been attributed to Owo on the grounds mainly of similarities, but others belong to one or more otherwise unknown traditions. Two figures of a group found near Jebba and Tada on the middle Niger have been dated to *c.* 1300 (linked to Ife) and to *c.* 1400–1500 (linked to Owo?). Then there is a large corpus of stone figures found at Esie and undated, but certainly old (Stevens 1978). These have tentatively been shown to exhibit some characteristics derived from Nok but are definitely hard to place. One scholar links them to Yoruba art, while another denies any direct link with either Yoruba or Ife.

One of the weak points of the hypothesis has been the chronological gap between the main body of Nok and the art of Ife. Only the two ceramic figures of Yelwa bridge it, but they are geographically eccentric and stylistically far removed from the main Nok styles. Moreover, they are removed in a direction away from Ife art. Then there is the fact that despite similarities, the main style of Ife is naturalistic and the main styles of Nok are not. To compound the

* See Shaw 1978; Lawal 1977; Fraser 1980, 1981a and b; Tunis 1981.

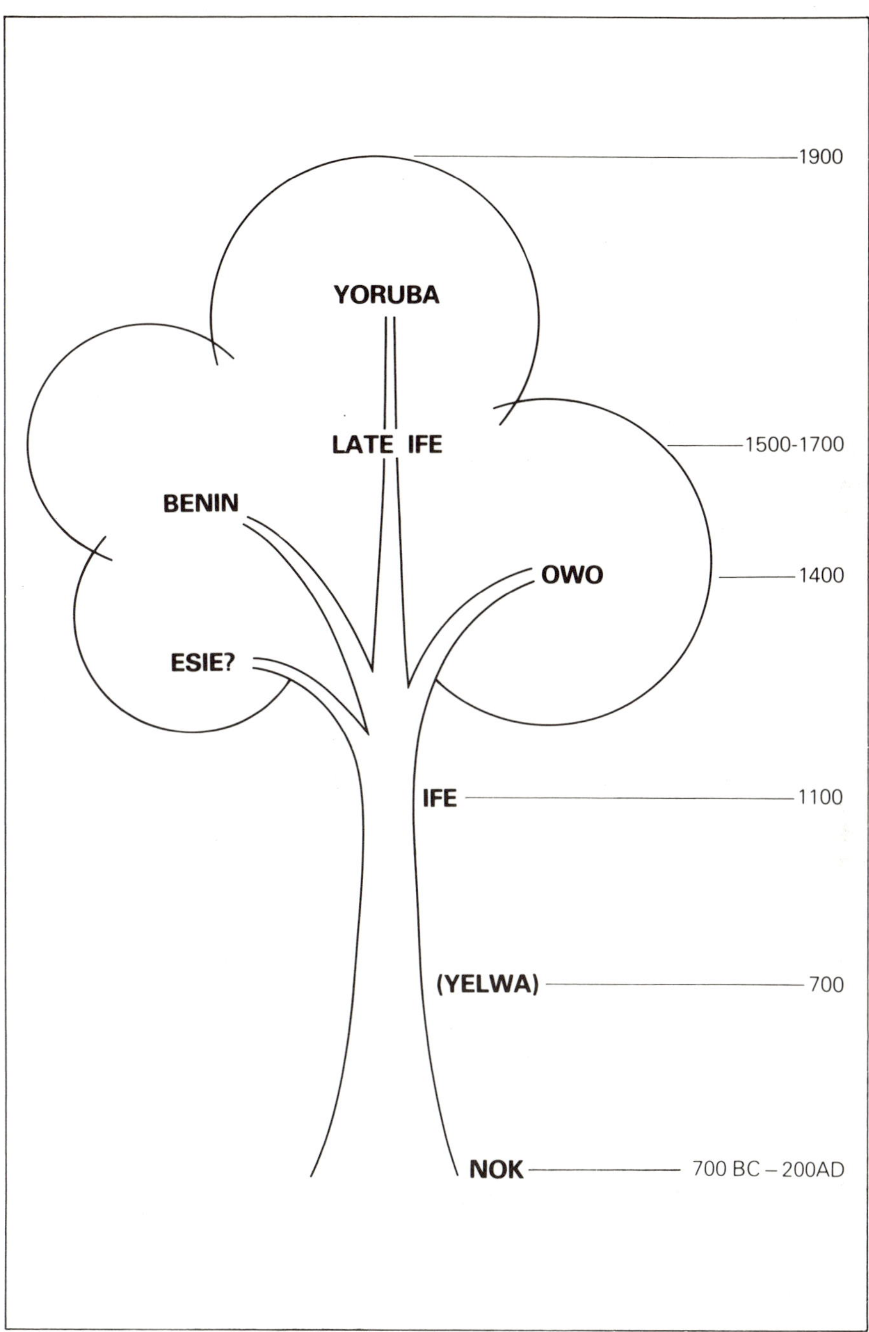

Fig. 10.1 *A tree model. Western Nigerian art styles*

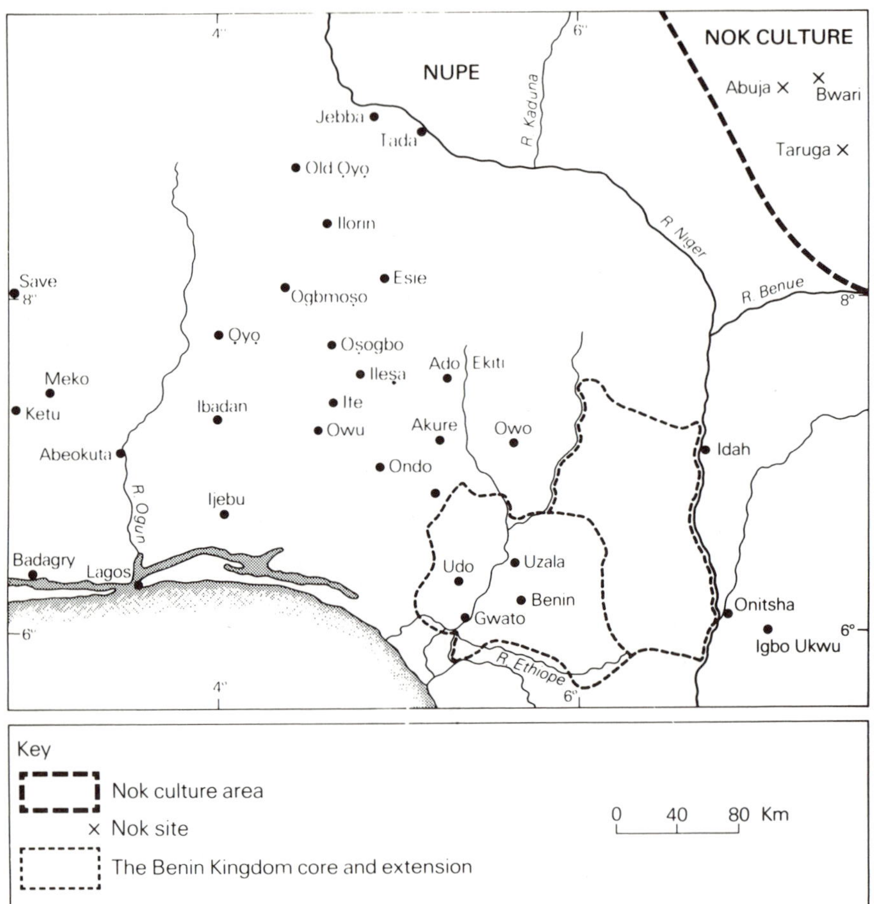

Fig. 10.2 *Major towns and archaeological sites in western Nigeria*

problem, it should be realized that Nok sculptures have not so far been properly published and that over the vast area and long periods covered by that term, several styles may in fact be lumped together. It is not at all certain that the *main* inspiration for the Ife corpus derives from Nok. Similarly, although Ife objects have been found in Benin and vice versa, Benin brasses probably do not derive *mainly* from Ife. The dates can be construed so that work at Benin partially overlaps with that of Ife, but the stylistic filiation is unconvincing (Fraser 1980, 1981a; Tunis 1981).

The links between Yoruba work and both Owo and late Ife are being better established especially for work in metal and ceramics. Part of the difficulty here stems from the use of different media, namely wood and stone sculpture. A major problem moreover is to decide whether perhaps the Esie stone sculptures may not be closer to later Yoruba wood sculpture than the latter would be to ceramic work from late Ife or Owo. Whatever the general proposed links, the tree model certainly fails in the attribution of only a single

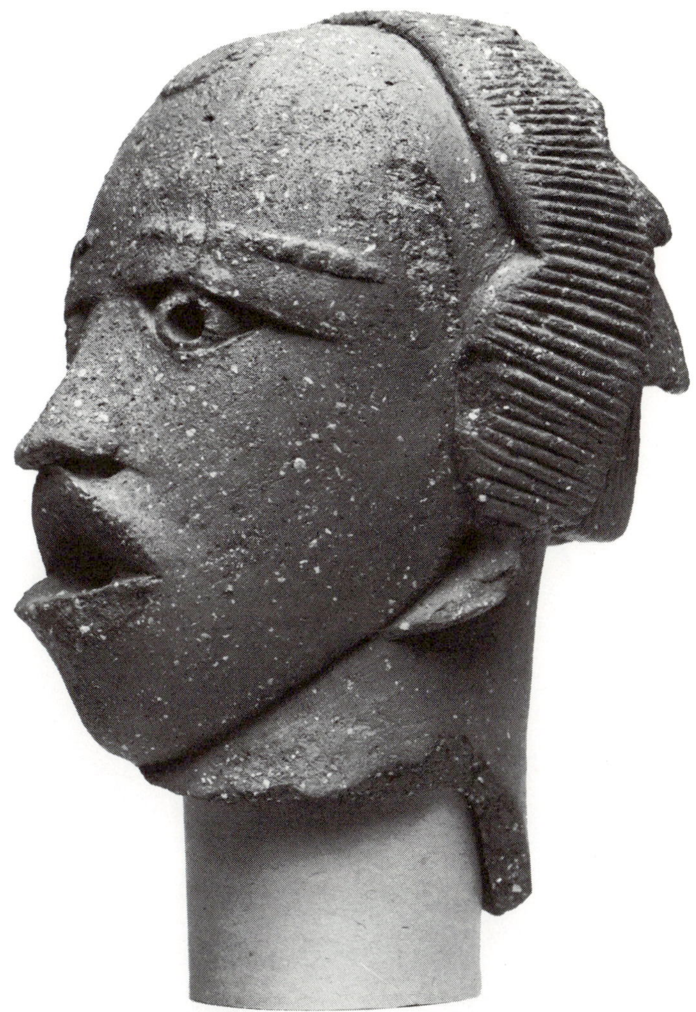

Plate 10.1 *Part of a figure. Pottery. Jemaa (Nigeria). Lagos Museum. Photo British Museum. Height 14ins. Found in 1943 at the Tsauni mine. Dated between 500 B.C. and A.D. 200. The object is usually labelled 'Nok culture', as are many others found in northern Nigeria, usually during tin mining. 'Nok' objects share a few traits such as the pierced eyeballs, but otherwise belong to many different styles*

'ancestor' to Yoruba art. Owo, Esie and Ife should be considered as some of its roots. Moreover, every sixteenth-century Yoruba city was also at the root of later art.

Beyond this, the model contains three major flaws. First, it tends to generalize from a set of specific works, the ceramic and copper alloy figures, to all of sculpture, which is unwarranted. Benin sculpture in wood or ivory differs markedly from the canons of Benin copper alloy heads, for instance, and Yoruba characteristics of statues of the earth mother, used in the Ogboni cult, cannot be extrapolated to stand for all Yoruba art.

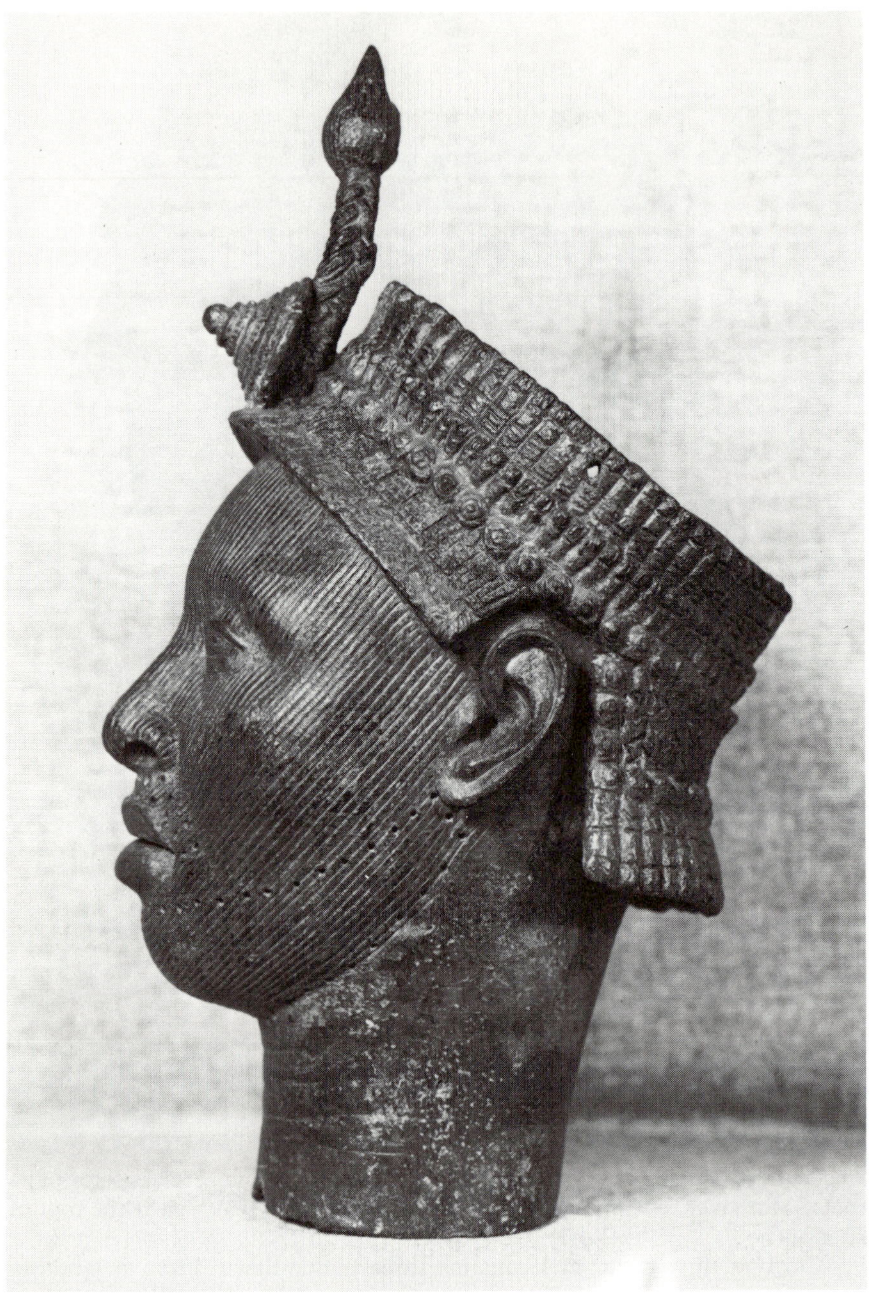

Plate 10.2 *Crowned head. Zinc brass? Ife, Nigeria. British Museum. Height 21cm. Acquired 1939. Made between the 12th and early 16th c. Remains undated. Such heads are interpreted as royal portraits, but they could be portraits of leading chiefs also, as we know nothing about Ife's government at that time*

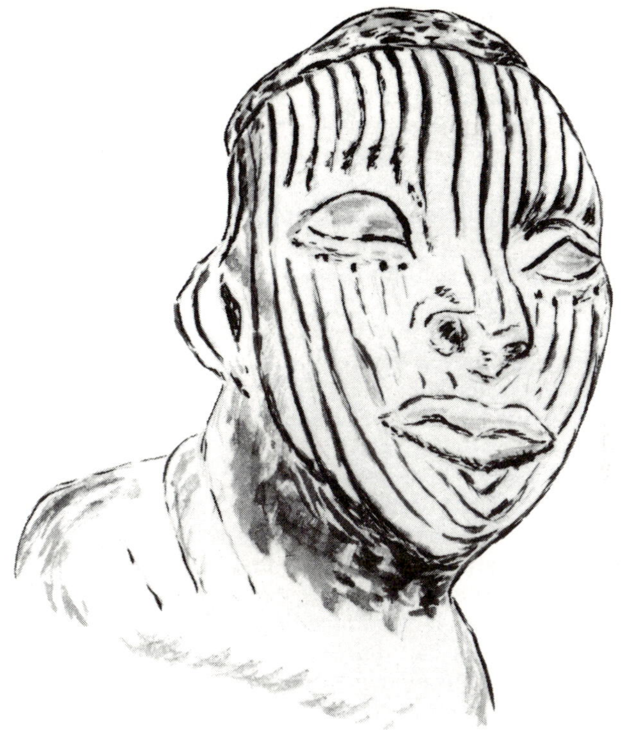

Fig. 10.3 *Head. Ceramic. Use unknown, perhaps in shrine. Owo, Nigeria. National Museum, Lagos. Height 17·4cm. Dated by association (date of the excavation), 15th c. The roundness of volume and the liveliness of expression (lips!) distinguishes it from similar sculpture at Ife. After T. Shaw 1978:185*

Secondly, it is evident that the tree model presupposes features of change which are valid in linguistics, but not for art. The model refers to a single totally integrated system (the language code), and attempts to establish a point in time, the node, at which languages split. Since the visual arts are not a totally integrated system, no such node can be found. Indeed, prime works are created out of multiple influences, whereas the tree model presupposes a single ancestor. The model takes into account only genetic links, leaving aside all later mutual influences. Again because such influences are of the greatest importance in the shaping of prime works in art, the model cannot be used to express changes in design and composition.

The last flaw is the belief that because one phenomenon follows another one, it *must* derive from it. In fact, Nok, Ife, Benin are a succession of styles over time and nothing more. The resemblances adduced between the styles of the representational ceramic and copper alloy sculpture are not so overwhelming as to prove filiation. On the contrary, intensive search for them merely establishes some influences for a few discrete features. It would be surprising if it were not so, given the localization of Owo, Ife, Benin and Yorubaland and the widespread occurrence of Nok ceramics almost a millennium before the appearance of the other styles. One can find some similarities between Nok work, later ceramics around Lake Chad (So) and even between Nok and Igbo Ukwu. Just the passage of such a vast amount of time, coupled with the huge territorial expansion of Nok styles, would lead to the expectation of such similarities.

To sum up: multiple centres for the production of ceramic and metal sculpture are old in western Nigeria. An urban or semi-urban way of life had developed there since the onset of this millennium and every city became a centre for the production of sculptures in various media. Multiple relationships and overlapping influences should be taken into account, hybrid inspiration being very common in art. The term Yoruba should best be dropped, and the hypothesis restated in terms of types of art and of cities seen as clusters of workshops. It then becomes evident that the term Nok refers to a different reality. Nok never was a city. It is a label applied to a set of traditions seven hundred years and more in duration over a huge area of Nigeria mostly between the Benue and the Kaduna rivers, north of the Niger. Truly satisfactory links with later work, as at Ife, could be found only after the clusters of Nok pieces have been published by locale and the relationship between the localities has been worked out. Thus the vague term Nok should be replaced by specific place names such as Kafanchan, Jemaa, Nok, Bwari, Abuja, Taruga, Nasarawa, Udegi, Katsina Ala, Yola, etc.

Despite its ultimate failure, the research hypothesis in the shape of a tree model had a great virtue. It attempted to take time into account, whereas none of the previous research had done so. But how then are we to visualize the overall development? The evidence allows us to state the following: from 700 to 500 B.C. ceramic sculpture was widespread in the Nigerian middle belt. It was produced in many centres and represents several stylistic sequences, as yet still unknown, but all labelled Nok. Ceramic traditions continued to the west of this area at Yelwa and to the north around Lake Chad where a still insecurely dated ceramic art flourished from the beginning of our era onwards. It is given the label So and represents the production of several centres as well. A progression of styles lasted over many centuries, perhaps only ending by A.D. 1600.

Towns appeared in southern Nigeria, the later Yorubaland. Ife, one of those, perhaps the oldest, produced ceramics, metalwork and stone sculpture between 1100 and the seventeenth century, although the dates are still provisional. As other towns developed in Yorubaland or to the southeast, they also developed such arts. Indeed, east of the lower Niger, evidence for such arts is found at Igbo Ukwu, which had never been a town, but must have been at least an important trading emporium. Igbo Ukwu clearly did not influence the art of Ife at all. Yoruba cities, however, probably all influenced each other, to unequal degrees as the prestige or power of each waxed and waned. Ife was one of them, Owo was another. Its ceramic traditions differ from those of Ife but are clearly influenced by Ife or a similar third source. The third source can be eliminated if the accounts that Ife was the wellspring of Yoruba cities and monarchy are accepted, as most historians do, although it may well be that such traditions refer only to relatively late dates before A.D. 1600 and not, say, to the situation around 1300 or so.

Benin slowly grew among other settlements in the forest, became the leading town by 1200, and developed its arts there. It later established connections with Ife as finds in both Ife and Benin show. Benin had connections with Owo based on evidence of similar iconographic motifs, but this type of evidence is weaker, for it does not show Owo objects in Benin city and vice versa. Still, the proximity and the later subservience of Owo to Benin allows mutual influences as a reasonable hypothesis. The sculptures found at Jebba and Tada as well as others for which a locality of origin has not been documented, show in fact how far such influences from Ife, Owo, Benin, could then be found.

So far, this account does not consider any media other than clay or metal. But Esie or later Yoruba sculpture used stone, wood and ivory. The undated stone sculptures from Esie may have come from a rural background, since they are not associated with any city. The technique of carving is similar to woodcarving techniques and we may suspect that woodcarving had been practised since remote times in Yorubaland because the Ifa board (Plate 1.1) made in the 1650s, or earlier, shows a refined technique and a well-developed genre, comparable to later Yoruba work. Note in passing the irony of using the term 'Yoruba' for these arts when the object was found at Ardra, a non-Yoruba-speaking area! Some of the ivory carvings in Yoruba styles and the carvings made in Benin for Portuguese in the sixteenth century point to the same inference. If ivory was carved, why not wood? Yoruba sculpture must be the continuation of the earlier sculpture that was thriving in the older Yoruba cities, places such as Ife, Owo but also Old Oyo, Ijebu Ode, Ilesha and perhaps others, all thriving in the sixteenth and seventeenth centuries. The whole complex of interrelated workshops in the earlier cities and rural traditions such as Esie or others is ancestral to that of later Yoruba art. A link between a work from Tada, attributed to 'late Ife' and a well-known political cult, the Ogboni of later cities, consists in an iconographic detail: the Ogboni salute. But there is no clear lineal link between later Ogboni brasses and Ife styles. That indicates how difficult it will be to unravel precise strands of development. Moreover, skeuomorph development also occurred because some features on ceramic and metal art from Ife are found on wood in modern Yorubaland. Still, the whole tradition of all interrelated Yoruba styles, and there are many, must be linked with the whole tradition of all known and unknown sites in the area in the sixteenth and seventeenth centuries. That means that the recent sculpture is a descendant, not only of Ife, nor even of Ife and Owo, nor even of all early Yoruba cities, not even of Yoruba cities and rural workshops, but also, in part, of the Benin world of sculpture, if only because in those centuries Benin was the overlord over southern Yorubaland and hence the point of reference for good taste. The catalogue entry for the Ifa board from Ardra mentions the supremacy of Benin. Benin art must also be counted among 'Yoruba' ancestry in sculpture because the city was then interacting with several Yoruba cities and it is the whole of the interacting network that is ancestral to later Yoruba art. Given these considerations, it becomes obvious that tree models will not do. A graphic sketch of a more appropriate model is set out in Fig. 10.4.

AN OPERATIONAL MODEL: STREAMS OF TRADITION

Any valid model for the evolution of form must take into account multiple origin, borrowing and continued mutual influences between neighbouring

I. Time and place where art appears.

Nok sites (many)	700 BC-400 AD
Daima	600 BC
Yelwa	700 AD
Igbo Ukwu	800-900 AD
Baha	1000 AD
Ife	1100-1500 AD. Late Ife: 1500-1700 AD.
Owo	1400s-now
Benin	1400s-now
Yoruba cities	1500's?-now

II. Each label comprises many styles.

'Classical Ife'

Stone figures: schematic
Stone figures: naturalistic
Stone thrones

Ceramic pottery (styles)
Ceramic pavements
Ceramic heads: schematic (two styles)
Ceramic heads: naturalistic.

Copper alloy or copper: heads and one mask.
Copper alloy: figures.

Ivory ?: lost.

Wood ?: lost.

Beadwork: lost

Textiles: lost
etc.

III. Streams of traditions: Naturalistic ceramic and copper alloy heads: 1100-1500 AD.

Note: Benin brass heads do *not* owe their major inspiration to Ife, but are influenced by Ife.

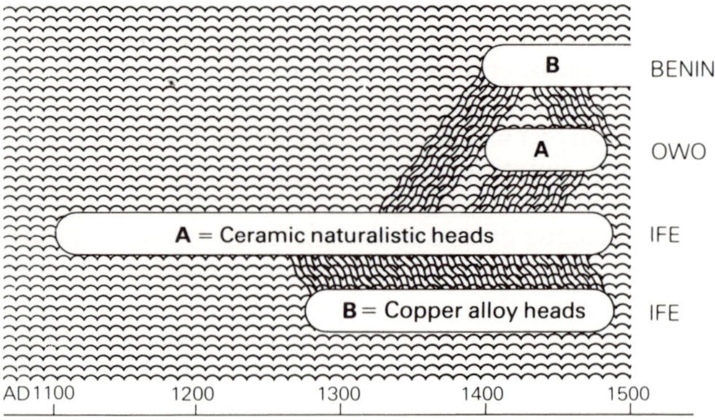

Fig. 10.4 *Style and Nigerian art history*

styles, while allowing also for renewed influence of art works crafted generations ago in the same area and perhaps in the same tradition, as in the case of Benin work from the eighteenth century imitating objects from the sixteenth (Ben Amos 1980a:30 34–7). At the same time, the real continuity in the art of any 'style' should be recognized. For small scale drift is also a major component of change. The evolution of style is like a large river, receiving water from neighbouring currents and giving off water to other currents, but nevertheless pushing a large mass of fluid downstream in time. Rivers can take on tributaries, lose tributaries, meander and fork, rather like the multiple outlets in the delta of the river Niger fed by the main river and by smaller rivers falling into the delta, or they can flow smooth and straight in the same channel. There are no single ancestors and yet there are ancestors and there are continuing streams. We need a model of streaming traditions.

With such concepts it is evident that there are not enough data on art, especially south of the Sahara to detail all the multiple interactions that were taking place. We must always assume then that we have more lacunae than data, whereas the tree model implies the contrary. When chronology indicates a broad synchronism of streams, mutual influences of such traditions on each other should be expected and found by stylistic comparison without prejudice to other links that also can be substantiated by style.

As an illustration we can survey the situation of sculpture west of Nigeria from *c.* 1100 to *c.* 1600. Three centres can be recognized then in the upper Middle Niger area: the environs of Jenne and of Bamako produced terra cotta in human form (De Grunne 1980; McIntosh and McIntosh 1981; Bedaux, *et al.* 1980), while the environs of Goundam yield varied work in metal and ceramics (Davies 1967:262, 265). By 1100, wood sculpture was practised, and some has survived near the cliffs of Bandiagara, not far from Mopti and the Jenne concentration (Bedaux *et al.* 1980; T. Northern, personal communication). Stone sculpture, undated so far except by stylistic association with Afro-Portuguese ivory (Dittmer 1967; Paulme 1981; Person 1961; Atherton and Kalous 1970) appeared further south near the upper Niger valley in Kissi country and then towards the coast of Sierra Leone. From the latter area, ivories were exported to Europe from *c.* 1500 to *c.* 1600. Contemporary written sources tell us that stone and wood sculpture were practised in the Niger bend during the fifteenth century and wood sculpture at the capital of the Mali Empire a century before, and probably since at least 1100, but no works from these areas have yet come to light. Finally, to the southwest, ceramic and metal works from modern Ghana, south of the big bend of the Volta, are known to have been created from 1400 onwards although pottery heads and figures are extant only from *c.* 1600 and later (De Grunne 1980:137–9).

Using the stream of tradition model, we must presuppose that each style centre influenced its neighbours. The multiple ateliers that can be recognized in the Jenne area are clearly all interrelated and form one stream. Despite obvious differences, there are also clear links with the Bamako area, from where we have mainly a single rivulet – perhaps because so few works have been recovered there. Links with Goundam are much less evident, except perhaps for metalwork. A few Jenne pieces can be put side by side with work from Bandiagara cliffs (Tellem) and one or two from Bamako strongly recall later wood carving tradition to the southeast: the traditions of Upper Volta and

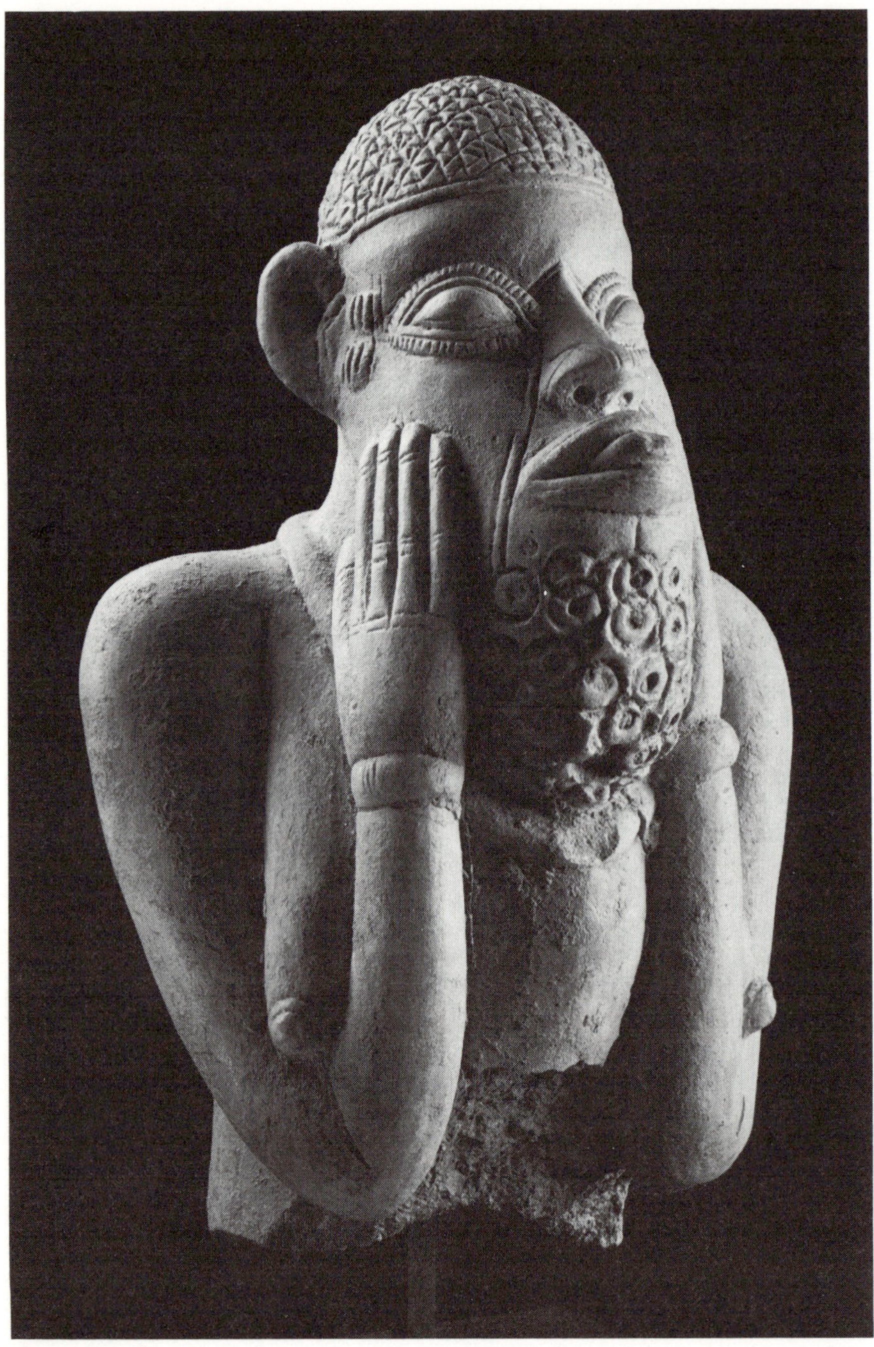

Plate 10.3 *Bust. Ceramic. Inner Niger delta, exact mound unknown. Mali. Private collection. Height perhaps 20cm. Undated. Similar figures have been dated between the 11th and 16th c.*

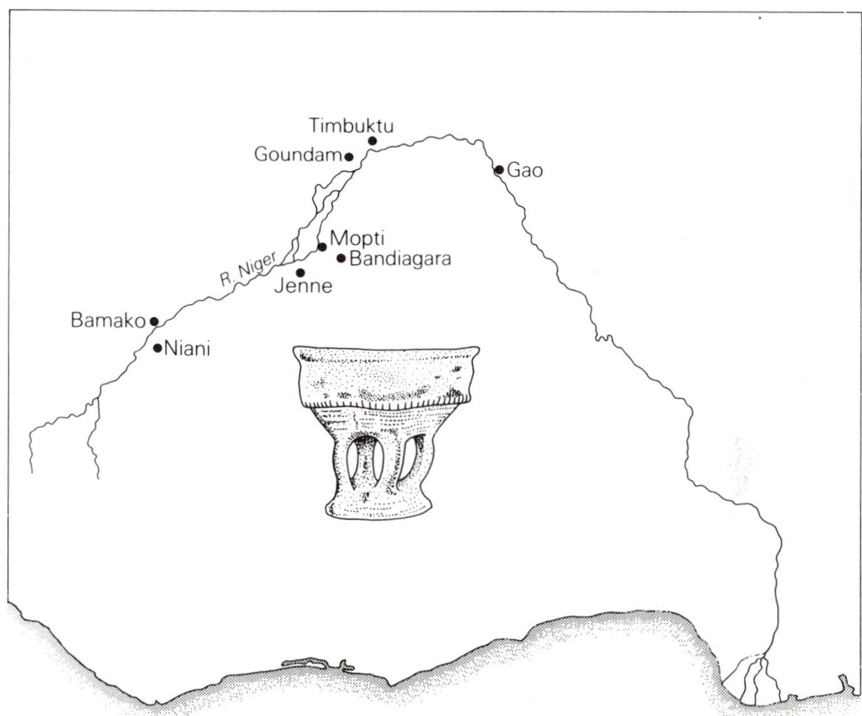

Fig. 10.5 *Distribution of four-legged pots along the Upper Niger before A.D. 1500*

Ivory Coast labelled 'Senufo'. That there really were contacts is proven by the presence everywhere along the Niger and at the Bandiagara cliffs of a well-defined ceramic vessel with three or four legs, found as far downstream as Gao and as far upstream as the region around the capital of the Mali empire, Niani (Fig. 10.5). Links between Jenne and the town of Begho in the lands beyond the lower Volta have been proven from 1350 or earlier onwards by ceramic evidence and by the system of goldweights. There is, as yet, no direct proof of links between this cluster and the cluster of stone and ivory work from the upper Niger and Sierra Leone, itself divided into several interrelated streams, but no detailed research has been undertaken and the differences in the media of the art works are obstacles barring easy identification of mutual influences.

When work after 1600 is compared with the situation earlier, some continuities appear. Thus, metalwork from Goundam, which had correspondences with metalwork from Mopti in the Jenne centre, is comparable with jewellery later worn by the inhabitants of the Sahara, while other pieces, mostly bracelets from Goundam, are directly comparable to bracelets on the lower Ivory Coast and in Liberia from the nineteenth century. This should not be surprising as lost-wax techniques for dealing with copper alloys diffused from northern Africa, presumably over the upper Middle Niger Valley (a casting mould near Mopti dates from A.D. 1000–1200, Bedaux *et al.*

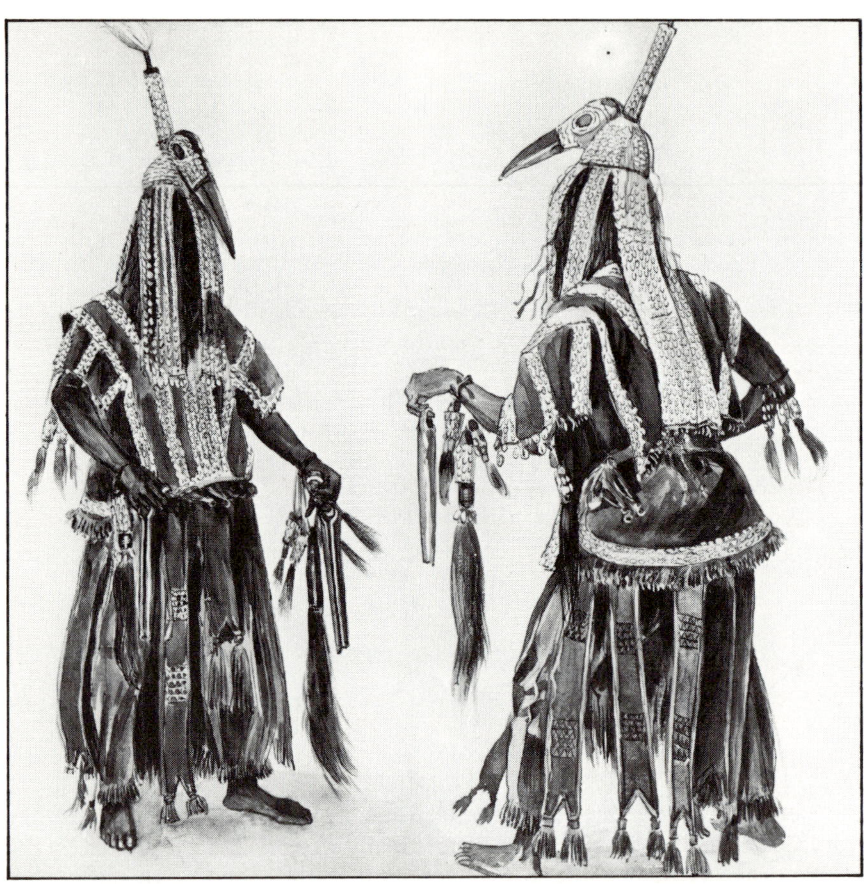

Plate 10.4 *Masked persons. Watercolour by Frobenius. Mossi, Upper Volta. Frobenius Institut. Original 1907–1909, entitled: 'Mossi priests in masks'. Probably chiefs of the land, representing the authority of the aborigines before the Mossi conquests. Birdmasks are ancient in West Africa being attested since the 1350s*

1980:146) to the south from the coast of Ghana to Liberia. As far as sculpture in wood is concerned, the later styles of the Bandiagara cliffs belong to a stream that is in part the direct continuation from the earlier Tellem works (see Plate 2.5) with some outside influence and local innovation. In Sierra Leone and in the Kissi area, the most significant feature however is a pronounced break between the ivory and stone work on the one hand and later carving in wood on the other. Very few influences cross that divide. But later wood carvings, especially from southern Sierra Leone, Liberia, the uppermost Niger, and portions of the Ivory Coast, share at least one icon, the bird-shaped mask (Bravmann 1974:47) that was reported for Mali by Ibn Battuta in 1352/3; even the red colour of the beak has been preserved in some cases (Plate 10.4). There must therefore be some continuity between these styles and wood carving in the 1300s, probably in southern Guinea. The obvious similarity between Afro-Portuguese ivories and styles of carving from eastern Liberia and the Ivory Coast – namely, that carving was done in the round, with a miniaturist's attention to detail and great care for the finish, is not a case where ivory work gave rise to wood sculpture. Rather, we should think that the later styles flow from a stream of carving in wood which also influenced the ivory work from the sixteenth century. And finally we begin to perceive that different clusters of ateliers in the Sahel made products *c.* 1900 that still share some features with the Bamako centre ceramics.

We have in this simplified sketch looked for both synchroneous relationships and filiation. We find clusters linked over time and for any given time amongst themselves and we conspicuously leave the lacunae as the main theme! Nevertheless, this does yield an operational framework for research in which all the sculpture of West Africa, west of the Volta and the Niger bend can be placed. Whilst it is evident that there are no direct relationships at all between the traditions we dealt with and either Nok or any of its cluster, future research probably will find transitions between the two, traces of which can be expected along the coast itself or from northern Ghana eastwards to northern Dahomey.

We have intentionally limited ourselves to sculpture. If we include architecture, the single most relevant feature to stress is the existence of an advanced mud architecture in the middle Niger from the last centuries B.C. onwards. The area of this architecture stretches from there over the Upper Volta, northern Ghana, Togo, Dahomey (Benin), to Nigeria. But the study of architecture is still in its infancy and we can say very little about it, except for the obvious: the mud architecture of the middle Niger belongs in that environment!

At this point the informed reader complains: you have illustrated the approach by using the one area for which somewhat adequate archaeological information exists. It at least gives you some hold over time, some straw to make bricks with. No doubt you could make a similar demonstration for stone architecture in southern Africa from *c.* 1100 onwards! Indeed, we can and the Zimbabwe ruins are just one stream in that delta of data. What if archaeological data are absent, however, or so sparse as not to make a difference? Is that not the situation in most of central and eastern Africa?

Such a perspicacious reader is right. Archaeology is as crucial to art history in Africa as elsewhere. Who would have foreseen a ceramic sculpture in Natal and Transvaal from *c.* A.D. 500 to 800, if the trowel had not uncovered it (Maggs and Davison 1981; Plate 10.5)? But archaeology without an operational framework of interpretation remains barren. The stream of traditions model provides that. It allows us to beware of quick conclusions, for instance that the wood sculpture in the form of heads topping poles and the stylistic features of the face in central Angola and along the Kwango and Middle Kasai must directly descend from the style of the first millennium pole found at Tumbica on the upper Kwango. That is tree-model reasoning and the chances of it being correct are abysmally small.

The same approach encourages us however to think in terms of real time depth, to see genuine links between space and time. At present we cannot reach much beyond the nineteenth century for most of the sculpture of southern Zaïre, but we can perceive affinities over large areas and think in terms of clusters of streams of tradition. Thus, for instance, icons as caryatids supporting stools are a typical theme from the Kwango to Lake Tanganyika.

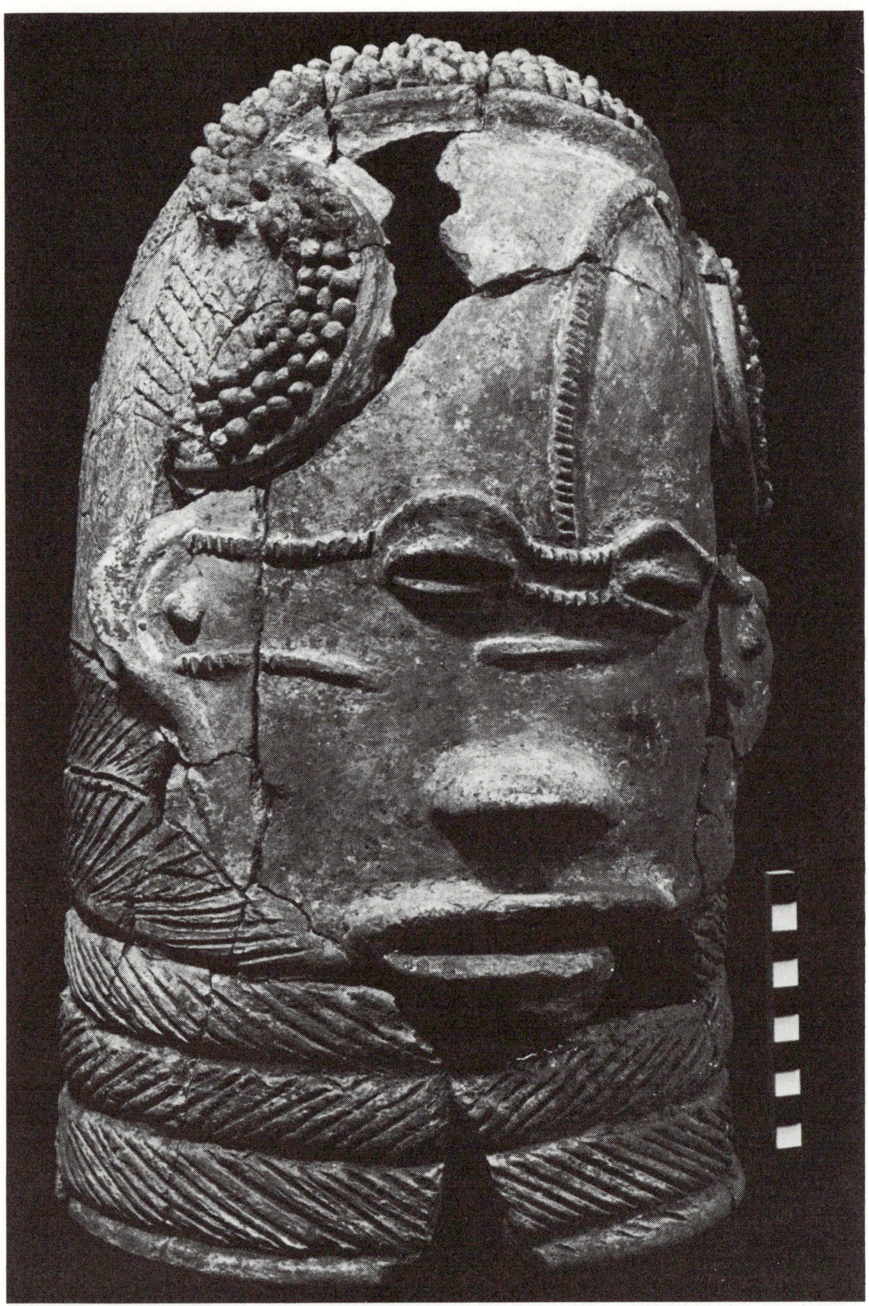

Plate 10.5 *Head. Ceramic. Use unknown. Lydenburg, Transvaal. Natal Museum. Height 38cm.* c. *A.D. 500. Since this photo was taken the mask has been restored with an animal crest on top of the head. Compare cover* African Arts, *1981, 14 (2). One of seven heads and the largest*

They do not prove that central Angolan and eastern savanna traditions share the same ancestry. But they do point to undeniable mutual influences. The study of spatial distribution tells us unmistakenly that the history of sculpture here is quite complex and reflects many different historical processes of drift and mutation.

THE FAILURE OF FORMAL FRAMEWORKS

By themselves formal sequences cannot provide a satisfactory framework for an art history because they are too limited even if sequences are dated. A general social and cultural history is crucial to a satisfying understanding of relationships in art history. Thus, when we deal with western West Africa, it is crucial to take into account that ancient Ghana, ancient Mali and Songhay were empires flourishing there; that Islam penetrated the area slowly, first at the courts, later in Songhay after 1493 as a state religion; that trade for gold first, kola later, linked the forest to the savanna to the desert and the need for salt linked the coast to the southern Sahel and the Sahel to the deposits of the Sahara. Our sketchy model of the evolution of sculpture becomes convincing only when we put it in full historical perspective. We account for breaks in tradition (Sierra Leone, middle Niger), for links over long distances (middle Niger-Ghana south of the Volta), for continuity (the cliffs of Bandiagara), for centres of production (Jenne to 1600). The skeleton is being covered by flesh.

The need for an overall historical framework is dramatically shown in cases where we do not have large numbers of art works from early sites. For eastern Zaïre we know that a sophisticated technology of iron existed from *c.* A.D. 800 onwards and some figurative work in fired clay was then practised (de Maret 1977). We know that by A.D. 1000 copper currencies emerged there (Bisson 1975), and trade from hand to hand was linking the area to the Indian Ocean. By then, or not much later, we know that chieftaincies had appeared and that some of their emblems are those of later Luba kings, while some of the customs, such as the way in which teeth were filed, were to survive until 1900. The whole cluster of the arts in and around the later Luba empire can be progressively disentangled as we come nearer to the present. We know that we have to allow for long time depths, and yet we can place the few early works in one overall valid framework.

Art works should be fitted into general history with greater care than has been the case in the past. For instance, too much is still made of migrations carrying icons and iconic tradition with them over long distances. There is not enough consideration of links between the sudden appearance of novel prime works and the demands by new social institutions. There is not sufficient awareness of leaving enough slack in interpretations for the unknown, even if rules of evidence are scrupulously followed. But it is possible to build up a tentative art history and it is imperative to break away from the flat map of styles to include the temporal dimension.

The immense value of the general historical framework is most apparent where it is lacking. Thousands of specimens of rock art in southern Africa and in the Sahara cannot make up for it. In the end, and speculation apart, we know very little about rock art (Lajoux 1977; Willcox 1963; Vinnicombe 1976; Woodhouse 1977, 1978; Rudner and Rudner 1970). Even if in the future precise distributions and chronologies are worked out, most questions will still remain begging, and only general archaeological finds of stone tools, other utensils, perhaps the remains of domestic and wild animals, and certainly living sites can alleviate the barrenness of a style classification in a total void. Even the iconography of such works can really only be enriched by finds relating to the general way of life.

In contrast, where the general historical evolution is well documented, the formal sequences of art history, as well as changes in the iconography and the technology acquire a rich significance. In northern Africa, the conditions obtain. We have enough historical background and enough dated works of art; at least in architecture. Stylistic similarities find their explanation through history. The Aghlabid rulers rebuilt the mosque of Qairawan as an expression of their legitimacy in the area and with means they could afford, as they had reorganized Tunisian society around their dynasty, its clients and its allies. They then commissioned the Zaytuna mosque in Tunis, which may have been built by the same architects and was certainly built using the same type of materials, the same techniques, the same standard elements. This was to impress the urban population, which was still impregnated with Christian Roman and Byzantine culture. The differences in the domes of Qairawan and the Zaytuna are telling. The first is a novel creation, but inspired by the domes in Iraq, home of the Caliphs. The second borrows some features from the Roman Byzantine architecture still visible near Tunis (Lezine 1966). The sequence of Fatimid portals, which we explored in Chapter 8, makes sense only with the political and religious background behind it.

In Nubia, the historical background is not as rich but the wall paintings provide a sturdy chronological sequence and the iconography is well understood. The architectural remains are not as yet dated with sufficient precision, but their sequence is clear and can be linked to the general historical evolution. Even the ceramic sequence, which is well dated, can be tied in with the other arts and with the social and cultural history. These arts as expressions of culture vary with cultural changes in religious dogma, with social change in the relative positions of monasteries, ordinary clergy, rulers or governors, and the relationships between both the ecclesiastical and political establishment on the one hand and the mass of farmers, fishermen, stock keepers and even traders on the other (Adams 1977). The sources complement one another and allow an overall historical hypothesis to be worked out.

Ethiopian painting is much less well dated, although the main sequences are evident. Far too few works as yet are dated at all, but wall painting at least can often be tied in directly with architecture. We also lack enough dated buildings, however, despite the hundreds of 'medieval' monolithic churches. But the general historical background, the economic, political, social and cultural forces at work, are well known from the fourteenth century onwards, and in outline, even earlier. This means that when more dates become available for works of art, it will be easy to place them into the general picture. Even now we can securely fit successive formal sequences and successive changes in the iconography of painting into more general change. We can measure Ethiopian reaction to Muslim advances in the sixteenth century both in the iconography (condemning Islam) and in stylistic evolution (dropping some Muslim motifs, but adding others). We see the impact of the Catholic missions on the evolution of paintings depicting the Virgin Mary in the seventeenth century, and we begin to measure the cultural impact of the Empire's collapse a century later in the paintings after 1750.

To conclude: techniques that yield stylistic sequences or that identify the shape of prime works and sometimes archetypes among prime works are necessary. But they deal with a development of form that does not lead directly to larger and deeper understanding, mainly because they are concerned with the least part of art history: that which documents the autonomous evolution of form and ignores the forces that bring about new icons, new genres, new 'traditions'. Grouping by area and by form leads nowhere, while grouping by area on geographical or linguistic criteria neglects formal variation and ignores socio-cultural matrices. The tree model is moderately fruitful because it draws attention to time, but it remains flawed because it considers only drift, not multiple influences, nor radical innovation. A stream model comes closer to reality and takes unknowns into account, but it too cannot account for the reasons for change, nor can it document and explain radical innovation. Only the reconstruction of the general social and cultural history can be the proper framework in which to establish valid art history. In turn, as is argued in the next chapter, art history is an essential ingredient to any history that claims to be general.

CHAPTER ELEVEN

ART IN HISTORY

History without works of art remains bloodless, unreal, to me – something that could have been, but never really was. Yet today art history has no place in general African history. None of the general overviews, not even the eight-volume-long series of the Cambridge University Press and the UNESCO general history of Africa, consider art as much more than a source of illustrations. The main journals carry very few articles on the topic, and at least one major school of historiography is hostile on principle, as it does not perceive a meaningful place for artistic expression in its explanation of history. We cannot assume that art is unimportant in general historical reconstructions, whether in Africa or elsewhere. It is too often dismissed as an irrelevant epiphenomenon. We must therefore argue the case for its relevance. Let us begin with an example.

STONE MANSIONS AT LAMU IN THE EIGHTEENTH CENTURY

Lamu is a town in Kenya with a long history. Built near one of the earliest trading settlements on the coast, it only reached its zenith almost a millennium later, in the eighteenth century. At that time the coast of northern Kenya was under the control of either Lamu or Pate, which were vying with each other for predominance. Trade with lands across the Indian Ocean was brisk and much wealth flowed into the towns. A number of leading citizens could afford to build stone mansions and live in them (De Vere Allen and Wilson 1979; Spear 1981:89–96).

Stone houses had been a feature of Swahili towns since the thirteenth century at least, but usually represented only a few buildings within a settlement built of wattle and daub. When prosperity was great, however, the majority of the buildings came to be of stone. So it was with Lamu in the 1700s, where mansions from that time are still standing, albeit mostly in ruins. They were the badge of civilization in the eyes of their dwellers and of the other townspeople. They dramatically separated the well-to-do from the *vulgum pecus* and people living in them also adopted different ways of life in matters of religious observance, making a living and even entertainment as well as in dress, speech and demeanour from the lesser folk. If they fell on hard times and could no longer keep up their mansion, they left their houses and with them the behaviour, mannerisms, tastes and predilections of their social layer. They usually moved to another town and merged with the less fortunate (P. Romero, personal communication). The stone house, then, was the crystallization of status in Lamu society.

Stone houses occurred in blocks, or wards *(mtaa)*, each block being under the authority of the head of a widely ramified family. The architectural evidence favours the notion that marriage was matrilocal so that women in a ward were closely related and visited each other within the *mtaa* without having to appear in the streets, something that was frowned upon in this Muslim society, and something that set their status dramatically apart from the lot of poorer folk.

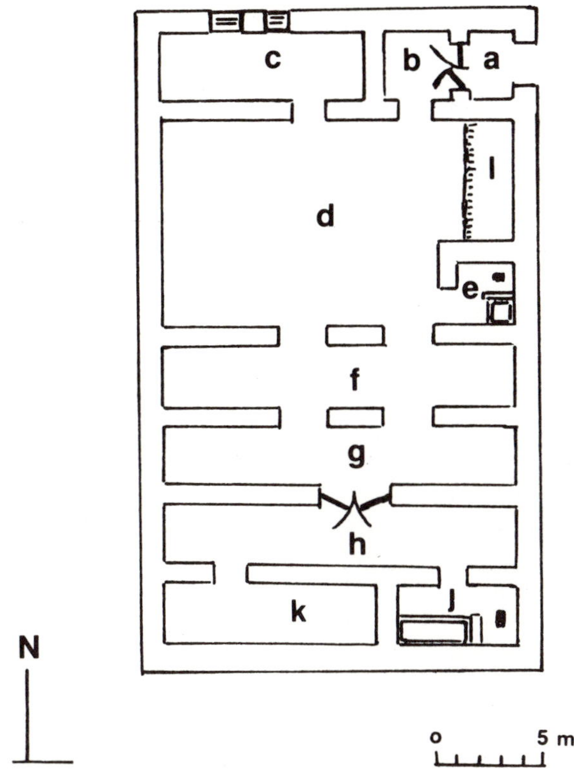

Fig. 11.1 *House, Lamu. Plan of a one-storey dwelling. 18th c. a porch) b inner porch; c guestroom; d courtyard; e front toilet; f outer living room; g inner living room; h women's quarters; j inner bathroom; k* nyumba ya kati; *l kitchen area. After De Vere Allen 1979:diag. 3*

Most houses were single storey, but two-storied buildings also existed and further distinguished the wealthiest people from the others. The average single storey house consisted of a porch with solid benches on the side and an inner porch leading to a courtyard (Fig. 11.1). Behind the porches was the guest room, the only room with windows, barring only ventilation holes in the toilet. One side of the courtyard served as a kitchen area with a toilet nearby, the other side was walled off. The bulk of the house lay on the back of the yard and its façade was oriented northward away from the rain. The block consisted of an outer living room, an inner living room, the harem, an inner bathroom and the

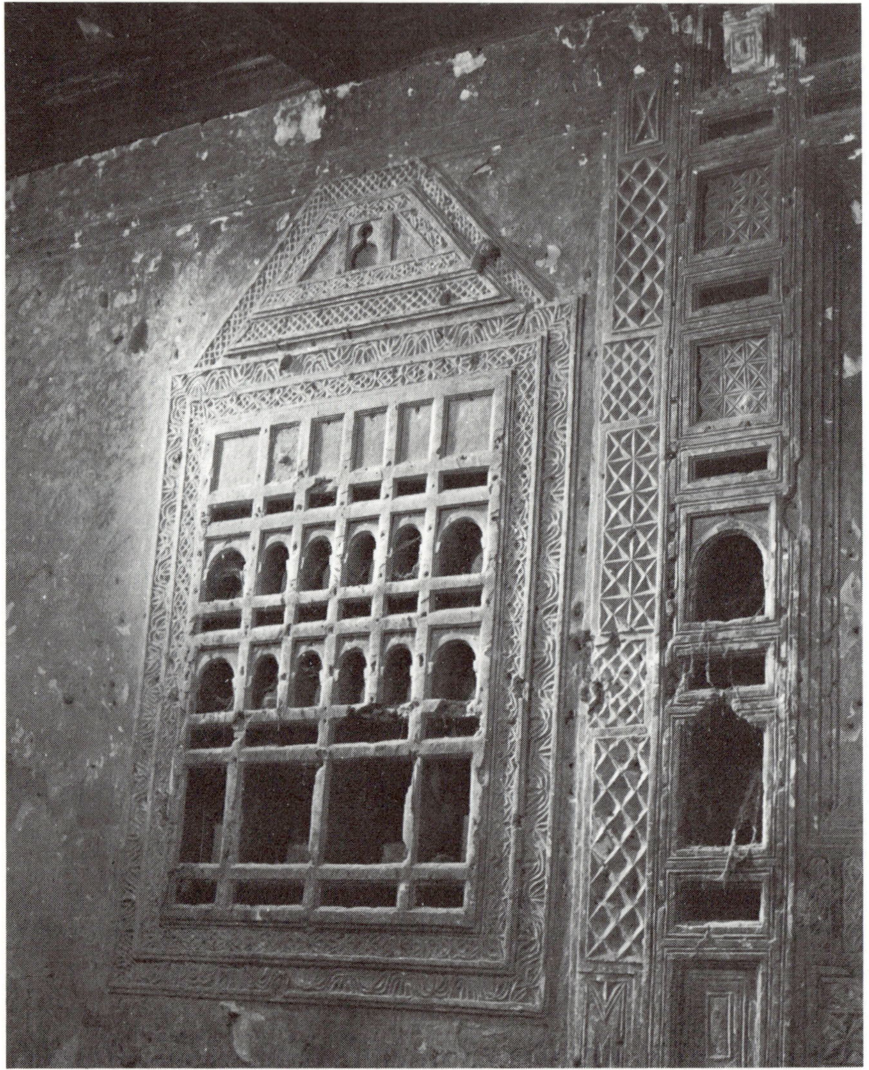

Plate 11.1 *Inner wall of Lamu mansion. Coral masonry, plaster. Inner walls, doorway, niches. Lamu, Kenya. 18th c. The niches vary in height, depth and slant for perspective. They give an illusion of depth. Brass lamps and Chinese plates or bowls were set in them*

nyumba ya kati, 'the inside room', at the back of the house. The living rooms received light from the courtyard through large apertures. They were densely furnished and served as work rooms as well as bedrooms. The harem only had a single entrance that could be closed by a door, and this opening was carefully out of alignment with the wide apertures from the courtyard to the living rooms. The harem was the most decorated room in the house. The whole wall facing the inner living room was covered with panels of wall niches. Such panels also occurred in smaller numbers in the inner living room, on either side of the harem doorway. The *nyumba ya kati*, 'middle room', at the back was the only one, however, that was left completely undecorated with stuccowork, which occurred to some extent everywhere else even though the decoration was never as rich as in the harem. More complex arrangements characterized the storied houses. There, as in the single storey buildings, the greatest care was taken to isolate visitors from the inside of the house and even to separate clearly the upstairs housing unit from the downstairs one. In all houses privacy was a prime consideration, not only in order to isolate women. Thus stone houses allowed a larger number of people including servants to live together with an acceptable standard of privacy, as compared with those in mud and thatch houses.

But houses were not built only with daily living requirements in mind, they were especially concerned with marriages and funerals, and in part births. The *nyumba ya kati* served to lay out the dead and take them out of the house through a hole in the back wall. Such rituals are so alien to Islam that today's informants vehemently deny them (P. Romero, personal communication). The arrangement of the living rooms and the harem, with their bays and doors and decorations, formed the proper stage for wedding ceremonies. First-class weddings were the supreme affirmation of a family's standing and of the groom's status and responsibilities at large. The stucco work, the niches, and other details were all arranged to display the wealth of the families and form a proper backdrop to the festivities, which might last a week. The whole house or house unit itself was usually new then, a present to the newlyweds, a building planned and prepared ever since the bride was born. The high point was the revelation of the bride on a bed in the harem against a wall space expressly stuccoed for effect.

The study of the eighteenth-century house can be pursued in many directions. It was the continuation of a tradition in which plans and decoration can be traced over time. Plaster decoration, for instance, replaced earlier coral rag carvings, much too cumbersome and expensive for the greater numbers who in that century aspired to a stone house but who were less wealthy than the smaller number of people belonging to the élite in earlier times. The details of decoration, of furniture, of imports such as ceramics, rugs and hangings, show a fine balance between imported items from all over the Indian Ocean and from China and items made on the coast in styles that were similar to, but diverged from, similar work in Islamic countries. These echo the results obtained by a study of the Swahili language. Many loans, yes, but fundamentally a strong local tradition. Houses can also be put in the context of social life. They were perhaps the most sizeable goods forming part of an estate, they were grouped in blocks expressing the material wealth of the block unit. They were the product of a great expense of labour, some unfree, and their owners were served by slaves. Details recalled links with mosques and with good Muslim traditions as in the small arches recalling mihrabs and even in their orientation towards Mecca.

Life in such houses could well be visualized. And they give concrete shape to the images of poetry from the age; describing both their éclat and – for the neighbouring town of Pate – their later ruin.

How many wealthy men have we not seen . . .
Their lighted mansions glowed with lamps of brass
And crystal, till night seemed like very day; . . .
Their homes were set with Chinese porcelain
And every cup and goblet was engraved
While, placed amid the glittering ornaments,
Great crystal pitchers gleamed all luminous.
The rails from which they hung the rich brocade
Were made – I swear by God, Source of all Wealth –
Of teak and ebony, row upon row of them,
Rank upon rank with fabrics hung displayed.
The men's halls hummed with chatter, while within
The women's quarters laughter echoed loud.
The noise of talk and merriment of slaves
Rang out, and cheerful shouts of workmen rose. . . .*

How can we fail to grasp the gulf of class difference in Lamu, the implications of patrician status, the interests patricians represented in city government, the aspirations of workmen and slaves? How can we fail to grasp the ambiguity of the proud and haughty, however pure, devout, rank conscious, and Muslim, but still tied to their menials by profound cultural ties? The hidden *nyumba ya kati,* the spatial arrangements in the house for delivery and birth reflected the same un-Islamic convictions also held by commoners. In every generation some of the exalted fell to the mud and thatch class, just as some of the humble rose. How can we fail to grasp the stakes when we see in the house and its trappings the prize defended by its holders and longed for by the poor?

Swahili houses testify to the material culture, the economy, social and cultural life on the Lamu islands in a more direct way than other sources, whose full meaning becomes clear only when confronted with this evidence. The importance of these houses as primary sources is clear when one realizes that historians until quite recently could not see any link between Swahili civilization and the civilizations of the villages around and behind the towns, civilizations that were those of the mud and thatch crowd. By examining material culture, J. de Vere Allen has been able to reinterpret basic reconstructions about the past of the East coast. He first showed that neither the houses, nor their furniture, are simple copies or imports from Muslim lands around the Indian Ocean or the Red Sea. He was thus led to stress the originality of Swahili culture. A study of the stone houses as *part* of cities then led to the insight that both 'upper class' and 'lower class' Swahili formed a single society with the lower class element obviously culturally related, sometimes almost identical with the neighbouring 'tribes' inland. The history of East African towns, which had been totally divorced from their hinterland and cultural heritage, could then be rewritten. It remains doubtful whether his insights could have been achieved in any other way.

* Quotation from the translation of *al Inkishafi* by J. de Vere Allen, Nairobi 1977, pp. 63–4.

ART OBJECTS AS SOURCES

The relevance of art history to history in general is of a double nature. At one level the use of art objects as sources for history must be assessed. At another the relevance of art history proper, that is, an account of the history of style, iconography and technology, must be considered in relation to history in general.

Art objects, as all objects, are traces of the past, and hence are sources. They are tangible and more or less permanent. They are direct witnesses to the time when they were made and used and having been of practical use they do not carry any bias, other perhaps than that induced by the hazards of survival. Collections of art works should be as fruitful as collections of objects recovered from sites by archaeologists. After all, quite a number of art works are archaeological finds whilst others are classified by methodologists as monuments, a species of archaeological material that was never buried! They testify to situations, rarely to events, except in some narrative compositions, and in Africa they are rare. Most of the narrative works do not even relate to history. Painting in the *oikoumene* refers rather to sacred history and among the plaques of Benin only some purport to portray an historic event. But it is true that great figures of the past are represented in art.

Representative art is a testimony to what it depicts. But we have seen that problems of interpretation are often thorny and presuppose that the artwork be accompanied by another source, oral or written or epigraphic, which explains its rendering. Nevertheless, some evidence is direct enough to be grasped immediately. Often historians do not quite realize how much a given body of art work can contribute as a source. A good illustration is given by the goldweights of southern Ghana and neighbouring parts of the Ivory Coast. They are first a record of weighing systems, related to North African and European systems. They also are a mute witness to the practices of the gold trade, the institution for which they were used. A repertoire of goldweights encompasses virtually all utensils common in the Akan world from *c.* 1600 onwards. We find the various forms of agricultural tools, fishing implements, tools for the craftsman, weapons (for old shields, see Garrard 1980:113), furniture and utensils for cooking, representation of dress, ritual objects, regalia, imports, the appearance of chiefs, traders, farmers, women of varying statuses, travellers, friends meeting, a whole little world of people engaged in their daily rounds and on their exceptional activities. Some 300 000 figurative weights have survived out of a total estimated at three million. One third consists of animals and plants and thus shows us the natural world interpreted by the Akan mind. A further one third consists of horns, knots, shields, daggers, hammers, axes and fans. Still that leaves yet another 100 000 to represent other artefacts. An estimated 8 000 human figure weights show man engaged in all sorts of activities. Here some portrayals may be unique, according to Garrard. Three men weighing gold dust or a man committing suicide belong to this group. There is no archaeological corpus that can match the wealth of this ensemble. If objects are indeed the footsteps of human activity, it can all be reconstructed here.

At the same time the goldweights also underline the special traps set by collections of objects and art works. We may be tempted to find that what was

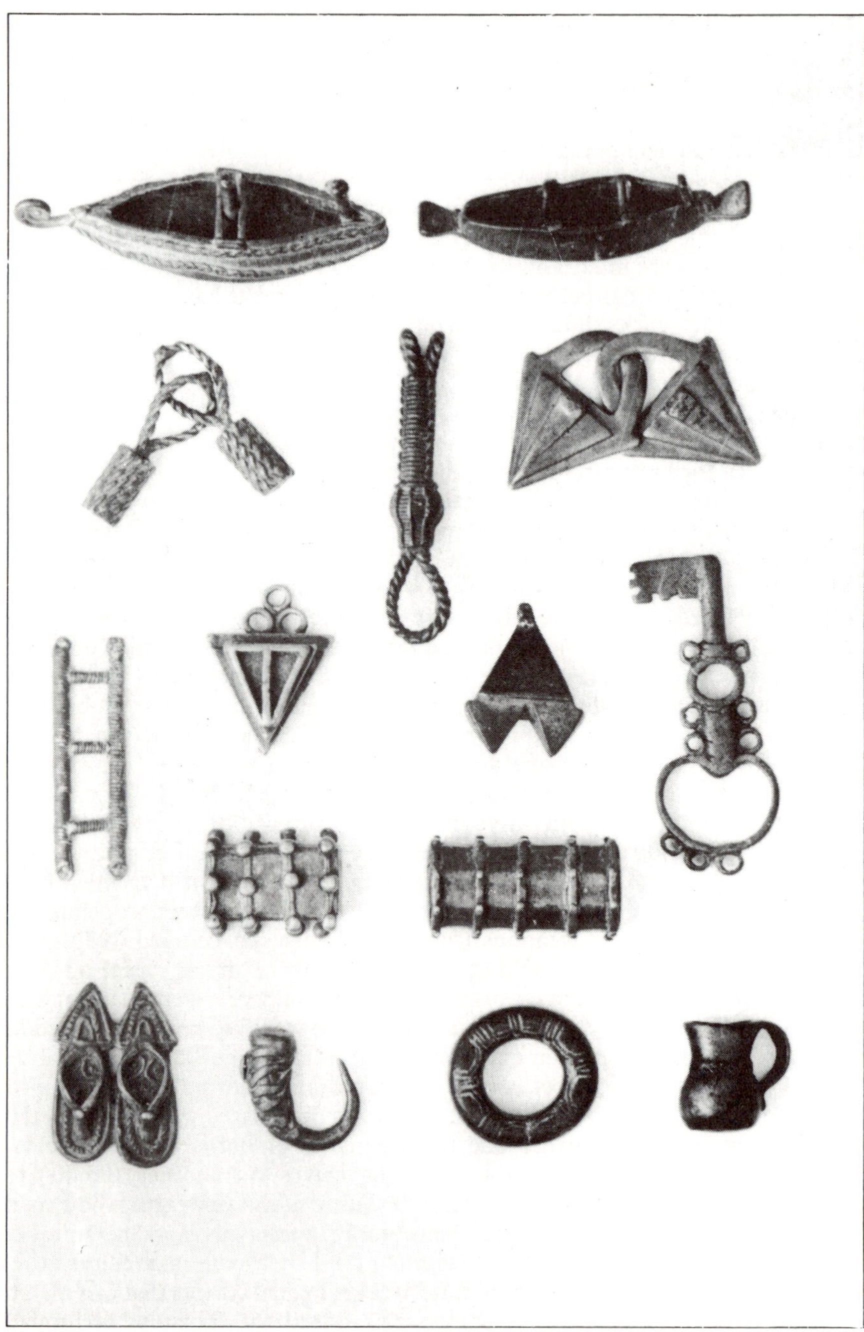

Plate 11.2 *Akan goldweights (after T. Garrard 1980; plate 54). Brass cast by the lost wax technique. Late period (1700–1900). The appearance of objects such as these boats, charms, ladder, key, treasure chests, sandals, claw, ring and jug and for some, even their existence in the period, is known only by models made as goldweights. The exact date of manufacture for each weight is unfortunately not known. The date 'late period' is inferred from the style*

not represented did not exist, and that which was not frequently depicted was a rare activity. Was suicide rare because only one surviving weight depicts it? Perhaps. But was gold weighing rare because only one weight shows it? Certainly not! Because compositions were limited in size (after all the objects had to conform to a given weight!) there are no goldweights showing the grand processions of rulers on days of national importance. There are thus limitations to the information portrayed. Negative evidence should not count with this type of source, especially with regard to assemblages.

Goldweights can be anachronistic, i.e., represent an object or a scene long after the object fell out of use or the activity had ceased. It survived in art by replication. From Benin we know that even recent carving includes a frieze of tiny Portuguese heads, replicated from those found on sixteenth-century work.

Goldweights often come with commentary. They often represent proverbs, making their meaning or symbolism explicit (Appiah 1979; Menzel 1968). Again there are dangers here. The proverbs constitute a potential storehouse of Akan practical philosophy, and of their cosmology, but we do not know that they were in the thoughts of the maker of the weights who could have had quite a different allusion or proverb in mind. Later the object itself suggested other interpretations and other proverbs. Thus we can be almost certain that the proverbs now cited along with the weights reflect nineteenth-century interpretations, and nothing that *certainly* is earlier. Again, anachronism is the main danger of interpretation accompanying the art work.

Modern interpretations must fully account for the stylistic conventions current at the time. These are themselves historical evidence. Just as we do not believe that Pharaohs were much taller than their subjects, we should not hold that all Nubians or West Asians or Libyans correspond to the stereotyped representations we find in Egyptian art. They are stereotypes and inform us about Egyptian prejudices at the time they were created and that is all.

A last general effect of works of art is that they may serve as the starting point for oral elaborations, precisely when interpretative speculation grew about them. Thus, Molet (1974) shows that several mythical animals entered Malagasy folklore from the bottom of Chinese dishes exported to the island. Some ceramics survived in deposits on the northwest coast and the dragons and other phantasms drawn in porcelain are the prototypes of the strange and sensational monsters in folklore, exactly as dragons are in our own folklore. Iconatrophy, as this phenomenon is called, is also well known from elsewhere, for example, in Ethiopia (Doresse 1972:215).

ART IN ECONOMIC AND SOCIAL HISTORY

Man-made objects testify to a technology. Representative art, such as the goldweights, extends our knowledge of objects and relates directly to process and production and consumption. Objects and art objects relate to trade in other ways. Mediums were imported as the copper alloys were in Igbo Ukwu or the brass in Benin, or foreign objects are mute witnesses to contact that must have taken place. North African Mamluk copper vessels from fourteenth- or fifteenth-century Egypt in northern Ghana are evidence of contact (Posnansky 1979:53; Cole and Ross 1977). Styles can be evidence of contact either by the presence of 'transitional' style or by foreign influences on local style. Thus, some fifteenth- and again eighteenth-century Ethiopian paintings show evident Far Eastern influences, perhaps Japanese (Leroy 1967:41; Chojnacki 1973:38). Architecture there, a century earlier, has links with Mogul India. We know of the Indian connections via Goa from other sources; we did not know at all about links with the Far East, however indirect they may have been. In most cases such links were trade contacts, especially when several objects are found together. Finally, art objects can tell us something about relative values of materials. If ivory was reserved for the king, it was valuable; if it served to make pestles to pound grain it was not. The first case was true in Benin, the second in the villages along the Sankuru. If we say that bronze or brass was the equivalent of gold in some societies, we base this on the restricted use of objects made in such metals, the types of object (e.g., jewels) and the social context inferred from the use (Herbert 1973).

In social history, art objects are as valuable a source as in economic history. For they are art objects and not just utensils marked as something special. They are tied to institutions. The skill displayed in them testifies to degrees of specialization of labour. The distribution of their use relates to social stratification. Above all, concentrations of art objects around certain institutions indicate their dominant role in society. If art is concentrated around courts in states, around men's meeting houses in portions of Gabon and Cameroon, around mosques, churches or such temples as exist among the Tsogo of southern Gabon, around medicine and healing as in eastern Kasai (Zaïre), or among several centres of attention, it tells us directly and unambiguously what the important foci of society were. Lastly, some forms of art, especially personal art, i.e., body art, or art typically linked to a person rather than to a community, were commonly used to mark social strata, emphasize status and role. Much of this evanescent art, such as scarifications, hairstyles, differences in dress, has survived in painting or in sculpture.

Social historians simply do not yet realize the full potential of art in such matters. Nor do they appreciate sufficiently that art is a direct source, emanating from the community itself, not from foreign reports as is so often the case in sub-Saharan Africa. Historians are now sensitive to archaeology as evidence for social strata, for instance, as evidenced by differences in grave goods, or as evidence for social coercion and control when e.g. 'imperial style' buildings appear isolated from the main centres of rule in the Roman Empire or in the Zimbabwe kingdom. They are still not directly interested in the gruesome evidence for coercion in Ife and Owo as shown by the tied and gagged sacrificial victims or the baskets of cut-off heads (ill. in Eyo and Willett 1980:41–2). They have not yet attempted (perhaps wisely, given the quarrels over seriation!) to use Benin plaques and stylistic change in the royal heads as evidence correlating to oral traditional data about the fluctuations of power in Benin between the king and various groups of chiefs. And yet the changing proportions in the representation of kings and others, or the increasing portion paraphernalia occupy on royal heads is testimony to relative positions and to increased isolation of the king in a ritual position.

The potential of art objects to provide a better understanding of social history is so great that we could align example after example of different conclusions that can be drawn from such evidence and have not been, whether it be about the growth and spread of such institutions as associations, or about changing social strata, or about the evolution of statuses or roles, or about expressions of ethnicity. Only by using such sources can a full realization of their potential be acquired. But beyond their value, even as documents about social history, works of art are unique as crucial data about ideology, legitimation and worldview.

ART AND INTELLECTUAL HISTORY

Sources for intellectual history in the portion of Africa where writing was unknown or unused are skimpy indeed. We are in danger of writing history as if acting forces were driven merely by ecological, economic or social trends which we postulate, but often cannot really 'see' in the past, and we know little about aspirations, values, cosmologies, the role of individual thought or even action. As an expression of culture art addresses these issues. Because of the problems of interpretation it poses, art cannot be a panacea for all other gaps in the record, but it certainly draws attention to this side of the past and sheds some light on it.

Changing ideology, legitimation and altering values can often be directly documented. For instance, among the Songo of Angola a new sort of icon was made in the second half of the last century. It showed a trader on an ox accompanied by a bird, a white oxpecker, the symbol of luck and wealth and masculinity (Bastin 1968/9: esp. 78, 80, Fig. 10). In works of a neighbouring society and of the same period, among the Chokwe, the motif of a well-defined mask and hat connotated power and wealth. With the expansion of the long-distance trade, the notion of wealth gained at the expense of the other elements that went into the make-up of power, and the motif appeared prominently on Chokwe thrones. The Songo icon and the Chokwe motif speak directly of change in values: wealth, obtained by trade brought prestige, a prestige that competed with increasing success against the older prestige vested in the chieftaincy.

The comparison of synchronic representations in different cultures vividly contrasts the meaning of roles that otherwise might seem similar. For the Kuba, womanhood was a dramatic and sad role, best expressed by the statue, *ngaat apoong,* set up in front of the initiation wall. She was seen explicitly as a sister and as a wife. As a sister she was doomed to be taken away from her near and dear to live among strangers. That was symbolized by her being tied to a circle – at other times in a circle – of raffia at the foot of the wall, just under the highest mask, that of her brother. The facial expression and pregnancy also relate to this (Plate 11.3).

On Kuba masks of women, *ngady amwaash,* the same role was expressed by the stylized tears. In contrast, the Chokwe in their masks and the Dan of Liberia and the Ivory Coast in their masks and rare statues of women, glorified female beauty and sensuous pleasure (Himmelheber 1960: 187). Elsewhere, as among the Akan or on the coast of Zaïre, motherhood was emphasized, even though it was the motherhood of chiefs in a matrilineal society. They were the originators of dynasties, the source of noble men. In southeastern Zaïre, femininity was obviously praised, but, despite their beauty, women were portrayed as holders of ambiguous mystical powers (see Plate 5.5), as servants

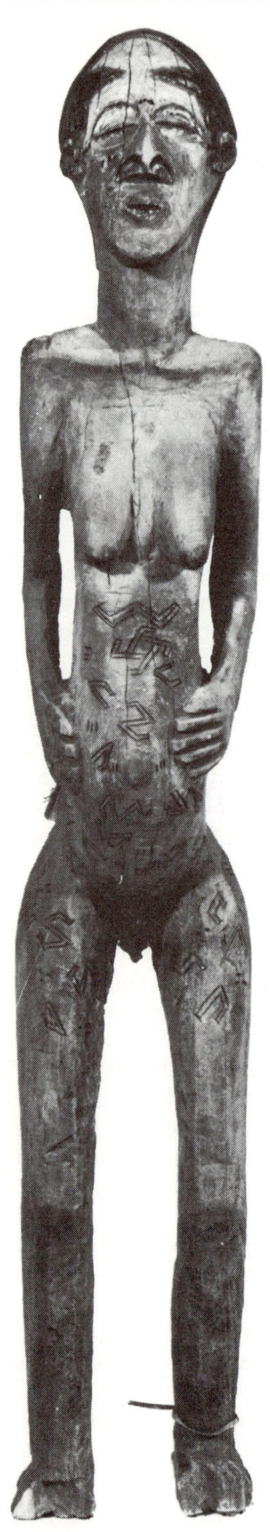

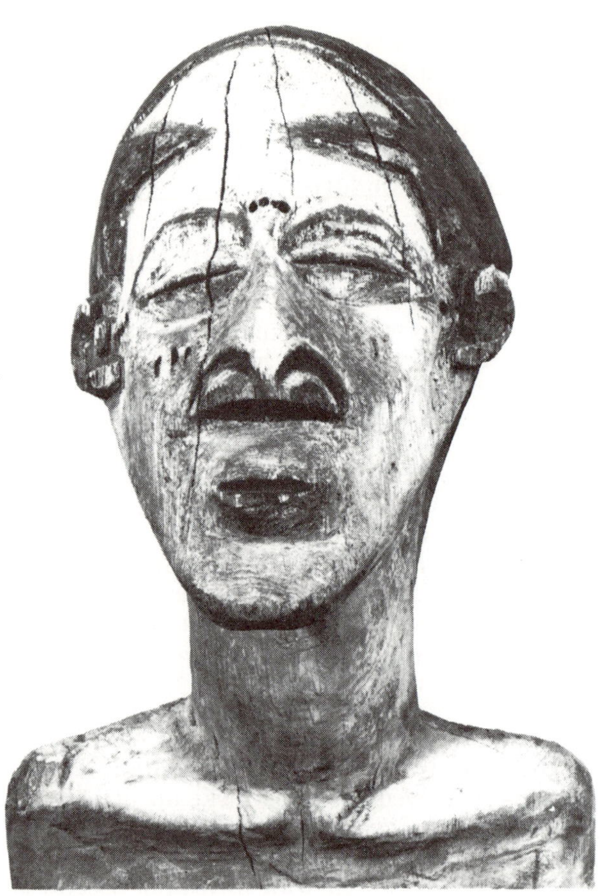

Plate 11.3 *Female figure. Wood, white clay, paint, hair. Used in boys' initiation. Mapey, Kuba country, Zaïre. Koninklijk Museum voor Midden Afrika, Tervuren. Height 146·5cm. Photo 1953. Made shortly before(?)*

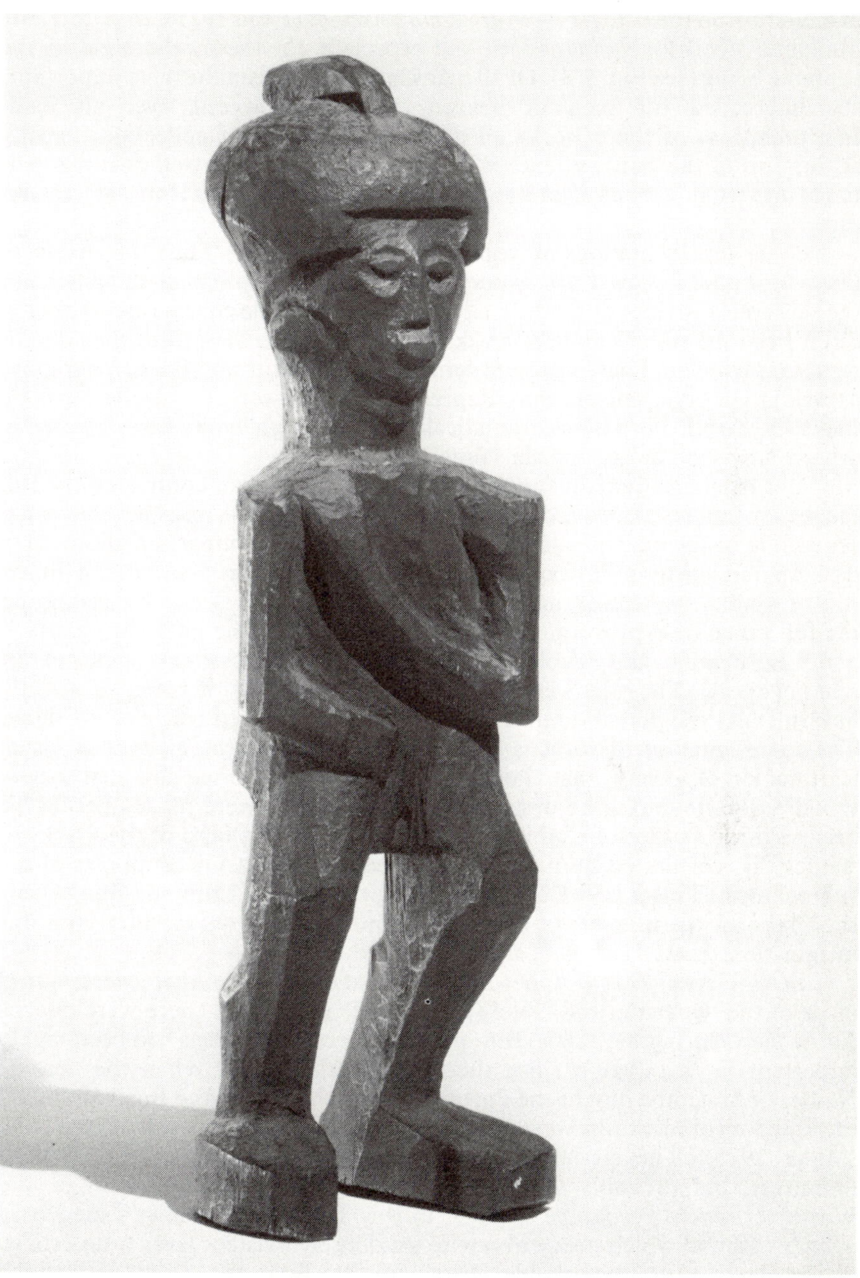

Plate 11.4 *Charm. Wood. Named* ishak indweemy *such charms represent female nature spirit. Exact use unknown. Kuba kingdom. Museum, University of Pennsylvania. Height 33cm. Acquired in Africa before 1920.* Ishak indweemy *styles remain still unknown. A statuette of similar style and size was acquired on the Kinshasa market in 1971 from a Kuba hawker*

of men, or – on the contrary – as great ancestresses (Flam 1971). In Nubia, the Madonna stood for womanhood, and especially for the motherhood of the supreme being (see Fig. 5.4). Of all mankind she had been the most important, she interceded for men in heaven, and she towered over all men. Interpretations of these works all date from the time of collection, usually at the turn of the century, except for Nubia. They are all well documented, based on a whole corpus of data and not contradicted by other icons, at least not directly.

Other representations of women complement these. Thus, for instance, Plates 6.6 and 8.5 show Kuba women in other roles: the pregnant daughter and the sensuous provider of food. In addition, Kuba female charm figures greatly differ from the statues and the masks discussed (Plate 11.4). But they do not represent women. They represent female nature spirits and the iconography, as well as the style reflects this. Representations of women elsewhere among the cases cited do not vary as dramatically, even though females are depicted in other roles, such as the female saints in Nubia.

Our examples remain superficial in that we have not contrasted the full range of meanings associated with womanhood in all these cases but only what are seen to be the main ideals. Nevertheless, even this comparison allows us to develop our sensitivity towards the variation in meanings associated with the role of woman, meanings that are then to be further developed by examining the full range of expression both in the visual and in the performing arts.

Legitimation and ideology are powerfully expressed in works of art relating to rule. The ruler's enclosure as well as the minbar in mosques directly link rule and religion and tell us how religion legitimized rule every Friday. The representation of persons crucial in founding myths gives us a visual legitimation of society, that allows us at the very least to see how that society visualized its founding heroes at the time the works were made. Earlier we discussed the statues of Chibinda Ilunga, the founding hero of the Chokwe, statues that celebrated hunting, physical power, the various supports of the supernatural. This is how Chokwe, relating the story of Chibinda Ilunga, saw their hero in the nineteenth century and not the way we see him with our imaginations now.

In a society along the upper Kwango, that of the Holo, there were statues made of the 'Queen of the Holo' (Plate 11.5), and indeed there were queens ruling there during the 1880s. But, more importantly, queens had been highly important in that region since the seventeenth century when the heroine Nzinga of Matamba fought the Portuguese and the Dutch and finally founded the kingdom of Matamba west of the Kwango River, just across from the Holo (Miller 1975). The statue of the queen reflects the Holo view of their foundress, but probably also that of the ideal woman ruler, Nzinga. No Westerner would recognize a queen in this statue of a woman seated on a cylinder around which heavy iron wire was loosely twisted. Even a superficial glance shows three remarkable characteristics: first, the sexlessness of the person: no breasts, no sex. This was not a woman, it was a ruler. High status is merely indicated by the coiffure and femininity only by the holes in the ears. Second, the face differs from conventional Holo representations giving it a strong expression of will and dynamic resolve rather than the usual serenity. That makes this the portrait of a ruler. And lastly there is the metal, which

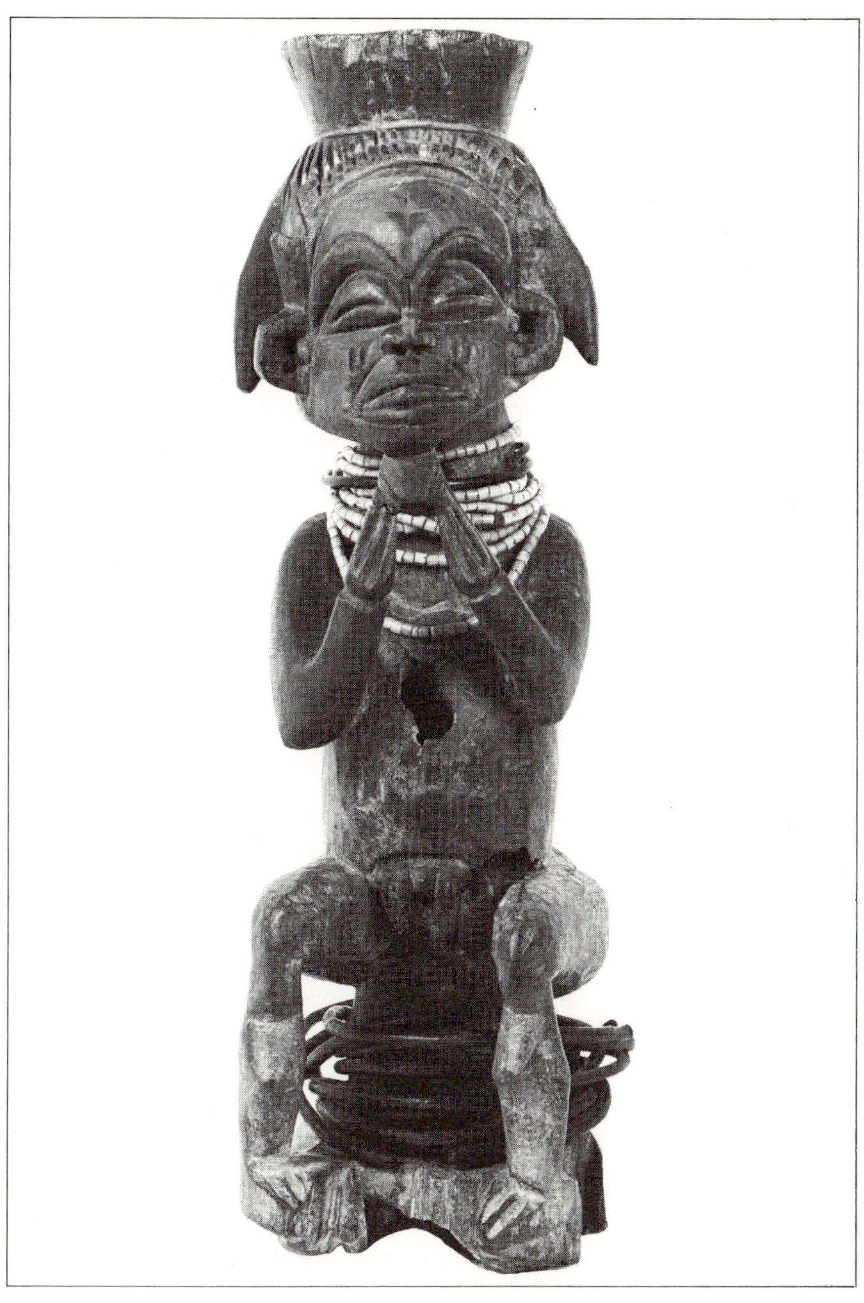

Plate 11.5 *Statue of a queen of the Holo. Wood, iron, yellow beads and one red one. Use unknown. Upper middle Kwango, Zaïre/Angola. Collection J. Hautelet. Height 39cm. Date of acquisition unknown*

alludes to the special status of the Holo in the area as famed blacksmiths. The lack of femininity and the ruthless will agree well with the written data existing about Nzinga of Matamba and contrast totally with the representations of her imagined by Europeans in the eighteenth century where she is very feminine and irresolute! (European illustrations: 17th c. Cavazzi 1965: vol. 2, 67, 68, 73; Bassani 1977:xiii; 18th c. Davidson 1961:18.) The contrast could not be greater. Thus the representations of ancestors or founders bring personality back into African history and show us the visual images later generations had about such personalities.

Art also expresses cosmology, sometimes explicitly as in Christian art or in the sculpture of the Dogon, sometimes only by implication. Explicit cosmology allows us easily to follow different threads that tie it to social organization. Thus, the emperors of Ethiopia and its warrior saints were almost interchangeable. In Nubia rulers protected by the Virgin were puny in relation even to saints and angels. In Islam finer differences in mosques emphasized local shades of theology. Thus, when the Almohads fought the Almoravids, they legitimized their bid for power by the assertion that the Almoravids deviated from Islam. Almohads stressed the 'oneness' of God (their name means 'one'), the theology of the oneness of God *(tawhid)*, and a humble and mystical approach to God. Their mosques were severe and plain. When they took Fes they whitewashed the rich decorative patterns in the honeycombed domes of the aisle leading up to the mihrab (Terrasse 1968). That expressed their legitimation of their bid for power. The power itself, they expressed in massive military architecture, in which proportions rather than decor were all important.

South of the Sahara, cosmology was rarely directly expressed, but the conventions of art imply it. From the proportions it is clear that on the Benin plaques kings towered over other men. The corpus of Kongo and related art of lower Zaïre stresses the real hidden world and the powers of charms, not of gods. Thus, an ivory horn of unknown age from Loango depicts the founding 'Queen of the Vili' seated on her elephant recalling the foundation myth and its cosmology. Hidden deep in the horn another statue has been detected by X-rays. The ensemble renders a worldview in iconic form, dissociating the visible and the real (ill. Neyt 1981:89).

Among works of art, regalia in kingdoms, sets of objects belonging to overarching institutions elsewhere, are especially valuable both to document legitimation and to provide insight into cosmology. Unfortunately, very few of such sets could be studied until recently. As long as the institutions had deep meaning, their icons were not accessible. Now such icons are beginning to be studied. What they reveal is that cosmologies and ideologies alike were far more complex than is usually imagined. They are a condensation of cosmology, theories of social organization, legitimations of existing order . . . and pose obvious problems of interpretation. Much of the local interpretations about these objects will be of recent vintage, because the original meaning of many features has been overlaid. Nevertheless the outlines of older meanings should still be discernible.

THE RELEVANCE OF ART TO HISTORY

Ultimately art history is relevant to general history because of two special properties: the concrete character of works of art and the fact that trends in art directly document meaningful change at large.

The houses of Lamu in the eighteenth century illustrate the concrete character of art. Art is the past coming to us without simplification, without generalization and it comes to us at a glance. It is an ideal mode of expression to render a situation directly rather than to describe it with all the selectivity description entails. This opaque character of art, this power of confrontation, baffles the historian, who is not used to being brought face to face with a foreign reality from the past. Art works do not narrate, they do not argue. They present a whole at once. This property implies a complexity of everything in one: medium, technology, use, social, emotional and mental significance, a frozen slice of life as it were. To explore and to understand a work of art fully one must relate it to everything that is known about the period and the place from where it stems. Even so, it almost always raises new problems to be solved and does not just confirm the already known. Its major challenge to historians though is that art acts as a total proof. After an historian has made all his dissections of data, traced all his causalities, built up his explanatory theory, it must stand the test of art. It should explain everything about this testimony to the 'spirit of the age'. The object from the past should fit naturally in the reconstruction of the past, and it is because of this power to challenge, to uncover precisely what remains unknown and what is known, that art works are important to historians.

Trends in art history should also reflect social and cultural history, for they are an expression of that history both in its superficial alterations and in its deep, often barely conscious changes. A few examples make this clear. We start with a clear-cut and simple case of culture contact. A drawing was made on the door of the house of the headman of the village of Lemba in 1885 or shortly before (Plate 11.6). It is a mixture of local style and European influences. Lemba was then some ten miles away from Leopoldville where the European post had only been established in December 1881. Barely three to four years later that fact was reflected not only in a passing sketch but as a received alteration in style consecrated by the eminent place in which it was displayed. It was taken away from Lemba during a raid by Europeans in December 1885 or January 1886 (Bula Nzau 1894:194–7; Krieger 1969: vol. 3, 56, Bild 180; Biographie Coloniale Belge 1951: vol. 2, 690–1). Art works indeed reflect events!

Art expresses changes in mentality of long duration. Thus we find that before the advent of the Almohad dynasty, Moroccans had already begun to elaborate a cult for the dead, something that, strictly speaking, is outlawed in Islam. They built an addition to the main mosque at Fes on the outside of the mihrab wall, near the focal point of the whole oratory, so that corpses could be put near the mihrab without being in the mosque, which they would have polluted. A little over a century later, in 1310, the Marinids laid out the first dynastic cemetery with an oratory and mausolea at Chella, while in the countryside, well-built domed tombs began to be erected for renowned saintly men. In very little time such tombs came to be surrounded by a mosque and a

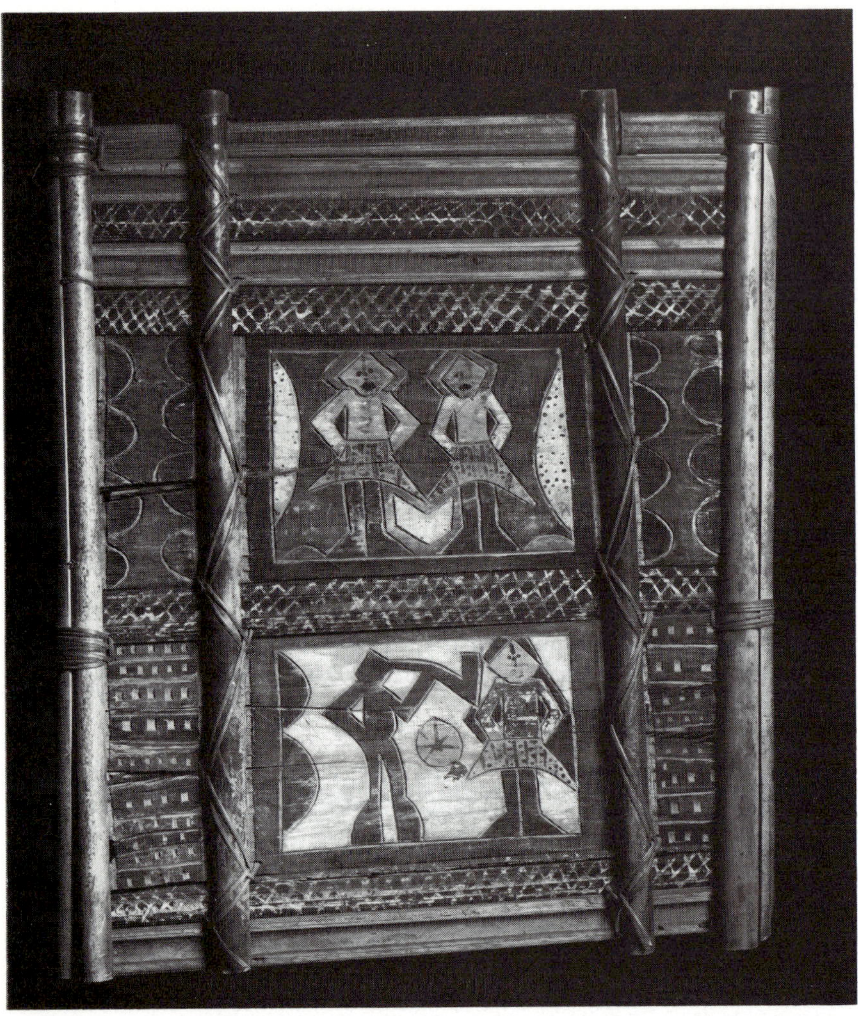

Plate 11.6 *Doorpanel. Wood, raffia stems, vines, paint black and white. Used in the house of the headman of Lemba village, Hum people, Zaïre (near Kinshasa). Museum für Völkerkunde, Berlin-Dahlem. Height 84·3cm. Painted 1882–1885*

school as the descendants and disciples of the holy men gathered and as the tombs became centres for pilgrimage. By the 1350s, brotherhoods were formed, founded by mystical holy men, whose lodges formed around the tomb sites of saints. Such *zawiya* were soon to become such a force in the land that all future governments in Morocco have had to cope with them. The architectural evidence shows this spread of the cult for the dead, for saints in particular, and correctly shows that the trend was older than the Marinid dynasty. The founding saints of Moroccan Sufism lived earlier under the Almohads, themselves mystically inclined. But as the mosque at Fes shows, the cult of the dead had begun to take hold even before the Almohads were well established, even before Sufi saints appeared. Despite their purism the Almohads could not arrest this development. It was only deflected and became a cult for the saints only. Art here testifies to a long and major shift in Moroccan society and in Moroccan mentality as it developed over two centuries (Terrasse 1932, 1968; Marçais 1954:281–4, 299–301; Laroui 1977:245–6).

More general and longer trends can also be correlated. Coptic art as a whole shows increasing tendencies towards stylization, away from the extreme naturalism which was its milieu of origin and became a highly ascetic art (du Bourguet 1967; Wessel 1965; Badawy 1978). In an evolution spanning well over five centuries the trend was never reversed. We can link it to the facts that Coptic art was Christian art above all and that it was an art for the dispossessed whether by and for monks, away from the Nile valley, or for the middle class and the poor in the valley itself. The evolution was a spiritualization of art, where meaning rather than full figuration counted for more and more. It is thus possible to account for the evolution of art, of social and of intellectual history at once. Nevertheless, difficulties remain, for monks did not become ever more ascetic with the passage of time, nor did the common people become more dispossessed, nor were all Copts always poor. Rather, the trend continued under its own momentum both in art and in religious expression. Moreover, even before the Arab conquest, stylization had become a profoundly perceived ethnic trend. Coptic religion and Coptic art were typical Egyptian features.

With this last example we reach two limits. The reader will appreciate that when we deal with such time spans and such complex correlations, our sketch becomes less and less convincing for lack of detailed evidence which requires more space than I have in this book. But we also reach a limit of what can be proved. If we went beyond this limit we could, for instance, argue that the development of geometrical arabesques to new heights and new mechanical precision of execution under the Marinids is to be related to the increased role of lawyers in public life and of law as a way of thinking with its sharp concepts and its long consequences. But the link is farfetched. This also was an age of rising mysticism. So why not correlate the conquest of voids by geometry with mysticism? Such links cannot be proved, merely suggested. Because they cannot be demonstrated by detailed correspondence they remain fruitless. But that last case does illustrate the particular danger of using art history within a general framework: namely, to let imagination run away with what become personal interpretations of an age.

Art history is important to general history. It brings sources, it brings us an immediacy from the past that cannot be replaced or ignored, and it gives us a further tool to probe the significance of both small breezes and long trade winds in the atmosphere of history. Art is a weathervane of history, and more. Art, produced by forces outside itself, expresses metaphors which in turn can lead to further cultural and social change.

REFERENCES AND FURTHER READING

BIBLIOGRAPHIES

BASKIN, L. J. P. (1968) *An Annotated Bibliography . . . on Ethiopian Art*, Addis Ababa

BURT, E. C. (1980) *An Annotated Bibliography of the Visual Arts of East Africa*, Bloomington, Indiana

COULET WESTERN, D. (1975) *Bibliography of the Arts of Africa*, Waltham, Massachusetts

CRESWELL, K. A. C. (1961) *A Bibliography of the Architecture, Arts and Crafts of Islam*, Cairo

GASKIN, L. J. P. (1965) *A Bibliography of African Art*, London

KAMMERER, W. (1950) *A Coptic Bibliography*, Ann Arbor, Michigan

OYENIYI, OSUNDINA (1968) *Bibliography of Nigerian Sculpture*, Lagos

JOURNAL ABBREVIATIONS

AA: *African Arts*
AAN: *Arts d'Afrique Noire*
AT: *Africa-Tervuren*
JAH: *Journal of African History*

REFERENCES

ADAMS, W. Y. (1977) *Nubia, Corridor to Africa*, Princeton, New Jersey

ALAGOA, E. J. (1972) *History of the Niger Delta*, Ibadan

APPIAH, P. (1979) 'Akan symbolism', *AA*, 13 (1), 64–7

ARKELL, A. J. (1950) 'Gold Coast copies of 5th–7th centuries bronze lamps', *Antiquity*, 24, 38–40

ATHERTON, J. and KALOUS, M. (1970) 'Nomoli', *JAH*, 11 (3), 303–17

ATIL, E. (1981) *Art of the Mamluks*, Washington

AYOUB, A. and GALLEY, M. (1977) *Images de Djazya*, Paris.

BADAWY, A. (1978) *Coptic Architecture and Archaeology*, Cambridge, Massachusetts

al-BAKRI (1968) 'Kitab almasalik wa'l mamalik (1067/8)'. Translated by V. Monteil, 'Routier de l'Afrique blanche et noire du nord-ouest', *Bulletin de l'Institut Fondamental d'Afrique Noire B*, 30, 39–116

BALANDIER, G. (1968) *Daily Life in the Kingdom of Kongo, from the Sixteenth to the Eighteenth Century*, New York

BASCOM, W. (1973) *African Art in Cultural Perspective*, New York
BASSANI, E. (1977) *Scultura Africana Nei Musei Italiani*, Bologna
BASSANI, E. (1978) 'Les sculptures Vallisnieri', *AT*, 24 (1), 15–22
BASTIN, M. L. (1965) 'Tshibinda Ilunga', *Baessler Archiv*, NF 13, 501–37
BASTIN, M. L. (1968/9) 'L'art d'un peuple d'Angola 1. Chokwe . . .3. Songo', *AA*, 2 (2), 40–6, 60–4; (3), 50–7, 77–81
BASTIN, M. L. (1976) 'Une statuette de Tshibinda Ilunga (Tshokwe, Angola) disparue d'un musée portugais (ou elle se trouvait depuis 1914) mutilée dans un but de fraude)', *AT*, 22 (1), 4–8
BATTUTA, (Ibn) (1966) *Tuhfat al-nuzzar fi ghara'ib al-amsar wa-'aja'ib al-asfar* (1352/3 voyage). Trans. V. Monteil, R. Mauny, A. Djenidi, S. Robert, J. Devisse, *Extraits Tiré des Voyages*, Dakar
BAUMANN, H. (1929) *Afrikanisches Kunstgewerbe* in Th. Bossert (ed.), *Geschichte des Kunstgewerbes*, 6 vols. Berlin, vol. 2, pp. 104 seq.
BAUMANN, H. (1964) 'Die Ethnologische Beurteilung einer Vorgeschichtlicher Keramik in Mittelafrika' in *Festschrift für A. Jensen*, Munich, vol. 1, pp. 13–58
BAUMANN, H. (1969) *Afrikanische Plastik und Sakrales Königtum*, Munich
BEDAUX, R. (1977) *Tellem:een Bijdrage tot de geschiedenis van de Republik Mali*, Utrecht (Tellem: a contribution to the history of the Republic Mali)
BEDAUX, R. (1980) 'The geographic distribution of footed bowls in the Upper and Middle Niger region' in B. K. Swartz and R. E. Dummett (eds), *West African Culture Dynamics*, The Hague, pp. 247–58
BEDAUX, R., CONSTANDSE-WESTERMANN, T. S., HACQUEBORD, L., LANGE, A. G., VAN DER WAALS, J. D. (1980) 'Recherches archéologiques dans le Delta interieur du Niger', *Palaeohistoria* (1978), 91–220
BEN AMOS, P. (1976) 'Men and Animals in Benin Art', *Man*, (NS) 11, 242–52
BEN AMOS, P. (1980a) *The Art of Benin*, London
BEN AMOS, P. (1980b) 'Patron-artist interactions in Africa,' *AA*, 13 (3), 46–7, 92
BERNATZIK, H. A. (1932) 'Meine Expedition nach Portugiesisch-Guinea', *Atlantis*, 4, 197–211
BERNATZIK, H. A. (1933) *Aethiopien des Westens*, Vienna
BIEBUYCK, D. (1973) *Lega Culture*, Berkeley, California
Biographie Coloniale Belge (1948–1977) Brussels, 7 vols.
BIRMINGHAM, D. and MARTIN, P. (eds) (1983) *History of Central Africa*, 2 vols., London
BISSON, M. (1975) 'Copper currency in Central Africa – the archaeological evidence', *World Archaeology*, 6 (3), 276–92
BONTINCK, F. (1979) 'La provenance des sculptures Vallisnieri', *AT*, 25 (4), 88–91
BRAIN, R. (1980) *Art and Society in Africa*, London
BRANDENBURG, D. (1966) *Islamische Baukunst in Aegypten*, Berlin
BRAVMANN, R. (1973) *Open Frontiers*, New York
BRAVMANN, R. (1974) *Islam and Tribal Art in West Africa*, Cambridge
BREUIL H. (1955) *The White Lady of the Brandberg*, Paris and London
BROWN, J. L. (1980) 'Miji Kenda Grave and Memorial Sculpture', *AA*, 13 (4), 36–9, 88
BRUEL, G. (1910) 'Les populations de la Moyenne Sanga', *Revue d'Ethnographie et de Sociologie*, 1, 3–32 (Pomo and Bomwali)
BULA NZAU (BAILEY), H. (1894) *Travels and Adventures in the Congo Free State and its Big Game Shooting*, London
Bundesministerium für Unterricht (1970) *Nubische Kunst aus Faras*, Vienna

THE CAMBRIDGE HISTORY OF AFRICA (1975–78) R. Oliver (ed.), Cambridge, vols. 2–5

CAVAZZI DE MONTECUCCOLO, G. A. (1965) *Istorica Descrizione dei tre regni: Congo, Matamba e Angola*, Bologna 1687, trans. G. M. De Leguzzano, *Descricão historica dos Tres Reinos: Congo, Matamba e Angola,* 2 vols, Lisbon (Historical Description of the Three Kingdoms: Congo, Matamba and Angola)

CHAFFIN, A. F. (1979) *L'Art Kota. Les figures de reliquaire,* Meudon

CHITTICK, N. (1974) 'Excavations at Axum: a preliminary report', *Azania,* 9, 195–205

CHITTICK, N. (1976) 'Radiocarbon Dates from Axum', *Azania,* 9, 179–81

CHOJNACKI, S. (1973) 'Ethiopian Paintings', *Religious Art of Ethiopia,* n.l. (Recklinghausen?)

CHOJNACKI, S. (1977) 'Two Ethiopian Icons', *AA*, 10 (4), 44–7, 56–61, 86

CLAERHOUT, A. (1971) *Afrikaanse Kunst,* Utrecht (African Art)

CLAERHOUT, A. (1978) 'Een ongewone edan-ogboni', *De Vrienden van het Etnografisch Museum Antwerpen,* 5 (2), 2–3 (An unusual edan-ogboni)

COART, E. (1927) *Les Nattes,* Brussels

COART, E. and HAULEVILLE, A. (1907) *La Ceramique,* Brussels

COLE, H. (1969a) 'Mbari is life', *AA*, 2 (3), 8–17, 87

COLE, H. (1969b) 'Mbari is a dance', *AA*, 2 (4), 42–51, 79

COLE, H. (1969c) 'Art is a verb in Iboland', *AA*, 3 (1), 34–9

COLE, H. (1975) 'The history of Ibo mbari houses: facts and theories' in D. F. McCall and E. Bay (eds), *African Images,* New York, pp. 104–32

COLE, H. and ROSS, D. (1977) *The Arts of Ghana,* Los Angeles

CORDELL, D. (1973) 'Throwing knives in Equatorial Africa: a distributional study', *Ba-Shiru,* 5 (1), 94–104

CORNET, J. (1972) *Art de l'Afrique noire au pays du fleuve Zaire,* Brussels

CORNET, J. (1975) *Arts of Africa. Treasures from the Congo,* New York

CORNET, J. (1976) 'A propos des statues ndengese', *AAN,* 17, 6–16

CORNET, J. (1978) *A Survey of Zairian Art: The Bronson Collection,* Raleigh, North Carolina

CORNET, J. (1980) 'Pictographies woyo', *Quaderni Poro,* no. 2, Milan

CRESWELL, K. A. C. (1952–9) *The Muslim Art of Egypt,* 2 vols, Oxford

CRINE-MAVAR, B. (1968) 'A propos de la stérilité artistique des Lunda', *Etudes Congolaises,* 11 (2), 59–67

CROWE, D. W. (1971) 'The geometry of African art: 1. Bakuba Art', *Journal of Geometry,* 1, 169–82

DANIELS, C. (1970) *The Garamantes of Northern Libya,* Stoughton, Wisconsin

DARK, P. J. C. (1973) 'Brass casting in West Africa', *AA,* 6 (4), 50–3, 94

DARK, P. J. C. (1975) 'Benin bronze heads: styles and chronologies' in D. F. McCall and E. Bay (eds), *African Images,* New York, pp. 25–103

DARK, P. J. C. (1981) 'Head and Tusk' in S. Vogel (ed.), *For Spirits and Kings,* New York, 136–40

DAVIDSON, B. (1961) *Black Mother,* Harmondsworth and Boston, Massachusetts

DAVIES, O. (1967) *West Africa Before the Europeans,* London

d'AZEVEDO, W. L. (1973a) 'Sources of Gola Artistry' in W. L. d'Azevedo (ed.), *The Traditional Artist in African Societies,* Bloomington, Indiana, pp. 282–340

d'AZEVEDO, W. L. (1973b) (ed.) *The Traditional Artist in African Societies,* Bloomington, Indiana

DECHAMPS, R. (1970/8) 'L'identification anatomique des bois utilisés pour des sculptures en Afrique', *AT,* 16 and 24

DE GRUNNE, B. (1980) *Ancient Terra Cottas From West Africa,* Louvain-la-neuve

DE HEUSCH, L. (1956) 'Le symbolisme du forgeron en Afrique', *Reflets du Monde,* 10, 57–70

DELANGE, J. (1974) *The Art and Peoples of Black Africa,* New York
DE MARET, P. (1977) 'Sanga: new excavations, more data and some related problems', *JAH,* 18 (3), 321–38
DE MARET, P. (1980a) 'Ceux qui jouent avec le feu: la place du forgeron en Afrique centrale', *Africa,* 50 (3), 263–79
DE MARET, P. (1980b) 'Les trop fameux pots a fossette basale du Kasai', *AT,* 26 (1), 4–12
DEMESSE, L. (1980) *Techniques et Economie des Pygmées Babinga,* Paris
DENNINGER, E. (1971) 'Use of paper chromatography to determine the age of albuminous binders and its application to rock paintings', *South African Journal of Science,* 2, 80–4
DENYER, S. (1978) *African Traditional Architecture,* London, New York
DE SOUSBERGHE, L. (1959) *L'Art Pende,* Brussels
DE VERE ALLEN, J. (1974a) 'Swahili architecture in the later Middle Ages', *AA,* 7 (2), 42–7, 66–8, 83–4
DE VERE ALLEN, J. (1974b) 'Swahili culture reconsidered: some historical implications of the material culture of the northern Kenya coast in the 18th and 19th centuries', *Azania,* 9, 105–38
DE VERE ALLEN, J. and WILSON, T. H. (1979) *Swahili Houses and Tombs of the Coast of Kenya,* London
DINKLER, E. (1970) *Kunst und Geschichte Nubiens in Christlicher Zeit,* Recklinghausen
DITTMER, K. (1967) 'Bedeutung, Datierung und Kulturhistorische Zusammenhange der "prähistorischen" Steinfiguren aus Sierra Leone und Guinee', *Baessler Archiv,* NF 15, 183–238
DJAIT, H. J. (1980) 'Written sources before the 15th century, in J. Ki Zerbo (ed.), *General History of Africa,* London, vol. 1, pp. 87–113
DORESSE, J. (1972) *La Vie Quotidienne des Ethiopiens Chrétiens (au XVII° et au XVIII° siecles),* Paris
DREWAL, H. (1980) *African Artistry: technique and aesthetics in Yoruba sculpture,* Atlanta, Georgia
DREWAL, H. (1981) 'Staff (Edan Oshogbo)' in S. Vogel (ed.), *For Spirits and Kings,* New York, pp. 90–1
DU BOURGUET, M. P. (1967) *The Art of The Copts,* New York
DUPRÉ, M. C. (1968) 'A propos d'un masque teke de l'Ouest Congo', *Objets et Mondes,* 8, (4);, 295–310
DUPRÉ, M. C. (1979) 'A propos du masque teke de la collection Barbier', *Connaissance des Arts Tribaux. Bulletin du Musé Barbier-Muller,* no. 2
DUPRÉ, M. C. (1980) 'l'art kota est-il vraiment kota?', *l'Ethnographie,* 83, 343–55

ELISOFON, E. and FAGG, W. (1958) *The Sculpture of Africa,* New York
Exoticophylacium Weickmannianum (1659), Anon., Ulm (Weickmann Catalogue)
EYO, E. (1978) 'Ekpe costume of the Cross River', *AA,* 12 (1), 73–5, 108
EYO, E. and WILLETT, F. (1980) *Treasures of Ancient Nigeria,* New York

FAGE, J. (1977) 'Upper and Lower Guinea' in R. Oliver (ed.), *The Cambridge History of Africa,* Cambridge, vol. 3, pp. 463–518
FAGG, W. (1959) *Afro-Portuguese Ivories,* London
FAGG, W. (1965) *Tribes and Forms in African Art,* New York
FAGG, W. (1970) *Divine Kingship in Africa,* London
FAGG, W. and PICTON, J. (1970) *The Potter's Art in Africa,* London
FAIRLEY, N. J. (1978) 'Mianda yaBen'Ekie', Ph.D. theses, University of New York, Stony Brook, English text (Matters of the Ben'Ekie)

FERNANDEZ, J. W. (1971) 'Principles of opposition and vitality in Fang aesthetics' in C. J. Jopling (ed.), *Art and Aesthetics in Primitive Societies: a critical anthology*, New York, pp. 356–73

FERNANDEZ, J. W. (1974) Review, *AA*, 8 (1), 76–7

FERNANDEZ, J. W. (1975) Letter, *AA*, 8 (2), 2

FISCHER, E. (1978) 'Dan Forest spirits: masks in Dan villages', *AA*, 11 (2), 16–23, 94

FLAM, J. (1971) 'The symbolic structure of Baluba caryatid stools', *AA*, 4 (2), 54–9

FLEMING, S. (1977) *Dating in Archaeology*, New York

FLEURIOT DE LANGLE, A. (1876) 'Croisières à la côte d'Afrique', *Le Tour du Monde*, 31 (1), 289–304

FOCILLON, H. (1943) *La Vie des Formes*, Paris

FRANCASTEL, P. (1951) *Peinture et Société*, Paris

FRASER, D. (1972) 'The fish-legged figure in Benin and Yoruba art' in D. Fraser and H. Cole (eds), *African Art and Leadership*, Madison, Wisconsin, pp. 261–74

FRASER, D. (1980) Review, *AA*, 14 (1), 15–22

FRASER, D. (1981a) 'A propos', *AA*, 14 (2), 27–8

FRASER, D. (1981b) 'Pair of armlets' in S. Vogel (ed.), *For Spirits and Kings*, New York, pp. 128–9

FROBENIUS, L. (1896) 'Die Kunst der Naturvölker', *Westermanns Monatshefte*, 79–329–340, 593–606

FROBENIUS, L. (1898) *Masken und Geheimbunde Afrikas*, Leipzig, vol. 79, pp. 329–40, 593–606

FROBENIUS L. (1907) *Im Schatten des Kongostaates*, Berlin

FROBENIUS L. (1933) *Kulturgeschichte Afrikas*, Zurich

GARDI, R. (1969) *African Crafts and Craftsmen*, New York

GARLAKE, P. S. (1973) *Great Zimbabwe*, New York

GARRARD, T. (1979) 'Akan metal arts', *AA*, 13 (1), 36–43, 100

GARRARD, T. (1980) *Akan Weights and the Gold Trade*, London

GAULME, F. (1981) *Le Pays de Cama*, Paris

GEBAUER, P. (1979) *Art of Cameroun*, New York

GERBRANDS, A. A. (1957) *Art as an Element of Culture Especially in Negro Africa*, Leiden

GERSTER, G. (1968) *L'Art Ethiopien: églises rupestres*, Paris

GHAIDAN, U. (1973) 'Swahili plasterwork', *AA*, 6 (2), 46–59

GOLLNHOFER, O. and SILLANS, R. (1963) 'Recherches sur le mysticisme des Mitsogo' in *Réincarnation et vie mystique en Afrique noire (colloque de Strasbourg)*, Strasburg, pp. 142–74

GOMBRICH, E. H. (1960) *Art and Illusion*, New York

GOODY, J. (ed.) (1968) *Literacy in Traditional Societies*, Cambridge

GRAEBNER, F. (1911) *Methode der Ethnologie*, Heidelberg

GRIAULE, M. (1948) *Dieu d'Eau*, Paris

GRIGORIEVA, M. (1980) *Hermitage, Leningrad*, Leningrad

GROTTANELLI, V. (1975) 'Discovery of a masterpiece', *AA*, 8 (4), 14–23, 83

GRUNER, D. (1977) 'Der Traditionelle Moscheebau am Mittleren Niger', *Paideuma*, 23, 101–40

HALDANE, D. (1978) *Mamluk Painting*, Warminster

HALLEN, B. (1979) 'The art historian as conceptual analyst', *Journal of Aesthetics and Art Criticism*, 37, 303–13

HAMMERSCHMIDT, E. and JAGER, O. (1968) *Illuminierte Aethiopische Hss*, Wiesbaden

HARTER, P. (1972) 'Les masques dit Bacham', *AAN*, 3, 18–45

HARTWIG, G. (1978) 'Sculpture in East Africa', *AA*, 11 (4), 62–5, 96

HAU, K. (1959) 'Evidence of the use of pre-Portuguese written characters by the Bini?', *Bulletin de l'Institut Français de l'Afrique Noire*, B.21, 109–54

HAU, K. (1964) 'A royal title on a palace tusk from Benin', *Bulletin de l'Institut Fondamental de l'Afrique Noire*, B.26, 21–39

HERBERT, E. (1973) 'Aspects of the use of copper in pre-colonial West Africa', *JAH*, 14 (2), 179–94

HERREMAN, F. (1978) 'Doorlichting van een kafigeledio', *De Vrienden van het Etnografisch Museum Antwerpen*, 5 (3), 2–4 (X-ray: kafigeledio)

HILL, D. and GOLVIN, L. (1976) *Islamic Architecture in North Africa*, Hamden, Connecticut

HIMMELHEBER, H. (1960) *Negerkunst und Negerkünstler*, Braunschweig

HOAG, J. D. (1963) *Western Islamic Architecture*, New York

HODGEN, M. (1942) 'Geographical distribution as a criterion of age', *American Anthropologist*, 44, 345–68

HOLY, L. (1967) *The Art of Africa. Masks and Figures from Eastern and Southern Africa*, Prague

HORTON, R. (1965a) *Kalabari Sculpture*, Lagos

HORTON, R. (1965b) 'A note on recent finds of brasswork in the Niger delta', *Odu*, 11 (1), 76–91

HRBEK, L. (1977) 'Egypt, Nubia and the Eastern Desert' in R. Oliver (ed.), *Cambridge History of Africa*, Cambridge, vol. 3, 10–97

HRBEK, L. (1980) 'Written Sources from the 15th century onwards' in J. Ki Zerbo (ed.), *General History of Africa*, London, vol. 1, 114–41

HULSTAERT, G. (1931) 'Over de volksstammen der Lomela', *Congo*, 1, 13–52 (About the peoples of the Lomela)

INSKEEP, R. R. (1979) *The Peopling of Southern Africa*, New York

ISAAC, E. (1968) *The Ethiopian Church*, Boston, Massachusetts

ISKANDER, Z. (1980) 'African archaeology and its techniques including dating techniques' in J. Ki Zerbo (ed.), *General History of Africa*, London, vol. 1, 206–32

JACOBSON, L. (1980) 'The White Lady of the Brandberg. A re-interpretation', *Namibiana*, 2(1), 21–9

JAEGER, O. A. (1965) *Antiquities of North Ethiopia*, Stuttgart

JOHNSON, M. (1977) 'Cloth strips and history', *West African Journal of Archaeology*, 7, 169–78

KAUENHOVEN JANZEN, R. (1981) 'Chokwe thrones', *AA*, 14 (3), 69–74, 92

KECSKESI, M. (1980) 'African Art at the Staatliches Museum für Völkerkunde, Munich', *AA*, 14 (1), 32–41

KI ZERBO, J. (ed.) (1980) *General History of Africa*, London, vol. 1, *Methodology and African Prehistory*

KRIEGER, K. and KUTSCHER, G. (1960) *Westafrikanische Masken*, Berlin

KRIEGER, K. (1965–69) *West Afrikanische Plastik*, Berlin, vol. 1 1965, vols 2 and 3 1969

KROEBER, A. (1948) *Anthropology*, New York

KROEBER, A. (1953) *Cultural and Natural Areas of Native America*, Berkeley, California

KUPER, A. and VAN LEYNSEELE, P. (1978) 'Social Anthropology and the "Bantu Expansion"', *Africa*, 48 (4), 342–56

LABURTHE-TOLRA, P. (1977) *Minlaaba*, 3 vols, Lille

LAJOUX, J-D. (1977) *Tassili n'Ajjer*, Paris
LAMB, V. (1975) *West African Weaving*, London
LAROUI, A. (1977) *The History of the Maghreb*, Princeton, New Jersey (Trans. R. Manheim)
LAVACHERY, H. (1954) *Statuaire de l'Afrique Noire*, Brussels
LAWAL, B. (1977) 'The present state of art historical research in Nigeria', *JAH*, 18 (2), 193–216
LAYTON, R. (1981) *The Anthropology of Art*, New York
LECOCQ, R. (1953) *Les Bamileke*, Paris
LEIRIS, M. and DELANGE, J. (1967) *Afrique Noire: la creation plastique*, Paris
LEM, F. H. (1948) *Sculptures Soudanaises*, Paris
LEROY, J. (1967) *Ethiopian Painting in the Late Middle Ages and During the Gondar Dynasty*, New York
LEROY, J. (1968) 'La peinture ethiopienne au Moyen Age' in G. Gerster (ed.), *L'art Éthiopien*, Paris, pp. 61–8
LEROY, J. (1973) *L'Ethiopie: archéologie et culture*, Paris
LEUZINGER, E. (1980) *The Art of Africa*, Baden Baden (Trans. from the German by A. Keep)
LEVTZION, N. (1973) *Ancient Ghana and Mali*, London
LEZINE, A. (1966) *Architecture de l'Ifriqiya, recherches sur les monuments aghlabides*, Paris
LOIR, H. (1935) *Le Tissage du Raphia au Congo Belge*, Brussels

McCALL, D. F. and BAY, E. (1975) *African Images: essays in African iconology*, New York
McINTOSH, R. and McINTOSH, S. (1981) 'Empire of Mali: evidence from Jenne-Jenno', *JAH*, 22 (1), 1–22
McNAUGHTON, P. (1970) 'The throwing knife in African history, *AA*, 3 (2), 54–60
MAES, J. (1938) *Kabila en Grafbeelden uit Kongo*, Brussels (Kabila statues and other funerary statues from Congo)
MAGGS, T. and DAVISON, P. (1981) 'The Lydenburg heads and the earliest African sculpture south of the Equator', *AA*, 14 (2), 28–33, 88
MAQUET, J. (1979) 'Art by metamorphosis', *AA*, 12 (4), 32–7, 90–1
MARÇAIS, G. (1954) *L'Architecture Musulmane d'Occident*, Paris
MARTIN, P. (1972) *The External Trade of the Loango Coast: 1576–1580*, Oxford
MAUNY, R. (1970) *Les siècles Obscurs de l'Afrique Noire: histoire et archéologie*, Paris
MEKHITARIAN, A. (1954) *La Peinture Egyptienne*, Geneva
MENZEL, B. (1968) *Goldgewichte aus Ghana*, Berlin
MENZEL, B. (1972) *Textilien aus Westafrika*, 3 vols, Berlin
MERCIER, M. (1928) 'Notes sur une architecture berbère saharienne', *Hesperis*, 8, 413–29
MERRIAM, A. (1973) 'The Bala musician' in W. D'Azevedo (ed.), *The Traditional Artist in African Societies*, Bloomington, Indiana, pp. 250–81
MICHALOWSKI, K. (1967) *Faras, die Kathedrale aus dem Wüstensand*, Einsiedeln
MILLER, J. C. (1975) 'Nzinga of Matamba in a new perspective', *JAH*, 16 (2), 201–16
MOLET, L. (1974) 'Origine chinoise possible de quelques animaux fantastiques de Madagascar', *Journal de la Société des Africanistes*, 64 (2), 123–38
MONNERET DE VILLARD, U. (1947) 'La Madonna di S. Maria Maggiore e l'illustrazione dei Miracoli di Maria in Abissinia', *Annali Lateranensi*, 11, 9–90
MONTI DELLA CORTE, A. A. (1940) *Lalibela*, Rome
MORTON WILLIAMS, P. (1960) 'The Yoruba Ogboni cult in Oyo', *Africa*, 30 (4), 362–74

NASSAU, R. H. (1904) *Fetichism in West Africa,* London
NENQUIN, J. (1960) 'Quelques poteries protohistoriques à face humaine trouvées au Katanga (Congo)', *Journal de la Société des Africanistes,* 30 (2), 145–50
NEYT, F. (1977) *La Grande Statuaire Hemba du Zaire,* Louvain-la-neuve
NEYT, F. (1979) *L'art Eket,* Paris
NEYT, F. (1981) *Traditional Art and History of Zaire,* Brussels
NICKLIN, K. (1980) Review, *AA,* 13 (2), 24–7, 83

OHNUKI TIERNEY, E. (1981) 'Phases in human perception/cognition/symbolization processes: cognitive anthropology and symbolic classification', *American Ethnologist,* 8 (2), 451–67
OJO, G. J. A. (1966) *Yoruba Palaces,* London
OLBRECHTS, F. (1941) *Bijdrage tot de Kennis van de Chronologie der Afrikaansche Plastiek,* Brussels (Contribution to the knowledge of the chronology of African sculpture and graphic arts)
OLBRECHTS, F. (1943) 'Contribution to the study of the chronology of African plastic art', *Africa,* 14 (2), 183–93
OLBRECHTS, F. (1959) *Les Arts Plastiques du Congo Belge,* Brussels (Trans. from the Dutch by A. Gilles de Pelichy)
OLIVER, R. and FAGAN, B. M. (1975) *Africa in the Iron Age,* Cambridge

PAULME, D. (1981) 'Figure pomdo' in S. Vogel (ed.), *For Spirits and Kings,* New York, 61–2
PAULME, D. and BROSSE, J. (1956) *Parures Africaines,* Paris
PECHUEL LOESCHE, (Dr) (1907) *Volkskunde von Loango,* Stuttgart
PERROIS, L. (1972) *La Statuaire Fang,* Paris
PERROIS, L. (1979) *Arts du Gabon,* Arnouville
PERSON, Y. (1961) 'Les Kissi et leurs statuettes en pierre dans le cadre de l'histoire ouest-africaine', *Bulletin de l'Institut Fondamental d'Afrique Noire,* B.23, 1–59
PHILLIPSON, D. W. (1977) *The Later Prehistory of Eastern and Southern Africa,* New York
PICTON, Y. and MACK, Y. (1979) *African Textiles,* London
PISKATY, K. (1957) 'Ist das Pygmäenwerk von Henri Trilles eine zuverlässige Quelle?', *Anthropos,* 52, 33–48
POLAKOFF, C. (1980) *Into Indigo: African textiles and dyeing techniques,* New York
POSNANSKY, M. (1979) 'Dating Ghana's earliest art', *AA,* 13 (1), 52–3, 100
POVEY, J. (1981) 'First word', *AA,* 14 (4), 1–11
PRESTON, G. N. (1975) 'Perseus and Medusa in Africa. Military art in Fanteland: 1834–1872', *AA,* 8 (3), 36–41, 68–71, 91
PREYS, G. (n.d.) 'Dossier Ethnographique no. 427', Royal Museum for Central Africa, Tervuren
PRUSSIN, L. (1968) 'The architecture of Islam in West Africa', *AA,* 1 (2), 32–55, 70–4
PRUSSIN, L. (1970) 'Sudanese architecture and the Manding', *AA,* 3 (4), 12–19
PRUSSIN, L. (1980) 'Traditional Asante architecture', *AA,* 13 (2), 57–65, 78
PRUSSIN, L. (1981) 'Building technologies in the West African savannah' in *Le Sol, la Parole et l'Ecrit: Mélanges Mauny,* Paris, vol. 1, pp. 227–45

RAGGHIANTI-COLLOBI, L. (1968) *British Museum: London,* New York
RANDLES, W. G. L. (1968) *L'Ancien Royaume du Congo,* Paris
ROSENWALD, J. B. (1974) 'Early Kuba figures', *AA,* 7 (3), 26–31, 92
ROSS, D. (1977) 'The iconography of Asante sword ornaments', *AA,* 11 (1), 16–25, 90
ROSSBACH, E. (1973) *Baskets as Textile Art,* New York
RUDNER, J. and RUDNER, L. (1970) *The Hunter and His Art,* Cape Town

RYDER, A. F. C. (1964) 'A note on the Afro-Portuguese ivories', *JAH*, 5, 363–6

SAPIR, E. (1916) *Time Perspective in Aboriginal American Culture: A Study in Method*, Ottawa (Reprinted in D. Mandelbaum, *Selected Writings of E. Sapir*, Berkeley, California, 1963)

SCHACHT, J. (1954) 'Sur les diffusions des formes d'architecture religieuse musulmane a travers le Sahara', *Travaux de l'Institut de Recherches Sahariennes de l'Universite d'Alger*, 11, 11–27

SCHACHT, J. (1957) 'An unknown type of Minbar and its historical significance', *Ars Orientalis*, 2, 149–73

SCHMIDT, P. (1981) *The Origins of Iron Smelting in Africa: a complex technology in Tanzania*, Providence, Rhode Island (Brown University)

SCHMITZ, C. A. (ed.) (1967) *Historische Völkerkunde*, Frankfurt am Main

SEBAG, P. (1965) *The Great Mosque of Kairouan*, New York

SHALOFF, S. (1970) *Reform in Leopold's Congo*, Richmond, Vermont

SHAW, T. (1970a) 'The analysis of West African bronzes: a summary of the evidence', *Ibadan*, 28, 80–9

SHAW, T. (1970b) *Ibgo Ukwu*, 2 vols, Evanston, Illinois

SHAW, T. (1978) *Nigeria: its archaeology and early history*, London

SHINNIE, M. (1965) *Ancient African Kingdoms*, London

SIEBER, R. (1980) *African Furniture and Household Objects*, New York

SILVER, H. S. (1981) 'Calculating risks: the socio-economic foundations of aesthetic innovation in an Ashanti carving community', *Ethnology*, 20 (2), 101–14

SIROTO, L. (1977) 'Njom: the magical bridge of the Beti and Bulu of southern Cameroons', *AA*, 10 (2), 38–51, 90

SIROTO, L. (1980) Review, *AA*, 14 (1), 76–9

SIROTO, L. (1981) Review, *AA*, 14 (4), 80–6

SOURDEL-THOMINE, J. and SPULER, B. (1973) *Die Kunst des Islam*, Berlin

SPEAR, T. (1981) *Kenya's Past*, London

SPRADLEY, J. P. and McCURDY, D. W. (1975) *Anthropology: the cultural perspective*, New York

STEVENS, P. (1978) *The Stone Images of Esie*, Ibadan

STONEHAM, D. (1980) 'Some thermoluminescence datings of terracottas from the inland delta of the Niger Mali' in B. De Grunne, *Ancient Terracottas from West Africa*, Louvain-la-neuve, pp. 276–82

TAGLIAFERRI, A. and HAM MMACHER, A. (1974) *Fabulous Ancestors: stone carvings from Sierra Leone and Guinea*, New York

TALBOT RICE, D. (1965) *Islamic Art*, London

TERRASSE, H. (1932) *L'art Hispano-Mauresque des Origines au XIIIe Siècle*, Paris

TERRASSE, H. (1968) *La Mosquée al Qaraouiyin à Fes*, Paris

THOMPSON, R. F. (1969) 'Abatan: a master potter of the Egbado Yoruba' in D. Biebuyck (ed.), *Tradition and Creativity in Tribal Art*, Berkeley, California, pp. 120–82

THOMPSON, R. F. (1973) 'Yoruba artistic criticism' in W. D'Azevedo (ed.), *The Traditional Artist in African Societies*, Bloomington, Indiana, pp. 19–61

THOMPSON, R. F. (1974) *African Art in Motion*, Los Angeles, California

THOMPSON, R. F. and CORNET, J. (1981) *The Four Moments of the Sun*, Washington

TUNIS, L. (1981) 'The Benin Chronologies', *AA*, 14 (2), 86–7

VANDENHOUTE, J. (1948) 'Classification stylistique du masque Dan et Guere de la Côte d'Ivoire Occidentale (AOF)' in *Mededelingen van het Rijksmuseum voor Volkenkunde*, Leiden, vol. 4

VAN DER MERWE, N. (1969) *The Carbon-14 Dating of Iron,* Chicago, Illinois
VAN DER MERWE, N. (1980) 'The advent of iron in Africa' in T. A. Wertime and D. J. Muhly (eds), *The Coming of The Age of Iron,* New Haven, Connecticutt, pp. 463–506
VAN NOTEN, F. (1972) 'La plus ancienne sculpture sur bois de l'Afrique centrale', *AT,* 18 (3/4), 133–6
VANSINA, J. (1955) 'Initiation rituals of the Bushong', *Africa,* 25, 138–53
VANSINA, J. (1968) 'The use of ethnographic data as sources in history' in T. O. Ranger (ed.), *Emerging Themes in African History,* Dar es Salaam, pp. 97–124
VANSINA, J. (1969a) 'The bells of kings', *JAH,* 10, 187–97
VANSINA, J. (1969b) 'Du royaume kuba au "territoire des Bakuba"', *Etudes Congolaises,* 12 (2), 3–54
VANSINA, J. (1976) 'Een negentiende-eeuwse stad in Centraal Africa: Nsheng', *AT,* 22, 47–56 (A 19th-century town in Central Africa)
VANSINA, J. (1978) *Children of Woot,* Madison, Wisconsin
VANSINA, J. (1979/1980) 'Bantu in the crystal ball', *History in Africa,* 6, 287–333; 7, 293–325
VINNICOMBE, P. (1976) *People of the Eland,* Pietermaritzburg
VOLAVKA, Z. (1979) 'The study of African art as an art historical discipline' in *25th International Congress of History of Art* (published proceedings), Bologna
VOLAVKA, Z. (1981a) 'Art and metal: review and preview of research strategy in African art history' in D. L. Ray, P. Shinnie and D. Williams (eds), *Into the 80's: Proceedings of the XIth annual convention of the Canadian Association of African Studies,* Vancouver, vol. 1, pp. 149–63
VOLAVKA, Z. (1981b) 'Insignia of the Divine Authority', *AA,* 14 (3), 43–51, 90–2
VOGEL, S. (ed.) (1981) *For Spirits and Kings,* New York

WANNYN, R. (1961) *L'Art Ancien du Metal au Bas-Congo,* Champles
WARREN, D. M. and KWEKU ANDREWS, J. (1977) 'An ethnographic approach to Akan art and aesthetics', *Working Papers in the Traditional Arts (Aesthetics),* Philadelphia, no. 2/3, p. 19
WERNER, O. (1970) 'Metallurgische Untersuchungen der Benin-Bronzen des Museum für Völkerkunde Berlin', Baessler Archiv, NF 18, 71–153
WESSEL, K. (1965) *Coptic Art in Early Christian Egypt,* New York [Trans. from German by J. Carroll and S. Hatton]
WILLCOX, A. R. (1963) *The Rock Art of South Africa,* Johannesburg
WILLETT, F. (1967) *Ife In the History of West African Art,* London
WILLETT, F. (1971) *African Art: an introduction,* London
WILLETT, F. (1978) 'An African sculptor at work', *AA,* 11 (2), 28–33, 96
WILLETT, F. and PICTON, J. (1967) 'On the identification of individual carvers: a study of ancestor shrine carvings from Owo, Nigeria', *Man,* 2 (1), 62–70
WILLIAMS, D. (1964) 'The iconology of the Yoruba *edan Ogboni*', *Africa,* 24, 139–66
WILLIAMS, D. (1974) *Icon and Image,* London
WILSON, T. H. (1979) 'Swahili funerary architecture of the north Kenya coast' in J. De Vere Allen and T. H. Wilson, *Swahili Houses and Tombs of the Coast of Kenya,* London, pp. 33–46
WISSLER, C. (1926) *The Relation of Nature to Man in Aboriginal America,* New York
WOODHOUSE, H. C. (1977) 'Bushman rock paintings', *AA,* 10 (4), 21–2, 88
WOODHOUSE, H. C. (1978) *Rock Art,* Cape Town

INDEX

Figures in roman type indicate references in the text; those in italics references in the captions.